CHIANTI ▲ 202

SIENA ▲ 208

SAN GIMIGNANO ▲ 225

PIENZA ▲ 232

VOLTERRA ▲ 236

TUSCAN ARCHIPELAGO ▲ 244

...continues to enjoy an international reputation.

**PISA**
Renowned for its spectacular 'Square of Miracles', one of the finest expressions of municipal pride, this dynamic university town has much to offer.

**LUCCA**
An exquisite, secluded city, still protected by its intact ring of walls.

**AREZZO**
This inland Tuscan city boasts an array of treasures, including one of the most beautiful squares in Italy and the fresco cycle of the *Legend of the True Cross*.

**SANSEPOLCRO**
The city of Piero della Francesca contains various masterpieces by one of the leading exponents of Renaissance art.

**CORTONA**
Etruscan walls, cobbled lanes, medieval houses and Renaissance and baroque palaces combine to create an unusually harmonious whole.

**CHIANTI**
If there is a heaven for wine, it is Chianti: a small region between Florence and Siena, whose landscape is dominated by grapevines.

**SIENA**
An extensive artistic heritage and a renewed sense of purpose. Siena is living proof that the Middle Ages can survive into the third millennium.

**SAN GIMIGNANO**
Walls and towers guarding the Via Francigena: this city is regarded as the epitome of a medieval city.

**PIENZA**
The Renaissance dream of Pope Pius II, realized by architect Rossellino.

**VOLTERRA**
One of the best preserved free towns in Italy surrounded by the spectacular dramatic landscape of the balze.

**TUSCAN ARCHIPELAGO**
A string of seven islands predominantly covered by dense Mediterranean vegetation in the largest protected marina area in the Mediterranean.

# TUSCANY

KNOPF GUIDES

## ● Encyclopedia section

**NATURE** Tuscany's natural heritage and most characteristic habitats, annotated and illustrated by specialist authors and artists.

**HISTORY AND LANGUAGE** The impact of national and international events on local history, from the earliest days to the present; information at a glance with key dates appearing in a timeline above the text; the Tuscan language in spoken and written form.

**ARTS AND TRADITIONS** Typical Tuscan customs and practices and their continuing role in contemporary life.

**ARCHITECTURE** The architectural heritage: traditional rural and urban dwellings followed by developments in civil, military and religious architecture with the emphasis on style and typology.

**AS SEEN BY PAINTERS** A selection of works by artists from the 14th century to the present day, presenting an informative overview of Tuscan art.

**AS SEEN BY WRITERS** An anthology of texts taken from works of all periods and countries, arranged thematically.

## ▲ Itineraries

Each of the eleven itineraries begins with a map of the area to be explored.
**◯ NOT TO BE MISSED** These sites, highlighted in gray boxes, should be seen at all costs.
**★ EDITOR'S CHOICE** Sites (also in gray boxes) singled out by the editor for special attention owing to their key importance or exceptional beauty.
**INSETS** Richly illustrated double-page insets turn the spotlight on subjects deserving more in-depth treatment.

## ◆ Practical information

All the travel information you will need before you go and when you get there.
**PLACES TO VISIT** A handy table listing the addresses and opening hours of all the monuments featured in this guide.
**USEFUL ADDRESSES** A selection of hotels and restaurants compiled by a specialist.
**APPENDICES** Bibliography, list of illustrations, index of names and index of people and places.
**MAP SECTION** Detailed maps of all the regions covered by the guide, followed by a topographical index and a map of the center of Florence.

◆ NORTHERN TUSCANY

◆ NORTHERN TUSCA

Each map in this section is designated by a letter while the letters and figures of the grid references make it easy for the reader to pinpoint sites featured in this guide (for example **B** C3).

# ● <u>Encyclopedia section</u>

The mini-map locates the itinerary within the wider area covered by the guide.

The itinerary map outlines the route to be taken and shows the main sites and places of special interest.

◆ C D4
This reference enables you to locate the site on one of the maps in the map section.

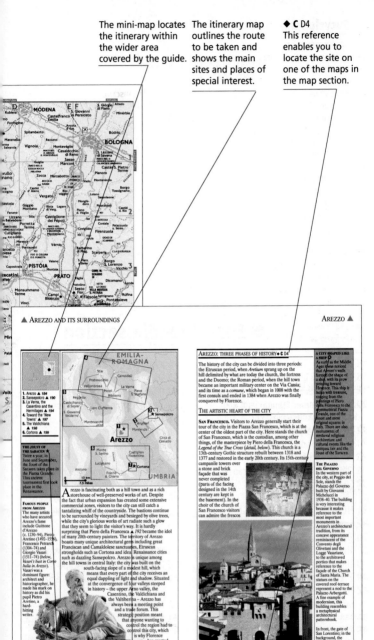

★ The star denotes sites, events and monuments singled out by the editor for special attention.

● ▲ ◆ The symbols within the text provide cross-references to a site discussed elsewhere in the guide.

✪ This symbol indicates places that should not be missed.

# ▲ Itineraries in Tuscany

# ◆ Practical information

**FLORENCE ▲ 115**
One of the most frequently visited cities of art in the world: a showcase of Medieval and Renaissance art and architecture.

**CHIANTI ▲ 201**
Castles, hamlets, villas and farmhouses in the land of wine and olive oil: a landscape that has been three thousand years in the making.

**AROUND FLORENCE ▲ 139.** Explore the Arno Valley, home of Leonardo da Vinci, and the Val di Pesa, dotted with Medici villas, hamlets and monasteries.

**SIENA ▲ 207**
The home of the Campo, the Palio, Simone Martini and Saint Catherine: this is one of the most symbolic cities of the Italian civilization.

**PISA AND LUCCA ▲ 145.** Two great cities with a glorious past divided for centuries by a bitter hatred and united by a magnificent Romanesque culture.

**AROUND SIENA ▲ 223.** Manmade landscapes, art treasures and the natural beauty of the hills from the Val d'Elsa to Mount Amiata.

**MASSA, CARRARA AND THE APUAN ALPS ▲ 163.** A long narrow strip of land lying between the Apuan Alps, scored by the white scars of marble quarries, and the Tyrrhenian coast.

**FROM VOLTERRA TO LIVORNO ▲ 235**
Unspoiled nature and sophisticated architecture; the ancient Via Aurelia along the coast; the Tuscan Archipelago.

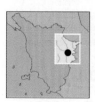

**PRATO AND PISTOIA ▲ 173**
Two cities now almost suburbs of Florence, but proud of their own distinctive cultural identity.

**GROSSETO AND THE MAREMMA ▲ 252**
From the geometric landscape of the reclaimed coastal plain to the inland plateaus.

**AREZZO AND ITS SURROUNDINGS ▲ 183.** A region endowed with numerous religious buildings and one of the cradles of the Renaissance.

→ NUMEROUS SPECIALISTS HAVE CONTRIBUTED TO THIS GUIDE. ALL THE INFORMATION CONTAINED IN THIS BOOK HAS BEEN CHECKED BY THEM.

**RAFFAELLA AUSENDA**
Milanese art historian, specializing in ceramic research. She works as a museum consultant and has published many essays devoted to Italian ceramics. *Author of Pottery.*

**NICOLETTA BAZZANO**
Research graduate in the History of Modern Europe. Her main interest is the history of politics in Italy between the 16th and 17th centuries. *Author of History.*

**GUYA BERTELLI**
Architect and researcher in the Faculty of Architecture of the Politecnico. She is one of the founders of the 'Institut pour l'Art et la Ville' in Givors (Lyons) and editor of the journal ARC (1996–8). Her works and designs have appeared in anthologies and specialist exhibitions. *Author of 20th-century Architecture.*

**MARIA NOVELLA BRENELLI**
Art historian involved in cultural promotion. She writes articles about art and travel for various publications. *Author of Pisa and Lucca.*

**ATTILIO BRILLI**
Teacher at the University of Siena. One of the leading experts in travel literature, he has edited the works of Ruskin, Irving, James, Wharton and others. His writings have been translated into various languages. *Author of From Fiesole to Villa Gamberaia; From Careggi to Castello; Around Florence; Massa, Carrara and the Apuan Alps; Arezzo and its surroundings.*

**ALBERTO CAPATTI**
Teaches History of the French Language at the University of Pavia and is an expert in the history of food. He edits the journal 'Slow' published by Slowfood, an international association. *Author of Cacciucco.*

**ENRICO CARACCIOLO DI BRIENZA**
A freelance journalist and photographer, he lives in Castagneto Carducci and contributes to publications in Italy and abroad. He specializes in bicycle touring; as well as publishing accounts of cycling trips, he works on travel guides for publishing houses and tourist organizations. *Author of From Volterra to Livorno.*

**LEONARDO CASTELLUCCI**
Florentine journalist and photographer, he has written various works on Tuscany. *Author of Ribollita.*

**MARIO CHIODETTI**
Professional freelance journalist and photographer. He contributes to daily newspapers and journals. He has mounted various exhibitions of photographic portraits and landscapes. *Author of The Maremma Nature Park and the Trappola marshes.*

**MAURO CIVAI**
He was born in Siena in 1951, where he completed his studies. Freelance journalist since 1974, he has been Director of the Museo Civico in Siena since 1982. He has organized various important cultural events and exhibitions for the Comune di Siena. He is a publishing consultant and has written various essays and works on Tuscan art, history and popular traditions. *Author of Tuscany as Seen by Painters; Chianti; Siena; Around Siena.*

**FLAVIO CONTI**
Architect, co-proprietor with his wife of an established architecture, restoration and industrial design practice. As well as his professional activities, he is a university teacher and a writer. He has written around one hundred publications on history, the history of architecture and industrial design. Committed to the protection of fortified buildings, he is president of the Istituto Italiano dei Castelli and editor-in-chief of the journal 'Cronache Castellare'. *Author of Architecture.*

**GIANLUIGI GAMBA**
Born in Milan where he still lives, he has devoted his life to teaching and music for over thirty years. He also has a passion for gardening and has made many trips throughout Italy and abroad, particularly the United Kingdom and France, to visit famous gardens. At the same time, he has created his own garden on Lake Iseo. He has written and translated educational works and books on music and has edited an encyclopedia of gardening. *Author of Gardens.*

**LUCA GIANNINI**
He was born in 1960 in Milan, where he studied at the university. A publishing consultant, he has designed and coordinated various publications. *Author of The Language; Florence*

**ALBANO MARCARINI**
A city planner, he was born in Milan in 1954. He studies cities and landscapes and designs routes and systems to improve mobility. He has edited various publications for the Touring Club Italiano, including the recent Guida ai Parchi e alle Aree Protette d'Italia. He publishes walking and cycling itineraries in the leading tourist journals. *Author of The Tuscan landscape; The Tuscan Apennines.*

**STEFANO MILIONI**
Journalist and writer specializing in food and wine and travel, he has been a contributor to the Roman daily newspaper Il Messaggero for fifteen years and writes for their food column. He has worked on the Italian edition of the Gault Millau and many other publications. He has written many works devoted to Tuscany. *Author of Cheese, salami and fish; Bread, honey, cakes and biscuits; Agriculture and horticulture; Olives and oil, vines and grapes; Stock farming; Grosseto and the Maremma.*

**MARCO MASETTI**
Expert on nature and the environment. *Author of The hills of Florence.*

**ANGELO MOJETTA**
Biologist, graduate from the University of Pavia, he lives and works in Milan where he alternates publishing and writing popular naturalist works with research in the field of freshwater and marine biology. He has written and translated numerous volumes devoted to water life and guides to submarine flora and fauna translated into various languages. *Author of Coastlines and islands; Apuan Marbles.*

**CORINNE PAUL**
Art historian and expert in 16th-century Italian literature. *Author of Guelphs and Ghibellines; The Medici.*

**ITALO SORDI**
He was born in Milan in 1936. His work in the field of Italian popular traditions revolves around material culture, pre-industrial technology and traditional theater, with specific emphasis on the ritual aspect of folklore, particularly carnivals. He has carried out a great deal of field research in these areas on behalf of the Discoteca di Stato, the Soprintendenza ai Beni Culturali di Milano, the Regione Lombardia and the Regione Sardegna. *Author of Religious festivals; Secular festivals; Popular literature.*

**CLAUDIO ZANINI**
Born in Trieste, he teaches art-related subjects. As an artist, he has shown his work in many one-man shows and group exhibitions in Italy and abroad. He has contributed to various art journals and publications. He is involved in writing for film and stage and has written TV screenplays for the Svizzera Italiana. He has published various stories and writes reviews of CD-ROMs devoted to art and tourism. *Author of Prato and Pistoia.*

**KNOPF GUIDES**

This is a Borzoi Book
published by
Alfred A. Knopf

Copyright © 2001
Alfred A. Knopf, New York

All rights reserved under International and
Pan-American Copyright Conventions.
Published in the United States by Alfred
A. Knopf, a division of Random House,
Inc., New York, and simultaneously in
Canada by Random House of Canada
Limited, Toronto.
Distributed by Random House, Inc.,
New York.

www.aaknopf.com

Knopf, Borzoi Books, and the colophon
are registered trademarks of Random
House, Inc.

Tuscany: ISBN 0-375-70960-6

First American Edition

Originally published in France by
Nouveaux-Loisirs, a subsidiary of
Editions Gallimard, Paris, 2000
© 2000 Editions Nouveaux-Loisirs.

**TRANSLATED BY**
Sue Rose

**EDITED AND TYPESET BY**
Book Creation Services Ltd, London

**TUSCANY**

■ **PRODUCTION**
Asterisco, Milano
■ **LAYOUT**
Fiammetta Badalato
■ **EDITORIAL**
Alda Venturi, Marco Del Freo,
Anna Ceruti
■ **PICTURE RESEARCH**
Irvana Malabarba, Pupa Bologna
■ **ILLUSTRATIONS**
NATURE: Alfonso Goi
NATURA: Annalisa Durante, Jean
Chevallier, François Desbordes,
Claire Felloni, John Wilkinson
ARCHITECTURE : Marina Durante,
Jean-Philippe Chabot,
Didier Domagala, Domitile Heron,
Pierre de Hugo, Bruno Lenormand,
Maurice Pommier, Michel Sinier
■ **MAPS**
Servizio Cartografico
del Touring Club Italiano
■ **ITINERARY MAPS**
Flavio Badalato
■ **COORDINATION**
Luca Giannini

**Printed in Italy by Editoriale Lloyd**

# Encyclopedia section

View of the hamlet of Fonterutoli in Tuscany, c. 1915–20.

The beach at Marina di Carrara, early 1900s

View of the Duomo in Florence from the Palazzo Vecchio, early 1900s

# Nature

Tuscany boasts some diverse mountain landscapes, including a ridge with peaks soaring to heights of over 6500 feet, basins of former lakes such as the Mugello, isolated massifs such as the Apuan Alps and Mount Pratomagno and vast tracts covered by rolling hills. The main rivers are the Arno, Tiber and Ombrone. The coastline varies between sandy beaches (Versilia) and high cliffs (Maremma). As a result, the region possesses a wide variety of vegetation, ranging from the evergreen shrubs on the Mediterranean coast to the fir woods of the Apennines, with holm oaks, cypresses and olive trees in between.

**THE CHIANTI REGION**
The vine-covered Chianti region ▲ *201* is internationally renowned for its wine, as well as its mild climate and landscape of rolling hills.

**THE SIENESE CRETE**
The barren, arid region of Le Crete ('crests') ▲ *228* is an exception to the Tuscan landscape. Largely formed of grayish clay, this region is devoted to crops and pasture.

**COASTLINES**
There is some breathtakingly beautiful countryside along the 200 or so miles of diverse Tuscan coastline, on Mount Argentario ▲ *258*, for example, or in the Uccellina mountains ▲ *255*. The latter were probably formed when sections of the Tyrrhenian coastline became completely silted up. This extensive process of siltation, which began at the end of the Pliocene era, continues to this day.

**MAQUIS**
The scrubland vegetation of the maquis is not always primarily composed of holm oaks: fragrant and aromatic plants, such as arbutus, heather and myrtle also occur. Covering the coastal hills, the maquis sometimes extends further inland, as can be seen in the Arno Valley.

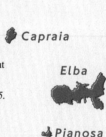

Massa

Lucca

Pisa

Livorno

*Gorgona*

*Capraia*

*Elba*

*Pianosa*

*Montecristo*

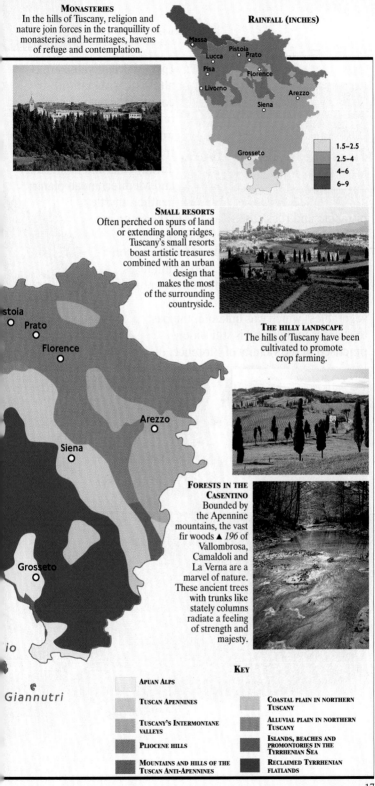

## MONASTERIES

In the hills of Tuscany, religion and nature join forces in the tranquillity of monasteries and hermitages, havens of refuge and contemplation.

**RAINFALL (INCHES)**

Massa
Pistoia
Lucca • Prato
Pisa • Florence
Livorno • Arezzo
Siena
Grosseto

1.5–2.5
2.5–4
4–6
6–9

stoia
Prato
Florence
Arezzo
Siena
Grosseto

io

Giannutri

## SMALL RESORTS

Often perched on spurs of land or extending along ridges, Tuscany's small resorts boast artistic treasures combined with an urban design that makes the most of the surrounding countryside.

## THE HILLY LANDSCAPE

The hills of Tuscany have been cultivated to promote crop farming.

## FORESTS IN THE CASENTINO

Bounded by the Apennine mountains, the vast fir woods ▲ 196 of Vallombrosa, Camaldoli and La Verna are a marvel of nature. These ancient trees with trunks like stately columns radiate a feeling of strength and majesty.

## KEY

APUAN ALPS

TUSCAN APENNINES

TUSCANY'S INTERMONTANE VALLEYS

PLIOCENE HILLS

MOUNTAINS AND HILLS OF THE TUSCAN ANTI-APENNINES

COASTAL PLAIN IN NORTHERN TUSCANY

ALLUVIAL PLAIN IN NORTHERN TUSCANY

ISLANDS, BEACHES AND PROMONTORIES IN THE TYRRHENIAN SEA

RECLAIMED TYRRHENIAN FLATLANDS

17

The alluvial plain surrounded by hills on which Florence was founded.

Extensive cultivated areas alternate with natural countryside over the hills of Florence ▲ *137*. The woodlands contain deciduous trees (oaks, sissile oaks, Turkey oaks and holm oaks) and Mediterranean plants: heather, myrtle, pistachio and rock rose. The hills in the south are crowned by vast expanses of stone pine and maritime pine which once provided the region with cones, resin and wood. Old farmhouses and castles bear witness to the time-honored system of mixed farming (grain and vegetables) which was linked in the past to sharecropping, and is still widely practised in the vicinity of Florence.

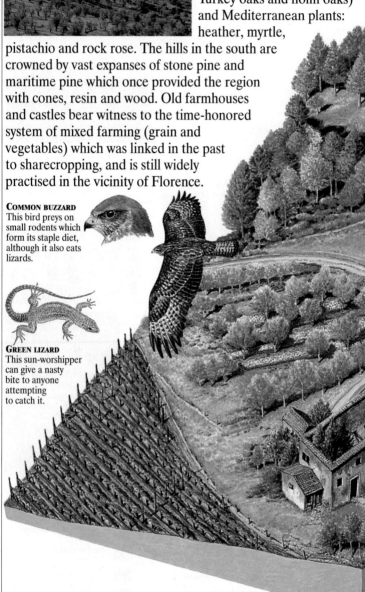

**COMMON BUZZARD**
This bird preys on small rodents which form its staple diet, although it also eats lizards.

**GREEN LIZARD**
This sun-worshipper can give a nasty bite to anyone attempting to catch it.

**HOODED CROW**
The hooded crow is as widespread in Italy as the all-black carrion crow is in western Europe. An omnivore, it lives in woods and pastureland.

male

female

**GOLDEN ORIOLE**
This bird is found in Tuscany from late April. Not easily seen, it may be detected by the male's lovely fluting song.

male

**KESTREL**
A species of falcon, it nests in ruined buildings, or uses old nests built by the hooded crow.

**TAWNY OWL**
At night, its hooting call echoes through the oak woods.

**ITALIAN CYPRESS**
Between 50 and 70 feet high, this tree is native to central Europe, and was introduced into Italy from Romania.

**SESSILE OAK**
This large acorn-bearing tree prefers a dry habitat on hillsides.

**SWEET CHESTNUT TREE**
Renowned for its edible nuts, it grows singly or in dense clumps.

**STONE (OR UMBRELLA) PINE**
The nuts are used in pastry-making and cooking.

**MARITIME PINE**
The resin is used to make turpentine.

# ● THE MAREMMA NATIONAL PARK AND THE TRAPPOLA MARSHES

The Uccellina coastline

The Maremma National Park (Parco Nazionale della Maremma) ▲ *255* is sandwiched between the Via Aurelia and the sea, south of Grosseto. Perhaps the last real *maremma*, or swampland, preserved in an unspoiled state, the park encompasses the Trappola marshes, the mouth of the Ombrone river and the Uccellina mountains. The term *maremma* refers to the flat land along the Tuscan coast, made marshy by frequent river floods. The Trappola marshes, between Principina a Mare and the mouth of the Ombrone, have sparse vegetation intermingled with semi-dry meadows, thickets of scrub evergreen and pines. During the migratory seasons of spring and autumn, they play host to a multitude of waterbirds. The northern part of the park is characterized by sandy coastlines, while the southern part has rocky cliffs interspersed with small coves.

**HOLM OAK**
This species occurs either as a bush in the maquis, or as a tree up to 80 feet high.

**STONE (OR UMBRELLA) PINE**
Unmistakable because of its umbrella-like foliage, the stone pine is typical of this coastline and is cultivated for its seeds.

**MYRTLE**
The berries of this highly aromatic evergreen shrub are used to make a fragrant liqueur, while the bark, leaves and flowers yield an essential oil used in perfumery.

Flowers on the Maremma dunes ▲ 252. The plants that grow along the sandy shores have adapted to the salty environment and can grow on a loose medium such as sand.

The Ombrone river at Trappola ▲ 255. These marshes were once a typical example of the Tuscan coastline. Mud-dwelling creatures, over-wintering birds and a variety of mammals (such as foxes, badgers and coypu) are attracted by the abundant food.

female

male

**WILD BOAR**
Males live a solitary life apart from mothers with young. Grubbing for food with their snouts, they leave deep furrows in the earth.

**BLUE ROCK THRUSH**
The male has splendid slate-blue plumage. It nests among rocks or in old ruins.

**SEA DAFFODIL (SEA LILY)**
The large fragrant white flowers of this plant decorate the sand dunes in places along the coast.

**PEREGRINE FALCON**
This bird nests on rocky cliffs. It preys on medium-sized birds, catching them in mid flight after spectacular dives.

**CRESTED PORCUPINE**
This nocturnal creature is one of the largest rodents. It lives in small groups in deep dens.

**EUROPEAN POND TERRAPIN**
This small turtle lives mainly in still or slow-flowing waters. It often stays on the surface of the water.

**THE APENNINES**
A 19th-century watercolor depicting a view of the Apennines from the Casentino.

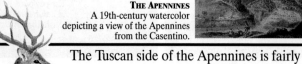

**RED DEER**
This deer is a typical Apennine mammal. Its numbers are growing since hunting is no longer permitted here.

The Tuscan side of the Apennines is fairly gentle, consisting of a series of parallel basins connected to a ridge. The ridge gradually becomes lower, dropping from peaks averaging between 6500 and 5500 feet down to 5000 feet. This graduated descent has a clear impact on the vegetation, which mainly consists of beech woods, providing dense coverage on slopes between 2500–3000 feet and 4500–5500 feet.

On the lower slopes, the beech trees combine with silver firs, while nearer the valleys the beeches give way to chestnut trees, often specially planted. These in turn are followed by oak woods, which mark the transition from mountain to Mediterranean vegetation.

**EDIBLE BOLETUS (CEP)**
The best-known mushroom used in cooking.

**CHANTERELLE**
A highly prized edible mushroom shaped rather like a spinning top.

**FLY AGARIC**
This brightly colored mushroom is poisonous.

**BARN OWL**
Nocturnal bird with extremely good hearing.

**TREECREEPER**
This bird nimbly spirals up tree trunks in search of insects and spiders.

**WEASEL**
A tiny predator which is skilled at catching mice and field mice.

**SALAMANDER**
This striking amphibian prefers damp wooded areas.

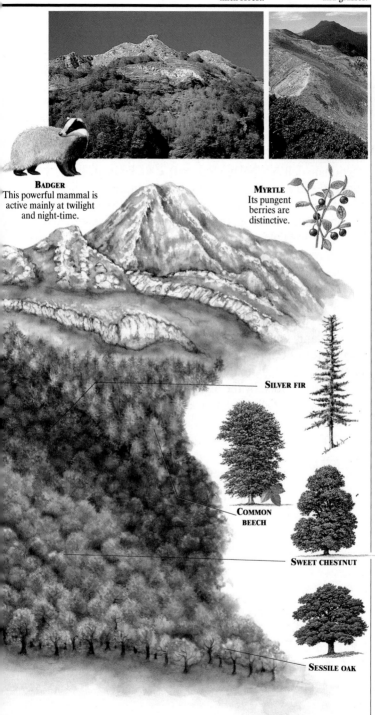

**DENSE WOODS**
Vast stretches of the
Tuscan mountains
are covered in
thick forest.

**ALTA QUOTA MEADOWS**
The peaks are covered
in a thin layer of small
shrubs, herbaceous plants
and grasses.

**BADGER**
This powerful mammal is
active mainly at twilight
and night-time.

**MYRTLE**
Its pungent
berries are
distinctive.

**SILVER FIR**

**COMMON
BEECH**

**SWEET CHESTNUT**

**SESSILE OAK**

Dartford warbler          Sardinian warbler          Scops owl

Even to the superficial observer, Tuscany's coastline appears to be divided into two distinct parts: the lower, sandy northern zone and the coast south of Livorno, where the shoreline is more varied, alternating stretches of sand and rock. Completing the picture, the seven islands of the Tuscan Archipelago, which form part of the Tuscan Archipelago National Park (Parco Nazionale dell'Arcipelago toscano) ▲ 244, lie in an arc between Livorno and Argentario in the clear turquoise sea. Nature here is just as diverse, although the sea continues to be the common denominator. Although the landscape along the shore and in the plains ranges from coastal dunes to inshore pines, the main type of vegetation on the islands and in the more rocky areas is maquis. Here, pines intermingle with forests of holm oak (particularly on Elba ▲ 244 and Gorgona) in company with the various species of hillside scrubland, or maquis (heather, myrtle, oleander, rosemary, arbutus), and many of the archipelago's native plants such as the Elban violet, and the toadflax and cornflower of Capraia ▲ 245. The fauna is just as varied, and natural wonders abound beneath the sea. The colors of the maquis are echoed by the algae and invertebrates which cover the submerged rocks, creating a variety of habitats frequented by schools of multicolored fish.

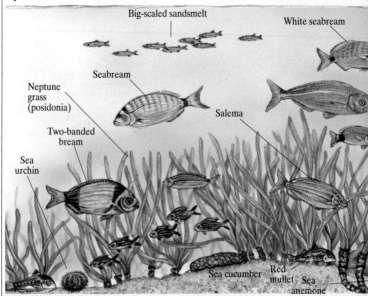

Big-scaled sandsmelt

White seabream

Seabream

Neptune grass (posidonia)

Salema

Two-banded bream

Sea urchin

Sea cucumber          Red mullet          Sea anemone

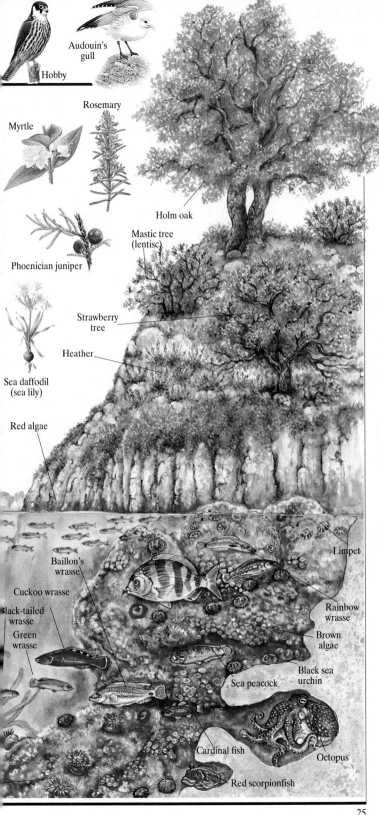

Hobby

Audouin's gull

Rosemary

Myrtle

Phoenician juniper

Sea daffodil (sea lily)

Holm oak

Mastic tree (lentisc)

Strawberry tree

Heather

Red algae

Limpet

Baillon's wrasse

Cuckoo wrasse

Black-tailed wrasse

Green wrasse

Rainbow wrasse

Brown algae

Black sea urchin

Sea peacock

Cardinal fish

Octopus

Red scorpionfish

*Fagioli al fiasco*: a simple dish that exemplifies Tuscan life and civilization.

The typical Tuscan farmer does not really conform to the popular image that equates working the land with hunger and poverty. In Tuscany, the time-honored tradition of cooperation between landowners and cultivators, coupled with a taste for the good life which has spread from the cities into country homes and a deep-rooted, vibrant popular culture, have produced generations of dynamic, modern farmers who welcome innovation and experimentation. This has, over the centuries, led to the development of diversified farming which has turned the region's many different structural and climatic conditions to good advantage. Teasing the Tuscans for being mediocre cooks is tantamount to paying tribute to their products, which are so varied and of such excellent quality that they require very little preparation before they grace the table.

### DELICIOUS MUSHROOMS
Mushrooms grow in abundance in Tuscany as 42 percent of the region is covered by woodland. The most sought-after ceps are gathered on the slopes of Mount Amiata, between Seggiano and Piancastagnaio, and in the northernmost part of the region, on the mountains that stretch from Pontremoli toward Borgotaro, in the province of Parma.

### TOP QUALITY CHESTNUTS
The entire Apennine zone and the slopes of Mount Amiata are covered by chestnut trees. Chestnuts abound, and with traditional Tuscan *vis polemica* (spirit of controversy), each area vaunts the excellence of their own. The best are those in the Mugello, which have been singled out by the European Union for a Protected Designation of Origin (PDO).

## THE PRODUCTION OF BEAUTY

In Pistoia, an industry has grown up around the beautiful Tuscan gardens, and flowers and plants are sold in markets throughout Europe.

## TYPICAL TUSCAN PRODUCTS

Cannellini beans and Tuscan cooking are inextricably linked. The best beans are mainly grown in the chalky mountain areas through which the Cecina river flows and in small places well known by gourmets, such as the area between Pitigliano and Sorano, and the region around Montemerano, in the province of Grosseto.

## HORTICULTURE

The production of vegetables, particularly cardoon, cauliflower, tomatoes and fennel, is centered around the hills of Lucca and Pistoia and in the Arno river plain. This area also produces another symbol of Tuscan gastronomy: Tuscan kale, which transforms ordinary soup into *ribollita* ('reboiled'), a thick, hearty vegetable soup.

## CARDOON

Cardoon soup is a must for those who have sophisticated tastes and a liking for old-fashioned flavors.

## CAULIFLOWER

Although rather overshadowed by the majestic Tuscan kale, the cauliflower has established itself as one of the main ingredients in rustic recipes.

## TUSCAN KALE

If this variety of winter cabbage were not so tasty, it would still be popular as an attractive ornamental plant.

## FENNEL

Fresh and fleshy, fennel tempers the aggressive bite of many Tuscan country recipes.

## TOMATOES

Although Tuscan dishes are rarely tomato-based, this fruit can enhance the flavor of the simplest dishes.

## SPELT

Although neglected for centuries elsewhere, the production of spelt never stopped in the fields of the Garfagnana, in the province of Lucca. Now rediscovered, this ancestor of wheat is cultivated everywhere, but the historical producers from the Garfagnana succeeded in safeguarding its quality when the EU awarded it a Protected Designation of Origin.

# ● OLIVES AND OIL, VINES AND GRAPES

Vineyards and olive groves: the clearest and yet most unobtrusive sign of human occupation in the Tuscan hills.

Olives and grapes are the two mainstays of the Tuscan farming community. These varieties take years to bear fruit, and so they are only planted when already firmly established in a territory. In other words, good oil and good wine not only require a favorable climate and fertile soil, but also a stable social context, a strong working relationship between those who own the land and those who work it. After the fruit is picked olives and grapes can only be processed slowly, with recourse to a great deal of technical know-how, expertise and experience. Oil and wine production takes a lot of time and effort and, in Tuscany, these activities have always attained the highest standards.

**OLIVE PICKING**
This humble, yet precious fruit is hand-picked after fine-mesh nets have been strung beneath the trees to prevent any being lost. The olives are then laid out on rush mats which are stacked in layers. This is to avoid overcrowding, which could cause undesirable mold and fermentation in the fresh olives.

**GREEN GOLD**
Pungent and delicate: two contrasting adjectives used to define Tuscan oil, which has achieved success in its own right for its unique flavor, a consummate blend of sophistication and character. The various different climates and types of soil in the region have resulted in some very different oils that are regulated by the Protected Designation of Origin. In addition to the generic description Toscano (Tuscan), the PDO recognizes the products of 8 regional subdivisions: Colline della Lunigiana, Colline Lucchesi, Monti Pisani, Montalbano, Colline di Firenze, Colline di Arezzo, Colline Senesi and Seggiano.

Labels do not just describe a wine, they provide information about families, castles and historic events.

## IL TREBBIANO
The ubiquitous Trebbiano, a sturdy but not overly refined vine, has encouraged the production of 'general' wines which, although pleasant, have very little character. It is easily surpassed by more superior vines that produce wines steeped in history, such as the sweet, sparkling Vernaccia di San Gimignano or the Moscadello di Montalcino, praised by Redi in his eulogy *Bacchus in Tuscany*.

## VIN SANTO
The strong, intensely-flavored Vin Santo is a faithful reflection of the Tuscan character, and people either love it or hate it. Going against all wine-making rules, it is matured in the stifling heat of attics instead of wine cellars. It successfully triumphs over this tortuous process, however, to glory in a unique blend of aromas and flavors.

## THE SANGIOVESE VINE
The Sangiovese vine is the historical forefather of the great Tuscan wines. Full of character, it has adapted well to various habitats to produce an endless number of clones. The Sangiovese vine has produced three of the great names in Italian wine-making: Chianti, Brunello di Montalcino and Vino Nobile di Montepulciano. However, it has also spawned many lesser-known gems like Carmignano, Morellino di Scansano, Montecarlo and Pomino.

## THE GRAPE HARVEST
A festive atmosphere, hard work and stress: the rewards of a whole year of labor are reaped during the few short days of the grape harvest.

## THE CELLARS
Peace and quiet reigns in the half-light of the wine cellars. Inside the casks, the wine matures, becoming a delicious nectar with many nuances of taste.

29

**GIOVANNI FATTORI**
*Contadino con maiali presso un carro di buoi*

History, custom and territory in Tuscany are so closely interwoven that even science and technology have to bow to the fruits of centuries of evolution. In other places, the phrase 'stock farming' conjures up worrying images of genetic engineering. Here, however, the emphasis is placed firmly on breeds that appear to have remained virtually unchanged for centuries.

**CHIANINA BEEF CATTLE**
Chianina bulls still retain the features of the *Bos Primigenius* painted on prehistoric cave walls. Highly prized by the Etruscans and the Romans, they are reared between Arezzo, Siena and Pisa in line with rigorous quality-control methods. The delicious cuts of beef are completely insufficient to meet market demand.

**MAREMMANA COW**
The Maremmana breed is found along the coast. This powerful indigenous bovine has been used for centuries as a farm animal and it is now rightly regarded as one of the seven most valuable Italian breeds.

**WILD BOAR**
Vast stretches of maquis and woodland in the Maremma have been fenced off, making it possible to breed the wildest of all animals, the boar. Rather than being reared, these animals are kept 'under control' here, ensuring a steady supply for an ever-expanding market sector.

**SHEEP**
In the last forty years, a steady influx of Sardinian immigrants has ensured the survival of the Tuscan pastoral tradition. There have only been marginal changes to a production process that dates back to the Etruscans, and this has guaranteed the quality of Tuscany's ewes-milk cheese, which continues to stand out from many other similar products from other Italian regions.

**AQUACULTURE**
After centuries, traditional eel farming in the lakes of Orbetello has made way for modern aquacultural facilities producing bass, giltheads and other valuable species.

# History and language

**524 BC**
The Greeks from Cumae defeat
the Etruscans at Ariccia

| 900 BC | 600 BC | 300 BC | 200 BC | 90 BC | 0 |
|---|---|---|---|---|---|

**900–700 BC**
Villanovan culture in
central Italy

**7–6TH CENTURY BC**
Growth of Etruscan
civilization: expansion
into Campania

**396 BC** The
Romans conquer
Veio

**295 BC** The Romans
defeat Etruscans and
Samnites at Arezzo

**90 BC** Tuscia obtains
Roman citizenship

## FROM THE BEGINNING TO THE FREE CITIES

### PREHISTORY

Small fossils, shells and tiny branches of coral show that tens of thousands of years ago present-day Tuscany was covered with water. As the great lakes dried up, they formed rivers, creating the alluvial plains that typify the region's landscape. The receding water also left extensive stretches of marshland along the coast.

The first human settlements date back to Middle Paleolithic times. They were built near rivers and in caves and rocky gorges, far from the unhealthy marshes. Archeological remains reveal the presence of Indo-European peoples throughout the 2nd millennium BC. They were in contact with the Mediterranean world, as shown by the discovery of Mycenaean artefacts in the Tolfa mountains. Toward the end of the 2nd millennium BC the Villanovan culture developed in the region bounded by the Arno and Tiber rivers and the Tyrrhenian Sea. This early Iron Age culture is regarded by archeologists as the preliminary stage in the birth and development of the Etruscan civilization.

### THE ETRUSCANS

In the 5th century BC the great Greek historian Herodotus wrote that the Etruscans, or Tyrrhenians, arrived on the Italian peninsula from Lydia before the Trojan War. In fact, the Etruscan language bears close similarities with many languages in Asia Minor. The magnificent Etruscan civilization developed as a result of the fusion of the indigenous population with these new people, who had landed in the region in the 8th century BC. The prehistoric settlements developed into densely populated cities, each of which, by the end of the 5th century BC, was governed by a king (*lucumo*). Political power was wielded by oligarchies formed by aristocrats, who lived like princes. The various Etruscan cities were never united in a single political structure, though some joined together to form leagues. The most important federation was the Dodecapolis, formed by the twelve cities of Cerveteri, Veio, Tarquinia, Vulci, Vetulonia, Roselle, Populonia, Volsinii, Chiusi, Perugia, Arezzo and Volterra. The Etruscans made a name for themselves as skilled traders and pirates: they controlled the Tyrrhenian Sea, the part of the Mediterranean named after them, and founded colonies along the coast of Campania. From the 5th century BC, their supremacy was threatened by the advance of the Greeks: after joining forces with the Carthaginians to defeat a Greek fleet at Alalia (540 BC), the Etruscans were vanquished at Ariccia (524 BC). The Etruscans had also spread south, through Lazio to Rome and beyond. The Tarquin rulers of Rome were an Etruscan dynasty, but after the republic was established, this city was to prove the end of the Etruscan world.

### TUSCIA

Under the Tarquins, Rome acquired an international role that it continued to play even after the republic was established. The successful war against Veio (405–396 BC) enabled Rome to extend its dominion as far as modern Pisa. From the second half of the 3rd century BC Tuscia (the Roman name) became an ally of Rome, providing it with military forces, ships and financial support. Roman colonies were gradually established in Tuscia, and the inhabitants were granted Roman citizenship in return for their loyalty to Rome. During the republican period, Tuscia, despite the birth of new towns like Florentia and the construction of consular roads which guaranteed contact with Rome, suffered an economic decline that was not halted by assistance from Augustus. Tuscia became the 'VII region' in the Augustan administrative system. Toward the end of the 3rd century AD, Emperor Diocletian formed a new administrative subdivision by combining the region with Umbria and placing it under the leadership of a *corrector*, who resided in Florentia.

| 500 | | 700 | | 1000 | | 1200 | | 1300 | 1350 |

**1074** Matilda of Canossa is Countess of Tuscany

**1284** The Genoese defeat the Pisans at Meloria

**1378** Ciompi Revolt in Florence

**568** Fall of the Lombards in Italy

**774** Reign of Charlemagne; the county of Tuscany is formed

**1015** Expedition by Pisa against the Saracen pirates

**1260** Defeat of the Florentine Guelphs at Montaperti

**1348** Black Death in Italy

# BETWEEN THE LOMBARDS AND THE FRANKS

After the fall of the Roman Empire Tuscia became part of the kingdom of the Ostrogoth king Theodoric, then passed into the hands of the Lombards after AD 568. It was vital for the Lombards to control Tuscia, to guarantee communication between their capital, Pavia, and the remote duchies of Spoleto and Benevento, since a large part of central Italy was under Byzantine dominion. Christianity had gained a strong foothold in Tuscan territories: Lucca had been an important episcopal seat since the 6th century, while an Irish bishop, San Donato, perpetuated the monastic tradition at Fiesole in the 9th century. After the victorious expedition of Charlemagne in Italy (772), Tuscany was set up as a province stretching from Siena to the Apennines.

# A MARITIME REPUBLIC

The city of Pisa soon escaped from the jurisdiction of the counts of Tuscany and in AD 1000 entered a period of great splendor that lasted for around two centuries. Pisa's participation in the First Crusade, with a fleet of 120 ships, secured trading privileges for the Pisans in all the eastern ports controlled by the Christians, enabling them to extend their dominion over the sea and seize the Balearic islands from the Saracens (1114–15). Pisa's maritime and commercial supremacy was brought to an end by the Genoese. Defeated in the naval battle of Meloria (1284), the city never regained its past glory.

# THE COUNTS OF TUSCANY

The counts of Tuscany did much to consolidate the region's position under the wrangling pontifical and imperial authorities. Count Ugo (953–1001) moved his residence from Lucca to Florence, bringing in a period of prosperity for the city after its loss of

prestige during the Lombard period. Countess Matilda (1046–1115) achieved fame for her role as mediator in the dispute between Pope Gregory VII and Emperor Henry IV. In January 1077, in the Countess's castle at Canossa, the excommunicated emperor made the famous 'penance in the snow'. He begged for and received a pardon from the Pope.

# THE FREE CITIES

Before AD 1000, the cities of Florence, Siena, Lucca, Arezzo and Pistoia also experienced a period of economic revival which went hand in hand with a new political system. The wealthiest and most influential citizens, lawyers and merchants banded together to found associations linked by a sworn agreement, the *foedus communis* (mutual compact). Once it was founded, the *Comune* gradually imposed its authority on all the city's inhabitants, changing from a private association to a kind of public institution. In the conflict between the imperial and papal authorities, the *comuni*, or free cities, of Lucca, Pistoia, Pisa and Siena continued to support the emperor. The Ghibelline cities, however, opposed Guelph Florence which, under the pretext of attacking the allies of the emperor, was threatening all Tuscan cities. Florence's expansion was temporarily halted by the Sienese at the battle of Montaperti (1260), but it continued in subsequent centuries with the subjugation of Arezzo (1298), Pistoia (1329), Prato (1351), Pisa (1406) and Livorno (1421).

# ● The Guelphs and the Ghibellines

The hostility between Guelfs and Ghibellines had its origins in the German conflict between the dukes of Bavaria and the imperial family of Hohenstaufen. As enemies of the emperor, the dukes and their allies sided with the Pope in the Investiture Controversy. Later, when the Italian *comuni* stood up to the Hohenstaufens, the same conflict spread to Italy, where it degenerated into family rivalries and wars between the *comuni*.

**THE INVESTITURE CONTROVERSY**
In 1059 Pope Nicholas II issued a decree which forbade the investiture of bishops by any secular powers. This ruling was upheld by his successors, and Emperor Henry IV responded by declaring Pope Gregory VII deposed. Henry was excommunicated and then pardoned at Canossa, but he finally forced Gregory to leave Rome. The conflict was eventually resolved in 1122 by the Concordat of Worms.

**ORIGIN OF THE NAMES**
The term 'Ghibelline' is derived from Waibling – the name of a castle in Germany owned by the Hohenstaufen dynasty. 'Guelph' comes from Welff, a legendary spokesman of the dukes of Bavaria.

**1076–1122.** The Investiture Controversy.
**1138–1254.** The throne is held by the Hohenstaufen emperors, who also rule Sicily 1195–1266.
**1154–83.** War between Emperor Frederick I of Swabia, and the Italian *comuni*.
**1167.** Supported by Pope Alexander III, the *comuni* combine to form the Lombard League in opposition to Barbarossa.
**1216.** Florence is drawn into the conflict.
**1226.** A new Lombard League is formed.
**1237.** Frederick II of Swabia routs the army of the *comuni*.
**1237–40.** Ghibelline hegemony in Florence.
**1240–60.** Florence is in the hands of the Guelphs.
**1250.** The city takes the Guelph emblem of a red fleur-de-lis against a white background as a standard. The exiled Ghibellines adopt the same standard with the colors reversed.
**1258.** Manfred, the emperor's illegitimate son, usurps the Sicilian throne and relaunches Ghibelline military activities in Italy.
**1260.** Battle of Montaperti. Leading the Ghibelline forces, Manfred conquers Florence.
**1260–68.** Florence is in the hands of the Ghibellines.
**1265.** Charles of Anjou enters Italy.
**1266.** Battle of Benevento. Charles of Anjou defeats and kills Manfred; in 1268, he defeats Conradin and seizes possession of the kingdom of Sicily.
**c.1300.** The Guelphs split into Black and White factions.

## FARINATA DEGLI UBERTI
After the victory at Montaperti, Manfred decided to raze Florence. Rebelling against his Ghibelline comrades, Farinata declared himself ready to lead an armed defense of the city and thereby saved Florence.

## THE BATTLE OF MONTAPERTI
In 1260, supported by the Ghibelline faction and Manfred, the Sienese defeated Florence. The Florentine Ghibellines, led by Farinata degli Uberti, made a triumphal comeback into the city.

## CONFLICT BETWEEN THE CITIES
At first united against the emperor in defense of their autonomy, the *comuni* soon found themselves in conflict over questions of foreign policy and were torn apart by rivalry and infighting between Guelph and Ghibelline families. Florence was predominantly Guelph.

## BLACK AND WHITE GUELPHS
Once the Ghibellines were defeated, the Guelphs split into two factions: Whites, opposed to the pope's hegemony, and Blacks, supporters of the pope. Banished in 1302, the Whites returned from exile in 1311, although without Dante and some of his comrades.

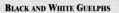

## A BLOODY EASTER
In 1216, in Florence, to circumvent sanctions imposed by the *comune*, the Buondelmonti and Amidei 'factions' attempted to disguise their own disputes as part of the overall political conflict, sparking off a quarrel that gradually spread to Florence's entire ruling class. By way of reconciliation, a marriage was arranged between the two families but, after being persuaded to marry a Donati woman, Buondelmonti did not make an appearance in church. In revenge, the Donati had him assassinated on Easter Day.

| 1400 | 1460 | 1470 | 1490 | 1510 | 1515 |
|---|---|---|---|---|---|
| **1434** Cosimo the Elder becomes *gonfalonier* and Count of Tuscany | **1469** Lorenzo the Magnificent becomes *signore* of Florence | **1478** Pazzi conspiracy against the Medici | **1494** The Medici are banished from Florence | **1512** Giuliano de' Medici returns to Florence and reinstates the *signoria* | |

## THE RISE OF THE MEDICI

### TUSCAN SIGNORIAL

In the early 15th century, Tuscany was divided into three extensive domains: the republics of Lucca, Siena and Florence. The presence of a strong merchant class enabled Lucca and Siena to defend their autonomy against Florence, where the Medici family had begun to play a dominant role. The rise of the Medici, who had grown rich from trade and money-lending, was boosted by their support from the city's ruling body. The election of Cosimo the Elder in 1434 to the post of *gonfalonier* (chief magistrate) consolidated their supremacy.

### LORENZO THE MAGNIFICENT

Nephew of Cosimo the Elder, Lorenzo ● *39* controlled the Florentine republic from 1469 to 1492, continuing like his uncle and father Piero, *signore* of Florence from 1464 to 1469, to keep the government under strict control. After escaping injury in the Pazzi conspiracy, in which his brother Giuliano died (1478), Lorenzo adopted a wise policy of moderation toward the other Italian powers and the city entered a long period of peace and prosperity. Lorenzo earned the nickname *Il Magnifico* (the Magnificent) for his work as a patron of the arts and, under his leadership, Florence became the major cultural center of Europe, a breeding ground for the new humanist sensibility and a mecca for the greatest artists of the time, who transformed its appearance. Brunelleschi, Donatello, Alberti, Ghiberti, Masaccio, Botticelli, Piero della Francesca, Leonardo da Vinci and Michelangelo left the stamp of their genius and the new Renaissance culture on Florence.

### THE FLORENTINE REPUBLIC

Lorenzo was succeeded by his son Piero, who proved to be a weak character, being unduly submissive when Charles VIII of France invaded Italy in 1494. Piero was finally chased out of the city by a popular uprising. Following the expulsion of the Medici, a republic was established. The Dominican friar Girolamo Savonarola was a prominent figure in the early days of the republic. His vehement, stirring sermons condemned the pagan spirit of the Renaissance and tried to guide the citizens toward a more pious and ascetic way of life. After accusing Pope Alexander VI Borgia of immorality, Savonarola was excommunicated in 1497. The whole city of Florence was then threatened with excommunication, but the Florentines were weary of the rigorous discipline imposed by Savonarola and so imprisoned him. The Palleschi, supporters of the Medici, joined forces with the Arrabbiati against the Piagnoni, who supported Savonarola. The Dominican friar was brought to trial, accused of treason and heresy, and was sentenced to be burned to death in the Piazza della Signoria in 1498. The republic continued for another ten years under the leadership of Pietro Soderini, who was elected *gonfalonier* for life in 1502.

| 1520 | 1530 | 1540 | 1550 | 1560 | 1570 |

**1527** Exile of the Medici and restoration of the Republic

**1537** Cosimo I de' Medici is Duke of Florence

**1548** The Biblioteca Laurenziana is opened

**1555** Siena is annexed to the Medici domain

**1561** The Cavalieri di Santo Stefano are founded in Pisa

# THE DUCHY OF FLORENCE

In 1512, with the help of Pope Julius II, Giuliano de' Medici restored Medici rule in Florence. After his death (1516), he was succeeded by his illegitimate son Ippolito, whose rule lasted several years. In 1527, after the sacking of Rome by the imperial forces, the Florentines exiled the Medici and reestablished the republican system. In the Treaty of Cambrai between Emperor Charles V and Francesco I of France (1529), the Emperor promised the necessary military assistance to reinstate Medici control in Florence. The imperial troops restored Medici control and the powerful family's return to Florence resulted in the abolition of republican institutions and the establishment of a principality. To ratify the family's unopposed supremacy, Alessandro was granted the title of Duke of Florence by Charles V (1530). However, Medici authority did not extend as far as the republics of Lucca and Siena, or several fortresses held by imperial forces along the coast.

# WAR WITH SIENA

Alessandro was murdered in 1537 by an assassin hired by his cousin Lorenzino. He was succeeded by Cosimo I, who initiated an extensive reorganization program to restructure the former republican institutions. The powers of various councils were substantially reduced, while the duke took personal control of vital centers of administration, assisted by the Pratica Segreta, an informal council of trusted advisors picked from the ranks of the aristocracy. In 1555, realizing a long-held Medici ambition, Cosimo I and the imperial troops conquered the city of Siena as part of the war between Valois France and the Emperor Charles V. Siena and its territory was annexed to the Medici domain which, in the mid-16th century, extended virtually over the entire region. The principality of Piombino, the so-called Stato dei Presidi, consisting of several coastal fortresses in the hands of the Spanish, and the Republic of Lucca were the only areas that did not come under their control. These areas continued to maintain the oligarchic regime established in the Middle Ages, safeguarding the republican form of government.

# THE GRAND DUCHY

In 1569, Cosimo I de' Medici was created Grand Duke of Tuscany by Pope Pius V. The title was inherited by his son Francesco I, who had been sharing governmental responsibilities since 1564 at his father's request. In the late 16th century, the dynasty of grand dukes proved very keen to continue the family's tradition of patronage. Thus the stunning Villa di Pratolino was built a couple of miles from Florence, within extensive, beautifully landscaped grounds, and the Uffizi Gallery, built to house the family's works of art, was established. Cosimo also extended the Palazzo Vecchio and installed the Medici in the Palazzo Pitti. Medici munificence was, however, with the limited political autonomy allowed to the Grand Duchy, a faithful ally of Spain. As a result, the attempt by Grand Duke Ferdinando, who succeeded his brother Francesco I in 1587, to abandon the traditional alliance with the Spanish king and forge closer ties with France did not have the desired results. In addition, there was a gradual economic decline in the 17th century, due to bad harvests, epidemics, and changes in the European markets. Medici Tuscany was suffering from the growing difficulties of the urban factories, which were rapidly losing ground in the traditional Levantine markets. The textile trade was particularly hard hit by this situation. The market for Florence's woolen goods collapsed and the city's banks went into a slump.

**THE COAT OF ARMS**
The battle cry of the Medici family's supporters was 'Palle, palle, palle' (Balls, balls, balls), which referred to the repeated device on the Medici coat of arms. In actual fact, these were bezants, coins of Byzantine origin, and the coat of arms appears to have been inspired by the sign of the Arte del Cambio, the guild to which the Medici belonged.

The Medici family, originally from the Mugello region, took up residence in Florence in the 12th century. They began to make a reputation for themselves around the mid-14th century, amassing an impressive fortune from trade and banking. With Salvestro, they supported the Ciompi Revolt ● 33, in defense of the common people. However, the true founder of the dynasty was Giovanni di Bicci, the richest Italian banker. In a century and a half, the wealthy merchants of the Medici family became a ruling family which provided the church with three popes and France with two queens.

**GIOVANNI DI AVERARDO DETTO BICCI (1360–1429)**

**COSIMO THE ELDER (1389–1464)**
A shrewd businessman, he controlled all the companies in which he was the main partner and increased his own fortune. Heading the opposition to the ruling body, he was popular with the people and governed from the sidelines. He was also a patron of the arts.

**PIERO IL GOTTOSO (THE GOUTY) (1416–69)**
A skilled businessman like his father, he took over the reins of the republic (1464–69).

**GIOVANNI (1421–63)**

**CARLO (d.1492)**

**LORENZO THE MAGNIFICENT (1449–92)**

**GIULIANO (1453–78)**

**PIERO II (1472–1503)**
Having no personal fortune at his disposal and not gifted with his father's political acumen, he was banished from Florence.

**GIOVANNI (1475–1521), POPE LEO X FROM 1513**
He placed great importance on the arts, having received a humanist education. A man of flawless morals, he began to indulge in nepotism after becoming pope.

**GIULIANO, DUKE OF NEMOURS (1479–1516)**

**IPPOLITO, CARDINAL (1511–35)**

**GIULIO (1478–1534), POPE CLEMENT VII FROM 1523**
His hostile policy toward Charles V caused the Medici to be exiled after the sacking of Rome.

**LORENZO II, DUKE OF URBINO (1492–1519)**

**ALESSANDRO (1511–37)**
Made Duke of Urbino by Pope Leo X, he was *signore* of Florence from 1513 to 1518, although the city was really governed by Cardinal Silvio Passerini. When he became duke in 1532, he commissioned Benvenuto Cellini to mint a new coin with his effigy in place of the old republican florin. He was assassinated by his cousin Lorenzino.

**CATERINA DE' MEDICI (1519–89)**
Wife of Henry II, King of France, she became regent in 1560 when her son Charles IX ascended the throne. She continued to hold the reins even after he came of age, subsequently exerting an influence over his successor, Henry III. The outbreak of the Wars of Religion saw a decline in royal power, but Caterina, who was gifted with great political acumen, succeeded in keeping the monarchy on an even keel.

Maria de' Medici became the second wife of Henry IV of Bourbon in 1600.

## LORENZO THE MAGNIFICENT

A patron of the arts, Lorenzo ● *36* was also an intellectual with humanist sympathies. A skilled diplomat, he made his name as an arbiter between the Italian powers. In a bid to found a princely dynasty, he married Clarice Orsini, from one of the oldest noble Roman families. He consolidated the fortune of the Medici, securing the appointment of his son Giovanni as cardinal at the age of fourteen.

## MARIA DE' MEDICI

In 1610, on the death of Henry IV of France, she was appointed regent and invested with full powers, but she left the real government of the country to Concino Concini, which made the monarchy very unpopular. Her son, Louis XIII, had Concini assassinated in 1617 and exiled his mother, who twice raised arms against him with the support of the great powers of Europe.

married Piccarda di Odoardo Bueri

**LORENZO (1395–1440)**

**PIERFRANCESCO (1430–76)**

**LORENZO (1463–1503),** *SIGNORE* OF PIOMBINO

**PIERFRANCESCO (1487–1525)**

### LORENZINO (1514–47)

It is not known whether he murdered Alessandro for political motives or for personal reasons. Alessandro had brought about the ruin of his family, but the assassination, which appeared to be the act of a madman, served no purpose whatsoever.

**GIOVANNI (1467–98)**

### GIOVANNI OF THE BLACK BANDS (1498-1526)

He raised black banners to mourn the death of Leo X, hence his nickname. Admired by Machiavelli and his friend, Pietro Aretino, he was a renowned soldier. Wounded by the troops of the Duke of Ferrara, he had a leg amputated and died several days later at the age of twenty-eight.

### COSIMO I (1519–74)

Although he once said of a rebel city: 'It's better to decimate it than to lose it', he was also fond of art and lavish entertainment. He commissioned Vasari to decorate the Palazzo Vecchio and build the Uffizi Gallery.

**FRANCESCO I, GRAND DUKE OF TUSCANY (1541–87)**

**MARIA DE' MEDICI (1573–1642)**

**FERDINANDO I, GRAND DUKE OF TUSCANY (1549–1609)**

**COSIMO II, GRAND DUKE OF TUSCANY (1590–1621)**

**LEOPOLDO, CARDINAL (1617–75)**

**FERDINANDO II, GRAND DUKE OF TUSCANY (1610–70)**

**COSIMO III, GRAND DUKE OF TUSCANY (1642–1723)**

### GIAN GASTONE (1671–1737)

The last Medici Grand Duke of Tuscany had no heirs. He kept out of politics, but abolished the death penalty and dissolved the political police.

**ANNA MARIA LUISA (1667–1743)**

● HISTORY

**1610** Galileo, philosopher and mathematician, is in Pisa

**1783** The Accademia dei Georgofili is founded

| 1580 | 1600 | 1730 | 1760 | 1780 | 1790 |

**1583** The Accademia della Crusca is founded

**1612** The *Vocabolario della Crusca* is published

**1737** The end of the Medici: Tuscany becomes part of Lorraine

**1765** Peter Leopold begins a program of reform

**1787** Promulgation of the Leopoldine code

# THE 17TH AND 18TH CENTURIES

## A SLOWLY GROWING ECONOMY

In the early 17th century Tuscany was struggling to play a leading role in Europe. Only Ferdinando I, of all the successors of Cosimo the Elder, displayed a genuine interest in the political, economic and cultural future of the region. He endeavored to continue Cosimo's centralizing policy and strongly promoted trade. The port of Livorno, open to foreign ships and merchandise, soon became an important trading center, despite the fact that most European trade was now routed through the Atlantic and not the Mediterranean. As a result, Livorno became the most densely populated Tuscan city after Florence and many thriving companies were based there. The city of Prato, with its flourishing textile factories, also succeeded in keeping pace with foreign competition, becoming the largest manufacturing center in the region. Prato was successful in spite of the restrictive laws imposed by the Medici, intended to protect the Florentine textile industry. In fact, measures granting substantial privileges to the craft guilds meant that Florence continued to retain its lead in many spheres of production. The other Tuscan cities found it very difficult to equal this supremacy, particularly as they were populated by an urban aristocracy more interested in acquiring noble titles than in boosting the economic life of the region. Yet when the need arose, the more dynamic members of the provincial nobility would occasionally take part in naval expeditions with the Cavalieri di Santo Stefano, an order of knights based in Pisa. The purpose of the expeditions was to attack Turkish and Barbary pirates or to defend their right to sail in the Tyrrhenian Sea.

## THE LAST OF THE MEDICI

The Medici dynasty slowly declined during the 17th century. In the early 18th century, the heir to the Grand Duchy of Tuscany became an issue which had to be resolved within the wider context of European stability. This was because neither of Cosimo III's two sons had heirs. On the death of Gian Gastone, the last of the Medici, the fate of the principality was decided by the great European powers who drew up the peace treaties after the War of Polish Succession (1738). Tuscany passed into the hands of the house of Lorraine in the person of Duke Francis Stephen, husband of Maria Theresa of Habsburg, the only daughter of Emperor Charles VI.

# THE ENLIGHTENMENT AND THE RESTORATION

## TUSCANY UNDER ENLIGHTENED RULE

Francis Stephen of Lorraine, the future Francis I of Austria, contented himself with a short formal visit to Florence in 1739, then left the government to a Regency Council composed of Lorraine and Lombard citizens. On the other hand, his successor, Peter Leopold, the second-born son of Maria Teresa of Austria and younger brother of Emperor Joseph II, directly assumed responsibility for the government of the Grand Duchy. He was assisted in economic and administrative affairs by Pompeo Neri and Francesco Gianni and, in religious matters, by Scipione de' Ricci, bishop of Pistoia. For the duration of his reign, between 1765 and 1790, Peter Leopold was the epitome of the enlightened despot. He paid particular attention to the problems of landed property, which he tackled with a consistent land reform program and collaboration with the local police. Free trade in grain within the Grand Duchy was set up in 1766. He also tried to reclaim the Maremma, a vast, sparsely populated alluvial plain between the Arno and Ombrone rivers, interspersed with malarial marshes. The intention was to convert it into an area producing grain for free export outside Tuscany's borders. In 1770, the guilds which were hindering the growth of production were abolished and a *Camera di Commercio delle Arti e delle Manifatture* (Chamber of Commerce) was set up. In the last decade of his reign, in a bid to assist the class of small rural landowners and increase the amount of available farmland, Peter Leopold tried to encourage the redistribution of large estates and sold some large properties belonging to the Grand Duchy. New legislation also ratified the important judicial reforms carried out by Peter Leopold. He left Tuscany in 1790 when he became emperor, and was followed as ruler by his son.

**1821** The review
*Antologia* is founded

**1846** First Italian
telegraph line is laid
between Florence and Pisa

| 1800 | 1810 | 1820 | 1830 | 1840 | 1850 |

**1807** Tuscany annexed
to the Napoleonic
empire

**1815** Restoration
of the Lorraine
Habsburgs in Tuscany

**1824** Leopold II is
Grand Duke of
Tuscany

**1848** Students from Pisa
University clash at
Curtatone and
Montanara

## THE KINGDOM OF ETRURIA

Tuscany's occupation by Napoleon's troops in March 1799. However, the provisional government set up by the French commissioner Reinhard only lasted a few months. In July, Austrian troops reinstated the government in the name of Ferdinand III. A quadrumvirate composed of the Grand Duke's supporters ruled in the name of the sovereign, who had been absent for several months. Following the Treaty of Lunéville in 1801, the territory of the

Grand Duchy of Tuscany became the Kingdom of Etruria and was given to Louis I of Bourbon, the principal heir of Parma. He was incapable of administering it justly, and allowed his wife Maria Luisa to exert a great deal of influence over matters of government. She continued to exercise power after the death of her husband, becoming regent for her son Louis II of Bourbon.
In 1807, French troops occupied Tuscany and Napoleon set up a provisional governing council headed by General Menou.

The following year, the region was annexed directly by the emperor, and Napoleon's sister, Elisa Bonaparte Baciocchi, already Duchess of Lucca and Princess of Piombino, took over the reins of government. In 1809, Tuscany, including the regions of Lucca and Piombino, was again made a Grand Duchy, still ruled by the emperor's sister.
In 1814, the Congress of Vienna decreed that the Grand Ducal throne should be given back to Ferdinand III of Habsburg-Lorraine, who governed with the help of Vittorio Fossombroni.

After Peter Leopold, the Grand Ducal throne was taken by his son Ferdinand III, who was unable to prevent

## TUSCANY RESTORED

The revival of Peter Leopold's code by Grand Duke Ferdinand III did not represent a sudden return to the past. The laws drawn up by Peter Leopold had in fact been worded in line with the ideals of the Enlightenment. They reflected the principles of

centralization of government, the annulment of privileges and the equality of all citizens before the law – the principles that had inspired the Napoleonic code. The activities of the government of the restored Grand Duchy were based

on the modern criteria of boosting the economy with a decisive redevelopment program, promoting free trade and strongly encouraging local industries (silk, wool and particularly steel and iron). From a strictly political standpoint,

however, Grand Duke Ferdinand sought to exercise control over all government positions, endeavoring to eliminate any trace of the elective principle in the appointment of local administrators.

41

● HISTORY

| 1860 Plebiscite for annexation to the Kingdom of Sardinia | 1865–71 Florence is capital. The city enters a period of regrowth | 1869 England acquires the island of Montecristo |

| 1850 | 1860 | 1865 | 1880 | 1890 | 1900 |

| 1859 Leopold II leaves Tuscany | 1861 Ricasoli forms the new government of the Kingdom of Italy | 1866 The Società Italiana per l'Educazione Popolare is founded in Florence | 1884 Cholera epidemic | 1898 Strike against the rising price of bread |

## FROM THE RISORGIMENTO TO ITALIAN UNIFICATION

### FLORENCE, CENTER OF RISORGIMENTO CULTURE

Public opinion was not in favor of the Grand Duke Ferdinand's reactionary, authoritarian policies, and people began to nurture hopes of some constitutional change that would reduce sovereign authority. They also championed a new brand of Catholicism which, rather than fostering backward looking principles, advocated a return to purity of faith. Intellectuals met in the literary club founded in Florence by Gian Pietro Vieusseux in 1819. The club developed a program that attempted to reconcile Catholicism with liberalism, within the context of a moderate constitutionalism, and to encourage the improvement of economic and agrarian techniques. From 1821, the ideas of the most important members of the club, Gino Capponi, Carlo Ridolfi, Niccolo Tommaseo and Raffaello Lambruschini, found expression in the periodical *L'Antologia*, founded by Vieusseux. When the periodical was shut down in 1833, on orders from Vienna, new publications such as *Il Giornale agrario, La Guida dell'educatore* and *L'Archivo storico italiano* took up the challenge of promoting innovative ideas in the fields of welfare, education and scientific progress.

### THE LAST GRAND DUKE

Leopold II, who ascended the Grand Ducal throne in 1824, endeavored to continue his father's policy: reclamation work in the Maremma went ahead, trade with the cities of Prato and Livorno was boosted by the construction of railroad lines, and communications between Florence and Pisa were improved by the construction, in 1846, of the first telegraph line on the Italian Peninsula. In the last months of 1847, popular liberal pressure compelled the Grand Duke to set up a Home Guard and a city council, and to grant greater freedom of the press. In 1848, as the Italian peninsula was unsettled by a wave of revolutionary events, he also granted a constitution for representative government: this did not prevent the exile of the Grand Duke, however, who returned to Florence the year after with the assistance of Austrian troops.

LEOPOLD II ARCIDUC D'AUTRICHE. *Grand Duc de Toscane.* Né le 3 Octobre 1797. — 1870 died.

### FLORENCE, CAPITAL OF ITALY

In 1865, awaiting the resolution of the 'Roman question' which made Rome the capital of the fledgling Kingdom of Italy, Florence became the temporary home of the government and parliament. After this short-lived period, the removal of the kingdom's governmental machinery to Rome in 1870 caused an economic recession which hit the whole region and which was only gradually overcome as a result of the expansion of the industrial and manufacturing sectors.

### UNIFICATION

Tuscany was also affected by the spread of Risorgimento unitarian ideas in the 1850s. In April 1859, a large popular demonstration led by the Mazzinian Giuseppe Dolfi convinced the Grand Duke to accept defeat and renounce sovereignty of the Grand Duchy. Vittorio Emanuele II, King of Sardinia-Piedmont, did not immediately accept the territory offered to him by the Tuscans. Unification did not come until 1860 when a plebiscite was held: in March of the same year, 366,571 Tuscans voted against 19,869 in favor of annexation with Sardinia-Piedmont.

# MODERN TIMES

## INDUSTRY AND LABOR UNIONS

In the last years of the 19th century and the early years of the 20th century, the presence of growing industrial centers such as the Orlando shipyards at Livorno, the wool mills of Prato, the paper mills in Lima and the industrial plants in Larderello, encouraged the organization of a labor union movement. It devoted itself to improving the conditions of the working classes and spreading socialist principles in both cities and rural areas. This period saw the appearance of the traditional electoral trend in favor of progressivist parties, which is still in evidence today.

## THE FASCIST DICTATORSHIP

After the rise to power of Benito Mussolini in 1922, even Tuscany had to submit to the fascist dictatorship. All attempts to oppose the regime, culminating in the publication of the periodical *Non mollare*, petered out in the face of violent attacks by armed squads of Blackshirts. During punitive expeditions in 1925 the Blackshirts carried out a series of savage murders in Florence. During World War Two, the port of Livorno and the cities of Pisa and Florence were particularly hard hit by air raids, which caused a great deal of damage to buildings and decimated the population.

## THE RESISTANCE

In 1943, a general feeling that the dictatorship was close to collapse speeded up the secret reestablishment of the political parties, initiating a battle which, after September 18, became a war against the Germans and the troops of the Italian Social Republic. Tuscany became a battlefield between Nazis and partisans, and the civilian populace was hit by reprisals carried out by Nazi troops who were attacked by increasingly well-organized partisan forces. In the postwar years Tuscany, like the other regions in central Italy, voted decisively in favor of the institution of the republic in the referendum of 1946.

## PRESENT-DAY TUSCANY

The region has now entered a new period of international prestige. This has come about partly through tourism, and partly through the economic and social infrastructure. Vineyards, olive groves and agriculture are still important, and well managed, generating income. Small and medium-sized firms and craft businesses now export luxury goods all over the world, particularly top quality leather and fabrics. Tuscany's cities are filled with medieval and Renaissance works of art and their historic centers have survived the destruction wrought by town planning programs, a process which has been a characteristic feature of most Italian cities in recent decades. These cities no longer attract wealthy visitors on the Grand Tour to complete their cultural education, as in previous centuries, but they act as a magnet to hordes of tourists from all over the world. Indeed, tourism is crucial for the future of the region. Moreover, the climate, mild in winter and temperate in summer, makes the region very popular with élite English and German tourists who want to escape the stresses of modern city life. They are attracted to the villas and old farms in the countryside and enjoy a return to nature. The region is not only famous for its masterpieces of art and its breathtaking landscape, but also for a cultural policy that is responsible for major events such as the Maggio Musicale Fiorentino, an annual festival of great international renown.

## THE ORIGINS

In some ways, it is natural to regard the three great fathers of Italian literature, Dante Alighieri (1265–1321), Francesco Petrarch (1304–74) ▲ *187* and Giovanni Boccaccio (1313–75) ▲ *144*, as models for the development of Italian, a non-existent language at that time: all three writers were deeply rooted in Florentine culture and were its main exponents. However, it did not follow that the inhabitants of the other regions of Italy would be happy to speak a language on loan from Florentine or Tuscan dialects. This is precisely what happened, with the result that Italian was for centuries a written, not spoken, language, read and used by very few.

## THE LANGUAGE QUESTION

Although these three major 14th-century figures had established the potential of the Florentine language, Leonardo Bruni (1374–1444) led a debate, in the following century, concerning the particular language that should be adopted for both speaking and writing: this was known as the 'language question'. Niccolò Machiavelli (1469–1527) supported the use of spoken Florentine; Pietro Bembo (1470–1547) in his *Discussions of the Vernacular Language* (1525), recommended Petrarch and Boccaccio (already somewhat remote) as the models for poetry and prose;

while in *The Courtier* (1528), Baldessare Castiglione (1478–1529) proposed the hybrid language used in the Italian courts. There were obviously other suggestions: some advocated Sienese instead of Florentine, while some thought the Tuscan dialect should be used as a model. But by the end of the 16th century, Bembo's archaic suggestion had triumphed over the other theories.

## DELLA-CRUSCANS AND ANTI-DELLA-CRUSCANS

The 17th century opened with the publication of a dictionary, the *Vocabolario degli accademici della Crusca* (1612). Founded in Florence in 1538, the literary Accademia della Crusca had been urged by Leonardo Salviati (1540–89) to make a systematic record of spoken Florentine. Although the century saw the flowering of dialect literature, the main controversy centered around the Della-Cruscans, members of the Academy, and the Anti-della-Cruscans, who accused the Academy of pedantry. Daniello Bartoli (1608–85), the official historiographer of the Society of Jesus and a leading prose writer, was one of the latter. Scientific prose also gave a stimulus to modernization: the writings by the Pisan astronomer and mathematician Galileo Galilei (1564–1642) are a splendid anti-rhetorical and dialect

VOCABOLARIO
DEGLI ACCADEMICI
DELLA CRUSCA,
IN QUESTA TERZA IMPRESSIONE
Nuovamente ricorretto, e copiosamente accresciuto.
AL SERENISSIMO
COSIMO TERZO
GRANDUCA DI TOSCANA
LOR SIGNORE.

IN FIRENZE, MDCXCI.

version of 16th-century Florentine. He was joined by a doctor and biologist, Francesco Redi (1626–98), who was an expert in languages, an excellent prose writer and the author of the famous dithyramb *Bacchus in Tuscany*.

These four shovels were the personal emblems of members of the Accademia della Crusca. They were designed to bear the pseudonym which concealed the identity of the institute's members. The emblems make reference to the world of grain, since the Academy's task was to protect the purity of the language (flour) from impurities (bran or chaff).

The real linguistic problem of the 18th century was the difficulty of breaking out of the provinces, since the language of international communication was French, which was widely spoken in Italy. The early 19th century saw a return to the purist 'order' (again, literary Florentine) in reaction to the theoretical and practical liberalism of many 18th-century writers. On the other hand, the Florentine model was still making its presence felt in the mid-19th century, to judge by writers such as the Milan-born Alessandro Manzoni (1785–1873) who felt the need to 'rinse his laundry in the Arno river' – in other words, cleanse his own language of dialect Lombard words and foreign words. Manzoni's suggested language model (the spoken Florentine of the educated classes) was so rigidly applied by his followers that it came to represent a new brand of academism. The 19th century closed with the lucid studies of the Italian linguist Graziadio Isaia Ascoli (1829–1907) who believed that only the circulation of ideas and culture could promote linguistic unity in Italy.

## A NEW DEVELOPMENT: ITALIANS SPEAKING ITALIAN

In 1861 (the year of Italian unification), an estimated 0.8 percent of the male population spoke Italian. Hardly more than 150,000 people were therefore able to put together a simple sentence in the language of Dante, Petrarch and Boccaccio, read it and sign their own name without making a mistake. It took another hundred years for the nation to emerge from the paradoxical situation of being a newly formed state without a distinctive linguistic identity. The motto, 'Now that Italy has been formed, we need to form the Italians' could also refer to the language. Television was the only method of communication that proved able to break down the barrier of traditional dialects. The Tuscan-Florentine model crumbled in the wake of television in particular and the mass media in general. Since the advent of television, Italians speak what linguists describe as regional Italian: a language with a simplified syntactical base which includes local and regional vocabulary. Although the consequences of this have been grave, they cannot be blamed on the mass media. The ever-increasing growth of the cities, domestic migration and the collapse of the patriarchal family unit, which has been partly replaced by the single-parent family, have caused ties with the countryside and with traditions, including spoken language, to be severed.

## TUSCAN RESISTANCE

Although there has almost always been a divide between written and spoken Italian, Tuscany is particularly resistant to homogenization of language. This is due to the specific situation in Florence and Tuscany, where there is a close similarity between language and dialect. This means that a Tuscan can read a 14th-century text with a high level of basic understanding, even without any special grounding in language or culture. This is primarily indicative of the 'slowness' of Italian, a European language which has not developed over the course of time as much as other languages such as English or French. Tuscany's 'resistance' can be seen on three levels: syntax, pronunciation and vocabulary. In terms of syntax, this region still uses the subjunctive as much as ever, and has not dropped the future perfect or historic past. Where pronunciation is concerned, the region has not fallen into line with the 'Lombard model' as regards tonic vowels, continuing to say 'bène' (open 'e') instead of the now current 'béne' (closed 'e') and 'perché' instead of 'perchè'. And as far as vocabulary is concerned, there is a remarkable tendency to favor the continued use of old-fashioned terms once associated with everyday usage, in spite of the ever-changing times.

45

## THE LANGUAGE OF SONG

Although the dialects used in the other regions of Italy were often very different from the language of Italian literature, in Tuscany the local dialect and standard Italian – the language of books – were to all intents and purposes identical. As a result, Tuscan farmers and artisans were familiar with works of highbrow literature, including great poems such as Dante Alighieri's *Divine Comedy* or Tasso's *Gerusalemme liberata*, even Marino's *L'Adone*, a state of affairs unimaginable elsewhere. Even more surprising, this meant that popular Tuscan culture succeeded in dominating not only literary language, but also the literary technique of versification. Tuscan ballad-singers (*below*) produced and circulated countless

narrative texts in Italian verse on a wide range of subjects, including historical chronicles, political satire, traditions and secular or religious myths. This familiarity with the language of poetry reached its creative pinnacle in the shows put on by the *improvvisatori* (improvisers), which are still very popular. These improvised performances take the form of a contest. The audience suggests a subject – which could be 'the blonde and the brunette' or 'the city and the countryside' or a topical political theme – that the two improvisers must develop in verse. Each improviser takes turns to sing an octave whose rhymes must be repeated in the following octave.

## THEATER

Theater has always occupied an important place in Tuscan popular culture, developing in a variety of ways which, particularly in rural areas, are sometimes unparalleled elsewhere. The texts, which are in verse and usually sung to traditional melodies, are written in literary Italian and are the work of local authors, farmers or artisans. These characteristic texts reflect Tuscany's time-honored tradition of literary culture and are a direct result of its familiarity with the great classics of poetry ● 45. The theatrical genres, which have a clearly defined formal character, include *Il Maggio* (*below*), *Il Bruscello* (*left*), *La Befanata*, *La Zingaresca* or *La Segavecchia*, and cover a wide variety of themes (all derived from 'ancient' models). They can be dramatic or comic-satirical epics with historical or social episodes, and draw on the repertories of literature, folk ritual and the Christian calendar. Events from Epiphany, carnival or Lent might be covered, as well as Christmas or Christ's Passion. The end results are often extremely dramatic and bursting with unexpected vitality.

# Arts and traditions

# ● POTTERY

From the 14th century onward, some fine examples of majolica pottery were produced in cities such as Siena and Florence: jugs and bowls for table settings, ewers and jars for hospital pharmacies. However, Pisa, Siena, Montelupo and Cafaggiolo were the main centers of production for the top-quality majolica ware that expressed the new Renaissance creativity. The pottery produced between the late 15th and 16th centuries at the castle of Cafaggiolo, near the Medici Villa ▲ *137*, was superior to the rest. The passion for oriental pottery in the 16th century led the Medici to found the first European (soft) porcelain factory in Florence; this short-lived venture flowered again in 1737 with the Ginori factory at Doccia.

**CAFAGGIOLO DISH**
This large dish (16 inches in diameter) displays the arms of the Florentine Tornabuoni family in a frame of green interlinked branches, probably a Medici emblem, to suggest the alliance between the two major Florentine families. The heraldic display is surrounded by a decorative pattern of blue and white motifs modeled on Chinese porcelain, and ornamental groupings composed of symbols of the *Signoria's* military power (ancient quivers and shields) and cultural emblems (books). The back of the dish is stamped with the trademark 'SP' at 'Chafaggiuolo'.

**'ZAFFER' EWER**
This majolica vase was produced in Florence in the first half of the 15th century. Its style of decoration is known as *'a zaffera a rilievo'*: the pattern is thickly painted in blue over a beige design. The highly stylized animal and plant motifs are derived from the patterns of oriental fabrics. There are stars beneath the handles: fifteen vases of this type carry this emblem of the Florentine hospital of Santa Maria Nova.

### GINORI PORCELAIN

In 1737 the leading factory of hard porcelain in Italy was founded by Marchese Carlo Ginori. The chief painter in the factory's early years was a Viennese artist, Karl Anreiter, who decorated sets of china with vivid polychromatic designs. This oval tray displays a figure in an 'oriental-style' costume derived from paintings by the 16th-century artist Jacopo Ligozzi.

### MEDICI PORCELAIN

Francesco de' Medici founded a laboratory at the Casino di San Marco in a bid to produce Chinese white porcelain. With the help of artists (including Buontalenti) and alchemists he succeeded in producing a material similar to the legendary oriental product. These extremely rare pieces are marked on the back with a picture of the dome of Santa Maria del Fiore. The shapes were often modeled on Medici jewelry, while the decoration shows the influence both of Chinese porcelain and the finest pieces of contemporary majolica.

### GALILEO CHINI

Having left the Ginori factory after it merged with Richard (1896), Chini (1873–1956) went into business for himself, naming his kiln in Florence after San Lorenzo. Here he produced some magnificent pottery that combined pictorial sensitivity with new shapes and the experimental use of different ceramic materials. He created some stunning masterpieces of Italian Art Nouveau and was awarded the Grand Prix at the Universal Exhibition in Paris in 1900, which earned him international renown.

### SIENESE 'TONDINO'

Benedetto was a sophisticated potter plying his trade in early 16th-century Siena. At the center of this small decorative dish, known as a 'tondino', there is a Renaissance emblem accompanied by the Petrarchan sonnet *Altro diletto che imparar non trovo*. The setting boasts an elegant *bianco sopra bianco* (white on white) decorative motif executed in white tin enamel on top of the tin glaze, to create a pattern that looks as if it has been embroidered onto the surface.

### LARGE VASE WITH PEACOCKS

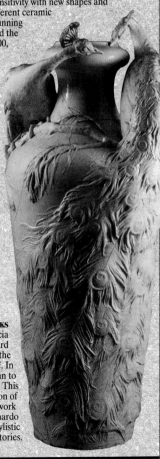

The reputation of the Ginori factory in Doccia continues to this day. In 1896 Augusto Richard became its new owner and the factory took the name of the *Società Ceramica Richard-Ginori*. In 1900, under Luigi Tazzini, the factory began to produce pieces in the new Art Nouveau style. This was made possible by the keen collaboration of leading modelers. These were inspired by the work of major contemporary sculptors such as Leonardo Bistolfi, and were also receptive to stylistic innovations made in other major European factories.

Members of a hooded brotherhood
in a Good Friday procession.

The Roman Catholic festivals are celebrated
with particular solemnity and splendor in urban
areas, often completely transforming the face
of the city, as do the carpets of colored sawdust
that cover the streets in Camaiore ▲ *172* (Lucca) for the
Corpus Domini procession. During the '*Luminare*' in Lucca and
Pisa, respectively on September 13 for the festival of the Volto
Santo and on June 16 for the festival of San Ranieri, the
buildings take on a phantasmagoric appearance in the flickering
light of thousands of oil lamps. In the rural villages and valleys
too, time-honored traditional events are still celebrated.

**HOLY WEEK
PROCESSIONS**
These atmospheric
torchlight
processions
often take
place
at night.
The torches
are carried
by believers
who follow the
cross and the
emblems
of the
Passion
with rapt
attention.

**SACRED DRAMAS**
Sacred verse dramas for Christmas,
Twelfth Night and Christ's Passion are
widespread. The actors of the Compagnia
del Maggio di Buti (Pisa) perform
Giordano's *Passaggio*.

**SCOPPIO DEL CARRO**
The spectacular ceremony of the *Scoppio del Carro* ('Explosion of the Cart') dates back to the
time of the Crusades. It is held at Easter in the Piazza di Santa Maria del Fiore in Florence.
During the singing of the Gloria, a small cart shaped like a dove, descending on a wire driven
by small rockets, ignites the fireworks contained in the large float pulled by white oxen.

## FLOATING PROCESSIONS

The festival of St Erasmus, the patron saint of sailors, is celebrated on June 2 at Porto Ercole (Grosseto) ▲ 258. The bust and the saint's relics are carried by seamen who lead a nocturnal procession across the sea in a ship hung with flags.

## CEREMONIAL FIRES

The practice of lighting bonfires to celebrate particular religious festivals is still widespread in Tuscany. The festival of San Giuseppe (March 19), in Pitigliano (Grosseto, *above left*)

▲ 260, is particularly elaborate. In Camporgiano (Lucca) the bonfire (*above right*) is lit on Christmas night. Built with branches of evergreen trees, it continues to burn as the bells ring out in jubilation.

## THE CORPUS DOMINI PROCESSION

At Camaiore (Lucca), in the days preceding the festival, specialists assisted by volunteers decorate the route to be taken by the procession carrying the Holy Sacrament. Using templates, they spread the streets with a brightly colored carpet of sawdust patterned with decorative motifs and religious scenes that differ from year to year (*below*).

## NIGHT FESTIVALS

Thousands of oil lamps, arranged on façades and in windows, transform the appearance of the city for the festival of the Volto Santo in Lucca and that of San Ranieri in Pisa ▲ 152 (*right*).

# ● SECULAR FESTIVALS

Soldier in Renaissance costume at the *Palio Marinaro* in Porto Santo Stefano ▲ *258*.

Tuscany's traditional festivals clearly reflect the region's historical urban and rural divide. Many of the festivals revolve around the central theme of a battle or contest. These can take the form of large-scale events such as Siena's Palio ▲ *214*, Pisa's Gioco del Ponte ▲ *152* and Florence's Calcio in Costume, or they can be simple yet quaint events such as the Bravvio delle Botti in Montepulciano, where representatives from each of the city's districts compete by rolling extremely heavy barrels toward a finishing line. It is impossible not to see these festivals as an accurate portrayal of the factional conflicts that once disturbed the peace of Tuscany's cities. In some cases, these ancient urban celebrations have been revived after a period of neglect, and have been reintroduced within the framework of dramatic historical reenactments.

**VIAREGGIO CARNIVAL**
Begun in 1873, the Viareggio carnival ▲ *172* has won international renown for the fantastic satirical figures that ride on huge floats made by local artisans.

**THE EMBLEM OF VICTORY**
The prize given to the winners of traditional costume contests is usually symbolic, and often takes the form of a *palio*, a kind of banner or standard decorated by local artists, hence the name of the contest.

**SHOOTING THE GYRFALCON**
This is a crossbow competition with a target resembling a bird of prey, the gyrfalcon. The extremely popular performances given by the flag-wavers are now a mandatory part of Tuscan historical commemorations.

### FOOTBALL PAGEANT

An antecedent of rugby and American soccer, this Florentine brand of football is played on June 24 with teams of twenty-seven players. The players used to compete in the streets and squares of Florence, particularly in honor of visiting foreign princes.

### JOUST OF THE SARACEN

Pairs of horsemen wearing armor and medieval costumes represent the districts of Arezzo ▲ *184* in this jousting contest. Lance in hand, they attempt to hit a life-size dummy representing a legendary Muslim king. The winner receives a 'golden lance'.

### JOUST OF THE BEAR

The bear, a heraldic animal in Pistoia ▲ *179*, holds up the target that has to be struck with a lance by racing horsemen who represent the city's four districts. This contest is held in honor of the festival of San Jacopo (July 25).

### GIOCO DEL PONTE

On the Ponte di Mezzo, which links the two banks of the Arno river in Pisa ▲ *152*, the two teams of Tramontana and Mezzogiorno try to drive their opponents back to the opposite end of the bridge. This sports contest is a reenactment of the often bloody clashes between the two factions.

53

# ● RIBOLLITA

Basically rustic in character, Tuscan cooking is characterized by the use of top quality, full-flavored olive oil and white beans. The Tuscans' nickname of *mangiafagioli* (bean-eaters) shows how much their diet revolves around this staple food. Olive oil and white beans are the two main ingredients of *ribollita*, a country dish traditionally prepared with sufficient quantities of seasonal vegetables to last the entire week, then reheated day after day (hence its name, which means 'reboiled').

**2.** Chop the carrot, celery, tomato and leek into large chunks and add them to the pan with the onion.

**3.** When lightly browned, add the beans, the *prosciutto* and about 8 cups of water.

**6.** Purée the beans using a mouli sieve or a food processor.

**7.** Add the purée to the other ingredients, together with the coarsely chopped cabbage. Cook over a low heat.

**10.** Ladle the soup into the bowl over the slices of garlic bread and sprinkle with grated parmesan.

## INGREDIENTS (6–8 servings)
2½lb fresh white beans
1lb red cabbage
½ cup Tuscan olive oil
2 slices of *prosciutto* or bacon
3 onions (red, if possible)

1 stick of celery with leaves, 1 carrot,
1 leek, 1 tomato, garlic (4–5 cloves),
rosemary, thyme
6–8 slices of bread
grated parmesan
salt, pepper

**1.** Dice the onions and half a clove of garlic and lightly fry in a large pan in 4 tablespoons of oil.

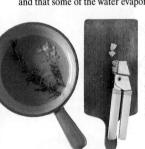

**4.** Add salt and pepper to taste, then leave to cook on a low heat, stirring frequently to ensure that the beans are cooked through and that some of the water evaporates.

**5.** Remove the *prosciutto* and take out a small quantity of beans (5 tablespoons).

**8.** Meanwhile, pour the rest of the oil into a saucepan and add a sprig of rosemary, a pinch of thyme and 2–3 cloves of crushed garlic. Lightly fry for 5 minutes, then add them to the soup.

**9.** Toast the slices of bread in the oven or under the grill, rub them with a clove of garlic and arrange them inside a bowl.

## RIBOLLITA
The leftover soup can be served the day after in a variety of ways. Try pouring the cold soup into a heat-resistant dish, cover the top with slices of fresh onion and add 3 tablespoons of olive oil. Cook in a medium oven until a golden crust has formed over the onions. Serve immediately.

*Cacciucco* is a fish soup made in Livorno and Viareggio. Its name is derived from *kaçukli,* which is Turkish for the small fish that form its main ingredients. Gastronomically speaking, it is a variation on a dish known as *brodetto* on the Romagnese coast and *zuppa alla marinara* in Rome. Although by the late 19th century this fish soup had become a popular middle-class dish, it was originally prepared on ships or served in taverns and, as a result, it is still served hot over slices of bread.

**SUITABLE TYPES OF FISH**
Rascasse, gurnard, dogfish, conger eel, mantis shrimps and squill. Mullet or goby can also be used. The small fish are gutted but left whole, complete with head; the larger fish should be cut up into chunks. Baby squid and cuttlefish go well with the mantis shrimps. You will need 3lb of fish for 4 servings.

**2.** Lightly fry in olive oil in a large pan.

**1.** Chop up some celery, onion and 2 cloves of garlic and add a pinch of paprika.

**3.** Add the mantis shrimps, cuttlefish and baby squid, and fry until golden brown.

**4.** Add a bay leaf and gradually pour in 2 tablespoons of strong vinegar and a glass of red wine. Allow the liquid to reduce by half.

**5.** Blanch 1½lb plum tomatoes, deseed and coarsely chop. Add to the pan and cook over a low heat for about 10 minutes.

**6.** Add the rascasse, gurnard, dogfish, conger eel and squill to the pan. Season with salt and pepper to taste and cook for at least 20 minutes.

**7.** Sprinkle with chopped parsley when almost done.

**8.** Cut and toast some slices of bread, rub with a clove of garlic and arrange in deep soup plates.

**9.** Ladle the *cacciucco* into the soup plates, ensuring that each serving contains all the different types of fish.

**10.** Serve with a young red wine.

In a rich, fertile region like Tuscany, blessed with a mild climate, food is plentiful and food conservation has never been an urgent priority. For this reason, the range of Tuscan gastronomic specialties is not as varied as in other regions, and the desire for innovation often plays a major part in their invention. It is by no means surprising that there are relatively few varieties of cheese and salami, while cakes, biscuits and products originally manufactured for the celebration of religious and popular festivals abound.

## CHEESES

Typical Tuscan cheeses are made mainly from ewes' milk (cattle were used for working the land) and the wide range of flavors is determined by the area of production and the ripening process. There are a number of varieties: they begin with the generic *pecorino* (ewes' milk cheese) and Tuscan *cacciotta* (soft cheese with added cow's milk), followed by Sienese *pecorino*, Garfagnana *pecorino* and Montagna *pecorino*, which is produced on the pastures on the slopes of Mount Amiata. The finest is the sublime *pecorino* from Pienza, which boasts an unmistakable tangy aroma and flavor. With a bit of luck, between May and June you can sample one of the varieties of *raveggiolo*, a fresh ewes' milk cheese with a full-flavored, creamy taste, that has to be eaten within a few days of production.

**SIENESE PECORINO**

**PECORINO FROM PIENZA**

**PECORINO FROM THE GARFAGNANA**

**PECORINO FROM MONTAGNA AMIATA/SEGGIANO VARIETY**

**RAVEGGIOLO**

### FINOCCHIONA

Although Tuscan *prosciutto* (salt-cured ham) has been awarded a Protected Designation of Origin (PDO), the finest example of Tuscan cured-pork products is *finocchiona*. With its rich, strong flavor and melting tenderness, it is a favorite with gourmets.

### BURISTO (MALLEGATO)

*Buristo*, also known as *mallegato*, is also common. It is made from pig's head, pig's blood, fat and entrails and flavored, depending on the area, with spices, raisins, pine nuts, lemon rind and candied citrus peel.

### LARDO DI COLONNATA

The most popular cured-pork product at present is produced in the Apuan Alps. *Lardo di Colonnata* ▲ *169* is pickled in marble basins that have been vigorously rubbed with cloves of garlic. The layers of *lardo* (fat bacon) are alternated with a seasoning of coarse salt, pepper, garlic, rosemary and sage. After six months, it is served thinly sliced on hot *crostini* (toasted bread rounds).

### WILD BOAR PRODUCTS

In the regions of Siena and the Maremma, the most popular cured-pork products are made from wild boar, ranging from *prosciutto* to fillet, salami and sausages and boasting a wide variety of curing processes and flavorings.

### PRESERVED FISH

Two traditional types of preserved fish come from the area around Orbetello. Smoked eels, are prepared by pickling small eels in a delicate red chilli sauce, then hanging them to dry in smoke flavored with wild fennel, bay, rosemary and thyme. Smoked mackerel is prepared by skillfully alternating the brining and smoking processes, both heavily seasoned.

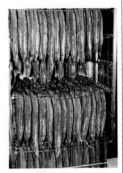

# ● Bread, honey, cakes and biscuits

### Bread
Even in the face of large-scale industrialization, Tuscan bread has retained its distinctive character: always unsalted, it comes in long or round loaves weighing between 1lb and 3lb. Further south, Tuscan bread is replaced by *pagnotta maremmana* which, although similar in appearance, is made from salted dough. *Pane di ramerino* (rosemary bread) can be enjoyed almost everywhere, particularly at Easter. These loaves, enriched with eggs and rosemary leaves, were made to celebrate Holy Week in the late Middle Ages.

**PANE TOSCANO (TUSCAN BREAD)**

**PAGNOTTA MAREMMANA**

### Honey
The production of Tuscan honey is as rigorously controlled as wine and Tuscany's beekeepers now produce some of the best honey in Italy. Tuscan honey is available in every possible flower variety and its main center of production seems to be in the area around Montalcino, between Siena and Grosseto.

**PANFORTE DI SIENA**

**BUCCELLATO**

### Cakes and biscuits
There are many Tuscan cakes and biscuits and each city has its own specialties. These include *brigidini* from Valdinievole, *africani* from Greve in Chianti, *befanini* from Viareggio, *buccellato* from the region around Lucca and *ossi di morto* from Montalcino. The most internationally renowned of these are the *biscottini* from Prato (often confused with *cantucci*), and the *ricciarelli* and *panforte* from Siena.

**BEFANINI DI VIAREGGIO**

RICCIARELLINI

SAPORI

**RICCIARELLINI** *alle mandorle*
DELICATEZZE TRADIZIONALI DI TOSCANA

**RICCIARELLI**

**CANTUCCINI**

# Architecture

# CIVIL ARCHITECTURE:
## TOWERS AND COURTYARDS

Medieval Tuscan cities, whose picturesque appearance can still be admired in some places, resembled a massive 'organ' of towers rising from a tight cluster of houses. These were mainly courtyard houses: buildings constructed around an empty central space in line with the classic Mediterranean plan. The towers were the fortified homes of wealthy citizens and noble families, and an impressive symbol of their power. The towers were therefore lopped or destroyed when one or other of these families was overthrown in the frequent conflicts.

### COURTYARD HOUSES
This vertical section shows clearly the typical structure of a courtyard house. These buildings were often labyrinthine, due to their infinite variations in height and shape and the intensive use of wooden overhangs and open galleries.

### THE COMPLICATED LAYOUT OF COURTYARD HOUSES
The chronic lack of space in overcrowded walled cities, the often irregular terrain and the age-old accretion of modifications made the layout of these houses very complicated. As a result, the buildings around one courtyard were often confused with those of an adjacent courtyard.

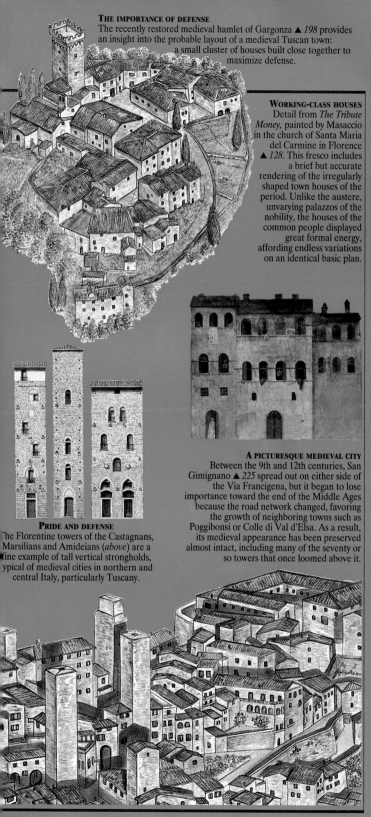

**THE IMPORTANCE OF DEFENSE**
The recently restored medieval hamlet of Gargonza ▲ *198* provides an insight into the probable layout of a medieval Tuscan town: a small cluster of houses built close together to maximize defense.

**WORKING-CLASS HOUSES**
Detail from *The Tribute Money,* painted by Masaccio in the church of Santa Maria del Carmine in Florence ▲ *128.* This fresco includes a brief but accurate rendering of the irregularly shaped town houses of the period. Unlike the austere, unvarying palazzos of the nobility, the houses of the common people displayed great formal energy, affording endless variations on an identical basic plan.

**A PICTURESQUE MEDIEVAL CITY**
Between the 9th and 12th centuries, San Gimignano ▲ *225* spread out on either side of the Via Francigena, but it began to lose importance toward the end of the Middle Ages because the road network changed, favoring the growth of neighboring towns such as Poggibonsi or Colle di Val d'Elsa. As a result, its medieval appearance has been preserved almost intact, including many of the seventy or so towers that once loomed above it.

**PRIDE AND DEFENSE**
The Florentine towers of the Castagnans, Marsilians and Amideians (*above*) are a fine example of tall vertical strongholds, typical of medieval cities in northern and central Italy, particularly Tuscany.

63

# ● CIVIL ARCHITECTURE:
## PIAZZAS AND PALAZZOS

View of the Piazza della Signoria in Florence ▲ 123, dominated by the equestrian statue of
Cosimo I: a symbol of autocracy erected in the square epitomizing the communal tradition.

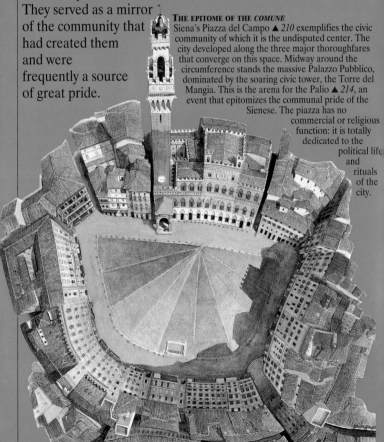

In a world as passionately devoted to the life of the *comune* as that of medieval Tuscany, the architectural trappings of self-government (the piazza for civic and religious gatherings and for the market, the *palazzo pubblico* or town hall to house the offices of the *comune's* magistracy) had a symbolic importance as well as a functional purpose. Many cities were constructed around them: public buildings and forums often ranked among the city's most characteristic and distinctive sights. They continued to play this role even after the political apparatus that had created them had collapsed, and thus exerted an influence on subsequent architectural achievements. As a result, a host of urban buildings and forums were built which, although extremely varied, were always of immense artistic and historical interest. They served as a mirror of the community that had created them and were frequently a source of great pride.

**THE EPITOME OF THE *COMUNE***
Siena's Piazza del Campo ▲ 210 exemplifies the civic community of which it is the undisputed center. The city developed along the three major thoroughfares that converge on this space. Midway around the circumference stands the massive Palazzo Pubblico, dominated by the soaring civic tower, the Torre del Mangia. This is the arena for the Palio ▲ 214, an event that epitomizes the communal pride of the Sienese. The piazza has no commercial or religious function: it is totally dedicated to the political life and rituals of the city.

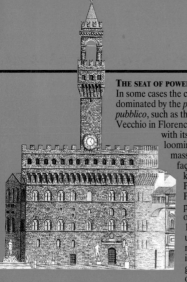

## THE SEAT OF POWER

In some cases the city square is dominated by the *palazzo pubblico*, such as the Palazzo Vecchio in Florence ▲ *123*, with its tall tower looming over the massive, austere façade. Initially known as the Palazzo dei Priori, the palace was opened in 1301 and used as a residence for important government officials.

## CITY SQUARE

In Pistoia, the seats of religious and civic power (the Duomo (**1**), the Palazzo del Podestà (**2**) and the Palazzo del Comune (**3**)) face onto the magnificent Piazza del Duomo ▲ *179*.

## SETTING THE URBAN STAGE

The Palazzo dei Cavalieri in Pisa ▲ *149* serves as a backdrop for the piazza of the same name, designed in the 16th century by Giorgio Vasari for Cosimo I de' Medici. The piazza was modeled on the plan of civic piazzas from previous centuries, which consisted of a vast open space dominated by a public building. But it represents a completely different reality: the assumption of absolute power by the ruling dynasty and the transformation of the old city center and its buildings into triumphant emblems of the new regime.

## BETWEEN CLOCK TOWER AND BELL TOWER

In Arezzo the religious buildings (especially the Romanesque apse of Santa Maria della Pieve and the Gothic-Renaissance façade of the Palazzetto della Fraternità dei Laici) are the most prominent. However, the theme is the same: the Piazza Grande ▲ *187* is surrounded by the city's most important buildings.

# ● CIVIL ARCHITECTURE:
## THE INVENTION OF THE PALAZZO

**BETWEEN ROOF AND FAÇADE**
The overhanging eaves of medieval buildings were replaced in the Renaissance by the antique-style cornice. This lavishly decorated, elaborately carved projection formed the crowning glory of a building.

The history of architecture is indebted to Tuscany for one of its basic styles: the private palazzo or palace. The idea itself dates back centuries (the term *palazzo* is derived from Latin), but its application to the homes of nobles and wealthy merchants, along with the styles that were to form the basis of modern civil architecture, was a product of Renaissance Tuscany. The palazzo, with its basically square plan and central courtyard, was modeled on the Roman *domus*. However, the Tuscan palazzo usually had three floors, unlike the typical Roman residence which only had one. It was a large isolated cube, the façades initially decorated with ashlar then later constructed using superimposed architectural levels.

**PALAZZO TOLOMEI ▲ 220**
Built in the early 13th century by Jacopo and Tolomeo Tolomei, this may be the oldest private palazzo in Siena and one of the oldest in the whole of Tuscany. The façade is punctuated by ogival two-light mullioned windows in line with Gothic tradition.

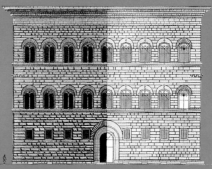

**PALAZZO STROZZI ▲ 129**
Begun in 1489 by its designer Benedetto da Maiano and continued by Simone del Pollaiolo, nicknamed Il Cronaca, this is a masterpiece of Renaissance civil architecture. The characteristic beveled rustication of the façade becomes less marked with each successive floor. The palazzo is crowned by a monumental Roman-style cornice which makes the building look even more imposing.

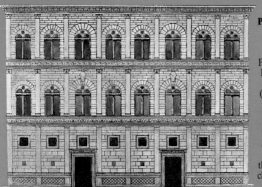

**PALAZZO RUCELLAI ▲ 129**
Designed by Leon Battista Alberti, this palazzo was built in Florence around 1455 by Bernardo Rossellino. It has a rusticated façade (although here 'smooth' or flattened ashlar is used) but the pilasters used to structure the façade are the key element here. It was in this structure that theories about the use of classical stories were first applied to the palazzo.

**TWO-LIGHT MULLIONED WINDOWS**
The classic two-light window of the Renaissance palazzo, surmounted by an arched lintel, was a modern variation on the ogival two-light window used in Gothic architecture.

**KNEELING WINDOW**
Designed by Michelangelo in 1517 to grace the end of the corner loggia of the Medici-Riccardi palazzo in Florence, this is a small self-contained 'temple', separate from the rest of the façade.

**NICHE WINDOW**
This window is a self-contained unit jutting out from the wall of the Palazzo Nonfinito in Florence.

**PALAZZO UGUCCIONI**
This conscious recreation of a Roman building, with its rusticated first floor and upper floors punctuated by pairs of columns, is the Florentine version of palazzos built by Bramante and Raphael in Rome. Erected between 1549 and 1559, it represented a new departure in architecture for the period.

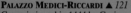

**PALAZZO MEDICI-RICCARDI ▲ 121**
Commissioned in 1444 by Cosimo the Elder, this became the archetypal noble residence in Florence, then throughout Italy. The private, inner courtyard at its center is the height of elegance. The façades, however, are impressively austere, their classic Tuscan rustication gradually becoming less pronounced with each floor. The palazzo was enlarged in the 17th century and the original layout altered.

1. Loggia
2. Plain stone façade
3. Smooth ashlar
4. Rusticated ashlar
5. Courtyard

# ● CIVIL ARCHITECTURE:
## NEW CITIES AND IDEAL CITIES

In the late Middle Ages, the Tuscan *comunes* and, much more rarely, the feudal lords, founded countless new-style cities primarily to protect the boundaries of their territory or take manpower out of the reach of neighboring *comunes* and rulers. New cities continued to be founded in the Renaissance (in fairly low numbers, although enjoying greater importance) under the impetus of theoretical studies concerning the 'ideal city'. These studies were the work of Renaissance architects who were keen to bring cityscapes into line with the new mathematical and rational principles. Some extremely interesting examples were built as a result, such as Pienza, Terra del Sole and Livorno.

**A CROWN OF TOWERS**
The town of Monteriggioni ▲ *225* sits within a circle of towered walls between Siena and Poggibonsi, overlooking the Via Cassia. Built by the Sienese in the 14th century as an outpost against the Florentines, it was visited by Dante, who described it in a poem. Ringed by a wall fortified by numerous square towers, it is a fine example of one of these new-style towns.

**ANTHROPOMORPHIC ARCHITECTURE**
A well-organized citadel is like a well proportioned man. This anthropomorphic view of architecture, consistent with the classical notion that man was 'the measure of all things', is portrayed here by Francesco di Giorgio Martini. This concept had a profound influence on Renaissance town planning.

**TERRA DEL SOLE**
Plan of Terra del Sole, a 16th-century new-style city built to defend the Florentine borders against Romagna. With its completely regular plan and mighty corner bastions, this city was the physical realization of the 'ideal city' so beloved of Renaissance theorists. It was also known by the classical-sounding name of Eliopoli, which clearly alluded to the glorious power of Grand Duke Cosimo I, who ordered its construction.

**THE THEORY TAKES SHAPE**
This 18th-century plan of the villa of Poggia Imperiale ▲ *137*, designed in the late 15th century by Giuliano da Sangallo, reflects the theoretical ideas of Francesco di Giorgio Martini. The plan shows the corner bastions, although not yet highly functional in form, that were to replace the traditional square or round towers several years later.

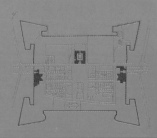

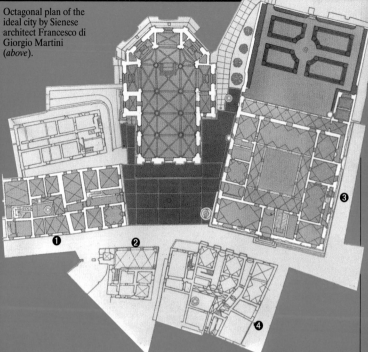

1. Palazzo Vescovile (bishop's palace)
2. Palazzo Pubblico (town hall)
3. Palazzo Piccolomini
4. Palazzo Ammannati

Octagonal plan of the ideal city by Sienese architect Francesco di Giorgio Martini (*above*).

**IN HONOR OF THE POPE**
To mark his accession to the papal throne in 1458, Pope Pius II (Enea Silvio Piccolomini) decided to transform his native medieval village of Corsignano into an elegant Renaissance city that was to take the name of Pienza ▲ *233*. He therefore commissioned architect Bernardo Rossellino to carry out a large-scale urban development program. This found expression in the piazza, the site of the city's most important buildings: the cathedral, the bishop's palace and the town hall. The end result is a stunning Renaissance gem, set among the original medieval buildings of the village.

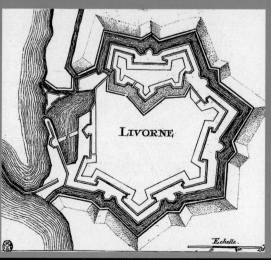

LIVORNE

Echelle.

**CITY OF THE FREE**
According to the writings of its designer Bernardo Buontalenti, the city of Livorno ▲ *247*, was born at exactly 'XVI ⅔ hours and 8 minutes' on March 28, 1577. The plan, based on a series of bastioned structures separated by water, is typical late Renaissance, but the way in which the city was populated, enticing inhabitants from other provinces with tax exemptions, guarantees and immunity, harked back to medieval practices.

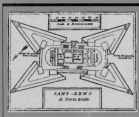

**FLOWER OF FLAME**
The characteristic profile of the Fortress of San Filippo at Porto Ercole ▲ 258, with its four mighty bastions defended by sweeping cannon fire: a truly impregnable 'flower of flame'.

Between the 15th and 16th centuries Tuscan architects were the main inventors of the bastion and the bastioned trace, the architectural tools that enabled fortified cities to withstand artillery attacks and defend themselves against enemy cannon fire. The application of this defensive system drastically altered the face of the city, enclosing it within an elaborate military shell that was sometimes more impressive than the city it was built to defend and transforming it into a real war machine. Many imposing and atmospheric vestiges of this phenomenon can still be found across the region.

**A SAFE EXISTENCE**
Overall view of Lucca within its ring of walls ▲ 159. This mighty line of fortifications, which took many decades of hard labor and enormous expense to build, safeguarded the existence of this small aristocratic republic for centuries. Preserved virtually intact, it has protected the city from the ravages of modern town planning.

**AN IMMENSE WAR MACHINE**
Bird's-eye view of Grosseto ▲ 252 and its walls, a large part of which are still standing. The advent of the cannon made it necessary to build massive defensive works to cope with the range of the new weapons. The destructive power of artillery in its turn necessitated an increasingly complex network of fortifications: bastions and curtain walls were gradually supplemented by ravelins, demilunes, tenailles, caponiers, covered ways and glacis. The result was a vast complex possessed of its own geometric beauty, but whose structure, unlike that of the castles of old, was incomprehensible to the layman.

Sketches of fortifications taken from the notebooks of the Sienese architect Francesco di Giorgio Martini, a leading Renaissance scholar of military architecture (*above*).

### THE STAMP OF GENIUS

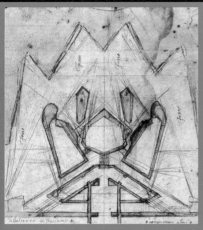

Autograph illustration by Michelangelo of the fortifications at San Miniato ▲ *137* in Florence. The great artist, put in charge of the Florentine Republic's fortifications, studied the results of the new military techniques in depth. He also came up with some ingenious solutions, such as the idea of defending particularly vulnerable walls with flexible defensive works, as they were less likely to be damaged by cannonballs than rigid ones.

### PROTECTING THE GATES

The three drawbridges defending St Peter's Gate in Lucca. A ravelin protects the gate from cannon fire.

### THE HEART OF THE DEFENSE

The characteristic heart-shaped bulwark of Santa Croce, more functional than the former round towers, protects part of Lucca's walls.

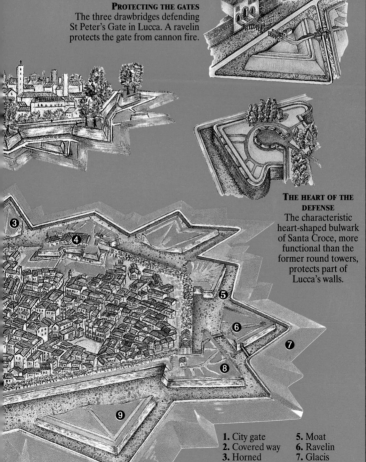

| | |
|---|---|
| **1.** City gate | **5.** Moat |
| **2.** Covered way | **6.** Ravelin |
| **3.** Horned defensive work | **7.** Glacis |
| **4.** Citadel | **8.** Bastion |
| | **9.** Demilune |

# CIVIL ARCHITECTURE:
## CASTLES AND VILLAS

**PETRAIA**

**PRATOLINO**

**CAFAGGIOLO**

During the Middle Ages feudal lords and *comunes* built castles, walled cities and fortified settlements throughout the region. In the Renaissance, as the civic authorities became more established and extended their power, castles were replaced by elegant villas with large Italian gardens boasting geometric designs and an architectural layout. The splendid Medici villas, built by the ruling dynasty, and the Lucchese villas, constructed by the aristocracy on the hills around Lucca, are particularly noteworthy.

**LAPPEGGI**

**MEDICI VILLAS**
Around 1598, Giusto Utens, a Flemish artist who may have been born in Carrara, was commissioned by the Grand Duke of Tuscany, Ferdinando I, to decorate the lunettes in the drawing room at the Villa Artimino ▲ *138, 143* with the principal villas owned by the family at that time. The paintings, executed in the same style and from a bird's-eye view perspective, provide an accurate contemporary catalogue of one of the most important phenomena of the Italian Renaissance.

**A PLEASURE PALACE**
The Medici Villa at Poggio a Caiano ▲ *142*, west of Florence, was built in the 1580s on the remains of a feudal castle. The only trace of this past, however, is the villa's severe H-shaped plan on top of a square base which is, in turn, surrounded by a regular square enclosure. This building is actually the epitome of the Renaissance villa, a superb 'pleasure palace' in a beautiful natural setting 'tamed' by man, where a gentleman could fully enjoy his *otia* (pastimes): polite conversation, philosophical contemplation and seemly artistic sentiment.

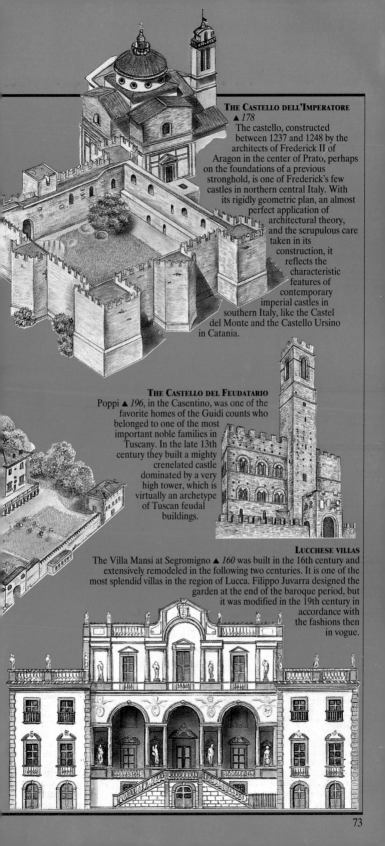

### THE CASTELLO DELL'IMPERATORE
▲ 178

The castello, constructed between 1237 and 1248 by the architects of Frederick II of Aragon in the center of Prato, perhaps on the foundations of a previous stronghold, is one of Frederick's few castles in northern central Italy. With its rigidly geometric plan, an almost perfect application of architectural theory, and the scrupulous care taken in its construction, it reflects the characteristic features of contemporary imperial castles in southern Italy, like the Castel del Monte and the Castello Ursino in Catania.

### THE CASTELLO DEL FEUDATARIO

Poppi ▲ 196, in the Casentino, was one of the favorite homes of the Guidi counts who belonged to one of the most important noble families in Tuscany. In the late 13th century they built a mighty crenelated castle dominated by a very high tower, which is virtually an archetype of Tuscan feudal buildings.

### LUCCHESE VILLAS

The Villa Mansi at Segromigno ▲ 160 was built in the 16th century and extensively remodeled in the following two centuries. It is one of the most splendid villas in the region of Lucca. Filippo Juvarra designed the garden at the end of the baroque period, but it was modified in the 19th century in accordance with the fashions then in vogue.

# CIVIL ARCHITECTURE:
## GARDENS

Tuscan gardens, the crowning glory of country houses, were regarded by the wealthy as an indispensable feature of city palazzos. These gardens reached the height of their splendor from the 16th century and although few have survived intact, particularly as a result of the 19th-century tendency to remodel them in imitation of English landscaped gardens, they are vividly portrayed in the contemporary documents. The writings of Leon Battista Alberti (1404–72) outline the cultivated Renaissance principles of garden design. Essential elements were open arcades, copses of fruit trees, cypresses enveloped in ivy, pergolas supported by marble columns, geometric paths lined with hedges and trees trimmed in accordance with the *Ars topiaria*, grottos, urns, statues and water features.

**VILLA GARZONI**
The spectacular garden of the Villa Garzoni ▲ *181* at Collodi, between Florence and Lucca, is a fine example of 18th-century Tuscan taste and culture. Built on a slope, it consists of a wood, a green theater and a bridge over a stream. At the entrance, a French-style parterre leads to a flight of steps punctuated by terraces and ornamented with urns, waterfalls, statues, plants and trees designed in 1786 by the architect Ottaviano Diodati.

## THE VILLA DI CASTELLO ▲ *138*

The lunette painted by Giusto Utens in the late 16th century provides a detailed illustration of this Medici Villa. The design of the gardens was commissioned in 1540 from the sculptor Niccolò Pericoli, known as Il Tribolo. Praised by Vasari as 'the richest, most magnificent and most ornamental garden in Europe', the garden was described enthusiastically by Michel de Montaigne who visited it in 1580.

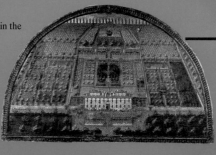

## THE PARCO DI PINOCCHIO

This park ▲ *181* was built in the 1960s as a result of a collaboration between the architect Zanuso, the sculptor Consagra and the landscape designer Pietro Porcinai. Set in a valley at the entrance to the small town of Collodi, paths lined with hedges of laurel wind their way past sculptures and water features illustrating the adventures of the wooden puppet created by Carlo Collodi.

## GROTTA DEL BUONTALENTI

This massive grotto, an elaborate combination of stucco, sculptures and frescos, greets visitors at the entrance to the Boboli Gardens ▲ *128*, the most splendid Tuscan garden in Florence. It has survived practically intact in its 18th-century incarnation.

## VILLA GAMBERAIA

The garden of the Villa Gamberaia ▲ *138*, in Settignano, enjoys a panoramic view over the Tuscan hills. This fine recreation of a Renaissance garden was designed along a longitudinal axis with a bench at one end. The flowerbeds which once formed the parterre were replaced in the 20th century by ornamental pools.

Romanesque architecture in Tuscany (mainly religious) was extremely varied, owing to the flowering of many regional schools, each with its own distinctive character. The Florentine style revolved around the use of colored marbles, the Pisan-Lucchese school was characterized by elegant rows of superimposed loggias, while Sienese Romanesque was more simple and austere. Lombard and French styles imported from the monastic orders also had a profound influence. But whatever the style, most of the buildings made clear reference to late classical and paleo-Christian architecture, a characteristic that is particularly evident in Florence and Pisa.

**LOZENGES**
The lozenge was a typical decorative motif of Pisan Romanesque. The result of esoteric theories as well as, possibly, the exchange of cultural ideas with distant places such as Armenia and Cappadocia, this motif is particularly visible on Pisa's city walls.

**BLIND COLONNADES**
A typical Romanesque ornamental feature, Tuscan blind colonnades were either decorated with black and white stripes or polychromatic geometric designs, as in the case of the Duomo in Pisa ▲ 147.

**A DOUBLE MIRACLE**
The famous Leaning Tower of Pisa ▲ 148 (in actual fact, the cathedral's bell tower) is doubly miraculous: its static, well-nigh impossible balancing act and its airy elegance are both breathtaking. The unexpected settling of the foundations, which caused it to lean, occurred only a short time after construction had begun. The architects attempted to remedy the problem by counterbalancing the upper part of the building, thereby partially halting the tilt. The graceful shape of the tower is achieved by the repetition over six successive floors of the characteristic loggia motif, which forms the most noticeable feature of Pisan-Lucchese Romanesque architecture.

## LOGGIAS
The superimposed loggias of Lucca's church of San Michele in Foro ▲ *157*, typical of Pisan-Lucchese Romanesque architecture, are treated with a considerable degree of figurative and chromatic freedom.

## TWO-COLOR DECORATION
The façade of the Badia Fiesolana, contained within a larger structure, is an excellent example of the use of different colored marbles which characterizes Romanesque architecture in and around Florence.

## CLASSICAL ALLUSIONS
This cross-section of San Miniato al Monte ▲ *137* in Florence, very similar to that of an early Christian basilica, clearly shows the influence of classical architecture on the structure of Romanesque buildings.

## THE 'BEL SAN GIOVANNI'
The huge octagon of the Florentine baptistery of San Giovanni ▲ *120* is, in its size and complexity, one of the major achievements of Florentine Romanesque architecture. The characteristic green and white marble decoration, coupled with the use of classical architectural stories, led the Renaissance population to believe that the baptistery was a Roman building. The interior is lavishly decorated with mosaics, making this building one of the finest examples of its type in Italy.

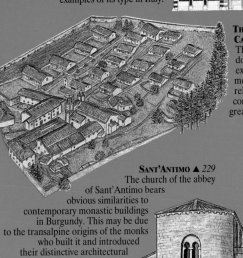

## THE HERMITAGE OF CAMALDOLI ▲ *195*
The ordered rows of cottages doubling as monastic cells express the austere, meditative side of Tuscan religious life, in marked contrast to the opulence of its great cathedrals.

## SANT'ANTIMO ▲ *229*
The church of the abbey of Sant'Antimo bears obvious similarities to contemporary monastic buildings in Burgundy. This may be due to the transalpine origins of the monks who built it and introduced their distinctive architectural style to Tuscany.

# ● RELIGIOUS ARCHITECTURE:
## THE AUSTERE SPLENDOR OF GOTHIC

Cimabue's *Crucifix* in the church of San Domenico ▲ *188* in Arezzo, an elegant symbol of Tuscan Gothic art.

There are various types of Tuscan Gothic. An important if minor movement drew its inspiration from French Gothic architecture: this found exclusive expression in monasteries, especially those built by the Cistercians. Another movement, in many ways the most prevalent, focused mainly on the decorative impact of transalpine architecture, producing lavishly ornamented buildings that were still Romanesque in structure. Last but not least, a third movement, typical of the mendicant orders, combined various Gothic elements, such as ogival arches, with a pared-down simplicity of form, creating large city churches designed specifically for preaching.

**MUNICIPAL SPLENDOR**
The lower part of the façade of the Duomo ▲ *213* in Siena was designed by Giovanni Pisano between 1284 and 1296. This cathedral is typical of Italian Gothic style, which focused more keenly on the decorative elements of the new architectural style than its structural aspects. The original church may have been intended as the transept for an even bigger cathedral that was started but never finished.

Imposing and austere, the ruins of the abbey of San Galgano ▲ 228 clearly show the influence of French Gothic architecture, introduced into Tuscany by the Cistercian monks who built the abbey between 1224 and 1288.

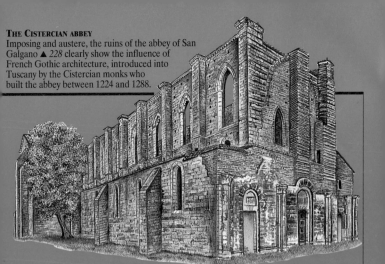

### STONE JEWEL-BOX
The little ornate church of Santa Maria della Spina ▲ 153 in Pisa was begun in 1323. Like an elegant stone jewel-box, it now stands on the Lungarno, although it was formerly constructed on a level with the river.

### GIOTTO'S CAMPANILE
With its slender, lavishly carved silhouette, the campanile of Florence's cathedral of Santa Maria del Fiore ▲ 119 is a perfect example of the Gothic style that prevailed in central Italy. Designed and begun by Giotto in 1334, it was completed after his death in 1359.

### DESIGNED FOR PREACHING
Typical of the new religious orders, Santa Maria Novella ▲ 130 in Florence was designed for preaching: space was devoted to the nave and aisles rather than the presbytery. The columns are spaced so they do not block the view of the preacher.

### TEMPLE OF THE WORD
As in many Franciscan churches, there are no vaults in the church of Santa Croce ▲ 136 in Florence. These were replaced by wooden trusses to reduce the cost of the building and save space. Only the chapels at the end and the choir, reserved for the monks, are vaulted.

# ● RELIGIOUS ARCHITECTURE:
## RENAISSANCE, MANNERIST AND BAROQUE STYLES

The interest that Tuscany had always taken in classical architecture resulted, in the Renaissance, in a conscious revival of classical forms, from architectural orders to the decorative features associated with them. This 'rebirth' led to a profound revolution in building design, construction and decoration that was to last until the turn of the 20th century. The elaborate forms and plans created by Tuscan architects spread throughout the world and gradually evolved, bringing about the birth of Mannerism and the baroque movement. Throughout the centuries, however, Tuscan architecture retained a formal restraint and dignity that continued to be its hallmark even during more exuberant periods such as that of the baroque.

**OLD AND NEW**
The façade of Santa Maria Novella in Florence ▲ *130* was completed by Leon Battista Alberti. He superimposed two classical orders, joined by huge volutes on the sides, on top of the preexisting white and green marble decoration, typical of medieval Florentine architecture and a feature of the original structure.

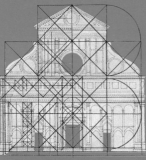

**PROPORTIONAL RELATIONSHIPS**
Renaissance architecture was based on simple mathematical and geometric relationships. Dimensions and proportions were generally obtained by using proportional plans correlated to create a harmonious whole. Here, a plan for the façade of Santa Maria Novella ▲ *130*.

**A RESTRAINED BAROQUE STYLE**
The extremely long façade of the Certosa di Pisa ▲ *154*, in the suburb of Calci, is an excellent example of Tuscan baroque: magnificence tempered by an innate sense of restraint and spatial clarity. The buildings in this region bear little resemblance to those in other areas of Pisa, which were less influenced by classicism.

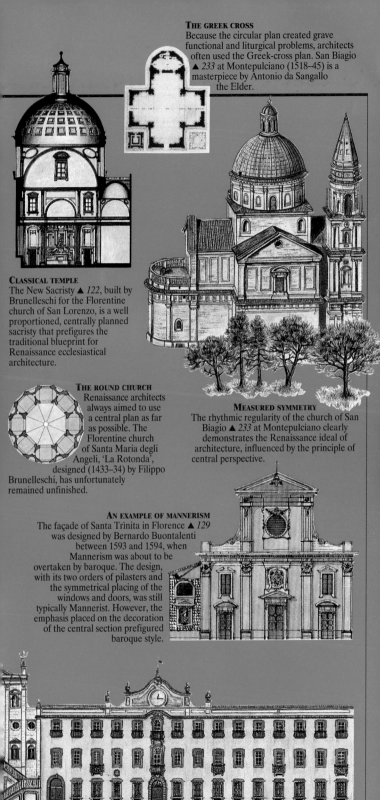

## THE GREEK CROSS
Because the circular plan created grave functional and liturgical problems, architects often used the Greek-cross plan. San Biagio ▲ 233 at Montepulciano (1518–45) is a masterpiece by Antonio da Sangallo the Elder.

## CLASSICAL TEMPLE
The New Sacristy ▲ 122, built by Brunelleschi for the Florentine church of San Lorenzo, is a well proportioned, centrally planned sacristy that prefigures the traditional blueprint for Renaissance ecclesiastical architecture.

## THE ROUND CHURCH
Renaissance architects always aimed to use a central plan as far as possible. The Florentine church of Santa Maria degli Angeli, 'La Rotonda', designed (1433–34) by Filippo Brunelleschi, has unfortunately remained unfinished.

## MEASURED SYMMETRY
The rhythmic regularity of the church of San Biagio ▲ 233 at Montepulciano clearly demonstrates the Renaissance ideal of architecture, influenced by the principle of central perspective.

## AN EXAMPLE OF MANNERISM
The façade of Santa Trìnita in Florence ▲ 129 was designed by Bernardo Buontalenti between 1593 and 1594, when Mannerism was about to be overtaken by baroque. The design, with its two orders of pilasters and the symmetrical placing of the windows and doors, was still typically Mannerist. However, the emphasis placed on the decoration of the central section prefigured baroque style.

# 20TH-CENTURY ARCHITECTURE:
## RESEARCH INTO NEW MATERIALS

Tuscan architecture in the 20th century, characterized by an underlying dialogue between tradition and innovation, witnessed a succession of identifiable phases: the eclectic experimentalism of the first years of the century, which welcomed Art Nouveau; the crises of the interwar period, torn between conservatism and support for modern trends; the uncertainty of the 1950s and 1960s, marked by an enthusiasm for rebuilding; and the confusion of contemporary trends, as evidenced by the exclusive, separate nature of individual works. The period was notable for the work of various important, commited and dedicated figures who left their mark on architecture and urban design: Michelazzi, André, Coppedè, Michelucci, Nervi, Morandi, Ricci, Savioli, Santi and Carmassi.

### SACRED ARCHITECTURE
The church of San Giovanni Battista (1964) by Giovanni Michelucci (1891–1990) at Campi Bisenzio. When it was being built, its location on the Milan-Naples highway earned it the nickname of the '100-kph-church'.

The experimental aspects of this church can be seen in the great 'tent' of the concrete roof surmounting the building's walls, which makes the heavy materials seem to ascend heavenward.

### VISUAL DYNAMISM
A visually complex building, the Florentine Villa Bayon at San Gaggio (1964–66), achieves maximum sculptural impact with the large keel-like roof whose volume is emphasized by its distance from the main body of the building below.

### MODERN ARCHITECTURE
The rigorously rationalist railroad station of Santa Maria Novella ▲ 130 (1932–34) in Florence, designed by the Gruppo Toscano. It reflects contemporary social and community demands in its careful interpretation of the relationship between the building's formal plan, structural clarity and functional character.

## 1960s
### EXPERIMENTALISM

Divided between non-figurative trends and brutalist language, the experimentalism of the 1960s was well represented by Leonardo Ricci and Leonardo Savioli, both students of Michelucci. Their most important works are in the village of Monterinaldi, near Florence, the Man a Forte dei Marmi house and the Villa Balmain (*right*) at Marciana Alta on the island of Elba, designed by Leonardo Ricci in 1958.

### CONSTRUCTIVE STRUCTURALISM

The dialogue between building techniques and esthetic appearance found expression in the structure of Florence's municipal stadium (1929–32), designed by Pier Luigi Nervi. The building boasts many expressive qualities, including the bold sculptural impact of the entrance staircase, the daring cantilevered roof over the stands and the structural distribution of the weight-bearing elements.

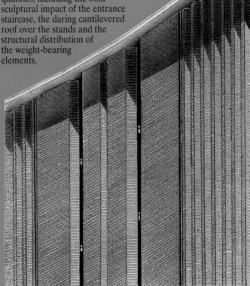

### THE MARK OF TRADITION

The work of Massimo Carmassi, one of the leading contemporary Tuscan architects, is characterized by his conscious emphasis on tradition. His research, begun in the 1960s, is based on the harmonious relationship between the use of local materials and the recovery of a regional vocabulary reinterpreted in a modern vein. (Residential building in Pontedera Vecchia; detail of the façade, 1998–99).

# ● RURAL ARCHITECTURE:
## FARMHOUSES

Although Tuscany boasts some breathtakingly picturesque cities, its true magic resides in the gentle beauty of its countryside, scattered with farms that have been cultivated for centuries. At the center of each estate was a sturdily built, welcoming farmhouse, the home of the farmer who looked after the estate. The farmhouse is a typically Tuscan building, a cross between a castle, a villa and a farm, often characterized by a squat tower marking the entrance. Blending in perfectly with the surrounding countryside, the farmhouse has served as a model for the rural architecture of much of central Italy.

**CASA ROSSA**
This was built in 1765 by Grand Duke Peter Leopold for Leonardo Ximenes who was in charge of the reclamation work carried out in the Maremma plain. The house controlled the three locks that linked the drainage lake to the sea.

**ALONG THE ARNO VALLEY**
Typical farmhouse in the Arno Valley with superimposed loggias and a large central tower with a dovecote. This is the 'luxury' version of a type of building found throughout eastern central Tuscany.

**SHARECROPPERS' HOUSES**
The large portico with superimposed depressed arches is a strange but characteristic feature of sharecroppers' houses in the region of Florence. These buildings, designed to house the family of the sharecropper who managed the estate, were usually quite small.

**THE TUSCAN FARMHOUSE**
A prime example, typical in design and function, of the traditional Tuscan farmhouse: a compact building, incorporating the home, stables and hay barn, placed at the center of a smallish estate. This was the house of the farmer who looked after the property. The design, although greatly altered, was originally modeled on that of ancient castles, as can be seen from the tower (sometimes a dovecote but more often containing a roof terrace) that usually stood at the center of the building.

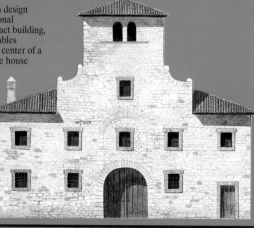

# Tuscany
# as seen by painters

'This region of Italy is blessed both for its natural beauty
and for its role as a civilizing force throughout the ages;
both the result of an almost divine harmony.'

Bruno Cicognani

the smallest details of everyday life. The houses are decorated with colorful plaster and the windows and balconies are adorned with vases of flowers about to be watered.

The rolling vine-covered Chianti hills and the bleak hillocks of Le Crete are also rendered with a miniaturist accuracy worthy of a skilled cartographer. The view of Pisa ▲ 147 (first half of the 14th century), in the church of San Nicola (**3**), is a vivid representation of the city. In the area bounded by the Arno river, the spectator can see the monuments that even then were famous, and a source of great pride to the Pisans: the Tower ▲ 148, already leaning, and the colonnaded façade of the superb cathedral ▲ 147.

The city of Fra Angelico (c.1400–55), which appears in the *Pala di San Marco* (**2**) in the Museo di San Marco in Florence ▲ 131, encapsulates the elegant characteristics of the ideal city, glimpsed in the distance like a promised land.

It may well have been the Tuscans' pride in their architectural and social achievements that prompted those living in large cities (Florence, Siena and Pisa) to decorate the walls of palaces and churches with images of their city. Ambrogio Lorenzetti (whose life is documented between 1319–47) depicted the effects of good government in his *Allegories of Good and Bad Government* (1338–40) ▲ 211 in the Sala della Pace in the Palazzo Pubblico in Siena (**1**). In this fresco, he portrayed the settled atmosphere and bustling activity of the city and surrounding countryside down to

| | |
|---|---|
| 1 | |
| 2 | 3 |

87

The 15th century saw the development of an iconography, which was also to flourish in subsequent centuries, that placed the protection of the city in the paternal hands of a saint. The Tuscans' growing faith in human potential then shifted to a belief in a devotional embrace, entrusting cities, large and small, to the care of a higher defender. A good example is the fresco by Sano di Pietro (1406–81), *San Pietro Alessandro benedice e protegge Siena* (**1**) set in an ancient, atypical *biccherna* (Revenue Office). It adorns the financial offices which used to be known by this unusual name in the Palazzo Pubblico ▲ *211*. The city resembles a relief model, and its finest buildings, the Duomo ▲ *213* and the Palazzo Pubblico, can be seen surrounded by impregnable walls. In a painting in the Museo Civico in San Gimignano (**3**), Taddeo di Bartolo (1362–1422) places the minutely detailed city ▲ *225* with its unmistakable turreted skyline in the hands of its protector. Similarly, in the picture depicting *Colle Val d'Elsa affidata da un angelo a San Marziale* (**2**), by a Florentine artist in the late 16th century, it is possible to recognize places and buildings that are still standing today in the center of Colle di Val d'Elsa ▲ *227*.

| 1 | 2 |
|---|---|
|   | 3 |

'Siena huddles beneath the cathedral that protects it from high above, like a mother hen covered with parallel bands of white and black marble.'

Bino Sanminiatelli

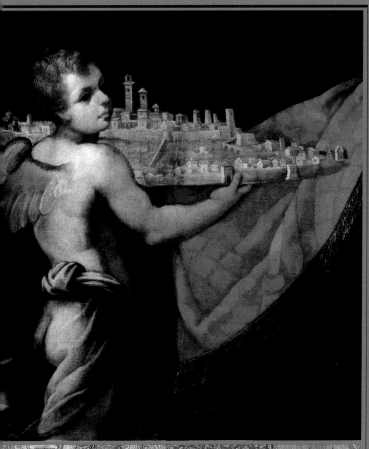

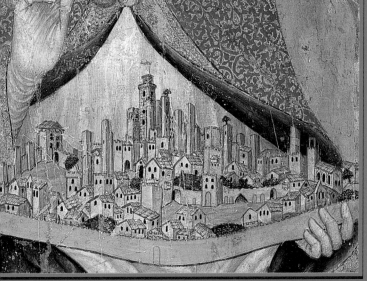

In the 16th century, with the steady growth of the Medici state, Tuscany entered a long period of peace and political stability. The first remarkable achievements in the art of cartography had already been produced. Around 1600, Francesco Vanni (1563–1610) sketched out a plan of Siena ▲ 208, one of the most thorough and successful plans of Siena of all time. A contemporary painting, *Il Beato Ambrogio Sansedoni implora la protezione della Vergine per Siena* (**1**), kept in the church of Fontegiusta ▲ 220, portrays the radiant, serene city from an unusual standpoint. In the foreground of the painting stands the massive structure of the ancient hospital of Santa Maria della

'Grosseto, a small hamlet of low houses surrounded by walls until the end of the last century.'

Enrico Guadagni

Scala ▲ 216, founded, as legend has it, in 832. Great emphasis is also placed on the fortifications, which were not only constructed for defensive purposes on the borders of the Medici state, but also in places where they could ensure control of the recently subjugated cities. The early 17th-century painting by Ilario Casolani (**2**), *La Madonna in gloria*, shows a bird's-eye view of Grosseto ▲ 252, its buildings surrounded by the mighty city walls constructed by Baldassarre Lanci.

| | |
|---|---|
| 1 | 2 |

From the 17th century onward, the number of foreign visitors to Italy, particularly writers and artists, soared as a result of the growing popularity of the Grand Tour. Renaissance Tuscany was obviously an essential port of call. These visitors were deeply affected by what they saw, recording their emotions, observations and delicately colored drawings in thick notebooks. Camille Corot (1796–1875) painted *Florence Seen from the Boboli Gardens* (**1**) ▲ *125* in 1834, a faithful recreation of the city of the fleur-de-lis, undistorted by the painter's romantic vision. The perceptive critic John Ruskin (1819–1900) contributed to the reevaluation of Gothic art, until then regarded as 'primitive', and heightened Tuscany's popularity with English-speakers. He kept accurate diaries of his travels, lavishly illustrated with drawings and watercolors. In this *View of Florence* (**2**), the city seems to disappear, swallowed up by the luminous, almost ashen light. Le Corbusier (1887–1965) also traveled through Tuscany, producing pictures such as these *Impressions of Fiesole* (**3**) ▲ *137* in which, with a few strokes, he lovingly portrayed ancient buildings flanked by stark cypresses.

92

'This landscape [the hills of Florence] possesses the
beauty of an ancient medallion and a priceless painting.
It is a perfect, unpretentious work of art.'

Anatole France

93

It is no coincidence that the most famous Italian artistic movement of the 19th century, renowned for anticipating French Impressionism in certain ways, originated in Tuscany between Livorno ▲ 247 and Grosseto ▲ 252, and consequently near the Tyrrhenian Sea. *Riposo* (**1**), painted in 1887 by Giovanni Fattori (1825–1908), is set against the backdrop of this sea which appears, as if by magic, at the limits of a barren, arid landscape. Fattori was the leading exponent of the Macchiaioli (members of the Impressionist movement in central Italy) and his painting was inspired by the tough working conditions of farmers in the Maremma ▲ 255. He depicts them simply but realistically, fully aware of the hardships experienced by these people who, despite suffering from malaria and centuries of poverty, were always dignified in their bearing. The famous *Rotonda dei bagni Palmieri*, painted by Fattori in 1866 (**2**), represents a kind of manifesto of the realistic Macchiaioli movement. This was opposed to academicism and denied the need for important subjects or historical allusions, until then more or less regarded as mandatory in art. The painting is composed of strong synthetic patches of color (or *macchia*, hence the name of the movement) and the focus is less on the large group of elegant women gathered in the fashionable seaside resort than the calm Tyrrhenian Sea, which becomes the real protagonist of the scene. Stretching horizontally across the entire surface of the painting, the sea corresponds exactly to the spectator's field of vision.

| 1 |
|---|
| 2 |

'They have now entirely disappeared […] the herds
of wild oxen which live and breathe for eternity in
the paintings and etchings of Giovanni Fattori.'

Lorenzo Viani

succeeded in making this scene so realistic, with its farmhouses and squared haystacks basking in the sunshine of a summer afternoon, that the painting itself seems to radiate warmth.

The Florence of Ottone Rosai (1895–1957) is an intimate city of working-class districts threaded with narrow lanes, where people meet up and enjoy the simple pleasures of life. Rosai's *Piazza del* *Carmine* (2) of 1920 suggests the serene spaciousness and monumental severity of this Renaissance place, although the painting is resolutely contemporary in spirit. Mino Maccari (1898–1990), an artist who spent his entire life savagely caricaturing the social conventions of his time, has symbolically brought together all the constituent elements of the Tuscan countryside in this *Paesaggio* of 1928 (1). The artist has

1

2

# Tuscany
## as seen by writers

## FLORENCE

### ON ARRIVING IN FLORENCE
*Stendhal was the pseudonym of Henri Beyle (1788–1842), French novelist. He lived for long periods in Italy, writing studies of Italian painting (*Histoire de la peinture en Italie, *1817) and travel books, as well as the novels for which he is best known.*

'The day before yesterday, as I descended upon Florence from the high ridges of the Apennine, my heart was leaping wildly within me. What utterly childish excitement! At long last, at a sudden bend in the road, my gaze plunged downward into the heart of the plain, and there, in the far distance, like some darkling mass, I could distinguish the sombre pile of Santa Maria del Fiore with its famous Dome, the masterpiece of Brunelleschi.

"Behold the home of Dante, of Michelangelo, of Leonardo da Vinci", I mused within my heart. "Behold then this noble city, the Queen of mediaeval Europe! Here, within these walls, the civilisation of mankind was born anew; here it was that Lorenzo de Medici so brilliantly sustained the part of Kingship, and established a Court at which, for the first time since the reign of Augustus, military prowess was reduced to a secondary role". As the minutes passed, so these memories came crowding and jostling one against the other within my soul, and soon I found myself incapable of rational thought, but rather surrendered to the sweet turbulence of fancy, as in the presence of some beloved object. Upon approaching the San Gallo gate, with its unbeautiful Triumphal Arch, I could gladly have embraced the first inhabitants of Florence whom I encountered...

Twice only was I forced to enquire my way of passers-by, who answered me with a politeness which was wholly French and with a most singular accent; and at last I found myself before the facade of Santa Croce.

Within, upon the right of the doorway, rises the tomb of Michelangelo; beyond, lo! there stands Canova's effigy of Alfieri; I needed no cicerone to recognise the features of the great Italian writer. Further still, I discovered the tomb of Machiavelli; while facing Michelangelo is Galileo. What a race of men! And to these already named, Tuscany might further add Dante, Boccaccio and Petraarch. What a fantastic gathering! The tide of emotion which overwhelmed me flowed so deep that it scarce was to be distinguished from religious awe. My soul, affected by the very notion of being in Florence, and by the proximity of these great men, was already in

'Lump the whole thing! Say that the Creator made
Italy from designs by Michael Angelo!'

Mark Twain

a state of trance. Absorbed in the contemplation of sublime beauty, I could perceive
its very essence close at hand; and I could, as it were, feel the stuff of it beneath my
fingertips. I had attained to that supreme degree of sensibility where the divine
intimations of art merge with the impassioned sensuality of emotion. As I emerged
from the port of Santa Croce, I was seized with a fierce palpitation of the heart; I
walked in constant fear of falling to the ground.'

STENDHAL, *ROME, NAPLES AND FLORENCE*,
TRANSLATED BY RICHARD N. COE, JOHN CALDER LTD, 1959

### LETTER TO MARY SHELLEY

*In 1818, suffering from ill health, money problems and 'social hatred' Shelley
(1792–1822) left England for good and went to Italy. The family settled in Tuscany, first
outside Livorno, then in Florence, and finally in Pisa.*

'As we approached Florence, the country became cultivated to a very high degree,
the plain was filled with the most beautiful villas, and, as far as the eye could reach,
the mountains were covered with them; for the plains are bounded on all sides by
blue and misty mountains. The vines are here trailed on low trellises of reeds
interwoven into crosses to support them, and the grapes, now almost ripe, are
exceedingly abundant. You everywhere meet those teams of beautiful white oxen,
which are now labouring the little vine-divided fields with the Virgilian ploughs and
carts. Florence itself, that is the Lung' Arno (for I have seen no more), I think is the
most beautiful city I have yet seen. It is surrounded with cultivated hills and from the
bridge which crosses the broad channel of the Arno, the view is the most animated
and elegant I ever saw. You see three or four bridges, one apparently supported by
Corinthian pillars, and the white sails of the boats, relieved by the deep green of the
forest, which comes to the water's edge, and the sloping hills covered with bright
villas on every side. Domes and steeples rise on all sides, and the cleanliness is
remarkably great. On the other side there are the foldings of the Vale of Arno above;
first the hills of olive and vine, then the chestnut woods, and then the blue and misty
pine forest, which invest the aerial Apennines, that fade in the distance. I have
seldom seen a city so lovely at first sight as Florence.'

PERCY BYSSHE SHELLEY,
*ESSAYS, LETTERS FROM ABROAD*,
TRANSLATIONS AND FRAGMENTS, VOL II, 1840

### A RUSSIAN VIEWPOINT

*The Russian novelist Fyodor Dostoevsky (1821–81) made several trips abroad, visiting
England, France, Italy and Germany. He lived very much a hand to mouth existence,
being always short of money, as this extract makes clear.*

'Only some parts of Sicily and Algiers can touch Florence for heat. Well, and so it
was as hot as hell, and we bore it like true Russians, who notoriously can bear
anything...

Our windows gave on a market-square with arcades and splendid granite-pillars; in
the square was a municipal fountain in the form of a gigantic bronze boar from
whose throat the water flowed (it is a classic masterpiece of rare beauty)...

You must know that the air, despite this heat and drought (it never once rained)
was wonderfully light; the green in the gardens (of which there are astonishingly few
in Florence; one sees hardly anything but stones) – the green neither withered nor
faded, but seemed brighter and fresher every day; the flowers and lemon-trees had
apparently only waited for the heat; but what astonished me most – me who was
imprisoned in Florence by untoward circumstances – was that the itinerant
foreigners (who are nearly all very rich) mostly remained in Florence; new ones even
arrived every day...When I saw in the streets well-dressed Englishwomen and even
Frenchwomen, I could not conceived why these people, who had the money to get
away with, could voluntarily stay in such a hell.'

LETTER FROM DOSTOEVSKY,
TRANSLATED BY E.E. MAYNE, 1917

### AN AMERICAN VIEWPOINT

*Mark Twain (1835–1910) satirist and humorist, is best known as the author of the* The Adventures of Tom Sawyer *and* The Adventures of Huckleberry Finn. *In* The Innocents Abroad, *a humorous account of a journey through the Mediterranean, he failed to be impressed with the city of Florence, or its great works of art.*

'We went to the Church of Santa Croce, from time to time, to weep over the tombs of Michael Angelo, Raphael and Machiavelli (I suppose they are buried there, but it may be they reside elsewhere and rent their tombs to other parties – such being the fashion in Italy) and between times we used to go and stand on the bridges and admire the Arno. It is popular to admire the Arno. It is a great historical creek with four feet in the channel and some scows floating around. It would be a very plausible river if they would pump some water into it. They all call it a river, and they honestly think it is a river, do these dark and bloody Florentines. They even help out the delusion by building bridges over it. I do not see why they are too good to wade.'

MARK TWAIN, *THE INNOCENTS ABROAD*,
CHATTO AND WINDUS, 1881

### IN SANTA CROCE WITHOUT A BAEDEKER

*After Cambridge, E.M. Forster (1879–1970) spent a year travelling in Italy with his mother. This trip was to provide much material for his early novels, such as* A Room with a View *(1908) in which he satirizes English tourists abroad, deeply suspicious of foreigners and lost without their Baedekers.*

'Tears of indignation came to Lucy's eyes, partly because Miss Lavish had jilted her, partly because she had taken her Baedeker. How could she find her way home? How could she find her way in Santa Croce? Her first morning was ruined, and she might never be in Florence again. A few minutes ago she had been all high spirits, talking as a woman of culture, and half-persuading herself that she was full of originality. Now she entered the church depressed and humiliated, not even able to remember whether it was built by the Franciscans or the Dominicans.

Of course, it must be a wonderful building. But how like a barn! And how very cold! Of course, it contained frescoes by Giotto, in the presence of whose tactile value she was capable of feeling what was proper. But who was to tell her which they were? She walked about disdainfully, unwilling to be enthusiastic over monuments of uncertain authorship or date. There was no one even to tell her which, of all the sepulchral slabs that paved the nave and transepts, was the one that was really beautiful, the one that had been most praised by Mr Ruskin.

Then the pernicious charm of Italy worked on her, and instead of acquiring information, she began to be happy. She puzzled out the Italian notices – the notice that forbade people to introduce dogs into the church – the notice that prayed people, in the interests of health and out of respect to the sacred edifice in which they found themselves not to spit. She watched the tourists: their noses were as red as their Baedekers, so cold was Santa Croce. She beheld the horrible fate that overtook three Papists – two he-babies and a she-baby – who began their career by sousing each other with the Holy Water, and then proceeded to the Machiavelli memorial, dripping, but hallowed. Advancing towards it very slowly and from immense distances, they touched the stone with their fingers, with their handkerchiefs, with their heads, and then retreated. What could this mean? They did it again and again. Then Lucy realized that they had mistaken Machiavelli for some saint, and by continual contact with his shrine were hoping to acquire virtue. Punishment followed quickly. The smallest he-baby stumbled over one of the sepuchral slabs so much admired by Mr Ruskin, and entangled his feet in the features of a recumbent bishop. Protestant as she was Lucy darted forward. She was too late. He fell heavily upon the prelate's upturned toes.'

E. M. FORSTER, *A ROOM WITH A VIEW*,
EDWARD ARNOLD, 1908

'I was most charmed with the *Venus* by Titian, which has a sweetness of expression and tenderness of coloring not to be described.'

Tobias Smollett

## FRA LIPPO LIPPI

*The poet Robert Browning (1812–89) eloped to Italy with Elizabeth Barrett in 1846, and they lived there until her death in 1861. This poem gives some idea of the extent to which Browning must have been steeped in the art of the Florentine Renaissance. The character of the painter Fra Lippo Lippi depicted here follows closely the version given in Giorgio Vasari's Lives of the Painters.*

I am poor brother Lippo, by your leave!
You need not clap your torches to my face.
Zooks, what's to blame? you think you see a monk!
What, 'tis past midnight, and you go the rounds,
And here you catch me at an alley's end
Where sportive ladies leave their doors ajar?
The Carmine's my cloister: hunt it up,
Do,—harry out, if you must show your zeal,
Whatever rat, there, haps on his wrong hole,
And nip each softling of a wee white mouse,
Weke, weke, that's crept to keep him company!
Aha, you know your betters! Then, you'll take
Your hand away that's fiddling on my throat,
And please to know me likewise. Who am I?
Why, one, sir, who is lodging with a friend
Three streets off—he's a certain . . . how d'ye call?
Master–a ...Cosimo of the Medici,
I' the house that caps the corner. Boh! you were best!
Remember and tell me, the day you're hanged,
How you affected such a gullet's-gripe!
But you, sir, it concerns you that your knaves
Pick up a manner nor discredit you:
Zooks, are we pilchards, that they sweep the streets
And count fair price what comes into their net?
He's Judas to a tittle, that man is!
Just such a face! Why, sir, you make amends.
Lord, I'm not angry! Bid your hang-dogs go
Drink out this quarter-florin to the health
Of the munificent House that harbours me
(And many more beside, lads! more beside!)
And all's come square again. I'd like his face–

His, elbowing on his comrade in the door
With the pike and lantern,–for the slave that holds
John Baptist's head a-dangle by the hair
With one hand ("Look you, now," as who should say)
And his weapon in the other, yet unwiped!
It's not your chance to have a bit of chalk,
A wood-coal or the like? or you should see!
Yes, I'm the painter, since you style me so.
What, brother Lippo's doings, up and down,
You know them and they take you? like enough!
I saw the proper twinkle in your eye–
'Tell you, I liked your looks at very first...
Let's sit and set things straight now, hip to haunch.
Here's spring come, and the nights one makes up bands
To roam the town and sing out carnival,
And I've been three weeks shut within my mew,
A-painting for the great man, saints and saints
And saints again...
Oh, the church knows! don't misreport me, now!
It's natural a poor monk out of bounds
Should have his apt word to excuse himself:
And hearken how I plot to make amends.
I have bethought me: I shall paint a piece
There's for you! Give me six months, then go, see
Something in Sant' Ambrogio's! Bless the nuns!
They want a cast o' my office. I shall paint
God in the midst, Madonna and her babe,
Ringed by a bowery, flowery angel-brood,
Lilies and vestments and white faces, sweet
As puff on puff of grated orris-root
When ladies crowd to Church at midsummer.
And then i' the front, of course a saint or two–
Saint John' because he saves the Florentines,
Saint Ambrose, who puts down in black and white
The convent's friends and gives them a long day,
And Job, I must have him there past mistake,
The man of Uz (and Us without the z,
Painters who need his patience). Well, all these
Secured at their devotion, up shall come
Out of a corner when you least expect,
As one by a dark stair into a great light,
Music and talking, who but Lippo! I–
Mazed, motionless, and moonstruck–I'm the man!'

THE POETICAL WORKS OF ROBERT BROWNING
CLARENDON PRESS, 1995

> 'It is said that Fra Angelico would never take up his brushes without a prayer. Whenever he painted a Crucifixion the tears would stream down his face...'
>
> Giorgio Vasari

# PISA

*Giacomo Leopardi (1798–1837) is famous as the greatest Italian Romantic poet. His poems are particularly noted for their pessimism and wistfulness, but in this description of Pisa he appears in a gay, even lighthearted mood.*

'The appearance of Pisa gives me far more pleasure than that of Florence; the lung' Arno is so beautiful a sight, so wide and magnificent, so gay and smiling, that one falls in love with it. I have seen nothing like it in Florence, Milan, or Rome and really I doubt whether in the whole of Europe many such sights could be found. It is a pleasure to stroll there in the winter, because the air is almost spring-like; and at certain hours of the day that part of the town is full of people, on foot or in carriages. One hears ten or twenty languages spoken, while brilliant sunshine lights up the gilding of the cafés, the shops full of frivolities, and the windows of the palaces and houses, all of fine architecture ... As for the rest, Pisa is a blending of a big town and a little one, of town and country – a romantic combination, such as I have never seen elsewhere. To every other charm, its beautiful language must be added – and I will add, too, that I am well, am eating with appetite, and have a room looking out westwards over a great orchard – with so wide a view that one can see far towards the horizon.'

GIACOMO LEOPARDI, *SELECTED PROSE AND POETRY*,
EDITED, TRANSLATED AND INTRODUCED BY IRIS ORIGO AND JOHN HEATH-STUBBS,
OXFORD UNIVERSITY PRESS, 1966

### THE BROWNINGS IN TUSCANY

*Elizabeth Browning (1806–61), poet and writer, was an invalid, ruled by a tyrannical father, until she met another poet and writer, Robert Browning (1812–89). In 1846 Elizabeth and Robert secretly married and left for Italy. They made their home in Florence, at Casa Guidi, from where they travelled throughout Italy, and it was noticeable how Elizabeth took on a new lease of life.*

'Now, for instance, instead of sipping a thimbleful of port and complaining of the headache, she tossed off a tumbler of Chianti and slept the sounder. There was a flowering branch of oranges on the dinner-table instead of one denuded, sour, yellow fruit. Then instead of driving in a barouche landau to Regent's Park she pulled on her thick boots and scrambled over rocks. Instead of sitting in a carriage and rumbling along Oxford Street, they rattled off in a ramshackle fly to the borders of a lake and looked at mountains; and when she was tired she did not hail another cab; she sat on a stone and watched the lizards. She delighted in the sun; she delighted in the cold. She threw pine logs from the Duke's forest on to the fire if it froze. They sat together in the crackling blaze and snuffed up the sharp, aromatic scent. She was never tired of praising Italy at the expense of England. "... our poor English", she exclaimed, "want educating into gladness. They want refining not in the fire but in the sunshine." Here in Italy was freedom and life and the joy that the sun breeds. One never saw men fighting, or heard them swearing; one never saw Italians drunk; – "the faces of those men" in Shoreditch came again before her eyes. She was

always comparing Pisa with London and saying how much she preferred Pisa. In the streets of Pisa pretty women could walk alone; great ladies first emptied their own slops and then went to Court "in a blaze of undeniable glory". Pisa with all its bells, its mongrels, its camels, its pine woods, was infinitely preferable to Wimpole Street and its mahogany doors and its shoulders of mutton. So Mrs. Browning every day, as she tossed off her Chianti and broke another orange from the branch, praised Italy and lamented poor, dull, damp, sunless, joyless, expensive, conventional England.'

VIRGINIA WOOLF,
*A WRITER'S DIARY*,
THE HOGARTH PRESS, 1953

### THE LEANING TOWER

*Charles Dickens (1812–70) made several visits to Italy. The first was in 1844 when he took his wife, children and servants – a party of twelve in all – on a year-long trip through France, Italy and Switzerland. Martin Chuzzlewit was published two days before his departure, but he still found time to take Italian lessons twice a week.*

'The moon was shining when we approached Pisa, and for a long time we could see, behind the wall, the leaning Tower, all awry in the uncertain light; the shadowy original of the old pictures in school-books, setting forth 'The Wonders of the World.' Like most things connected in their first associations with school-books and school-times, it was too small. I felt it keenly. It was nothing like so high above the wall as I had hoped. It was another of the many deceptions practised by Mr. Harris, Bookseller, at the corner of St. Paul's Churchyard, London. HIS Tower was a fiction, but this was a reality – and, by comparison, a short reality. Still, it looked very well, and very strange, and was quite as much out of the perpendicular as Harris had represented it to be. The quiet air of Pisa too; the big guard-house at the gate, with only two little soldiers in it; the streets with scarcely any show of people in them; and the Arno, flowing quaintly through the centre of the town; were excellent. So, I bore no malice in my heart against Mr. Harris (remembering his good intentions), but forgave him before dinner, and went out, full of confidence, to see the Tower next morning.

I might have known better; but, somehow, I had expected to see it, casting its long shadow on a public street where people came and went all day. It was a surprise to me to find it in a grave retired place, apart from the general resort, and carpeted with smooth green turf. But, the group of buildings, clustered on and about this verdant carpet: comprising the Tower, the Baptistery, the Cathedral, and the Church of the Campo Santo: is perhaps the most remarkable and beautiful in the whole world; and from being clustered there, together, away from the ordinary transactions and details of the town, they have a singularly venerable and impressive character. It is the architectural essence of a rich old city, with all its common life and common habitations pressed out, and filtered away.

SIMOND compares the Tower to the usual pictorial representations in children's books of the Tower of Babel. It is a happy simile, and conveys a better idea of the building than chapters of laboured description. Nothing can exceed the grace and lightness of the structure; nothing can be more remarkable than its general appearance. In the course of the ascent to the top (which is by an easy staircase), the inclination is not very apparent; but, at the summit, it becomes so, and gives one the sensation of being in a ship that has heeled over, through the action of an ebb-tide. The effect UPON THE LOW SIDE, so to speak – looking over from the gallery, and seeing the shaft recede to its base – is very startling; and I saw a nervous traveller

> 'Truly. One might as well try to describe the face of one's
> angel as these holy places of Pisa ...'
>
> Edward Hutton

hold on to the Tower involuntarily, after glancing down, as if he had some idea of propping it up. The view within, from the ground – looking up, as through a slanted tube – is also very curious. It certainly inclines as much as the most sanguine tourist could desire. The natural impulse of ninety-nine people out of a hundred, who were about to recline upon the grass below it, to rest, and contemplate the adjacent buildings, would probably be, not to take up their position under the leaning side; it is so very much aslant.

The manifold beauties of the Cathedral and Baptistery need no recapitulation from me; though in this case, as in a hundred others, I find it difficult to separate my own delight in recalling them, from your weariness in having them recalled. There is a picture of St. Agnes, by Andrea del Sarto, in the former, and there are a variety of rich columns in the latter, that tempt me strongly.

It is, I hope, no breach of my resolution not to be tempted into elaborate descriptions, to remember the Campo Santo; where grass-grown graves are dug in earth brought more than six hundred years ago, from the Holy Land; and where there are, surrounding them, such cloisters, with such playing lights and shadows falling through their delicate tracery on the stone pavement, as surely the dullest memory could never forget. On the walls of this solemn and lovely place, are ancient frescoes, very much obliterated and decayed, but very curious. As usually happens in almost any collection of paintings, of any sort, in Italy, where there are many heads, there is, in one of them, a striking accidental likeness of Napoleon. At one time, I used to please my fancy with the speculation whether these old painters, at their work, had a foreboding knowledge of the man who would one day arise to wreak such destruction upon art: whose soldiers would make targets of great pictures, and stable their horses among triumphs of architecture. But the same Corsican face is so plentiful in some parts of Italy at this day, that a more commonplace solution of the coincidence is unavoidable.

If Pisa be the seventh wonder of the world in right of its Tower, it may claim to be, at least, the second or third in right of its beggars. They waylay the unhappy visitor at every turn, escort him to every door he enters at, and lie in wait for him, with strong reinforcements, at every door by which they know he must come out. The grating of the portal on its hinges is the signal for a general shout, and the moment he appears, he is hemmed in, and fallen on, by heaps of rags and personal distortions. The beggars seem to embody all the trade and enterprise of Pisa. Nothing else is stirring, but warm air. Going through the streets, the fronts of the sleepy houses look like backs. They are all so still and quiet, and unlike houses with people in them, that the

greater part of the city has the appearance of a city at daybreak, or during a general siesta of the population. Or it is yet more like those backgrounds of houses in common prints, or old engravings, where windows and doors are squarely indicated, and one figure (a beggar of course) is seen walking off by itself into illimitable perspective.'

CHARLES DICKENS,
*PICTURES FROM ITALY*,
BRADBURY AND EVANS,
1846

# ● Tuscany as seen by writers

## Siena

*Charles Dickens (1812–70) visited Siena during a long trip with his family in 1844. It was his first visit to Italy, subsequently described in* Pictures from Italy.

'On the evening of the second day from Pisa, we reached the beautiful old city of Siena. There was what they called a Carnival, in progress; but, as its secret lay in a score or two of melancholy people walking up and down the principal street in common toy-shop masks, and being more melancholy, if possible, than the same sort of people in England, I say no more of it. We went off, betimes next morning, to see the Cathedral, which is wonderfully picturesque inside and out, especially the latter – also the market-place, or great Piazza, which is a large square, with a great broken-nosed fountain in it: some quaint Gothic houses: and a high square brick tower; OUTSIDE the top of which – a curious feature in such views in Italy – hangs an enormous bell. It is like a bit of Venice, without the water. There are some curious old Palazzi in the town, which is very ancient; and without having (for me) the interest of Verona, or Genoa, it is very dreamy and fantastic, and most interesting.'

CHARLES DICKENS, *PICTURES FROM ITALY*,
BRADBURY AND EVANS, 1846

## Fiesole

*Iris Origo (1902–88) was an Anglo-American biographer and historian. In* Images and Shadows *she describes her childhood spent between Europe and America. After her father's death she and her mother settled at the Villa Medici at Fiesole, described here. She later married Antonio Origo and they moved to la Foce, a large farm in Tuscany. There they tried to bring back prosperity to the land and its impoverished inhabitants.*

'Sometimes, my grandparents came to Villa Medici to visit their daughter – Gran enjoying the house and garden and Gabba the walks and drives in the hills – but both of them a little bored by the constant intellectual and artistic talk, and trying to reassure themselves by repeating, 'But of course Sybil always did like this sort of thing!'

They brought England with them – but indeed England was already there. Florentine society at that time was not so much cosmopolitan as made up of singularly disparate elements – an archipelago of little islands that never merged into a continent. The worlds of the various colonies – Russian, French, German, Swiss, American and English – sometimes overlapped, but seldom fused into one, and the English colony itself, though the largest and most prosperous, was far from being, in its own eyes, a single unit. "They are, of course," as E. M. Forster's clergyman delicately expressed it, "not all equally ... some are here for trade, for example." The real gulf, however, lay not between one kind of resident and another, but between the mere tourist and the established Anglo-Florentine, who felt himself to have become as much part of the city life as any Tuscan. Some of these

> 'Absolutely for the first time I now saw what medieval
> builders were and what they meant.'
>
> John Ruskin

residents sank roots so deep that when, at the outbreak of the Second World War, the British Consulate attempted to repatriate them, a number of obscure old ladies firmly refused to leave, saying that, after fifty years' residence in Florence, they preferred even the risk of a concentration camp to a return to England where they no longer had any tie or home.

The English church in Via La Marmora, Maquay's Bank in Via Tornabuoni, Miss Penroses's school (where their children met all the little Florentines whose parents wished them to acquire fluent English), the Anglo-American Stores in Via Cavour, Vieusseux's Lending Library and, for the young people, the Tennis Club at the Cascine – these were their focal points. If they lived in a Florentine palazzo it was at once transformed – in spite of its great stone fireplaces and brick or marble floors – into a drawing-room in South Kensington: chintz curtains, framed water-colours, silver rose-bowls and library books, a fragrance of home-made scones and of freshly made tea ("But no Italian will warm the tea-pot properly, my dear").'

IRIS ORIGO, *IMAGES AND SHADOWS*,
JOHN MURRAY LTD, 1998

## A VIEW OF THE HILLS

### PASSAGE OF THE APENNINES – A FRAGMENT

*Shelley (1792–1822) composed some of his greatest poems in Tuscany, including* Ode to the West Wind, To A Skylark *and* Adonais, *in memory of Keats. He drowned in a storm in 1822, on a return trip from visiting Byron and Hunt at Livorno.*

'Listen, listen, Mary mine,
To the whisper of the Apennine,
It bursts on the roof like the thunder's roar,
Or like the sea on a northern shore,
Heard in its raging ebb and flow
By the captives pent in the cave below.
The Apennine in the light of day
Is a mighty mountain dim and gray,
Which between the earth and sky doth lay;
But when night comes, a chaos dread
On the dim starlight then is spread,
And the Apennine walks abroad with the storm'

PERCY BYSSHE SHELLEY, *POEMS*,
MODERN LIBRARY, 1994

### GREEN AND BLUE HILLS

*Virginia Woolf (1882–1941) was one of the great innovative novelists of the twentieth century, using techniques such as stream of consciousness which are now part of mainstream fiction. She was also a distinguished critic and journalist, as well as a tireless letter writer and diarist. Her diaries are a unique record of the creative process, with all its pleasures and problems.*

'This should be all description – I mean of the little pointed green hills; and the white oxen and the poplars and the cypresses and the sculptured shaped infinitely musical, flushed green land from here to Abbazia – that is where we went today; and couldn't find it and asked one after another of the charming tired peasants, but none had been 4 miles beyond their range, until we came to the stonebreaker and he knew. He could not stop work to come with us, because the inspector was coming tomorrow. And he was alone, alone, all day with no one to talk to. So was the aged Maria at the Abbazia. And she mumbled and slipped her words, as she showed us into the huge bare stone building: mumbled and mumbled, about the English – how beautiful they were. Are you a Contessa she asked me. But she didn't like Italian country either. They seem stinted, dried up; like the grasshoppers and with the manners of impoverished gentle people; sad, wise, tolerant, humorous.

There was the man with the mule. He let the mule gallop away down the road. We are welcome, because we might talk; they draw round and discuss us after we've gone. Crowds of gentle kindly boys and girls always come about us and wave and touch their hats. And nobody looks at the view – except us – at the Euganean, bone white, this evening; then there's a ruddy red farm or two; and light islands swimming here and there in the sea of shadow – for it was very showery – then there are the black stripes of cypresses round the farm; like fur edges; and the poplars and the streams and the nightingales singing and sudden gusts of orange blossom; and white alabaster oxen with swinging chins – great flaps of white leather hanging under their noses – and infinite emptiness, loneliness, silence: never a new house, or a village; but only the vineyards and the olive trees, where they have always been. The hills go pale blue, washed very sharp and soft on the sky; hill after hill.'

VIRGINIA WOOLF, *A WRITER'S DIARY*,
THE HOGARTH PRESS, 1953

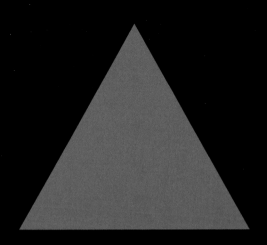

# Itineraries in Tuscany

▲ Maremma

Volterran landscape ▼

Vineyards in Chianti ▼

Sienese countryside ▶

▲ Grosseto

▲ Abbey of San Galgano                          ▼ Pienza

▲ Lucca

▲ Monteriggioni ▼ Pistoia

▲ Viticcio, island of Elba

▲ Golfo di Baratti

▼ Argentario coast

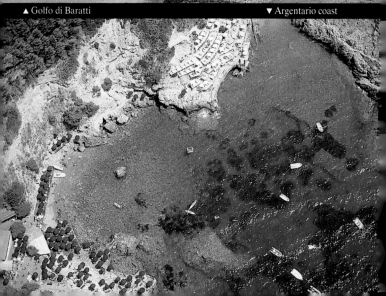

# Florence

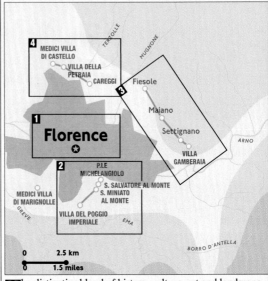

**DAVID**
One of the most representative figures of the Florentine Renaissance, *David* has been the city's emblem since the first Medici rulers ● 38. The statue, carved by Michelangelo between 1502 and 1504, is exhibited at the Galleria dell'Accademia ▲ 132.

The distinctive blend of history, culture, art and landscape that has assured the universal fame of Florence and Tuscany has been thousands of years in the making. The itineraries suggested in this chapter will explore every aspect of this age-old civilization, starting with the incomparable city of Florence and its beautiful neighbor, Fiesole. Florence's palaces, gardens and numerous works of art have been described through the ages by writers of all nationalities. The masterpieces that grace the city are studied in art schools all over the world. But these masterpieces are everywhere, not just in museums: beautiful sights greet the visitor on every street corner and on the façade of every palazzo.

Untouched by time, they are as fresh and vibrant as they

> 'There is no place [in Florence] that is not imbued
> with the noble, magnificent spirit of the Medici.'
>
> Franz Grillparzer

were when they first emerged from the studios of the artists and artisans who labored to make this Tuscan capital unique. Giotto, Michelangelo, Brunelleschi and Leonardo da Vinci are just a few of the major artists who have left their stamp on the city. The history of Florence is the history of human genius in pursuit of beauty.

## HISTORICAL BACKGROUND ◆ **B** F4 **C** B2

In the 9th century BC, Villanovans settled on the site where the Arno river meets the Mugnone, but it was not until the Romans settled here that the area began to be a real city. By the 3rd century AD, *Florentia* had more than 10,000 inhabitants. The small city was ruled in turn by the Byzantines and the Lombards, but regained importance and prosperity under the Carolingian dynasty. Between 1173 and 1175, the city's growth necessitated the construction of new walls incorporating the left bank of the Arno river, which replaced the smaller circle built by Matilda of Canossa in 1078. During the 13th century, as the conflict between Guelph and Ghibelline factions ● *33, 34* escalated along with strife between the wealthy and the poor, the city's supremacy was consolidated by its success in trade and banking, which led to a surge of building activity and cultural growth. In the following century, various tragic events (the flood of 1333, the famine followed by the Black Death of 1348) decimated the population and brought the economy to its knees, while in 1378 the revolt of the Ciompi (wool-carders and dyers) was brutally quelled. However, economic recovery and territorial expansion at the beginning of the 15th century paved the way for the birth of the enlightened Renaissance period.

**THE MEDICI ERA** ● *36*. Infighting within the oligarchy of bankers and merchants contributed to the rise to power (1434) of Cosimo de' Medici, known as Cosimo the Elder, who began his family's three centuries of power over the city, although this dominion was not always peaceful or glorious.

**MONEY AND BUILDING SITES**
Until 1252, the Florentines used the Pisan mark for currency. In that year, however, Florence began to mint its own gold coins, florins, which were struck in the *Zecca* (mint) next to the Palazzo Vecchio. The coins bore the effigy of John the Baptist, patron saint of the city, on one side and the fleur-de-lis, its symbol, on the other. From then on, Florence dominated the European money market. Between 1296 and 1299, this wealth was used to build the Palazzo della Signoria and the Duomo which, being financed by the city and not the church, became a proud symbol of the city's new identity.

**THE 'BONFIRE OF THE VANITIES'**
To encourage the Florentines to purify themselves, Savonarola built pyres in the Piazza della Signoria to burn jewelry, books, precious objects and works of art considered to be too pagan. The friar's terrible prophesies and attacks on corruption aroused the people, but eventually led to his own execution. The ecclesiastical authorities hanged Savonarola with two other monks, then burned his body on May 23, 1498 in the same piazza. This marked the end of one of the most dangerous heretics in the history of the Church of Rome.

After a brief republican period, ushered in by the fiery sermons of Girolamo Savonarola, Cosimo I took over the reins in Florence in 1537 and in 1569 became the first Grand Duke of Tuscany. He left his stamp on the city when he commissioned Vasari to build the Uffizi and convert the Palazzo Vecchio into a ducal palace. After the fall of the Medici dynasty in 1737, power passed into the hands of the Grand Dukes of Lorraine ● *40* who, influenced by the progressive ideas of the Enlightenment, launched an extensive reform program. Leopold II ● *42*, the last Grand Duke, was forced to abdicate in 1859 and the people finally voted for the union of Tuscany with the Kingdom of Sardinia and Piedmont.

**THE PRESENT DAY.** Proclaimed capital of Italy in 1865 (which it remained until 1870), Florence's new role called for an urgent facelift. The city began an intensive building program to make use of surrounding land. Since the start of the 20th century, tourism has played an increasing role, making Florence one of the most important places in Italy. Despite the attendant problems, the city is still a lively cultural and social center, and the seat of various universities and cultural organizations.

## PIAZZA DEL DUOMO ◆ **A** D3

The two squares, the Piazza del Duomo and the Piazza di San Giovanni, that surround and protect the two monuments of the Duomo and the Baptistery did not acquire their present appearance until the 19th century.

**LOGGIA DEL BIGALLO.** At the corner of the Via de' Calzaiuoli, this building is a combined example of secular and religious architecture, with its spacious loggia (1352–8), two-light windows on the upper floor and three spired tabernacles. It was the home of the Compagnia della Misericordia and the Compagnia del Bigallo, which were devoted to the care of orphans.

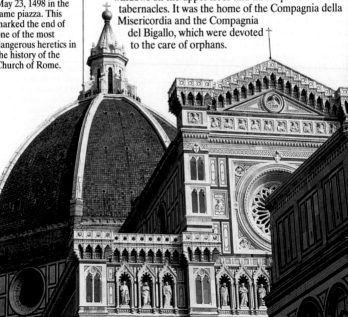

> 'I saw Dante, Petrarch, Machiavelli, Pazzi, Politan, Michelangelo and thousands of others gazing out of the windows of the gloomy palaces that line the street and block out the light.'
>
> Alphonse de Lamartine

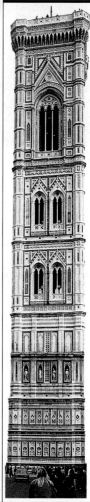

**DUOMO (SANTA MARIA DEL FIORE).** Not only was the cupola of the Duomo (*above*) an inspired architectural achievement, it was the symbol of Florence's ambitions. Arnolfo (who designed the Duomo and began work in 1296) and Francesco Talenti (who continued it in 1356) had given the Florentines a magnificent church, but one that lacked a cupola. The solution to this problem was to become Brunelleschi's life work. Drawing on his research into Roman architecture, he resolved the problem with two daring innovations: the abolition of the centering (the huge wooden framework or armature) and the construction of a self-supporting double vault with a usable space between the two shells. In this way, he succeeded without undermining Arnolfo's original design, which was based on a skillful marriage of Gothic elements (ogival arches, tall two-light windows) with extended, harmonious and brightly lit spaces that, like the cupola, were evocative of classical buildings. The result was a masterpiece of style and craftsmanship: special quick-drying mortar and light materials had to be used, and a new system of construction devised, since they could not use the traditional wooden centering. The work took from 1420 to 1436.

**GIOTTO'S CAMPANILE ● 79.** Giotto was responsible for the design and realization of the lower floor, decorated with hexagonal panels. He began work in 1334 and continued until his death in 1337. The building work was then placed under the supervision of Andrea Pisano, the artist who, with Luca della Robbia, was responsible for the decorative relief panels, works reminiscent of the *Original Sin* and *Redemption Through Work*. The entire third floor was decorated by Pisano, whose distinctive style can be seen in the different characterizations of the various laborers and the lozenge-shaped decorative panels showing, among others, symbolic figures of the planets, virtues, liberal arts and sacraments. Francesco Talenti then took charge of the work between 1348 and 1359, creating the three upper floors and replacing the pyramidal apex of the original design with a horizontal crowning. Giotto's design was totally original compared to traditional models: the tall building is defined by corner buttresses and lightened by two rows of two-light windows and one large three-light window at the top.

**PARADISE GATE**
Four of the panels (1425) by Lorenzo Ghiberti
for the east door of the Baptistery. They are
exhibited at the Museo dell'Opera del Duomo.

**'ZUCCONE'**
The Prophet Habakkuk, carved by Donatello for the campanile of the Duomo, is now displayed in the Museo dell'Opera. The figure he created was so realistic that the artist, in a fit of anger, kicked it, shouting, 'Speak, you idiot!' Perhaps this is why the statue is still known as *Lo Zuccone* (The Dunce) in Florence.

**BAPTISTERY OF SAN GIOVANNI ● 77** (*above*). Reconsecrated in 1059, this may be the oldest religious building in the city. The clear-cut lines of its octagonal shape are emphasized by the green and white striped geometric design of the marble facing. This Romanesque building shows an obvious classical influence in the windows with triangular and curvilinear pediments and in the interior, where a large segmented dome rests on the external walls, punctuated by pillars and architraved columns surmounted by imitation windows. The baptistery is decorated with 13th-century mosaics in the apse and has bronze doors (*above*) adorned with biblical figures by Andrea Pisano and Lorenzo Ghiberti.

**MUSEO DELL'OPERA DEL DUOMO.** The organization responsible for the construction of a monument and its maintenance was called the Opera: the Opera del Duomo di Firenze was founded in 1296 and from 1331 came under the Autorità dell'Arte della Lana (the wool merchants guild) whose coat of arms, the *Agnus Dei*, it adopted. The present building was built near the workshop of the architect Ghiberti. Since 1891, the museum has housed artistic objects from the monumental complex. It contains an assortment of Florentine sculpture from the late 13th century to the 15th century, with original works that once adorned the Duomo, the baptistery and the campanile: statues from the old façade of the cathedral (Arnolfo di Cambio, Donatello, Nanni di Banco); Michelangelo's unfinished *Pietà*; the two *cantorie* (marble choir balconies) by Luca della Robbia and Donatello; panels and statues from the campanile and the anguished wooden *Mary Magdalen*, again by Donatello (who also sculpted the statue of Habakkuk; *opposite page*). The great sculptor created many statues for the cathedral and the campanile between 1418 and 1425.

## A MEDICI ENCLAVE ◆ A D3

Between the 15th and 16th centuries the Medici transformed the area north of the Duomo with the construction of the family palace (owned by the Riccardi family from 1659), the complex of San Lorenzo, the monastery of San Marco and other minor buildings.

**PALAZZO MEDICI-RICCARDI.** After Cosimo rejected Brunelleschi's bold designs, he gave the commission (1444–62) to Michelozzo, who created the prototype of the aristocratic palace in Renaissance Tuscany ● 67. Traditional medieval motifs were given a new lease of life by the geometric design of the building, its rhythmic rows of windows, the repetition of the horizontal lines and the use of different facings (rusticated ashlar, smooth ashlar, plain stone) to emphasize the progression of the three floors. The palace has a square plan and an inner courtyard. Before it was enlarged in 1670, it resembled a cube with only ten windows on each side, reflecting a symmetrical style that had already begun to evolve.

**SAN LORENZO ● 81.** The simple gray stone façade gives no indication of the magnificent interior of this basilica (1420–70), a symbol of the vast power of the Medici who could lay claim to an entire church rather than the conventional family chapel. San Lorenzo is in fact one of the most lavish churches in Florence, built over the remains of a church consecrated to St Ambrose in 393. Its ground plan was designed by Brunelleschi in strict accordance with the laws of proportion and perspective. The same relentlessly logical approach is apparent in the plan of the OLD SACRISTY (1421–6), a simple cube-shaped room topped by a vaulted dome: the purity of geometric forms is offset by the dark moldings and stucco ornaments by Donatello. These were not to Brunelleschi's liking, however, as they disrupted the architectural harmony. A staircase in the FIRST CLOISTER with its two levels (*right*) leads up to the BIBLIOTECA LAURENZIANA (Laurentian Library).

**BIBLIOTECA LAURENZIANA.** The library, which houses the largest collection of manuscripts in Italy, was commissioned in 1523 by Clement VII from Michelangelo and completed in 1568 by Ammannati and Vasari. It has some inspired features: the VESTIBULE, with

### IN HONOR OF THE MEDICI
In 1459–60, Piero il Gottoso commissioned Benozzo Gozzoli to paint the walls of the chapel in the Palazzo Medici-Riccardi. The frescos on the ceiling, the *Procession of the Magi*, represent the Council of Florence of 1439: the courtiers are mainly portraits of members of the Medici dynasty and their entourage.

### SAN LORENZO ✪
The works of art decorating the basilica span a long period of time, from the 14th century to the 19th century. The major pieces include the unusual wooden *Madonna and Child* (c. 1382), attributed to Giovanni Fetti, the elegant marble tabernacle (c. 1460) by Desiderio da Settignano, the two bronze pulpits (1460–6), the unfinished work of Donatello, and the interior façade (1523) by Michelangelo.

contrasting colors of stone and plaster, the STAIRCASE, designed by Michelangelo, all straight and curved lines, and the READING ROOM, a horizontal room that forms a marked contrast to the linear vestibule.

**MEDICI CHAPELS.** Michelangelo's design for the outer façade of San Lorenzo was rejected (the façade was never actually completed), and as compensation Leo X and Giulio de' Medici commissioned him (1520) to build the NEW SACRISTY ● *81*, a funerary chapel for the family of Lorenzo the Magnificent. The structural plan and use of gray stone in this building represent a clear homage to Brunelleschi. Later (1640), Matteo Nigetti built the opulent octagonal mausoleum known as the CAPPELLA DEI PRINCIPI (Chapel of the Princes) under San Lorenzo's impressive dome. Entirely faced with porphyry, granite and rare stone, this was probably the most lavish example of Florentine baroque and the last true monument to the glorious reign of the Grand Dukes.

## PIAZZA DELLA REPUBBLICA ◆ A D3

This piazza was the nucleus of the Roman city, whose plan is still visible in the surrounding road system that survived Giuseppe Poggi's urban renewal program in the 19th century. The Via dei Calzaiuoli that connects the two most important monuments in Florence is a product of these improvements: its name is all that remains of its medieval past.

**PIAZZA DELLA REPUBBLICA.** This vast empty square bears eloquent witness to the creative poverty of the 1881 program, which demolished the Mercato Vecchio (built over the Roman Forum) to enlarge it and make it more 'dignified'.

**ORSANMICHELE.** An almost unique example in Florence of the influence of the ornamental style of European late Gothic, this building replaced the former loggia of the Grain Market (Arnolfo di Cambio, 1290) to which it owes its distinctive two-storied structure: the upper floor, with its high vaults and windows, was once used as a storehouse and now houses the MUSEO DI ORSANMICHELE; the lower floor, after the arcades with their elegant three-light windows with interwoven arches were bricked up, became a church dedicated to the Virgin.

**PALAZZO DAVANZATI.** The period rooms of this tall, elegant 14th-century palace (*left*) and the Museo della Casa Fiorentina (housed here since 1956), have been restored to recreate daily life in a medieval nobleman's palace. It has shops and workshops on the first floor, reception rooms and the owner's private apartments on the main floor, the rooms of other family members on the third floor, and the servants' quarters and kitchens on the fourth floor. Unlike the military appearance of the neighboring TORRI DEI FORESI, this palace immediately provides an insight into life in the flourishing city of Florence in the early 14th century. It was bought in 1578 by Bernardo Davanzati and belonged to the family until 1838. In 1904, Elia Volpi acquired it, restoring its past glory and embellishing it with his art collections.

## PIAZZA DELLA SIGNORIA ◆ A D4

As in Siena ▲ *210*, the center of political and civic life in
Florence was originally (13th century) a completely 'secular'
piazza, in which the buildings of municipal power stood
independently from the bishop's palace and the cathedral.
**PALAZZO VECCHIO** ● *65*. In 1540, Cosimo I began living in the
palace that had been the seat of the republican government,
thus emphasizing that the city's power was now in his hands.
In 1565, when he moved into the Palazzo Pitti, this former
residence became known as the 'old' palace. Designed by
Arnolfo di Cambio as a fortress, the interior celebrates the
absolute power of the Medici, particularly that of Cosimo I,
who relied on Vasari's inventiveness to do full justice to his
ambitions. With great sensitivity, Vasari left the heavy façade
unaltered and instead remodeled the building's interior,
coordinating the work of a large team of artists: they
decorated the Quartiere degli Elementi (1555–8), then the
Quartiere di Leone X (1555–62) and di Eleonora di Toledo
(1558–65) and, last but not least, the opulent Salone dei
Cinquecento (1563–72) and the two elegant, private studies,

**ALBERTO DELLA
RAGIONE COLLECTION
OF CONTEMPORARY
ART**
After the splendors of
Renaissance art, this
collection, housed in
a palace on the Piazza
della Signoria, marks
an unexpected return
to the 20th century.
Here, visitors have
the chance to admire
a collection of the
works of the most
important Italian
artists of the century,
donated to the city of
Florence in 1970.

The Palazzo Vecchio
seen from the Uffizi
Gallery.

**THE PEOPLE'S STATE
OF THE PRIORS**
The priorate (an
executive body)
dates back to 1282
when the city was
in practice ruled by
the heads of the
various *Arti* or
guilds. There were
initially three
priorates, but, as
new guilds were
formed, this number
rose to six, twelve
and at certain times
even sixteen. Dante
was a prior between
June 15 and
August 15, 1300.

No artist was closer to the Medici than Sandro Botticelli (1445–1510). Various paintings in the Uffizi Gallery make direct reference to the Medici family, the most blatant being the *Adoration of the Magi* (1475): the Magi have the faces of Cosimo and his sons Piero and Giovanni, while Giuliano and Lorenzo, Botticelli himself, Angelo Poliziano and Pico della Mirandola are among the onlookers. On the other hand, *Spring* (1477–8) ▲ *127* and the *Birth of Venus* (1482–4; *detail below*), mythological allegories painted for the Villa di Careggi ▲ *138*, are the finest representations of the cultural climate during the reign of Lorenzo the Magnificent.

the Tesoretto of Cosimo I and the Studiolo of Francesco I (1570–5). But the winds of change had already begun to blow several years earlier. In 1534, the year in which Michelangelo left Florence for good, the statue of *Hercules and Cacus* by Baccio Bandinelli was erected in front of the Palazzo Vecchio: its triumphant, brutal show of strength, placed in front of Michelangelo's *David*, clearly symbolized the changing climate of Florentine culture. The *David* was replaced in 1873 with a copy: the original is now on display in the Galleria dell'Accademia.

**LOGGIA DELLA SIGNORIA.** This is also known as the Loggia dell'Orcagna or dei Lanzi, because in the 16th century the Lanzichenecchi (German bodyguards) of Cosimo I had their quarters here. Its three lofty pointed arches (1376–82) reveal a taste for bright, sunlit, open spaces that prefigures Brunelleschi's first classical attempts. Built for public ceremonies, it became a sculpture workshop and finally an open-air museum. It now houses Giambologna's *Rape of the Sabines* as well as, after a lengthy restoration, Benevento Cellini's *Perseus*.

## THE UFFIZI ◆ A D4

**THE PIAZZALE AND THE PALAZZO.** In 1560, next to the Palazzo Vecchio, Vasari started work on a building for Cosimo I to bring all the administrative offices under one roof. Two parallel buildings, with elegant Doric porticos, connect the Piazza della Signoria with the Arno, enclosing a long, narrow space, like an open-air drawing room. This is closed at the back by a light and airy window crowned by a loggia with splendid views on both sides: across the Arno to the hills beyond on one side and the dramatic vista to the Piazza della Signoria on the other. Francesco I (1580) used the

third floor as a museum, commissioning the octagonal
TRIBUNE from Buontalenti. These art collections were
augmented by subsequent members of the family.

**THE GALLERY** ▲ *126*. One of the leading museums in the world,
this gallery began as a collection of ancient statues and
historical finds but was extended by the Medici, who also
collected items of natural history, weapons and objects of
scientific and technical interest. In the late 18th century, the
dukes of Lorraine began reorganizing this wealth of material
which ranges from antiquity to the 18th century (up to the
20th, if you take a walk through the CORRIDOIO VASARIANO).
In May 2000, the 'Grand Uffzi Project' was announced, which
will extend the exhibition area and allow some of the
currently archived works to be displayed.

## THE OLTRARNO: THE PITTI PALACE AND
THE BOBOLI GARDENS ◆ A C5 D5

Until the early Middle Ages, when the Ponte Vecchio was the
only bridge in the city, the left bank of the Arno was clustered
with markets and workshops. The working-class nature of the
Oltrarno, well described by Palazzeschi and Pratolini, still
exists, in sharp contrast with the austerity of the Palazzo Pitti,
the religious centers of Santo Spirito and Santa Maria del
Carmine and the stately façades of the noblemen's houses.

**PONTE VECCHIO.** A bridge would have stood at the narrowest
part of the river since antiquity. The present one, built in
1345, is one of the symbols of the city. It is crowded with
goldsmiths shops (which in the 16th century would have been
butchers and greengrocers) and overlooked upriver by the
Corridoio Vasariano.

**PALAZZO PITTI.** The largest palace in Florence, begun in 1458
for the banker Luca Pitti, was the residence of the Medici
family, then the House of Lorraine for three centuries. Finally,
when Florence was the capital of Italy ● *42*, it was owned by
the House of Savoy who had the rooms in the royal quarters

**THE BOBOLI
GARDENS ★**
These include
fountains and water
features, groves,
avenues of cypress
trees, grottos and
terraces, an
amphitheater, a little
island and countless
classical statues, both
grotesque and bucolic.
The gardens originally
served as a 'botanical
laboratory' for the
Grand Duke's court:
potatoes, mulberry
bushes, dwarf pear
trees and other exotic
fruit trees from all
over the world were
grown here for the
first time. There are
111 magnificent acres
overlooked by the
massive structure of
the Forte di Belvedere
and by the Palazzina
della Meridiana.

This suggested tour of one of the most important museums in the world spans less than 100 years of Florentine Renaissance art. Machiavelli, when describing this unique period in Western culture, said: 'This province seems to have been born to give new life to dead things, as can be seen from its poetry, painting and sculpture'.

**MASOLINO AND MASACCIO**
*Virgin and Child with St Anne* (c. 1424). The composition was started on a large scale by Masolino (1383–1440), who painted the figures of St Anne and the angels. Masaccio (1401–1428) added the monumental virgin and the vigorous child. The figures painted by Masaccio delineate the space in which they have been placed and define the area occupied by the other grouped figures.

**PAOLO UCCELLO** (1397–1475) A visionary painter, Uccello was commissioned by Cosimo de' Medici ● *36* to paint the victory (1432) of Florence over Siena at the Battle of San Romano. He devised a nocturnal landscape seen from a bird's-eye perspective, setting up a dialogue between the intricate interplay of geometric forms in the background and the planes created by the forest of lances.

**FILIPPO LIPPI** (c. 1406–69)
It is very difficult to define the work of this monk from Santa Maria del Carmine ▲ *129*. One need only compare his works in the Uffizi to see how the style changes. It can be solid and realistic (*Coronation of the Virgin*), or much more stylized and spiritual, as in his Nativities. This *Madonna and Child* (*left*) was painted around 1465. The Madonna is fragile and delicately executed (anticipating Botticelli, Lippi's pupil), while the Christ has the sturdiness of a Masaccio figure. Lippi's model was his mistress, which reveals something about his free and independent spirit.

**ANTONIO POLLAIOLO** (1431–98)
Antonio Pollaiolo was one of the leading artists in Florence in the 1460s and 70s, together with his brother Piero (c. 1443–96) and Andrea del Verrocchio (1435–88). *Hercules and the Hydra* reveals his affinity with the prevailing concerns of Florentine culture: his powerful, dynamic figures radiate energy and are presented like monuments against the background of a luminous landscape, portrayed with analytical precision.

**LEONARDO DA VINCI**
(1452–1519)
Leonardo painted
this magnificent
*Annunciation*
(1472–75) when he
was just over twenty.
Here he left behind
his training in
Verrocchio's
workshop: his careful
analysis of the
relationship between
light and shadow
clearly shows his
desire to transcend
the limits imposed by
contour lines, typical
of Florentine art.
This principle, known
as *sfumato*, can be
seen in the angel's
face, which is defined
by the backlit trees.

**SANDRO BOTTICELLI**
(1445–1510) The
painter who best
interpreted the
cultural climate under
Lorenzo the
Magnificent ● *36*,
painted *Spring*
(1477–8) for another
Medici, Lorenzo di
Pierfrancesco. The
painting was inspired
by Neoplatonic
doctrines that
combined Christian
revelation with pagan
wisdom. The work,
which represents
deification through
the medium of love,
is characterized by
graceful rhythm and
deliberate negation
of space.

**MICHELANGELO** (1475–1564)
The *Holy Family with San Giovannino*
(1504–5), known as the *Doni Tondo*. It was
produced in the unique climate of
competition between Michelangelo,
Leonardo da Vinci and the young
Raphael in early 15th-century
Florence. One of these 'challenges'
was launched by Leonardo whose
*St Anne with Virgin, Child and
Lamb* presented the figures in
a pyramidal composition.
Michelangelo's response was
unconventional: a spiraling group
of masses emphasized by a clean-
cut contour line and vivid colors. In
the middle ground, to the right, San
Giovannino gazes down at the Holy
Family. In the background, the human
race before revelation are portrayed as
naked figures: a 'pagan' element, a hallmark
of Michelangelo's style, that was to become an
accepted feature of sacred representation.

**THE SPATIAL UNITY OF SANTO SPIRITO** ✪
Highly indicative of Brunelleschi's artistic precepts, the interior of Santo Spirito shows the influence of classical and medieval Tuscan architecture (as does, too, his Duomo in Pisa ▲ 147) and represents a new concept in harmonious, unified space. The unbroken rhythm of the forty side chapels contributes to this effect. The original decorative scheme would have been repeated forty times (altars with altarpieces and hangings), to create an even stronger impression of unity. Much of this original decoration can still be seen in the apse and left transept: a pocket of 15th-century style preserved intact.

redecorated to reflect the lavish, overblown style of the late 19th century. The stark, somewhat oppressive courtyard with its three orders of rusticated ashlar, built (1558–70) by Bartolomeo Ammannati for Cosimo I and his wife Eleonora di Toledo, only makes sense when taken in relationship to the magnificent Boboli Gardens. Seen from there in perspective, the whole building seems as necessary as a theater backdrop.

**THE PALAZZO PITTI MUSEUMS.** The palazzo is also a prestigious museum complex. It houses the Galleria Palatina, a splendid example of a prince's picture gallery, with Italian and European paintings from the 16th and 17th centuries; the Galleria d'Arte Moderna, the Museo degli Argenti and the Museo delle Carrozze. The 18th-century Casino dei Cavalieri houses the Museo delle Porcellane (Porcelains Museum).

**FORTE DI BELVEDERE.** Grand Duke Ferdinando I ordered this fortress (1590–95) to be built on top of the hill that was also the site of the Boboli Gardens. Designed by Bernardo Buontalenti and Giovanni de' Medici, the building completed Vasari's complex defensive system. At the heart of the fort stands the PALAZZINA DEL BELVEDERE (1560–70), which may have been designed by Bartolomeo Ammannati: this is only open to the public for exhibitions.

## THE SANTO SPIRITO DISTRICT ◆ A C3 C4

Variety is the keynote between the Palazzo Pitti and San Frediano. The stately architecture of Via Maggio is little more than a stone's throw away from the picturesque medieval vistas of Borgo San Jacopo, while not far from the elegant palaces lining the Lungarno Guicciardini you are plunged into the noisy, working-class atmosphere of the district around Borgo San Frediano, which is also the site of two Renaissance gems: Santo Spirito and Santa Maria del Carmine.

**SANTO SPIRITO.** The powerful Augustinian order built one of its most important centers here in Florence. The present conventual complex was begun in 1250 and the first church (*below and left*) was constructed in 1260. The addition of libraries, studios, schools and hospices led to the decision to build a new and more beautiful church, commissioned in the 15th century from Filippo Brunelleschi. The plan was so

costly that the monks decided to set an example, economizing by skipping one of their daily meals for a year. In this church, Brunelleschi progressed from the linear purity of the plan for San Lorenzo to a more elaborate use of space: the curved profile of the side chapels guides the eye constantly back to the central axis of the nave, while the repetition of the design in the presbytery transforms this church into a centrally planned building of classical influence. He died before he could finish his work and the campanile of 1503 is the work of Baccio d'Agnolo, while the double dome was designed by Il Cronaca and Salvi d'Andrea.

**SANTA MARIA DEL CARMINE.** This 13th-century building, completed in the 15th century, was entirely rebuilt in 1775 after a fire. Its fame is largely due to the frescos in the BRANCACCI CHAPEL where Masaccio's collaboration with Masolino da Panicale enabled him to formulate a revolutionary new style of painting.

**SANTA TRÌNITA.** Beyond the slender arches of Ammannati's original SANTA TRÌNITA BRIDGE (1567–9), faithfully reconstructed after its destruction by the retreating Germans in 1944, stands the basilica of Santa Trìnita. Its severe Mannerist façade (1593–4) by Buontalenti conceals one of the oldest Gothic interiors in the city (14th century). The frescos (1483–6) in the SASSETTI CHAPEL by Ghirlandaio combine the Florentine tradition with the stylized Flemish elements that had become fashionable after Hugo van der Goes' *Portinari Altarpiece* (now in the Uffizi) arrived in Florence.

**VIA DE' TORNABUONI.** It has become virtually mandatory for any internationally renowned stylist to have a sales outlet on this street which, lined with imposing palaces, is one of the most elegant thoroughfares in the city.

**PALAZZO STROZZI ● 66.** This famous Renaissance palace (1489) was inspired by Michelozzo's Palazzo Medici, although it is much taller. The cornice and elegant inner courtyard surrounded by two orders of loggia are the work of Simone di Pollaiuolo, nicknamed Il Cronaca.

**PALAZZO RUCELLAI ● 66.** The Renaissance building, which was built in several stages (1455–70) by knocking together several preexisting houses, is a powerful affirmation of geometric purity and classicism. Alberti's palazzo dictates concerning 'graceful' ornamentation are clearly visible in the vertical and horizontal division of the façade and the use of smooth ashlar, while the delicacy of the three superimposed storeys conveys an 'absence of arrogance'.

**THE BRANCACCI CHAPEL ✪**
The restoration (1990) of the paintings in the Cappalla Brancacci has revealed both the true colors used by Masaccio, unexpectedly similar to those used by Fra Angelico, and Masolino da Panicale's formal mastery. Masolino's delicate structures form a contrast to the extraordinary power and realism of Masaccio's work.

**MARINO MARINI AT SAN PANCRAZIO**
Since 1988, the church of San Pancrazio (deconsecrated in 1808) has been the home of the Museo Marino Marini, which contains various works by the Pistoian artist (1901–80). It stands next to the small temple of Santo Sepolcro, designed for Giovanni Rucellai by Alberti.

**MASACCIO'S TRINITY** ✪
The *Trinity* painted by Masaccio for Santa Maria Novella is one of the pinnacles of 15th-century art. A triumphal arch seen in perspective has a sequence of three planes (God the Father, Christ, the Madonna and St John), concluded by the kneeling figures of Lorenzo Lenzi and his wife, the two donors. The 'hollow wall' effect described by Vasari was created by Masaccio's application of the mathematical laws of perspective.

## AROUND PIAZZA SANTA MARIA NOVELLA ◆ A C3

It was here, in the 13th century, at the opposite end of the city from the Franciscan church, that the Dominicans chose to site the church of Santa Maria Novella. An order of great erudition, religious intolerance and political conservatism, the Dominicans left their mark on the city with this lavish church, begun in 1278. Two contrasting architectural styles are juxtaposed in this part of Florence: Alberti's innovative treatment of the church and the functional continuity between the interior and exterior of the railway station. There is always something happening in this vibrant area of the city, which offers a lively program of cultural and historical events.

**SANTA MARIA NOVELLA** ● *79, 80*. The present church was begun in 1278 on the ruins of an old one. Cardinal Malebranca, invited to the city to put a halt to the strife between the Guelphs and Ghibellines, commissioned Arnolfo di Cambio to build the cathedral. In 1458, asked by Giovanni Rucellai to complete the 14th-century façade, Leon Battista Alberti came up with an inspired solution to the problem of linking the new pediment to the preexisting lower part and concealing the Gothic buttresses of the arches: he 'invented' the two large volutes on the sides, creating a model that was to be widely imitated and one that successfully integrated the Romanesque heritage (two-color decoration) with the architectural tradition of Ancient Rome. The interior contains many priceless works, including the frescos by Ghirlandaio in the TORNABUONI CHAPEL, those by Nando di Cione in the Strozzi Chapel, an early *Crucifix* by Giotto and the wooden one by Brunelleschi, created to prove a point to Donatello, as well as the outstanding *Trinity* (1424–7) by Masaccio, a secular meditation on the relationship between man and God, here depicted on an almost equal footing.

**SANTA MARIA NOVELLA RAILROAD STATION** ● *82*. Designed by Giovanni Michelucci with a team of pupils (1933–5), the station is a successful example of functionalism. It was rare in the 1930s for a large public building to blend in with the preexisting layout; in this case, the architect managed to strike a perfect balance between the building and its urban setting.

## PIAZZA SAN MARCO ◆ A E2

The confines of the convent of San Marco still resound with Savonarola's sermons. The Medici did not escape his barbs and the leading member of the family, Cosimo, completely remodeled the Dominican complex in order to square his account with God, spending 40,000 florins, part of his huge revenue from usury. The commission was given to Michelozzo, who supplemented the stark convent with the light, airy elegance of an unusually long library, intended for use as a school.

**MUSEO DI SAN MARCO.** Giovanni da Fiesole, who was commissioned to decorate the convent, was more than capable of translating the strict doctrines of the Dominicans into color and form. As early as the *Linaiuoli Altarpiece* (1433–4), with the Virgin surrounded by angel musicians, he had adopted Masaccio's ethics although rejecting his realism, and had attained a new depth of serenity in his treatment of religious imagery. He showed further development in the *Pala d'Annalena* (c. 1434–5). His use of perspective to create spatial unity made this the first example of a Renaissance altarpiece, a 'sacred conversation' executed in intimate tones that found even greater expression in the frescos in the convent's cells, the true pinnacle of his achievements. Here the paintings are truly meditative in theme, like the famous *Annunciation* of 1442.

**THE REFECTORY OF SANT'APOLLONIA.** Among other frescos, the refectory of the convent of Sant'Apollonia contains Andrea del Castagno's painting of the *Last Supper* (c. 1450), which became the model for all subsequent interpretations until Leonardo da Vinci. The setting is designed as a continuation of the real space in the refectory, and the eyes and gestures of the disciples focus on the dramatic central group in which Judas stands out in the foreground, his dark face looming over that of his master through Castagno's skilled use of perspective: a daring solution that has never been repeated.

**THE ALTARPIECE OF SANTA TRÌNITA AT THE MUSEO DI SAN MARCO** ✪
The altarpiece was commissioned from Lorenzo Monaco by the Strozzi family and left unfinished on the death of the artist (1425), who had painted the spires and the predella, today on display at the Galleria dell'Accademia ▲ *132*. Fra Angelico therefore found himself working on a pre-prepared triple-arched format. He interpreted the trilobate, ogival span as a large window looking out onto the scene, thereby creating a much freer formal composition: the central group of the deposition, a band of mourners on the left and the contemplative figures on the right. In the painting, the story (told by the characters) and nature (the urban landscape on the left ● *86*, the cirrus-streaked sky illuminating the countryside on the right) form a completely harmonious whole.

**GALLERIA DELL'ACCADEMIA.** Although it also houses some important Florentine paintings from the 14th to the 17th centuries, the gallery is widely regarded as the 'Museo di Michelangelo' and it possesses many of his original casts. His *David* (1502–4) ▲ *116* is closely associated with Medici ideology and the prevailing passion for antiquity: the iconography is that of Hercules, the Florentine rulers' favorite hero, but when the statue was placed in front of the Palazzo Vecchio, it also became a symbol of the new republic's strength and liberty, a cause clearly supported by Michelangelo. Other masterpieces, in various stages of completion, are the four gigantic *Prigioni* (c. 1530), intended for the mausoleum commissioned by Pope Julius II, and the *St Matthew* (1506).

## PIAZZA DELLA SANTISSIMA ANNUNZIATA ◆ A E2

The equestrian statue of Ferdinando I del Giambologna and two elegant baroque fountains stand at the center of this unusually shaped and harmonious square.

**OSPEDALE DEGLI INNOCENTI.** This building, begun in 1419, was the only part of the original plan for the piazza to be built by Brunelleschi. This is not only a masterpiece of civil architecture, but a monument to Florence's social conscience, since the city employed one of the top architects in the service of the most underprivileged citizens: foundlings. Brunelleschi's customary meticulous attention to geometric proportion produced a functional and attractive building as well as a superb COLONNADE.

**SANTISSIMA ANNUNZIATA.** The largely baroque interior of this basilica contains some of the most important frescos of the 16th century. The ones in the CHIOSTRINO DEI VOTI clearly reveal the unsettling and innovative responses of Pontormo and Rosso Fiorentino to the erudite and flawless classicism of Andrea del Sarto, described by Vasari as a 'faultless' painter. This new language had a marked impact on Andrea del Sarto himself, as can be seen by the naturalism and spontaneity of his *Madonna del Sacco*, painted in 1525 for the CHIOSTRO DEI MORTI.

**MUSEO ARCHEOLOGICO.** This museum, which was a result of the Medici's interest in antiquity, was enlarged by the Lorraine collection and also includes various Egyptian pieces collected by Leopold II (this is the second largest collection in Italy after the Egyptian Museum in Turin). The museum boasts an outstanding collection of Etruscan art and is a must for all students and devotees of this ancient civilization.

One of the *Prigioni* (Prisoners) exhibited at the Galleria dell'Accademia in Florence. Two other statues are kept in the Louvre.

**OPIFICIO DELLE PIETRE DURE**
The Opificio delle Pietre Dure is located at Via degli Alfani 78, near the Accademia di Belle Arti. Founded in 1588 by Ferdinando I de' Medici, the workshops of the Opificio were exclusively devoted to the restoration of inlaid work using semi precious stones. Over the centuries, it has widened its area of competence and is now one of the most prestigious art restoration institutes in the world, with a famous school and a well-equipped scientific laboratory.

The *Birth of the Virgin (detail)*, fresco (1514) by Andrea del Sarto, in the basilica of Santissima Annunziata.

# THE SANTA CROCE
DISTRICT ◆ A E4

For centuries this has been the busiest, most working-class district in Florence, full of merchants and manufacturers, and housing the administrative offices of the magistracy.

**PIAZZA SAN FIRENZE.** Behind the Palazzo Vecchio, near the heart of the medieval city, is Piazza San Firenze, the home of some of Florence's most important buildings.

**BADIA FIORENTINA.** Founded in 978 (which makes it the oldest monastery in the city), this building was remodeled by Arnolfo di Cambio (1285) and then again in the 17th century. The baroque interior, in the form of a Greek cross, contains various works of art, including the remarkable *Virgin Appearing to St Bernard* (1485) by Filippino Lippi. The church is also known for another famous vision: it was here that Dante saw Beatrice for the first time.

**PALAZZO AND MUSEO NAZIONALE DEL BARGELLO.** The Bargello (a synonym of the more prosaic *sbirro* or policeman) was the Capitano di Giustizia or Chief of Police, who lived here from 1574, under the Medici. It was the Medici who turned this palace into a prison and who walled up the loggias and whitewashed over the frescos in the Cappella della Maddalena. Restoration work in the 19th century rejuvenated the lovely porticoed INNER COURTYARD, with octagonal columns surmounted by ogival arches. Since 1865 it has housed one of the most famous MUSEUMS ▲ *134* in the world, not least because of its extraordinary variety of exhibits. The collections of works by Donatello, Verrocchio and the Della Robbia brothers are exceptional, and a whole room is devoted to Michelangelo, whose *Tondo Pitti* (c. 1504) is displayed among other masterpieces.

**THE ARCHEOLOGICAL MUSEUM**
The Etruscan finds at the Museo Archeologico in Florence create a telling, down-to-earth picture of a civilization too often described as 'mysterious'. The François Vase from Chiusi (570 BC), the *Mater Matuta* from Chianciano (470 BC), the famous *Chimera from Arezzo* (4th century BC), the *Sarcophagus of the Amazons* (4th century BC, above) the Roman-influenced *Arringatore* or *Orator* (late 2nd century BC) and countless other finds chart the history of the fascinating nation that once occupied a large territory in central Italy.

**THE MUSEO DI FIRENZE COM'ERA ★**
Housed in a former convent at Via dell'Oriuolo 24, the museum of the history of Florence illustrates the changing face of the city over the centuries. The collection includes the remarkable *Vedute delle Ville Medicee* (1599) by the Flemish painter, Giusto Utens, which depict the architecture and gardens of the Grand Dukes' villas in and around Florence ● 75.

In 1865, just after Florence became the capital of the kingdom of Italy, the city opened a new museum dedicated to applied arts and medieval art. The museum was housed in the city's oldest purpose-built civic building: the 13th-century Palazzo del Capitano di Giustizia. This impressive palace had, since the 16th century, been the seat of the Bargello, and thus of the law courts and prisons. Bequests and donations have made it one of the most famous museums in the world.

**BUST OF COSIMO I**
This splendid bronze (1545–47) was sculpted by Benvenuto Cellini at the height of his technical powers. The monumental classical work of art is combined with telling psychological detail.

**LEDA AND THE SWAN**
Sixteenth-century Florentine majolica. Florence's long ceramic tradition dates back to the 15th century. It was not until the latter half of the 16th century that various neighboring towns (particularly Montelupo and Cafaggiolo) began to produce pottery of a superior quality to that of the capital.

**'MERCURY'**
Commissioned from Giambologna by Cosimo I in 1564 for Emperor Maximilian II, this bronze displays a flowing purity of line that makes it the epitome of Florentine Mannerism.

134

## BACCHUS

Michelangelo was little more than twenty when he sculpted this unsteady *Bacchus* (1496–7), whose eyes, in the words of Ascanio Condivi (the artist's pupil and biographer), 'are in the overwhelming grip of his love for wine'.

## THE COMPETITION OF 1401

The finalists of this competition for the commission of the north door of the baptistery were Filippo Brunelleschi, who produced the panel below, and Lorenzo Ghiberti, the winner with his entry above. These two panels, depicting the *Sacrifice of Isaac*, are among the earliest examples of Renaissance sculpture.

## ST GEORGE SLAYING THE DRAGON

On the bas-relief at the base of his magnificent *St George* (1416), Donatello provided the first example of a stiacciato relief. The scene, with the holy Crusader at the center, is flanked by a colonnade depicted in geometric perspective.

**CASA BUONARROTI**
The Casa Buonarroti at Via Ghibellina 70 was built by Michelangelo the Younger (1568–1647), grand-nephew of the famous artist, on the site of the three houses bought by Michelangelo in 1508. Michelangelo the Younger was a brilliant scholar who swelled the family collection, as did his successors Filippo (1661–1733) and Cosimo (1790–1858). Cosimo bequeathed the palace to the city, which converted it into a museum in 1859.

The tomb of Michelangelo Buonarroti, in the church of Santa Croce.

**SANTA CROCE** ● *79.* The somewhat 'funereal' fame of this church as the final resting place of illustrious men such as Michelangelo, Alfieri, Galileo and Foscolo sometimes overshadows the remarkable works of art it also contains. In the magnificent interior, the walls are lined with funerary monuments. A Renaissance shrine contains the TOMB OF LEONARDO BRUNI, the humanist and chancellor of the Florentine Republic. It was built by Bernardo Rossellino in 1444–5 and was to become the model for countless Renaissance tombs. There are two of Donatello's works here, both displaying the artist's anti-classical tendencies: the tranquil *Annunciation* (1435) and the hyper-realistic *Crucifixion* (1425), criticized by his friend, Brunelleschi, who accused him of 'putting a peasant on the cross'. Visitors can also admire frescos by Giotto at the height of his powers in the BARDI AND PERUZZI CHAPELS (1320–26).

**CAPPELLA PAZZI.** Before all members of the Pazzi family were exiled or executed after the conspiracy of 1478, Andrea de' Pazzi financed the construction of a funerary chapel to house the family tombs. Brunelleschi was given the commission. He placed a great deal of emphasis on natural light, which floods in through the skylight and bull's-eye windows and is reflected by the white walls. The spandrels of the cupola are decorated with paintings of the evangelists by Luca della Robbia, apparently to a design by Brunelleschi himself.

**MUSEO DELL'OPERA DI SANTA CROCE.** Situated in the second cloister designed by Brunelleschi, this museum was seriously damaged in the flood of 1966: Cimabue's *Crucifix*, only part of which was saved, has become a desolate emblem of art as a victim of the elements.

## IL VIALE DEI COLLI ◆ A F5-6

A picturesque network of 19th-century ring roads, the
Viale dei Colli climb toward the summit of the hills toward
Le Croci, then lead to the Villa del Poggio Imperiale.

**PIAZZALE MICHELANGIOLO.** The square (1875) was built
to the designs of Giuseppe Poggi, who headed the urban
development program while Florence was capital of Italy. It is
named after the great artist, whose famous statue of *David* (a
copy) stands here. The view from the piazzale is stunning,
taking in the entire heart of Florence.

**SAN MINIATO AL MONTE** ● *71, 77* (*below*). Like the baptistery
of San Giovanni, this church (1013–1207) displays some of the
most distinctive features of Florentine Romanesque with its
allusions to ancient Roman architecture and the clear-cut
linear design of the two-colored intarsia work; the potential
monotony of the repetitive geometric motifs is avoided by the
introduction of a vivid mosaic of the *Cristo Benedicente*.

**VILLA DEL POGGIO IMPERIALE.** Reconstructed over ancient
buildings in the early 17th century
by Grand Duchess Maria
Maddalena of Habsburg, the
widow of Cosimo II, this villa was
then remodeled in neoclassical
style. The façade, with its central
loggia, is adorned by ancient
statues. In 1865, it became the
home of a prestigious girls' school.

## FROM FIESOLE TO VILLA GAMBERAIA ◆ B F4 C B2

From the late 14th century
onward, the major Florentine
families built houses in the hills
north of Florence, including the
hill towns of Fiesole and
Settignano.

**FIESOLE.** The countryside around
Florence is characterized by a
remarkable symbiosis between
mankind and nature. From the
15th century to the present day,

Fiesole's beautiful setting and many artistic monuments have
attracted admirers. The town's ARCHEOLOGICAL ZONE and
ARCHEOLOGICAL MUSEUM are particularly notable. No less
valuable is its heritage of Renaissance art. Even though Mino
da Fiesole and Fra Angelico were not born here, they have
left behind some priceless works: the former in the DUOMO
(the tomb of Leonardo Salutati), the latter in the CHURCH OF
SAN DOMENICO (*Crucifix, Madonna and Child*), several miles
further south. This is also the site of the MEDICI VILLA, the
VILLA L'OMBRELLINO with its 16th-century loggia, the VILLA
BELLAGIO, the last home of the painter Arnold Böcklin and
the VILLA DOCCIA or SAN MICHELE, whose façade
overlooking the valley is extended by a long portico.

**MAIANO.** The sandstone quarries mined here since the Middle
Ages are responsible for the long tradition of stonecutters and
sculptors, including Benedetto and Giuliano da Maiano.

**SAN SALVATORE AL MONTE** ✪
A flight of steps
from Piazzale
Michelangiolo leads
up to one of the most
beautiful churches in
the city: San Salvatore
al Monte, the work
(1499–1504) of Il
Cronaca. This
building was a favorite
of Michelangelo,
who called it '*la bella
villanella*' (his pretty
country lass). The
interior displays the
innovative use of two
superimposed rows of
pilasters.

**TWO GEMS NORTH
OF FLORENCE**
About 15 miles to the
north, along the S65
highway, stands the
Castello di Trebbio
(1436), probably built
by Michelozzo for
Cosimo the Elder.
Further on, you will
come to the Medici
Villa di Cafaggiolo
(1454), the favorite
residence of Lorenzo
the Magnificent,
immortalized in a
famous view painted
by Giusto Utens.

**MEDICI VILLAS** ✪
As early as the 15th century, the importance placed by the Medici family on real estate had encouraged the construction of country residences that reflected the humanistic ideal of the *locus amoenus*: a place devoted to leisure activities and the pursuit of knowledge. In the following century, the villas were modernized in line with the new style, exploiting the contrast between the geometric patterns of Italian gardens and the more natural appearance of the park.

**Villa Gamberaia** (17th century), near Settignano
**Medici Villa della Petraia** (c. 1594), at Castello.
**Medici Villa 'La Ferdinanda'** ▲ *143* (1598), at Artimino.
**Medici Villa di Cafaggiolo** ▲ *137* (1454), 19 miles north of Florence.
**Medici Villa di Careggi** (15th century), at Careggi.
**Medici Villa di Castello** (1477), seat of the Accademia della Crusca, in Castello.
**Medici Villa di Marignolle** (c. 1485), at Marignolle.
**Medici Villa di Poggio a Caiano** ● *72*, ▲ *142* (15th–16th century), at Poggio a Caiano.

The VILLA DA MAIANO, once the property of the Pazzi family, was restored in the 19th century by John Temple Leader.
**SETTIGNANO.** This hamlet (*bottom*) is famous as the birthplace of artists such as Desiderio and brothers Bernardo and Antonio Rossellino. In the CHURCH OF SANTA MARIA there are some 16th-century frescos with *Saints* and a *Trinity* attributed to Santi di Tito and a painted terracotta of *Santa Lucia* (c. 1430) by Michelozzo.
**VILLA GAMBERAIA** ● *75*. In the early 15th century, the father of the two sculptors Bernardo and Antonio Rossellino owned this country house. It was remodeled in the 17th century by the Capponi family, who laid out the garden embellished with statues, fountains and water features.

## FROM CAREGGI TO CASTELLO ◆ **B** F4 **C** B2

**CAREGGI.** This is the site of the MEDICI VILLA, enlarged (1459) and renovated, probably to designs by Michelozzo.
**MEDICI VILLA DELLA PETRAIA.** Remodeled in 1594 by Bernardo Buontalenti, this villa has a series of frescos (*Fasti di Casa Medici*, 1636–48) by Volterrano and a magnificent GARDEN which still partly retains its 16th-century layout.
**MEDICI VILLA DI CASTELLO** ● *75*. Built in the 15th century, this was modified (1538) by Tribolo and then Buontalenti. It is famous for its GARDEN, which had a statue-lined walk designed in celebration of the Grand Duchy. Some beautiful fragments survive, including the *Statua dell'Apennino*, the *Grotta degli Animali* and the *Fontana di Ercole e Anteo*.

# Around Florence

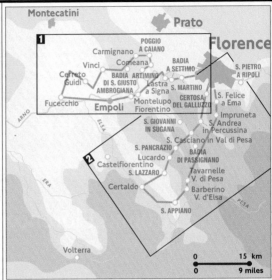

1. In the Arno Valley
   ▲ 141
2. From Florence to the
   Val di Pesa ▲ 143

**HOW PEOPLE USED
TO TRAVEL**
A 19th-century guide
gives a graphic
description: 'At one
time, people used to
ride around the
Empoli region,
disembarking with
great discomfort,
breathless and dusty,
from the ancient,
ramshackle carriages;
and if they were
seized by the urge to
head for the beautiful
hills lining the right
bank of the Arno,
they were ferried
across the smooth-
flowing river in a boat
that progressed by fits
and starts depending
on the surface of the
water or the vagaries
of the wind.'

This itinerary follows in the footsteps of Pontormo, the
tormented Mannerist painter whose work can be seen
in many locations at Empoli, Carmignano and Poggio a
Caiano. However, the itinerary also passes through Vinci,
the home of Leonardo da Vinci, where a fascinating museum
displays models of his inspired inventions. A 19th-century
traveler, marveling at the picturesque beauty of the
Arno Valley (below), described it as 'the Milky Way of
the road to Hesperia', while the views of the Pesa valley
with its crown of parish churches and castles are equally
breathtaking. The wide tracts of countryside here,
with rolling hills and tall, straight cypresses, are
typically Tuscan.

## IN THE ARNO VALLEY ◆ B E4 C A3

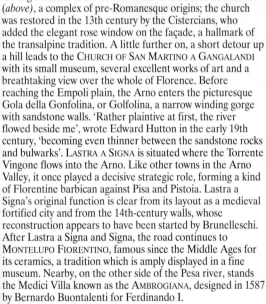

Like ancient historical sentinels, two abbeys mark the start of this itinerary which winds its way through the lower Arno Valley, passing through places dear to Pontormo, the leading Mannerist artist.

**FROM BADIA A SETTIMO TO MONTELUPO.** The first abbey you come to after leaving Florence is the BADIA DI SAN SALVATORE A SETTIMO (*above*), a complex of pre-Romanesque origins; the church was restored in the 13th century by the Cistercians, who added the elegant rose window on the façade, a hallmark of the transalpine tradition. A little further on, a short detour up a hill leads to the CHURCH OF SAN MARTINO A GANGALANDI with its small museum, several excellent works of art and a breathtaking view over the whole of Florence. Before reaching the Empoli plain, the Arno enters the picturesque Gola della Gonfolina, or Golfolina, a narrow winding gorge with sandstone walls. 'Rather plaintive at first, the river flowed beside me', wrote Edward Hutton in the early 19th century, 'becoming even thinner between the sandstone rocks and bulwarks'. LASTRA A SIGNA is situated where the Torrente Vingone flows into the Arno. Like other towns in the Arno Valley, it once played a decisive strategic role, forming a kind of Florentine barbican against Pisa and Pistoia. Lastra a Signa's original function is clear from its layout as a medieval fortified city and from the 14th-century walls, whose reconstruction appears to have been started by Brunelleschi. After Lastra a Signa and Signa, the road continues to MONTELUPO FIORENTINO, famous since the Middle Ages for its ceramics, a tradition which is amply displayed in a fine museum. Nearby, on the other side of the Pesa river, stands the Medici Villa known as the AMBROGIANA, designed in 1587 by Bernardo Buontalenti for Ferdinando I.

**EMPOLI, PONTORMO'S CITY.** Situated in a plain on the left bank of the Arno, at the intersection of the Florence and Siena roads, Empoli was once renowned as the granary of Tuscany and an important trading center. Its name is probably derived from *Emporium*. The entire Empoli area is now given over to industrial and commercial activities, even though there is much to see in its historic center: the CATHEDRAL with its marble arches inspired by Florentine Romanesque, the PALAZZO DEL GHIBELLINO, the CHURCH OF SANTO STEFANO and the CHURCH OF SANTA MARIA A RIPA. The highlight is the MUSEO DELLA COLLEGIATA DI SANT'ANDREA, whose six rooms contain some remarkable works of art, including masterpieces by Tino da Camaino, Masolino da Panicale, Filippo Lippi and Raffaello Botticini. A particularly enigmatic work, the painting of *St Michael and St John the Evangelist* by Jacopo Carrucci, nicknamed il Pontormo (1494–1557), is in the church of San Michele at PONTORME, the painter's birthplace, now a suburb of Empoli.

**CHURCHES AND ABBEYS AND THEIR TREASURES ✪**
**Badia di Passignano** ▲ *203*; reliquary of St John Gualberto (14th–15th century).
**Badia di San Giusto:** (12th century).
**Badia di San Salvatore:** tomb of countesses Gasdia and Cilia (11th century); shrine by Giuliano da Maiano (15th century).
**Church of San Martino a Gangalandi:** font (1432) and apse attributed to Alberti.
**Church of San Pietro a Ripoli:** polychromatic trusses (14th century).

Masolino, *Cristo in Pietà* (1425), Museo della Collegiata, Empoli.

**THE PADULE DI FUCECCHIO**
Heading north from Fucecchio, the Via Lucchese passes through the Fucecchio swamp (*right*), a lake formed by the stagnant waters of three streams that were dammed up and drained during various reclamation programs in the 18th century. This has resulted in an unusual 'mixed' landscape, part swamp and part farmland.

**FUCECCHIO.** Fucecchio played an important role in Tuscan history during the 13th and 14th centuries. A Guelph town, it was a place of refuge for those defeated at Montaperti ● *33, 35* ▲ *209*, finally becoming part of Florence's domain in 1323. Although the town has picturesque views, there are only a few traces of ancient times. Fucecchio's position straddling the Via Francigena, in an area made treacherous by its notorious swamp, traditionally gave the town a strategic advantage over Cerreto Guidi and other neighboring localities. The fact that it commanded the road to Rome also made it very desirable.

**CERRETO GUIDI.** This small hilltop town overlooks the Arno Valley. It was once the site of the oldest castle of the counts of Guidi. A magnificent villa was built by Cosimo I de' Medici on its ruins in the mid-16th century. The breathtakingly beautiful approach to the MEDICI VILLA is a sturdy double ramp, the 'Medici bridges', designed by Bernardo Buontalenti. As a result of the Medici presence in the area, the CHURCH OF SAN LEONARDO possesses some remarkable works of art including an outstanding baptismal font by Giovanni della Robbia.

**VINCI.** The picturesque, towered hamlet on the hillside north of Cerreto Guidi is famous as the birthplace of Leonardo da Vinci. The Conti Guidi castle (12th century) houses the beautiful MUSEO LEONARDIANO which contains a collection of models and reconstructions of Leonardo's designs, taken from his *Codex Atlanticus* notebooks.

**CARMIGNANO.** All that survives of the old castle destroyed by the Florentines is the Torre del Campano, on the highest part of the hill. The most famous monument, however, is the CHURCH OF SAN MICHELE, part of an old 13th-century monastery, approached by a Renaissance portico. The single-nave church acquired its baroque appearance in the 17th century and was partly restored to its original form after World War Two. Its most outstanding work of art is *The Visitation* by Pontormo, the artist whose works can be seen time after time on this itinerary.

**PONTORMO'S 'VISITATION' ✪**
Painted c. 1530, this picture displays the distinctive personal style Pontormo displayed in the altarpiece for Santa Felicita in Florence. It has been pointed out that the rhomboidal form of the women is derived from a famous engraving by Dürer. However, the painting is still surprising for its symmetrical doubling of the two women about to embrace – the young Mary and the elderly Elizabeth – and the women at the back, enigmatically staring into space, or perhaps into the future.

**POGGIO A CAIANO.** The Medici Villa of Poggio a Caiano ● *72* was built from 1480 onward to a design by Giuliano da Sangallo. There is a spacious area in front of the villa enclosed by a wall with corner turrets and surrounded by a garden. In contrast to the other Medici villas, the design of this villa, inspired by humanist models, represented a new departure, as can be seen by the elegant vestibule with ionic columns, surmounted by a tympanum and a fine glazed terracotta frieze. The frescos (1519–21 and 1579–82), including works by Pontormo, Franciabigio and Andrea del Sarto, for which the villa is famous, are in the central salon on the second floor. The uncharacteristic subject of the lunette painted by Pontormo makes it unique in his work. Although the relaxed fluidity of line is typical of Pontormo's style, this airy, serene interlude seems completely foreign to his usual melancholy style. The fresco of *Vertumnus and Pomona* around the window was part of the program of decoration for the room, commissioned by Leo X in honor of his father, Lorenzo de' Medici.

**COMEANA.** This small town is renowned for its Etruscan remains: the TOMBA DEI BOSCHETTI (7th century BC) and the burial mound, the TUMULO DI MONTEFORTINI.

**MEDICI VILLA DI ARTIMINO** ● *72.* Known as 'La Ferdinanda' or the 'Villa of a Hundred Chimneys', it was built for Ferdinand I by Buontalenti in the late 16th century. Used as a hunting lodge, it has a harmonious façade flanked by two towers. The villa, which houses the MUSEO ARCHEOLOGICO COMUNALE, is the ideal starting point for walks, especially to the Romanesque CHURCH OF SAN LEONARDO.

## FROM FLORENCE TO THE VAL DI PESA ◆ B EF5 C AB3

With its continual switchbacks, this winding road appears to be defying the rapid progress of the Florence-Siena freeway, which it continually crosses.

**CERTOSA DEL GALLUZZO.** Protected by high walls, this is one of the major monastery complexes in Tuscany. It was founded in 1342 by Niccolò Acciaioli and over the centuries has benefited from various Florentine legacies. It has buildings from various periods, the first of which is the Palazzo Acciaioli (14th–16th century), the home of the PICTURE GALLERY. The 14th-century CHIESA DEI MONACI is full of artistic treasures, including the choir stalls (late 16th century) and the elegant *Monumento Funebre di Niccolò*, the founder of the Carthusian monastery. The lavish CHIOSTRO GRANDE, with decorations from Giovanni della Robbia's workshop, is entirely Renaissance in style.

**SAN CASCIANO IN VAL DI PESA.** This town extends over the hills that separate the Greve river from the Pesa and is one of the most renowned towns in Chianti. Of particular interest is the MUSEUM OF THE SACRED HEART with an early *San Michele* attributed to Coppo di Marcovaldo and a *Madonna and Child* by Ambrogio Lorenzetti. The beauty of the surrounding countryside, which alternates sloping vineyards

The façade of the Medici Villa di Artimino: a simple façade, flanked by two sloping corner towers (*top*). The staircase is a 20th-century reconstruction based on a design by Buontalenti. A view of the Certosa del Galluzzo (*above*).

**FOLLOWING IN PONTORMO'S FOOTSTEPS**
After the *Visitation* at Carmignano and the frescos at Poggio a Caiano, admirers of the bright colors of Jacopo Carrucci, known as Pontormo, must see the five lunettes depicting *Scenes from the Passion*. These frescos were painted in the Chiostro Grande of the Certosa del Galluzzo between 1523 and 1525. They are now in the picture gallery of the monastery complex.

with steep hillsides covered with cypresses and holm oaks, makes San Casciano an ideal base for picturesque walks to the many churches and abbeys in this region, from SANT'ANDREA IN PERCUSSINA to SAN GIOVANNI IN SUGANA.

**THE VIA CERTALDESE.** The solitary Via Certaldese, lined on both sides by churches and castles, is one of those roads that seem to have been built expressly to recall the charms of Sienese landscape painting, characterized by hillocks, isolated churches and the straight-backed vigil of cypress trees. The churches are among the earliest examples of Romanesque art. SAN PANCRAZIO a Lucardo, SAN LAZZARO a Lucardo and SAN MARTINO a Lucardo all derive their name from the castle of Lucardo, between the Pesa and Elsa rivers.

**CERTALDO AND THE GHOST OF BOCCACCIO.** The artist Boccaccio is associated with Certaldo: the reconstructed house where he was born now contains an excellent library. The surprising thing about this town, which appears to glow red with the color of the bricks, is its picturesque layout on two staggered levels, the upper part, or CASTELLO, and the lower part or BORGO, extending along the Via Francigena. Only the Castello has preserved its original medieval aspect.

**OTHER DESTINATIONS.** Buildings of red brick, always reminiscent of Florence or Siena, work their magic in the towns of BARBERINO VAL D'ELSA, with its prestigious ring of walls, and TAVARNELLE IN VAL DI PESA. You will then come to the PIEVE DI SANT'APPIANO, the oldest church (10th century) in the Val d'Elsa, dedicated to the saint who, as the tradition goes, converted the valley to Christianity.

**IMPRUNETA AND THE SURROUNDING COUNTRYSIDE.** On the way back, after San Casciano, a detour towards Greve will bring you to Impruneta, a beautiful town that grew up around the old CHURCH OF SANTA MARIA. Elevated to the status of a basilica by the miraculous icon of the Madonna that is kept there, the church is a patchwork of styles due to the many changes made over the centuries. However, its porticoed façade with a clock tower, and the early campanile, cast an unmistakable spell over the semicircular piazza that resembles a sundial. The return journey back to SAN FELICE A EMA and Poggio Imperiale ● 68 ▲ 137 offers a particularly attractive drive through typical Tuscan landscape.

# Pisa and Lucca

# ▲ PISA AND LUCCA

**A BRIEF TIME OF GLORY**

This began in the 11th century and came to an end in 1284, with the city's defeat (40 ships lost, 9000 prisoners) by Genoa at the battle of Meloria. But the real reasons for the city's decline were internal. Having abandoned its commercial and maritime vocation, Pisa concentrated on the manufacture of leather and wool from the 13th century. The region deteriorated due to intensive stock rearing, becoming increasingly unhealthy, while demand for labor led to an exodus from the countryside.

**A CITY-PIAZZA** ✪

In 1063, Pisan ships returned laden with booty from the expedition against the Muslims, and the city ordered a cathedral to be built. This marked the birth of the Piazza del Duomo and the architectural gems that stand on the 'Square of Miracles'. The best approach to the square is from the Lungarno, bringing you into the piazza opposite the Leaning Tower, with the Duomo and the Baptistery on the left.

Although divided by bitter rivalry and bloody conflicts, Pisa and Lucca are united by a culture that has found expression in some wonderful Gothic buildings. Visitors will admire the exemplary layout of both these cities. Their historic centers, enclosed within the circle of their walls, still boast some priceless art treasures and are the site of mighty civic buildings facing stark churches and surprisingly graceful cathedrals. In Pisa, the most important is the Piazza del Duomo, a perfectly proportioned space scattered with buildings covered in marble tracery as delicate as lace. It resembles an immense field strewn with white marble prisms by an inspired god. Visitors can stroll around these massive buildings, admiring their purity, their sculptural quality and the graceful modernity of their decoration which seems to have been fashioned from light. Anyone visiting the Piazza del Duomo will understand Goldoni's famous remark: ' I was supposed to stay in Pisa for several days and I spent a full three years there'. It was here, in this treacherous area, frequently flooded and in constant need of drainage, that architects and workers labored to design a city full of priceless works of art. A picturesque itinerary heads from Pisa toward the mouth of the Arno river, where the landscape becomes Mediterranean evergreen in the lush forests of the Tenuta di San Rossore. Wooded lanes lead to the restless Tyrrhenian Sea, cutting through dunes and pine forests. In the opposite direction, the itinerary heads for the ancient beauty of hamlets like Calci, Cascina, Vicopisano, Pontedera and San Miniato. Lucca, enclosed within its bastioned walls, still appears intact with its densely packed houses, noblemen's palaces and towers; the openwork façades of the churches also catch the eye. Lucca's surroundings, dotted with elegant 'palace-villas', invite visitors to enjoy a tranquil stop in a landscape that echoes the harmonious restraint of these buildings in its gently sloping hillsides scored with cultivated fields. From Lucca, the valley of the Serchio winds up the hillside to Bagni di Lucca, a popular thermal spa, and Barga, with its perfectly preserved medieval layout. The itinerary then continues into the lush region of the Garfagnana, sandwiched between the steep valleys of the Apuan Alps and the Apennines, passing through Castelnuovo, the main town in the valley.

One of the most famous cities of art in Italy,
Pisa ◆ **B** C4-5 was once a powerful maritime republic.
This glorious past can be seen in its medieval monuments and
in the prestigious role it was called upon to play by the Medici
dynasty, which ordered the construction of the Piazza dei
Cavalieri and the Studio Universitario. Having reached the
apex of its economic and military power, its sudden defeat in
1284 by Genoa at the naval battle of Meloria marked the
beginning of an irreversible decline, and the city was
conquered by Florence in 1406. Pisa passed from the Medici
into the hands of the Dukes of Lorraine, who began a
program of urban renewal. After a French interlude, it was
again governed by Lorraine until being annexed to the
Kingdom of Italy in 1860. Heavy bombing raids in 1944
caused serious damage to the city, only partially repaired.

The loggias of the
façade of the
Duomo are a typical
decorative element in
Pisan Romanesque
● 76.

## PIAZZA DEL DUOMO

The monumental complex that stands on the Piazza del
Duomo, the so-called 'Square of Miracles', is the most
important example of Pisan Romanesque style.
**DUOMO.** Begun in 1064 under Buscheto, the cathedral was
completed by Rainaldo in the early 13th century. The lower
section of the façade, articulated by blind colonnades
enclosing the three portals, is surmounted by four rows of
tiered loggias, decorated with sculptures and intarsia work.
This building, with black and white striped walls and
colonnades and pilasters running around its entire perimeter,
creates an impression of remarkable stylistic unity. An
unusual oval dome soars above the junction of the transept
and the nave. Strips of black and white stone and the
'mosque-like effect' created by the forest of columns make
the magnificent INTERIOR seem even larger. This style of
decoration gives it an oriental appearance (the contribution
of Arab decorators has been documented). The many works

**THE PORTA DI
SAN RANIERI** ✪
The 24 panels
depicting *The Life
of Christ* (1180),
designed by Bonanno
Pisano for the
Duomo's transept
doors, combine
classical, Byzantine
and Romanesque
influences. The
language of the
narrative is both fluid
and incisive.

THE INCLINATION OF
THE LEANING TOWER
● 76
The tower's
inclination from the
vertical, immediately
attributed by Vasari
to the settling of the
foundations, is
around 5° and 30"
toward the south, a
tilt that increases on
average by about 6"
per year. Work has
begun to halt further
leaning, and to date
the tower has been
closed for about a
decade, preventing
visitors from climbing
the inner spiral
staircase to the top of
the tower. Galileo
Galilei once
conducted his famous
experiments
concerning falling
bodies from the top
of this tower.

of art include the PULPIT by Giovanni Pisano ▲ *151*, the tomb
of Emperor Henry VII by Tino di Camaino, and paintings by
Andrea del Sarto in the presbytery. GALILEO's LAMP hangs
opposite the pulpit. The scientist discovered the phenomenon
of the pendulum by watching this lamp swinging back and
forth. The apse contains a large 13th-century mosaic of the
*Redentore tra la Virgine e San Giovanni Evangelista* by
Cimabue; beneath are pictures by Sodoma and Beccafumi.
**BAPTISTERY.** This magnificent Romanesque building (*below*)
was begun in 1152, continued in the 13th century by Nicola
and Giovanni Pisano and completed in the 14th century.
It is surrounded by a delicate tracery of arches and loggias
crowned by Gothic motifs with an octagonal dome topped by
a truncated pyramid. Inside is an octagonal BAPTISMAL FONT
(1246) by Guido Bigarelli da Como and Nicola Pisano's
beautiful PULPIT ▲ *150*; the five relief panels of its parapet are
decorated with episodes from the life of Christ. The walls are
lined with statues by Nicola and Giovanni Pisano, whose work
also appears on the exterior.
**CAMPANILE OR LEANING TOWER** ● 76. Begun in 1173, the
building was brought to a halt by the settling of the
foundations in the soft ground. Completed in the14th century,
it echoes the elegant motif of the superimposed loggias which
are a characteristic feature of all Pisan architecture.
**CAMPOSANTO.** This elegant building closes the north side of
the piazza. It was begun in 1277 by
Giovanni di Simone and completed in
the 15th century in late Gothic style.
The interior walls were covered with
frescos that were partly lost during
the bombing in 1944. Its four wings
contain many masterpieces: the tomb
of the counts of Gherardesca (1320),
frescos by Taddeo Gaddi (*Tebaide*),
Spinello Aretino, Antonio Veneziano
and Benozzo Gozzoli; sculptures by
Giovanni Pisano and his school and by
Lorenzo Bartolini (*Inconsolabile*).

THE CAMPOSANTO,
AN ICONOGRAPHIC
BIBLE ★
Within the
Camposanto is the
old cemetery, where
illustrious Pisans
were buried. From
the 14th century, the
walls were lined with
Roman funerary
monuments and
tombs (1st–4th
century), which had
once stood against
the walls of the
Duomo. Many
of these pieces
form a valuable
iconographic
repertory, enabling
masters like Pisano
to reuse classical
motifs.

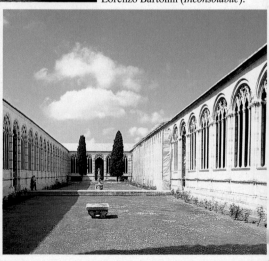

> 'Strangely enough, the buildings in the Piazza represent the complete cycle of human life: in this square are the baptistery, the cathedral, the Leaning Tower, the hospital and finally the graveyard.'
>
> H. Friedlander

Particularly noteworthy is the Ammannati chapel with an altar by Tino di Camaino. The Salone degli Affreschi contains the *Triumph of Death* (*right*), attributed to Bonamico Buffalmacco. Near the entrance is a bust of Franz Liszt, who was inspired to compose his *Totentanz* by the *Triumph of Death*.

**MUSEO DELL'OPERA DEL DUOMO.** This is housed in the Palazzo dei Canonici del Duomo (13th–17th century) and contains works from the principal buildings on the piazza. The many sculptures include the *Madonna del Colloquio* by Giovanni Pisano, four statuettes by Nino Pisano, the *Madonna and Child* and the *Crocifisso d'Elci*, also by Giovanni Pisano.

**MUSEO DELLE SINOPIE.** Housed in the Spedale Nuovo della Misericordia (13th century), this museum has a collection of 14th-century drawings and *sinopie*, preparatory drawings on plaster of the frescos in the Camposanto. They were discovered during restoration work.

## PIAZZA DEI CAVALIERI

The former hub of the republican city, the piazza, commissioned by Cosimo I from Vasari, is surrounded by a group of 16th-century noblemen's buildings constructed in honor of the order of knights, the Cavalieri di Santo Stefano.

**PALAZZO DEI CAVALIERI ● 65.** Converted by Vasari in 1562, it is now occupied by the Scuola Normale Superiore, founded by Napoleon. The statue of Cosimo I stands opposite the curvilinear façade decorated with graffito.

**PALAZZO DELL'OROLOGIO.** This was built as the infirmary of the Cavalieri (1607) and stood on the remains of the Torre della Muda or Torre della Fame ('Hunger Tower'), where Count Ugolino della Gherardesca, blamed for the defeat at Meloria, was left to starve to death (as related by Dante in his *Inferno*).

**THE TRIUMPH OF DEATH**
This iconographic subject made its appearance after the plague of 1348. The Camposanto has various frescos from the latter half of the 14th century dedicated to this theme. The one featured above shows death in the center claiming a group of young men, while angels and demons fight over the souls of the dead. Critics are almost unanimously agreed that this fresco is by Bonamico Buffalmacco.

*The Ivory Madonna and Child* (1299–1300), by Giovanni Pisano, is perhaps the most important work in the Museo dell'Opera del Duomo (*left*).

**CASE-TORRI**
The distinctive Via Santa Maria, lined with noblemen's houses from the 17th and 18th centuries, is also the site of some 13th-century *case-torri* (towers built for living in). These consist of a framework of high stone arches, between which the various floors, made of lighter materials, are subdivided by other arches. The first-floor portico and loggia above were left open.

149

THE PULPIT IN PISA'S BAPTISTERY (1260) ▲ *148*
This is one of the best examples of the transition from
Romanesque style to Gothic, by Nicola Pisano.

The work of the Pisano family marked a watershed in the history of 13th-century sculpture. Perpetuating the tradition of classicism, Nicola Pisano (c. 1215–1284) gave Christian religious art a renewed sense of history, infusing it with the dramatic force of the present, so characteristic of Gothic language. He placed greater emphasis on dramatic potential in the pulpit for the Duomo of Siena, done in collaboration with his famous pupil Arnolfo di Cambio (c. 1245–1310) and his son Giovanni (c. 1245–1318). Although Giovanni trained in his father's workshop, he was profoundly influenced by the transalpine Gothic vocabulary, developing it to the point of shattering classical models with the strength of his remarkable intensity and dynamism.

**STRENGTH**
A statue of Hercules embodies the virtue of strength in the pulpit (1260) of the baptistery in Pisa ▲ *148*, by Nicola Pisano. Classical elements clearly abound in this sculpture, showing the vast store of motifs Pisano was able to borrow from the iconographic 'bible' of the Camposanto ▲ *148*.

**THE NATIVITY**
In this relief panel, also from the pulpit in Pisa's baptistery ▲ *148*, the Madonna is idealized like a classical statue and placed at the center of the scene, resting on her elbow like many figures on Etruscan tombs. St Joseph resembles a classical Hercules and all the figures radiate a serene dignity within a well-ordered, harmonious space.

## THE MASSACRE OF THE INNOCENTS

This is one of the relief panels from the pulpit (1298–1301) in the church of Sant'Andrea in Pistoia ▲ *180*, executed by Giovanni Pisano. The brutality of the tragedy is conveyed by an impression of continual movement, a frenetic state of agitation, and an overwhelming energy. The drama resides in the fragmentary nature of this experience: the focus is now on everyone, not just the central nucleus.

### PERGAMO DEL DUOMO DI PISA (1302–11) ▲ *148*

The richness and dramatic force of this pulpit, by Giovanni Pisano, with its columns, lions and statues, makes it a masterpiece of Italian Gothic sculpture. The pulpit has had a checkered history: dismantled and removed after the fire of 1595, it was reassembled in its present form in 1926; some parts which had been lost were reconstructed.

### A PORTRAYAL OF SUFFERING

A mother with her murdered child; detail from the *Massacre of the Innocents*, from the pulpit of Sant'Andrea in Pistoia, by Giovanni Pisano.

### MODESTY

This is one of the cardinal virtues supporting the pulpit in Pisa's Duomo. With the liberal arts, the theological virtues, the personification of the Church, the figure of Christ towering over the evangelists and the Archangel Michael together with Hercules (symbol of victory over evil), these figures represent a portrait of medieval learning.

151

# ▲ PISA

Simone Martini, *Madonna with Child and Saints* (1319–21), a polyptych from the church of Santa Caterina, now housed in the Museo Nazionale di San Matteo.

**A CLOAKROOM FOR THE KNIGHTS**
The side aisles of the church of Santo Stefano dei Cavalieri were actually two wings added in 1682 as cloakrooms for the knights. They were converted into side aisles in 1868.

**THE GIOCO DEL PONTE**
This ancient costumed tournament, started by Lorenzo the Magnificent in 1490, is held in June on the Ponte di Mezzo, the oldest bridge in Pisa (rebuilt after World War Two). The two teams, from the two parts of the city divided by the Arno, attempt to push their respective opponents back to the far end of the bridge, using a carriage ● 53.

**THE REGATA OF SAN RANIERI ★**
This extremely old contest ● 50 is held on the Arno river on June 17, preceded by a costumed procession. The competition is between the boats representing the city's four districts: Sant'Antonio, San Martino, Santa Maria and San Francesco. The evening before the contest, the districts are dramatically illuminated by characteristic little oil lamps.

**SANTO STEFANO DEI CAVALIERI.** The church, designed by Vasari (1565–9), boasts a carved wooden ceiling (1605) and is lavishly decorated with numerous paintings by Vasari and others. Saracen battle standards and trophies hang on the walls, recalling the glorious past of an order of knights founded to combat the threat of the Turkish pirates.

## THE EASTERN DISTRICTS NORTH OF THE ARNO RIVER

In the oldest part of the city are churches built by the preaching orders, whose superb crucifixes by the Pisan school are in the Museo Nazionale di San Matteo. At the end of Via San Zeno, next to the church, is a 13th-century gate affording an attractive view of the medieval walls.

**SANTA CATERINA.** Built by the Dominicans in the 13th century, this church has a Pisan Romanesque façade, with blind colonnades surmounted by two rows of slender Gothic loggias and a rose window. The vast nave contains a painting by Lippo Memmi and Francesco di Traino, *Apotheosis of St Thomas Aquinas* (1363), and the statues of the *Annunciata* and the *Archangel Gabriel* (1368) by Nino Pisano.

**SAN FRANCESCO.** Begun in 1211 and finished in the 14th century, the façade dates back to 1603. The interior with its wide nave has a ceiling with exposed trusses. Six chapels line the tribune whose vault is decorated with frescos by Taddeo Gaddi. The marble altarpiece of the *Madonna and Child with Saints* is by Tommaso Pisano. There is a beautiful suspended bell tower supported by corbels linked by an arch.

**MUSEO NAZIONALE DI SAN MATTEO.** The former Benedictine convent (11th–13th century) contains one of the largest collections of Tuscan sculpture, painting and ceramics ranging from the 12th to the 15th centuries. The works by

> 'Fortunately for us, Pisa stands unscathed and invulnerable on the banks of the Arno. The communal standard with the white cross flutters during all the festivities held on the Ponte di Mezzo.'
>
> Lorenzo Viani

early masters include some interesting crosses painted in the 12th century. The paintings dating from the 14th–15th centuries, besides the polyptych by Simone Martini (*left*), include the *Madonna dell'Umilità* (1425) by Gentile da Fabriano and the *Madonna and Child* by Fra Angelico. The sculptural works by Andrea and Nino Pisano are outstanding, as is the magnificent bronze bust of San Lussorio (1427) by Donatello.

**SAN MICHELE IN BORGO.** The façade decorated with marble intarsia work charts the transition from Romanesque to Gothic style and reiterates the Pisan motif of the superimposed loggias.

## THE SOUTHERN DISTRICTS

Lungarno Galilei and Lungarno Gambacorti run alongside this curving stretch of the Arno on the south bank, where in the 19th century new districts sprang up around the old neighborhood of Chinzica.

**SAN MARTINO.** The Gothic church (1332) with its marble façade contains the altarpiece (*San Martino e il povero*) attributed to Andrea Pisano in the Cappella del Sacramento.

**SAN SEPOLCRO.** This unusual stone building with an octagonal ground plan stands among the old *case-torri* and palaces on Via San Martino. Dating from the 12th century, it is crowned by a high dome. Inside is the tomb of Maria Mancini Colonna, one of Louis XIV's favorites, who died in 1715.

**SANTA MARIA DELLA SPINA** (*below*) ● *79*. This church, finished between 1323 and 1360, derives its name from a thorn from Christ's crown of thorns, which used to be kept here. Damaged by flooding, it was dismantled and rebuilt in 1871. A masterpiece of Pisan Gothic, it has an interesting façade and an apse crowned with three soaring pinnacles. The interior contains statues by Andrea and Nino Pisano.

**SAN PAOLO A RIPA D'ARNO.** The façade, a harmonious example of Pisan-Lucchese architecture echoes the motifs of the Duomo. The interior has been restored and terminates in an apse with a 14th-century stained-glass window. The columns support Arabic-style ogival arches. Behind the apse stands the CHAPEL OF SANTA AGATA, a small octagonal structure.

**THE NEIGHBORHOOD OF CHINZICA**
This old district, extending from Via San Martino to the Ponte di Mezzo, was originally inhabited by oriental merchants who had their storehouses here. As the legend goes, the district adopted the name of Chinsica dei Sismondi who gave the alarm during a Saracen invasion in 1004. The traditional crossbow contest, known as the 'Kinzica di Sismùondi', is held every year on June 2.

**KEITH'S GRAFFITI**
The American artist Keith Haring loved Pisa. Several months before he died, in February 1990, he painted a large mural on the walls of the church of Sant'Antonio in the piazza of the same name, in the southern part of the city.

**A MOUNTAIN BETWEEN PISA AND LUCCA**
Mount Serra (3009 feet) separates the two cities which have been rivals since time immemorial. In Canto XXXIII of his *Inferno*, Dante described Mount Serra as '...the mountain that blocks the Pisans' view of Lucca'. Parochial considerations apart, its summit affords one of the finest panoramic views in the region.

**THE TENUTA DI SAN ROSSORE**
Lying between the Serchio and Arno rivers, this hunting preserve stretches for 8100 acres north of Pisa. It is populated by wild boar, fallow deer, foxes, porcupine and many species of birds. The flora is Mediterranean and tropical. First owned by the emperor, then the Pisan bishops, it passed in turn to the Medici family, the Grand Dukes of Lorraine and the King of Italy. With Lake Massaciuccoli ▲ *172* and the forest of Migliarino, this forest forms part of the *Parco Naturale Migliariano San Rossore Massaciuccoli*, founded in 1979.

One short itinerary leads to the coast, where the Arno flows into the Tyrrhenian sea after running alongside the Tenuta di San Rossore. The other leads in the opposite direction, to Calci and the nearby Certosa di Pisa.

**THE COAST.** Four miles from Pisa on the road to Marina di Pisa, a turning leads to the Romanesque basilica of SAN PIETRO A GRADO (10th–11th century), standing in isolated countryside. Made of Livornese tufa and white and black marble, it is surrounded by pilasters and decorated with suspended arches and majolica ornamentation. It contains 14th-century frescos by Deodato Orlandi and a Gothic ciborium which, according to tradition, marks the spot where St Peter preached when he came here in AD 44. The popular resort of MARINA DI PISA is reached by skirting the TENUTA DI SAN ROSSORE, an ancient forest (*below*) situated between the Arno and Serchio rivers and the Tombolo pine forest.

**CALCI.** About 9 miles from Pisa in the opposite direction, this delightful hamlet is situated in the picturesque Valgraziosa valley on the slopes of Mount Serra. It has a beautiful Pisan Romanesque PARISH CHURCH dedicated to St John and St Ermolao, dating back to the late 11th century. Its elegant façade has two rows of arcades and the interior contains a finely carved 12th-century baptismal font.

**THE CERTOSA DI PISA** ● *80*. Not far from Calci stands one of the largest monastic complexes in Italy, founded for an enclosed order. The massive white 14th-century building was remodeled in the 18th century. Standing at the back of a spacious square, the complex, which has a magnificent and monumental façade, is composed of a monastery, church, guest quarters and cloisters. A superb 17th-century fountain stands at the center of the large cloister. The baroque church contains 17th- and 18th-century sculptures and frescos. The building houses the MUSEO STORICO E ARTISTICO DELLA CERTOSA with paintings, frescos and sculptures and the MUSEO DI STORIA NATURALE E DEL TERRITORIA PISANO, which holds the scientific collections of the University of Pisa.

## FROM PISA TO SAN MINIATO ◆ **B** C4-5-D4-5

Retracing the winding course of the Arno river for just over 30 miles, the S67 highway passes through a typically Tuscan landscape with hills and flood plain, scattered with well-preserved hamlets and modern conglomerations of houses and factories.

**CASCINA.** Still partly surrounded by medieval walls, the city on the left bank of the Arno has some noblemen's palaces and old churches such as the PIEVE DI SANTA MARIA, pure Pisan Romanesque in style, dating back to the 12th century. There are some fine Romanesque and Gothic sculptures. Cascina is also famous for its furniture.

**VICOPISANO.** Crossing the Arno at Cascina, just before Fornacette, brings you into sight of the picturesque fortifications of Vicopisano. The architect Brunelleschi collaborated on this work after the hamlet was captured in 1407 by the Florentines, who transformed it into a fortress. Not far from the central Piazza Cavalca stands the PARISH CHURCH, a stark 11th–12th-century building in Pisan Romanesque style. The interior, with a nave and two aisles, contains a wooden carving of the *Deposition* (12th–13th century). Heading back along Via Lante from the piazza, you come to the TORRE DELL'OROLOGIO, various other towers and a 15th-century house. A little further on stands the 14th-century TORRE DELLE QUATTRO PORTE with its ogival arches.

**PONTEDERA.** Returning on the S67 highway, you come to this medieval hamlet at the confluence of the Era river with the Arno; it was originally a castle built by the Pisans at the start of the 13th century and attacked on several occasions by the Florentines. The 17th-century CHIURCH OF SANTI JACOPO E FILIPPO still possesses some Romanesque elements. The interior contains the *Madonna del Rosario* (1595) by Cigoli and a 14th-century wooden statue of Santa Lucia.

**SAN MINIATO.** This hill town (*below*), overlooking the Arno plain, was the seat of the imperial vicars in Tuscany and the birthplace of Matilda of Canossa. The 14th-century CHURCH OF SAN DOMENICO, with its remodeled façade and interior, has a *Madonna and Child with Four Saints* by Domenico Michelino and the *Tomb of Giovanni Chellini*, built by Bernardo Rossellino. The DUOMO, built on a site with panoramic views in the 13th century, has a campanile known as the 'Torre di Matilde' and a splendid interior. The adjacent MUSEO DIOCESANO DI ARTE SACRA contains works by Filippo Lippi and Andrea del Verrocchio. Some ancient palaces are also worthy of note: the PALAZZO DEI VICARI DELL'IMPERATORE (12th century); the Renaissance PALAZZO GRIFONI and PALAZZO FORMICHINI. All that remains of the 13th-century hilltop TORRE DI FEDERICO, is a single tower, where Pier delle Vigne was imprisoned.

**THE LEGENDARY 'VESPA'**
The Piaggio Company in Pontedera manufactures the Vespa, which in postwar Italy became, along with the Fiat 500, the symbol of mass motoring.

**THE TORRE DI FEDERICO AT SAN MINIATO**
This is where Pier delle Vigne met his unfortunate end. He was the secretary and court poet of Frederick II who for a long time held him in great esteem until he was slandered by envious courtiers. Frederick II then had him incarcerated and blinded with a red-hot iron. As the story goes, Pier, mad with grief and pain, committed suicide (1249) by smashing his head against the wall of his cell.

The circular Piazza del Mercato; with San Frediano at the top.

Set like a precious gem within the circle of its walls, Lucca ◆ **B** C4 has lost none of its appeal over the centuries, and its magnificent monuments have survived virtually intact. It is almost as if the city's fortifications have protected it from the ravages of time. Occupied in turn by Ligurians and Etruscans, then a colony of Ancient Rome, Lucca came under barbarian domination until 1162, when it became a free town. Despite infighting and conflicts with neighboring cities, it entered a period of steady economic growth owing to its thriving silk industry and banking activities. Throwing off the yoke of Lombard-Pisan influences, its artistic output also attained a position of supremacy. In the mid-16th century, the city became an independent republic. This lasted until 1805, when it became a Napoleonic Principality. It then passed into the hands of the Bourbons and was annexed to the Grand Duchy of Tuscany.

## ON THE RUINS OF THE ROMAN CITY

**LUCCA, AN UNCHANGED CITY ✪**
Time seems to have stood still in the lovely city of Lucca. It has an intact circle of walls that do not appear forbidding or warlike; narrow, winding streets with gates standing ajar; half-hidden gardens; and as many towers, campaniles and monuments as any other city of Tuscany, but more discreet.

*Ascension*, 12th-century mosaic on the façade of San Frediano.

Lucca's geometric road network betrays its Roman origins. This is particularly evident in the orientation of Via Fillungo and Via Cenami and that of Via San Paolino, Via Roma and Via Santa Croce. Vestiges of the walls ● *70*, reused fragments and, most important, the structure of the stark medieval houses that form the ellipse of the amphitheater also bear witness to the city's Roman past.

**PIAZZA DEL MERCATO.** The piazza was built within what was once the Roman amphitheater (2nd century). This was partly demolished in the Middle Ages so that the materials could be reused, while the wedge-shaped sections (*cunei*) around the inner ring were used as houses, prisons and storehouses. In 1830, the Bourbons commissioned the architect Lorenzo Nottolini to restore the amphitheater's public function. The buildings in the central section were therefore cleared so that the harmonious elliptical structure was once again visible. It is still possible to make out various remains of what was once two rows of 54 arches.

**SAN FREDIANO.** Built in the 12th century over the remains of an ancient basilica (still visible), this church displays the characteristic features of Pisan Romanesque, even though it has been extensively modified. At the top of the central section of the façade, divided by pilasters, is an architraved loggia with a large mosaic of the *Ascension* (*left*), attributed by many to Berlinghieri. Behind it, silhouetted against the sky, is the top of its impressive white crenelated campanile. The interior, with a nave and

> 'There are very few churches in Lucca without a Romanesque façade and they are not very important.'
>
> Luigi Baldacci

two aisles supported by reused columns and capitals, has been embellished by many works over the centuries: the baptismal font and pavement date from the 12th century, the lavish marble polyptych (*Madonna and Child with Four Saints*) by Jacopo della Quercia from 1422 and the frescos in the chapel of St Augustine from 1509.

**VIA FILLUNGO.** This road, running at a tangent to the amphitheater, is one of the city's main axes. Stretching from the medieval Porta dei Borghi to the Canto d'Arco, it is lined by old houses and dominated by the 13th-century TORRE DELLE ORE which has been the city's clock tower since 1471. When it was remodeled in 1754, the tower was given a mechanical clock, made by the Swiss clockmaker Louis Simon, which is still in working order.

**SAN MICHELE IN FORO** ● 77. This huge marble church, built between 1070 and the mid-12th century, looms over the piazza of the same name, which occupies the area corresponding to the Roman forum. On the church's façade (15th century), the loggias of Pisan inspiration, covered with lavish polychromatic decoration, create a graceful interplay of light and shade. Although the colossal marble statue of the Archangel Michael on the top is still Romanesque in style, the two shrines on either side, which emphasize the church's vertical thrust, consolidate its uniquely Gothic character. The interior contains two fine works: the glazed terracotta *Madonna and Child* by Andrea della Robbia and the painting by Filippino Lippi, *Sts Helena, Jerome, Sebastian and Roch*. In the piazza, on the corner of Via Vittorio Veneto, stands the PALAZZO PRETORIO, with its elegant loggia. This was begun in 1494 by Matteo Civitali and today houses the Prefecture.

**CASA DI PUCCINI.** The house where Giacomo Puccini was born in 1858 stands on Corte San Lorenzo. It is now a museum containing personal items, portraits and the piano he used when writing his opera *Turandot*.

**PALAZZO MANSI.** This wonderful nobleman's residence dating from the late 16th century, has been the seat of the MUSEO and the PINACOTECA NAZIONALE since 1977. Visitors can wander through the spacious apartments of the main floor, from the luxurious Sala degli Specchi to the vast Salone della Musica, until they reach the famous Sala dell'Alcova with its renowned tapestries, said to be haunted by the ghost of Lucida Mansi, condemned to Hell for her vanity.

**THE TORRE DELLE ORE**
Situated on Via Fillungo, the most celebrated street in Lucca, this tower owes its fame to an old legend. Lucida Mansi, a Lucchese noblewoman, asked the devil to preserve her beauty for thirty years. One moonless night, thirty years later, the devil was seen standing on the tower as the tolling of the bell marked the end of the pact. The tower was also called the 'Tower of the Lawsuit' because, when the Republic decided to buy the building, it was so hard to establish ownership that it took over twenty years to complete the transactions.

**THE MUSEO AND PINACOTECA NAZIONALE AT THE PALAZZO MANSI**
A variety of artistic schools are represented in this collection of works, whose main nucleus dates back to the donation made in 1847 by Leopold II. There are paintings by the Venetian, Lombard, Roman and Flemish schools as well as a large collection of Tuscan masters, including outstanding works by Beccafumi, Bronzino, Pontormo (*Portrait of a Young Man*, 1525, *above*) and Andrea del Sarto.

## From the 'Three Piazze' to Villa Guinigi

**THE TOMB OF ILARIA DEL CARRETTO** Although Ilaria, Paolo Guinigi's second wife, died very young in 1405, her funerary monument, a masterpiece by Jacopo della Quercia (1408) in the Duomo, has ensured her immortality. She lies outstretched on the tomb with her head on the pillow and her lapdog curled at her feet, a symbol of loyalty. Her face is framed by her headdress and her eyelids are closed as if she had just fallen asleep.

The Guinigi houses and tower (*below*). A detail of the façade of the Duomo (*below right*).

Remodeled in the 16th century, the piazzas of San Martino, San Giovanni and Antelminelli became open spaces partly bounded by walled gardens with windows overlooking the street. This unusual design, carried out within the existing narrow medieval road network, afforded some delightful and unexpected views. As a result, visitors emerging from extremely narrow streets and lanes are greeted by the sight of the beautiful asymmetrical façade of the Duomo.

**DUOMO DI SAN MARTINO.** Founded in the 6th century by Bishop Frediano, this cathedral was rebuilt in the 12th century in pure Romanesque style and various modifications were carried out until the 15th century. With its three rows of loggias with a dazzling variety of pillars, the marble FAÇADE is a marvel of airy grace. Its lower section has a deep three-arched portico supported by large pilasters. The interior contains works by Tintoretto and Ghirlandaio. The TEMPIETTO DEL VOLTO SANTO (1482–4) by Matteo Civitali (who also created the altar of San Regolo, 1484) has a famous 11th–12th-century wooden crucifix, perhaps of oriental origin, mentioned by Dante in his *Inferno*. In the sacristy is the TOMB OF ILARIA DEL CARRETTO. The inner façade has the group of *San Martino a Cavallo e il Mendico*, by an unknown 13th-century Lombard-Lucchese master, which used to be on the outer façade.

**CASE GUINIGI.** The brick palaces and 14th-century tower are the last, impressive modified versions of the Romanesque-Gothic house. Together with an ancient loggia, these buildings stand on the Via Guinigi, which has preserved its delightful medieval aspect despite the destruction of three of the four

> 'A road lined with plane trees descends toward Lucca, enclosed in the seamless circle of its mighty walls covered in trees, so that seen from above the city looks like it is wearing a crown.'
>
> Lorenzo Viani

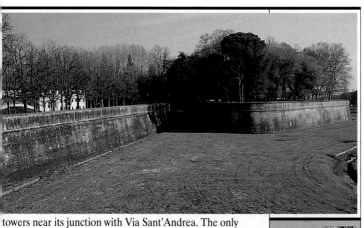

towers near its junction with Via Sant'Andrea. The only survivor of the many towers that used to characterize Lucca's cityscape is the TORRE GUINIGI, built in the 14th century and crowned by some fine holm oaks growing at the top.

**VILLA GUINIGI.** Built (1413) by Paolo Guinigi, *signore* of Lucca, it now houses the MUSEO NAZIONALE DI VILLA GUINIGI. The building, later known as Quarquonia, forms a striking contrast to earlier villas with its impressive brick structure and the interplay between the different colors of the materials used: the gray stone, white limestone and red brick are echoed by the colors of the landscape. The building has a spacious portico, while the entire second floor has a continuous line of typical rounded three-light windows.

**THE WALLS ● 70.** Lucca is one of the few Italian cities which has preserved its circle of walls intact (*above*). These wide, well-maintained walls are composed of twelve mighty curtain walls, ten triangular bastions and the PIATTAFORMA DI SAN FREDIANO. The first circle dates back to the Roman era, while the second was built after 1000 to take in the spreading hamlets outside the walls. The two surviving gates into the medieval city are PORTA SAN GERVASIO, in the south, and the PORTA DEI BORGHI, in the north. The third and present circle, built in response to the development of artillery and the growing expansionist ambitions of the Florentines, was completed in 1645. From that time onward, the walls restricted urban growth, thereby preserving the harmonious layout of the city. Under Maria Luisa of Bourbon-Parma, in the early part of the 19th century, the walls were planted with a double row of trees, equipped with benches and transformed into a pedestrian-only public promenade.

## FROM THE LUCCA PLAIN TO THE GARFAGNANA ◆ B C4-C3

From Lucca, a short detour to the east of the Serchio river leads to some of the villas, at Camigliano, Marlia and Segromigno, built by wealthy Lucca families on the hills marking the boundary of the Lucca plain. Heading through the Serchio valley on the S12 highway, then taking the S445 highway into the lower Garfagnana, you will be greeted by a beautiful diverse landscape, alternating crops, hills, woods, vines, delightful hamlets, parish churches and castles.

**THE MUSEO NAZIONALE DI VILLA GUINIGI ✪** Villa Guinigi is a typical example of the late romantic museum. It has an excellent collection displaying the culture and art of Lucca and its territory. The archeological section has a rich store of funerary equipment from Ligurian and Etruscan tombs (10th–9th century BC), as well as many architectural fragments (a Romanesque capital, *above*). The most valuable medieval piece is a Lombard parade shield. The paintings include *Ecce homo* by Matteo Civitali and the *Madonna della Misericordia* (1515) by Fra' Bartolomeo.

**VILLA TORRIGIANI.** This villa is 6 miles from Lucca on the 'via delle ville' (the 'villa road'). A monumental driveway, over half a mile long, leads to the Villa Torrigiani, one of the best examples of baroque architecture in Tuscany. In the mid 17th century it was bought by Count Nicolao Santini, ambassador of the Republic of Lucca at the court of Louis XIV, who converted it into a magnificent residence with a park inspired by the gardens at Versailles. The secret garden, known as the 'Flora' garden, was also built, with grottos and water features that still work and can be seen in the Grotta dei Venti.

**SEGROMIGNO IN MONTE.** A couple of miles from Camigliano, near the 12th-century church, is the VILLA MANSI ● *73*. Bought in 1675 by the family of silk merchants of the same name, the villa is regarded as one of the most representative works of Lucca culture and society. Originally built in the late 16th century, it was substantially remodeled in the two subsequent centuries. Filippo Juvarra transformed the park for the Mansi family. The space around the villa was laid with lawns and the park was embellished with nymphs and water features.

**MARLIA.** At the foot of the first hills stands the former VILLA REALE, now privately owned. This 16th-century building was drastically remodeled in 1811 by Elisa Bonaparte Baciocchi ● *41*, who made it her country retreat. The park, landscaped with woods, rivulets and a romantic-style lake, also had a green theater and a camellia walk in keeping with traditional 17th-century Italian gardens.

**SAN PANCRAZIO.** Near to the Villa Reale in Marlia stand two villas dating back to the 16th century. The VILLA GRABAU, built by the Diodati family, wealthy Lucca merchants, was owned by various families who, over the centuries, transformed the building's original structure and were responsible for its present neoclassical

appearance. In 1868, the villa was sold by the Cittadella Counts to the Grabau family, who were of German descent. The park, also worthy of note for its prolific and varied plants, is composed of various architectural gardens, including the lovely English or landscaped garden with its dense copses, the semi-oval terraced Italian garden, structured by high hedges interspersed with marble female statues, a majestic 17th–18th-century orangery and the green theater used in the summer for open-air concerts. VILLA OLIVA, formerly Buonvisi, was designed by Matteo Civitali for Lodovico Buonvisi. It has an elongated main building with the characteristic open loggia above two salons

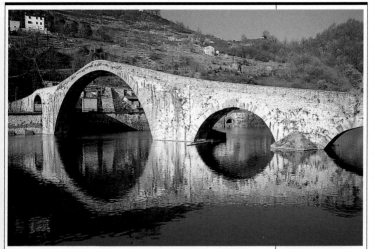

in the central section. The large park boasts grottos with water features, statues, waterfalls, pools with water jets and fountains.

**CHURCH OF SAN GIORGIO DI BRÀNCOLI.** Take a 3-mile detour at Vinchiana, on the S12 highway, through the river valley of the same name to this CHURCH, a remarkable Romanesque building with a crenelated campanile. The interior, with a nave and two aisles, contains an 11th-century holy-water font by the Comacini masters, a 12th-century pulpit supported by two lions and the vestiges of a 15th-century fresco by the Luccha school.

**DIECIMO.** Back on the S12 highway and continuing toward Bagni di Lucca, the CHURCH OF SANTA MARIA A DIECIMO is 2 miles from Borgo a Mozzano. This late 12th-century building possesses a typical Lucca campanile. The portal on the façade has an architrave carved with plant volutes.

**BORGO A MOZZANO.** This town has two main centers, Borgo and San Rocco, joined by a street lined with various palaces. The PARROCHIALE DI SAN JACOPO has a wooden statue of *San Bernardino da Siena* by Matteo Civitali and a terracotta of the *Annunciation* by Benedetto Buglioni. The most important monument is the 14th-century PONTE DELLA MADDALENA, a hog-back bridge that arches steeply over the Serchio river, commonly known as the 'Devil's bridge'. As the legend goes, only the devil could have built such an audacious structure in such a short time.

**BAGNI DI LUCCA.** This busy thermal spa, made up of a series of scattered hamlets, is situated in a lush landscape traversed by the Torrente Lima. Its warm, beneficial waters were renowned as early as the 11th century. The spa resort experienced a boom in the 19th century when Lucca was a Napoleonic principality and did particularly well under the Bourbons who transformed it into a popular resort for the nobility. The hamlet known as LA VILLA boasts many fine noblemen's houses, including the particularly splendid 16th-century VILLA BUONOVISI (owned by a family of rich Lucca merchants) where Byron and Shelley used to stay, the 17th-century PALAZZO MANSI and the VILLA DUCALE, built by the Baciocchi princes in 1811–12.

The 14th-century Maddalena bridge (known as the 'Devil's bridge') in Borgo a Mozzano.

**GIACOMO PUCCINI AT BAGNI DI LUCCA** At the end of 1870, Puccini, who had not yet completed his studies, came to Bagni di Lucca to play the piano in a dance band every evening. To save money, he dined at the house of Adelson Betti, father of the famous violinist, Adolfo. Puccini often came back to Bagni di Lucca and composed the second act of his opera *La Fanciulla del West* here.

**PLASTER FIGURES AT THE MUSEUM AT COREGLIA**
At Coreglia Antelminelli, the Palazzo Vinci houses the Museo della Figurina di Gesso. It charts the history and activity of the *figurinai*, craftsmen and itinerant salesmen who handed down the art of making plaster figurines from father to son. Forming tight-knit companies, they traveled all over the world, selling their vast range of exquisite figurines.

**THE GROTTA DEL VENTO ★**
The Cave of the Wind is in the *Parco*

*Naturale delle Alpi Apuane* ▲ 169, near Fornovalasco, at the end of the road after Vergemoli. The cave gets its name from the wind whistling through the entrance. Inside are beautiful grottos and galleries: the Lago dei Cristalli, the Sala del Ciondolo, the Baratro dei Giganti, the Sala delle Voci, the Salone dell'Acheronte and the Salone dell'Infinito.

**COREGLIA ANTELMINELLI.** Crossing back over the Serchio river at FORNOLI, take the S445 highway into the lower Garfagnana. The first detour (5 miles) leads to the old bastion of the Castracani degli Antelminelli family, now a holiday resort. The town center has partly preserved its former appearance as a medieval fortress. The extensively modified CHURCH OF SAN MICHELE (13th century) is a must. Its façade has a statue of the saint attributed to Matteo Civitali, while inside is a beautiful engraved processional cross, dating from the 15th century. The PALAZZO COMUNALE with its Renaissance façade is also worth a visit.

**BARGA.** A short detour (2 miles) will take you to this lovely medieval hamlet, overlooked by the stark bulk of the Duomo, begun in the 11th century and modified in the 17th century. It has a characteristic crenelated tower and the interior contains some fine terracottas by Luca Della Robbia. The TEATRO DELL'ACCADEMIA DEI DIFFERENTI (18th century) puts on musical seasons reviving little-known works.

**CASTELVECCHIO PASCOLI.** Continuing on the S445 highway, you will come to the village that takes its name from the poet Giovanni Pascoli who, in 1895, bought the Cardosi Carrara country house and lived there until his death in 1912. The villa has naturally been converted into a CASA MUSEO devoted to the artist. In the chapel, the poet lies next to his sister Maria in a marble tomb designed by Leonardo Bistolfi.

**CASTELNUOVO DI GARFAGNANA.** This old town was the capital city of the province of Garfagnana when the House of Este was in power. The most important monuments are the ROCCA (*below*), the home of Ariosto when he was the Este duke's commander, and the Duomo, remodeled in the 16th century and restored after World War Two.

**VAGLI.** Following the course of the Serchio river will bring you to the artificial Lago di Vagli, created in 1941–53, submerging the ancient village of Fabbrica di Careggine, which can still be seen when the lake is periodically drained. The water is used to supply the electric power station of Torrite. Passing the lake, you will reach Vagli di Sotto, an old Lombard domain. In the village's medieval center, the CHURCH OF SAN REGOLO, enlarged in 1584, has retained some of its original exterior features.

# Massa, Carrara
# and the Apuan Alps

**THE VIA FRANCIGENA**
This was one of the major pilgrimage roads in medieval Europe. The main branch of the Via Francigena cut across Tuscany from northwest to southeast, starting approximately in the area of Luni a Radicofani, skirting Carrara and Massa and passing through Lucca ▲ 156, Monteriggioni ▲ 225, Siena ▲ 208 and San Quirico d'Orcia ▲ 232 to reach its final destination of Rome. It was lined with abbeys, convents and stopping places for the pilgrims.

Telemaco Signorini, *Marina a Viareggio* (1860).

One of the prevailing memories of a visit to this narrow strip of land between the sheer mountains and the sea is bound to be that of the dazzling glare from the Apuan mountains, caused by light reflecting off the snowfields of marble. But your imagination will also be fired by this area's colorful history: the chanting pilgrims who stayed in the Romanesque churches along the Via Francigena, the booksellers of Pontremoli who used to travel the world with their suitcases of books, or the first visitors to the shores of Viareggio or Forte dei Marmi in pursuit of pleasure. Following in their footsteps, this itinerary takes in all the historical towns in the Lunigiana and the Versilia. In the spirit of Michelangelo, it explores the crags of the marble mountains and visits Massa, Carrara and the castles built by the Malaspina family. Descending towards Lake Massaciuccoli, the air seems heavy with the unmistakable languor of Puccini's melodies.

## MASSA ◆ B B3

Although vestiges of the city walls, an inspired example of urban planning, are few and far between, it is impossible to forget that in the mid 16th century the city was surrounded by walls in the shape of a large five-pointed star, with a tail incorporating the Castello Malaspina and the medieval hamlet: a star with a trail like a comet, with all the attendant symbols. The medieval town had been transformed in the 16th century into *Massa Nova* or *Cybea*, named after its founder, Alberico I Cybo-Malaspina, who designed one of the most complex examples of an ideal city. The modern visitor will find it hard to visualize such a lavish and symbolic design, even though odd fragments reveal traces of the city's unique layout.

**CATHEDRAL.** Built in the latter half of the 15th century, this building has a modern façade (1936) and a baroque INTERIOR: in the CAPPELLA DEL SANTISSIMO SACRAMENTO, above the CYBO-MALASPINA SEPULCHER, there is a Madonna, a fragment of a fresco by Pinturicchio.

**THE ROCCA.** Built on a spur around a medieval nucleus, this early castle is connected by an airy loggia to the Palazzo dei Malaspina, whose construction continued into the 15th and 16th centuries. The Rocca can be reached by crossing the palace's courtyard. A walk along the curtain walls gives a fine, unimpeded view of the coastal strip.

## CARRARA ◆ B B3

Visitors over the centuries have received the impression, due to the destruction of many historical monuments, that the city was hastily built, albeit with one of the most durable and valuable materials in the world: marble. Visitors to this somewhat contradictory city may feel like a kind of King Midas, turning everything they touch to marble, lining the streets with statues and fountains as well as more humble things such as marble fragments, piers, entablatures and steps.

**THE HISTORICAL CENTER.** Although, like Massa, associated with the Cybo-Malaspina dukes, Carrara does not possess any surviving monuments linked to these rulers, apart from the

16th-century palace of the ACCADEMIA DI BELLE ARTI (*left*), which boasts a fine collection of primarily Roman sculptural material (1st–3rd century AD). The city prides itself on being a crossroads of different cultures, as displayed by the various individual monuments.

The altar in the Cappella del Santissimo Sacramento, in Massa's cathedral.

**THE CYBO-MALASPINA SEPULCHER**
This underground chapel in the cathedral contains the burial urns of the princes and dukes of Massa. Their gravestones are set in the floor.

The loggia of La Rocca dei Malaspina at Massa.

**THE SANTUARIO DELLA MADONNA DELLA MISERICORDIA**
In Massa's Piazza Garibaldi stands the oratory of Nostra Signora della Misericordia, commissioned by Cybo to house a miraculous image of the Madonna. This small centrally planned building has a dome sitting on an octagonal drum supported by small towers. It is reached through an elegant vestibule.

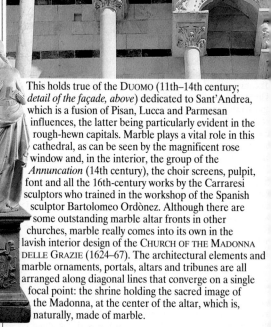

Two statues from the group of the *Annunciation* in the Duomo in Carrara, a 14th-century work that shows a clear French influence.

This holds true of the DUOMO (11th–14th century; *detail of the façade, above*) dedicated to Sant'Andrea, which is a fusion of Pisan, Lucca and Parmesan influences, the latter being particularly evident in the rough-hewn capitals. Marble plays a vital role in this cathedral, as can be seen by the magnificent rose window and, in the interior, the group of the *Annunciation* (14th century), the choir screens, pulpit, font and all the 16th-century works by the Carraresi sculptors who trained in the workshop of the Spanish sculptor Bartolomeo Ordònez. Although there are some outstanding marble altar fronts in other churches, marble really comes into its own in the lavish interior design of the CHURCH OF THE MADONNA DELLE GRAZIE (1624–67). The architectural elements and marble ornaments, portals, altars and tribunes are all arranged along diagonal lines that converge on a single focal point: the shrine holding the sacred image of the Madonna, at the center of the altar, which is, naturally, made of marble.

## THE LUNIGIANA ◆ B B2

**MARBLE QUARRIES ★**
All roads out of Carrara that do not head toward the sea lead to quarries. The spectacular quarry of Fantiscritti, with the bridges of what was once the Ferrovia Marmifera (marble railroad), is a good example of this panoramic lunar landscape, dazzling in the sunshine at any time of year and characterized by *ravaneti*, piles of waste material, and the white arabesques of roads leading to higher quarries. Another fascinating quarry is Colonnata, unexpectedly bright after a long road shaded by ancient chestnut trees.

Anyone stopping at Pontremoli, in upper Lunigiana, must pay a visit to the church of San Pietro, even though it was rebuilt after the war. Embedded in the right-hand wall is what could be called the region's identity card: a sandstone slab depicting a labyrinth. This symbol, which forms a pair with a similar one carved on a pilaster on the façade of the Duomo in Lucca, was both an allegory of the long and tortuous path of Christian life and also a road sign, a street map informing the pilgrim that he was on the right road. It could be said that Lunigiana was governed by the sign of the labyrinth, since the entire region was crossed by the Via Francigena, along which the road to the Cisa Pass was built. The region of Lunigiana, which derives its name from the ancient city of Luni, now refers to the Magra river valley. Its defining characteristics are linked to the fact that it was a border region. This can be seen, for example, by the Romanesque churches, often furnished with guest quarters, that stand on the ancient Via Francigena, as well as the many menacing castles that controlled passes and bottlenecks to impose tolls and harass wayfarers.

**FOSDINOVO.** The oldest part of this ancient town, in a commanding position on the spur of a hill, is the CASTLE, bought in 1340 by the Malaspina family, who owned it until 1797. The PARROCCHIALE DI SAN REMIGIO contains the marble tomb of Galeotto Malaspina, who died in 1367.

**AULLA.** Aulla's pivotal role in the Lunigiana is due to its location at the convergence of the Magra and Aulella rivers. This strategic position has its drawbacks, however: it was heavily bombed during World War Two. In the past, its position at the crossroads of the Lunigiana, some distance from the sea, made it the focal point for a collection of saints' relics that were too vulnerable to Saracen raids in churches along the coast. Relics from Spain and Provence even made their way here. On the other hand, anyone heading out of Aulla on the road to Fivizzano will soon come to churches dedicated to St Thomas à Becket, in PALLERONE, and to St James, near CANOVA, as well as in PODENZANA, with the sanctuary of the Madonna della Neve (17th century), in confirmation of the fact that this historical road is 'Santiago's Italian road'. As is often the case in these border areas, the other key attraction in Aulla is the FORTEZZA DELLA BRUNELLA (*below*), built in the early 16th century by the Genoese in line with the new techniques imposed by the advent of firearms.

**FIVIZZANO.** A detour east toward the Cerreto Pass will bring you to Fivizzano, still enclosed within the walls built by Cosimo I. Worthy of note is the picturesque PIAZZA MEDICEA which is surrounded by Renaissance palaces and has a large fountain built by Cosimo III.

**VILLAFRANCA IN LUNIGIANA.**
This is reached by heading back along the course of the Magra. The strategic importance of this 'Frankish' town is highlighted by the remains of the castle owned by the Malaspina family, known as IL MALNIDO. Barbarossa gave the Malaspinas the right to impose taxes and tolls along the Via Francigena.

**PICTURESQUE HAMLETS ★**
About 5 miles from Villafranca, a branch of the Via Francigena passes several hamlets. The layout of **Filetto** betrays its origins as a Byzantine *castrum*. **Malgrate** has a castle (12th century) which the Malaspina family made into a residence. The castle or *castello* in **Castiglione** was remodeled (1451) when it became the seat of the Capitanato di Giustizia. It is now the 'Niccolò V' Center of Humanist Studies with a large library of Florentine history.

**THE MUSEO DELLE STATUE-STELE DELLA LUNIGIANA**
At Pontremoli, the hilltop Castello del Piagnaro (9th–15th century) houses the museum of carved stone figures dating back to 3300–2000 BC and the start of the Iron Age (mid 1st millennium BC). The steles represent men (holding daggers or axes), women (recognizable by their breasts) and figures who have no clear role, perhaps children.

**THE FIRST MARKET STALL**
Pontremoli is the chosen home of the first traveling booksellers. Generations of Pontremoli citizens and inhabitants from neighboring villages, with suitcases full of books (frequently 'banned' titles), have made bookselling their *raison d'être*. Every year, they award the prize for the top-selling Italian book.

**PONTREMOLI.** The landscape here seems to have been formed expressly to encourage the growth of a town like Pontremoli, an ancient fortified market town mentioned as early as 990 by Sigerico, the Archbishop of Canterbury, in his *Diary*. The town stands at the confluence of the Torrente Verde with the Magra, in a narrow valley ringed by hills of chestnut trees. The hills are crossed by various ridge-top roads that connect the Tyrrhenian Sea with the Po valley, including the Mount Bardone Pass, and the Cisa Pass that leads to Pisa. As was often the case with towns of strategic importance, Pontremoli passed from one *signoria* to another until it was acquired by the Grand Duchy of Tuscany in 1650. This was a good year for Pontremoli, which enjoyed immediate recognition as a duty-free zone, and the attendant economic and commercial growth led to a remarkable artistic flowering. From the 17th century onward, people were referring to a 'new city', a small baroque capital that boasted fine ecclesiastical and civil architecture. The rich artistic heritage and the extensive network of clients who commissioned works from the Lombard, Emilian and Tuscan schools can be seen in the ornamental work of the CATHEDRAL, which represents an anthology of 18th-century Italian painting from late baroque caprice to neoclassical rigor. It is also evident in the ORATORY OF THE MADONNA DEL PONTE (1738), an elegant example of lightness and rococo grace, heightened by marble, stucco and wood decorations as well as statues and ornaments. These elements are interwoven to form a piece of religious theater whose stage is the high altar. The altarpiece showing the *Immaculate Conception* by Gherardini serves as a backdrop. The baroque design of the church is paired with the restrained elegance of the civil buildings from various periods including the PALAZZO PETRUCCI with its statues, the PALAZZO BOCCONI, the 18th-century PALAZZO PAVESI-RUSCHI and the PALAZZO PRETORIO. Just outside the city, the CHURCH OF THE SANTISSIMA ANNUNZIATA, with its small temple by Sansovino and paintings by Francesco Natali and Luca Cambiaso, is well worth a visit.

## THE APUAN ALPS ◆ B C3

Isolated from the other mountain ranges, the Apuan Alps form an Anti-Apennine chain running parallel to the Tyrrhenian shoreline. With their peaks and crags, wrote Vernon Lee, the Apuan Alps look like a group of giants resting their elbows on the table. These giants must have obsessed Michelangelo, who copied their gestures, twisting limbs, superhuman strength and fatal immobility, translating them into the bodies of prophets and sibyls.

**THE APUAN ALPS FROM MASSA.** PIAN DELLA FIOBA is the site of a botanical garden. The town stands just below the summit of MOUNT ALTISSIMO (5213 feet), scarred by the open quarries which, according to tradition, once belonged to Michelangelo. STAZZEMA is one of the largest towns in the Alta Versilia; the Romanesque church of Santa Maria Assunta

(13th century) stands at the entrance to the town. Descending
toward Forte dei Marmi, you come to SERAVEZZA, an
important marble-producing center and, since the 19th
century, a favorite holiday resort. It has a Medici palace
(1555) designed by Bartolomeo Ammannati.
**THE APUAN ALPS FROM CARRARA.** COLONNATA represents the
missing link between marble and food since the town is
renowned both for its black marble and the famous *lardo*
● *59*, pickled here in marble basins. CAMPO CECINA is famous
for its 19th-century Walton quarries, named after the English
contractor who promoted new quarrying techniques.

## THE VERSILIA ◆ B B3 C4

The Apuan Alps looming over the coast are a characteristic
feature of the Versilia, a strip of land between the mountains
and the sea that stretches from the mouth of the Cinquale to
Lake Massaciuccoli. This area saw the appearance of the first
bathing establishments (*below*) in Italy, which have helped to
create the legend of this region as a luxury holiday destination
with resorts such as Forte dei Marmi and Viareggio.
**FORTE DEI MARMI.** This resort is named after the fortress
still standing in the main piazza built by Leopold I in 1788,
and the pier once used for loading marble. This elegant
seaside resort was a meeting-place for artists and writers
of all nationalities, who helped to secure its fame throughout
the world.

THE 'CAPANNINA'
DEL FORTE
This originally started
out as a small group
of tables on the beach
of Forte dei Marmi,
surrounded by the
classic reed matting
used to protect trees
from the salt. Known
in the interwar years
as a meeting place for
the leading names in
finance and art, the
Capannina, a
restaurant and
nightclub, has since
become a symbol of
the 'good life' in the
Versilia.

Situated directly behind the narrow strip of the Versilia ▲ *169*, the sheer Apuan Alps soar to an altitude of more than 6000 feet with Mount Pisanino (6388 feet). Steeped in history, these peaks have a particularly arid appearance with valleys, steep rocky slopes, moraines and Alpine cirques formed during periods of glaciation and accompanied by numerous karst phenomena that created, for example, the Antro del Corchia, the major karst system in Italy. But the heart of the Apuan Alps is made of marble, the top-quality marble favored by sculptors and architects. From Carrara to the Versilia, many different types of marble are quarried, ranging from white and gray marbles to the green-veined cipolin marble and red marbles, culminating in the rare *fior di pesco* and pink coral marbles.

**A TIME-HONORED TRADITION**
In the vicinity of the Apuan Alps, between Massa, Carrara and Pietrasanta, artisans and artists transform blocks of marble into modern sculptures, or copies of more famous statues such as Michelangelo's *Pietà*. As well as traditional tools, sculptors now use pneumatic hammers and other mechanical tools, although this in no way detracts from these craftsmen's manual expertise, as they are highly skilled in the most sophisticated manufacturing techniques.

A detail from Giotto's Campanile ▲ 119, with its polychromatic facing, and of the central marble shrine of Santa Maria della Spina in Pisa ● 79 ▲ 153.

## THE QUARRIES

Centuries of quarrying have created some unique landscapes in these mountains, now protected by the Parco Naturale delle Alpi Apuane. With cranes placed in the most unthinkable positions and cables cutting into the mountainside, the quarries in the Apuan Alps are scarred by regular gashes and fissures. Lower down can be seen sprawling piles of marble waste, and the sheer access roads used to transport the blocks of marble to the mountain slopes where they are stored until bought by purchasers from around the world.

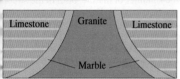

## THE FORMATION OF MARBLE

Marble, a crystalline limestone, is formed from limestone rock which, under the influence of pressure or heat, becomes recrystallized. As a result of this phenomenon which, in the case of Carrara marble, took place in the Jurassic Period, limestone devoid of any impurities produces white marble; if, however, it contains other minerals besides calcite, the marble can assume a variety of colors.

## DIFFERENT TYPES OF MARBLE

Carrara marble is subdivided into seven types, which include the valuable snow-white monochrome marbles (*bianco*, *statuario*, *venato*) and the polychromatic marbles widely used in building. The most famous types of marble include the gray-veined *bardiglio*, *arabescato* and the various red marbles.

**BARDIGLIO CARRARA SCURO**

**BARDIGLIO FIORITO**

**ARABESCATO CORCHIA**

**PAONAZZETTO**

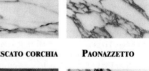

**ROSSO COLLEMANDINA**

**CALACATTA VAGLI ROSATO**

Sculpting marble requires the use of specific tools: stonemason's hammer (1), stonecutter's chisel (2), hammer (3), chisel (4), double-point chisel (5), bushhammer (6), gradines (7).

**BRECCIA STAZZEMA**

**ROSSO RUBINO**

*Spiaggia* (1920), by Moses Levy (*above*).

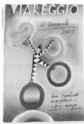

**VIAREGGIO'S SUCCESS STORY**
Viareggio was a small fishing village when in 1861 Giuseppe Barellai founded several hotels, the first in Italy. It soon became a famous seaside resort, because of the beautiful beach and mild climate.
As well as being famous for its floats at Carnival ● *52* Viareggio is also renowned for the literary award presented in August before an international audience.

**PIETRASANTA.** This town was founded in 1255 along the Via Francigena at the foot of the hills. The geometrical layout has a formality that is relaxed in the main piazza, whose monuments are built on different levels, and in the picturesque walls that climb to the top of Sala hill, the site of the Lombard ROCCA DI SALA. Here and there, the eye is caught by the shimmer of marble, both in the streets and in particular on the façade of the DUOMO DI SAN MARTINO (13th–14th century), with its lovely rose window attributed to Lorenzo Riccomanni, forming a striking contrast to the red brick campanile. It also gleams on the façade of the former CHURCH OF SANT'AGOSTINO (now an exhibition center), which has an elegant loggia with Gothic arches.

**VIAREGGIO.** Passing through CAMAIORE ● *50*, with its beautiful COLLEGIATE CHURCH, the road leads back to the coast at Viareggio, another famous beach resort and an elegant garden city sandwiched between the two pine forests of Levante and Ponente. The resort's main attraction is the array of Art Nouveau and Art Deco buildings and decorative features that line the elegant seafront promenade and the streets behind.

**TORRE DEL LAGO PUCCINI.** This villa, on the banks of the extensive marshlands at Massaciuccoli, was where Giacomo Puccini wrote many of his operas and where he is now buried. It makes for an extremely picturesque visit.

**LAKE MASSACIUCCOLI.** Together with the forest of Migliarino and the Tenuta di San Rossore ▲ *154*, the marshlands at Massaciuccoli (*below*) form a natural park, richly populated with diverse species of woodland plants and animals. The lake is all that remains of a vast lagoon, formed in the Quaternary Period by the Arno and the Serchio rivers, then isolated when the coastline shifted. At the eastern end are the remains of a Roman baths and villa.

# Prato and Pistoia

**PRATO: A CITY FOR 17,500 FLORINS**
The first human settlement on the site of present-day Pistoia dates back to the Bronze Age. The city's commercial calling was clear from the Middle Ages onward. In 1351, it was bought by the Florentines, who paid 17,500 gold florins to Queen Giovanna of Naples.

**MUSEO DI PITTURA MURALE**
Not far from the Palazzo Comunale, the convent of San Domenico houses a museum that has a collection of detached frescos, *sinopias* and graffito from Prato and the surrounding territory, ranging from the 14th to the 17th centuries.

Cristiano Banti, *Boscaiole*.

Overshadowed by the splendor of neighboring Florence and somewhat dismissively regarded as an industrial city, Prato has many delightful surprises in store. Within the city's walls, visitors can marvel at an array of masterpieces including the pulpit by Donatello and the fresco series by Filippo Lippi in the Duomo. The *Centro per l'Arte Contemporanea 'Luigi Pecci'* ▲ 176 lies just outside the city. There is also a remarkable number of beautiful monuments in the medieval center of Pistoia. These cities are surrounded by the rolling landscape of the Valdinievole, its hamlets nestling in the lush countryside or perched on the hilltops. Further toward the Tuscan-Emilian Apennines, the landscape, densely forested with chestnut trees and conifers, becomes more rugged. The route through the Lima Valley with its pretty vacation resorts eventually leads to the forest of Abetone, its border crossing and its snow-covered ski slopes. The whole territory boasts areas of great natural beauty where the encroaching suburban sprawl gives way to countryside, as well as places of profound historical interest and some marvelous works of art found not only in the two cities, but also in every small town. The history of this region mirrors that of Italy as a whole, characterized by civic pride, domination, conflict and a hunger for supremacy that also promoted intellect, artistic enterprise and the establishment of the laws and values of a Renaissance culture that was to illuminate the entire Western world.

PRATO ◆ **B** E4 **C** AB2

**THE MUSEO DEL TESSUTO**
Prato is renowned as one of the leading textile-manufacturing cities. The museum, situated in the loggias of the Palazzo Comunale, charts the history of techniques and technology from the paleo-Christian era to the present day. Machinery, tools and a variety of antique and modern fabrics bear witness to the continued growth of Prato's textile industry.

Renowned in particular for its wool industries, Prato, like its sister Tuscan cities, contains some extraordinary works of art and architecture within the 14th-century hexagon of its walls. It also boasts ancient Roman origins, even though the first town center was founded in the Lombard period. From the 12th century, it became a free town, entering a period of remarkable growth that continued when it became part of the Florentine Republic (1351) ● *36*. It had some troubled times in the 17th century from which it did not recover until the mid 19th century, when the development of the textile industry promoted urban expansion. The Piazza del Comune and the Piazza del Duomo, enlarged in 1293, form the hub of the city center, which is skirted by the Bisenzio river.

**PIAZZA DEL COMUNE.** This is the site of the classical-style PALAZZO COMUNALE and the Palazzo Pretorio (*top, left*), the former seat of government which has retained the appearance of a *casa-torre* with its external staircase and balcony. It houses the MUSEO CIVICO, with a varied collection of paintings by Filippo and Filippino Lippi, Bernardo Daddi, Giovanni da Milano, Luca Signorelli and others.

**DUOMO.** Dedicated to Saint Stephen, this cathedral is one of the oldest examples of Romanesque-Gothic architecture. The elegant façade is striped with bands of limestone and green marble; on the right-hand corner (*top, right*) is the PULPIT OF THE SACRED GIRDLE (1434–8) by Michelozzo and Donatello, who carved the dancing *putti*. The original panels are now kept in the Museo dell'Opera del Duomo. The interior, with a nave and two aisles supported by green marble columns, contains some splendid series of frescos by Filippo Lippi (*Storie di San Giovanni Battista* and *Storie di Santo Stefano*), Paolo Uccello, and the school of Agnolo Gaddi. Also worthy of note is the TABERNACOLO DELLA MADONNA DELL'ULIVO (1480), by Giuliano and Giovanni da Maiano and the PULPIT (1469–73) probably designed by Mino da Fiesole and Antonio Rossellino. Behind the Duomo stand the twin Buonconti towers, the oldest surviving towers of the sixty that once characterized the city skyline.

**FILIPPO LIPPI'S SALOME** ✪
The most widely admired episode from the *Storie di San Giovanni Battista* by Filippo Lippi is that of Herod's Banquet, which shows an admiring audience of courtiers watching Salome's dance. According to tradition, the dancer is modeled on Lucrezia Buti, the young novice whom Lippi married after leaving the monastery of Santa Margherita.

# ▲ CENTRO PER L'ARTE CONTEMPORANEA 'LUIGI PECCI' IN PRATO

**MICHELANGELO PISTOLETTO,** *Rear View of a Naked Man* (1962–7)
A representation of the spectator on the threshold of virtual space.

Kapoor, Cucchi, Merz, Lewitt, Pistoletto, Burri and Staccioli are some of the contemporary artists whose works are featured in the Centro per l'Arte Contemporanea 'Luigi Pecci' ▲ *174*, an ultra-modern structure designed by the functional artist Italo Gamberini and set in a landscape rich in history and tradition. A couple of miles from the Autostrada del Sole, in the modern part of Prato, the museum complex, covering 130,000 square feet, comprises exhibition rooms, auditorium, bookshop, restaurant and amphitheater. The center, which has been active on the international scene since 1988, provides a continual program of exhibitions and events. It also possesses a permanent collection of works by artists active in the last thirty years.

**JANNIS KOUNELLIS,** *Untitled* (1985–95)
Kounellis makes use of everyday materials and tools neglected by traditional artists which she often brings together in serial installations whose meaning is heightened by the use of repetition. Her tools are reclaimed from the repertory of industrial archeology with the aim of reviving the memory of distant suffering and strength, as in this work that uses dark, heavy metals such as iron, lead and steel.

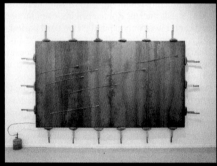

**THE MUSEUM**
The geometric patterns formed by the load-bearing structures of the museum building, highlighted with red-lead paint, are exposed, offsetting the lightness of the walls and the serried ranks of prismatic skylights on the roof. These elements give the museum the stark appearance of a factory; one, however, that manufactures a varied range of cultural and informative products and sets up a dynamic dialogue with the surroundings.

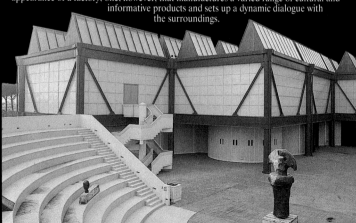

**MARIO MERZ, *The Spiral Appears* (1990)**
In this installation, the artist (one of the leading exponents of Arte Povera) combines elements that engender different sensations and concepts. Systematic neon numbers taken from the Fibonacci sequence appear above each pile of old newspapers, as if to suggest they represent an absolute sequence, pure thought. Behind them, an espalier of bundles of sticks conjures up the image of an arid, desiccated natural landscape. Humble, everyday materials are given new meaning purely by the fascination exerted by the neon lights: a uniquely suggestive combination.

**ENZO CUCCHI, *Untitled (Mountain)* (1989)**
This work, by one of the exponents of *Transavanguardia*, is a simple outline, deliberately devoid of any symbolic meaning. Repeated on a grand scale, it trusts to light to trace its own contour.

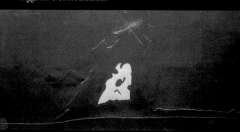

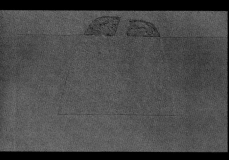

**ALBERTO BURRI, *Black* (1984–5)**
Burri's restrained tonal range, typical of much of his output (after the *Sacchi* series which has made him internationally famous), has produced an intense negative radiance in this work which, with the sharply defined geometry of its forms, conjures up a nocturnal landscape.

**SOL LEWITT, *Irregular Tower* (1997)**
An exponent of conceptual art and interested in serial art and the logic of mathematical formulae, the American artist has assembled 994 equal cement parallelepipeds, forming a sort of tiered tower on one side: a serial structure that could bear similarities to musical composition.

**THE MERCATALE**
Close by the banks of the Bisenzio river lies the Piazza Mercatale, a vast square, partly covered by gardens, used as the site of markets and fairs since the 12th century. The lovely Porta del Mercatale (1308) on Via Garibaldi is well worth a look.

**THE CONVITTO NAZIONALE CICOGNINI**
Not far from the Palazzo Datini, this boarding school was a lively cultural center in the mid 19th century. Illustrious Italians such as Bettino Ricasoli, Gabriele D'Annunzio and Curzio Malaparte studied here.

**MUSEO DELL'OPERA DEL DUOMO.** The Palazzo Vescovile, 16th-century in style (although it retains one side of the 12th-century Romanesque cloister in the courtyard), houses a museum of works from the Duomo or linked to the cult of the Sacred Girdle, such as the RELIQUARY OF THE SACRED GIRDLE (1446) by Maso di Bartolomeo. The works include the seven RELIEF PANELS from the pulpit by Donatello and the painting of *Saint Lucy*, attributed to Filippino Lippi.

**SANTA MARIA DELLE CARCERI.** Built by Lorenzo the Magnificent on the site of a former prison, the church (1485) designed by Giuliano da Sangallo is remarkable for its harmonious proportions and marble facing. Built in the form of a Greek cross, it is regarded as a masterpiece of early Renaissance architecture. The interior is decorated with terracotta roundels by Andrea della Robbia (*detail, right*) and stained-glass windows (1491) by Alessandro di Giovanni Angolanti.

**CASTELLO DELL'IMPERATORE ● 73.** This castle was built in 1237 by Frederick II and has remained a valuable example of Swabian architecture. The geometric lines of the massive towers and the crenelated walls (*below*) are particularly striking. Spiral staircases lead to the top of the towers and to the communication tunnels.

**SAN FRANCESCO.** This church has a beautiful façade crowned by a Renaissance tympanum. The chapterhouse contains FRESCOS (c. 1395) by Niccolò di Pietro Gerini; the adjacent refectory also contains some 14th-century frescos.

**PALAZZO DATINI.** This is one of the few examples of a 14th-century palace with a fresco façade. It was built by the merchant banker Francesco di Marco Datini and now houses the ARCHIVIO DI STATO.

## PISTOIA ◆ B E4 C A2

The historical center within Pistoia's 14th-century walls has an extraordinary concentration of buildings and monuments. The streets are lined with churches and palaces built at a time when power and beauty went hand in hand. The Piazza del Duomo is a fine example of a medieval city square and the site of the most important religious and civic buildings.

**PIAZZA DEL DUOMO ● 65.** Equally prestigious, the austere seats of civic power stand opposite the religious buildings of the cathedral and the baptistery: the PALAZZO PRETORIO (1367), that houses the court of justice, and the PALAZZO DEL COMUNE or DEGLI ANZIANI (14th century), with its solid façade made of *pietra serena* (soft blue-gray stone), embellished by an unusual spacious portico that gives onto the square. The interior houses the MUSEO CIVICO, with a collection of paintings from the 14th to the 17th centuries.

**DUOMO DI SAN ZENO.** This cathedral dates backs to 923 but was remodeled in Pisan Romanesque style in the 12th and

13th centuries when the portico was added. The mighty campanile stands next to it. The interior contains some remarkable works including the *Madonna di Piazza* by Verrocchio with his pupil Lorenzo di Credi, the tomb slab of Bishop Donato de' Medici by Rossellino or Verrocchio, a beautiful *Crucifix* (1275) on wood by Coppo di Marcovaldo and his son Salerno and the baptismal font (1497) by Andrea da Fiesole to a design by Benedetto da Maiano. The most outstanding work is the huge silver *Altar of St James*, made by Sienese, Pistoian and Florentine silversmiths (1287–1457): even Filippo Brunelleschi, at the start of his career, added a couple of figures.

**BAPTISTERY.** A fine example of Tuscan Gothic architecture that may have been designed by Andrea Pisano, this building dates

**THE ANCIENT JOUST OF THE BEAR ★**
This colorful contest ● 53 in which the model of a bear (the heraldic symbol of the city) has to be hit by riders representing the city's four districts, is held on July 25 in the Piazza del Duomo to celebrate the festival of San Jacopo (Saint James). Jacopo was none other than Giacomo Maggiore, whose remains are kept in Santiago, in Galicia. He became the patron saint of Pistoia when, in 1100, the bishop of Compostela gave Atto, the bishop of Pistoia, a holy relic from the saint's body.

The Duomo in Pistoia (*top*); on the corner stands the Palazzo dei Vescovi.

**PALAZZO DEI VESCOVI**
This recently restored building, the bishops' palace for almost eight centuries, stands next to the cathedral. The interior contains the Sagrestia de' Begli Arredi, stolen sacrilegiously by Vanni Fucci, as recorded by Dante in his *Inferno*. The building now houses the Museo Capitolare di San Zeno, which has a collection of valuable liturgical objects.

## THE FORTRESS OF SANTA BARBARA

At the southeast corner of the circuit of walls, built on the site of a castle erected by the Florentines and demolished by subversive Pistoians in 1343, this fortress is unusual as it was built not to defend the city but to attack it. 'It has in the center,' related an account of 1569, 'a tower that dominates the entire city with its cannon, *rinforzato* and culverin.' Cosimo I de' Medici obviously did not trust the Pistoians who were chafing under his government. In 1571, the fortress was joined to the quadrilateral of Pistoia's walls; it was disarmed in 1773.

## SEVERED HEADS

Displaying the severed heads of enemies has always been a brutal indication of supremacy. Proud Pistoia did not want to do without these ornaments in public places. At the corner of each street, the stone heads of beheaded enemies leer at passersby.

## THE LEONCINO WELL

In front of San Giovanni Fuorcivitas lies the Piazza della Sala where, in the Lombard period, justice was administered. It has a fine central well, carved by Cecchino di Giorgio in 1453. The architrave is adorned by the *Marzocco*, the Florentine lion, with one paw placed on the Pistoian coat of arms. This was a homage to Pope Clement VII who saved the city from Charles V.

back to the mid 14th century (*right*). It has three portals with reliefs and statues; the interior contains Lanfranco da Como's lovely baptismal font (1226).

**SPEDALE DEL CEPPO.** This building, named after the hollowed-out log (*ceppo*) used to collect alms, was founded in 1277 and enlarged after the plague in 1348. In 1514, the elegant porch (*below*) was added, and decorated by the della Robbias with a magnificent frieze. Inside, the ACCADEMIA MEDICA FILIPPO PACINI has a collection of surgical instruments from the 17th, 18th and 19th centuries.

**SANT'ANDREA.** This church dates back to the 8th century. The decoration of the façade, by Gruamonte in the 12th century, and the soaring interior illustrate the typical Pistoian concept of spatial design. The nave contains some outstanding works by Giovanni Pisano including the PULPIT (1301) ▲ *151*.

**SAN FRANCESCO.** Founded in 1289, this church, despite various remodelings that culminated in the 20th-century restoration program, has preserved its simple, stark appearance. The CAPPELLA MAGGIORE is decorated with frescos by the Bolognese school of 1343; the ones in the Bracciolini chapel were done after 1419.

**MADONNA DELL'UMILTÀ.** Designed by Giuliano da Sangallo, this church was built in 1495 to celebrate a miracle. The dome, which dates back to the mid 16th century, was designed by Vasari and completed in 1575–85 by Bartolomeo Ammannati.

**SAN GIOVANNI FUORCIVITAS.** The elegant black and white decoration of this church, begun in the mid 12th century, perfectly complements its architectural structure. The interior contains, among other works, the outstanding *Visitation* (1445) by Luca della Robbia, the polyptych by Taddeo Gaddi (1553–5), the PULPIT by Guglielmo da Pisa (finished in 1270) and the holy water stoup by the school of Nicola Pisano.

**CHURCH AND CONVENT OF SAN DOMENICO.** This large Gothic complex (late 13th century) was enlarged in 1380. It has some interesting remnants of 14th-century frescos.

## FROM PISTOIA TO COLLODI ◆ B ED4 C A2

The Valdinievole ('Valley of Mists') threads its way through the Apennine hills, climbing gently through flowery meadows, rows of olive trees, vineyards, chestnut trees and poplars. A peaceful drive along the S435 highway will take you through Montecatini, Pescia and Collodi, home of Pinocchio.

**MONTECATINI TERME.** This town, nestling in the green countryside, is divided by the magnificent PARCO DELLE TERME, the site of health spas and springs. These were renowned in the 14th century, but it was Grand Duke Peter Leopold I ● *40*, in the late 17th century, who exploited their

full potential. A visit to the baths enables visitors to admire neoclassical, Art Nouveau and neo-Renaissance buildings with sumptuous bars and bathing pools: TERME LEOPOLDINE (1777), EXCELSIOR (1915), STABILIMENTO TETTUCCIO (1781). There are breathtaking views from MONTECATINI VALDINIEVOLE, which is reached by funicular railway.

**PESCIA.** This medieval hamlet is divided into five districts, known as *quinti*, and is famous for its market and the Biennale dei Fiori. Do not miss the DUOMO, remodeled in the late 17th century, the Gothic CHURCH OF SAN FRANCESCO, with a fine painting by Bonaventura Berlinghieri (*San Francisco e storie della sua vita*, 1235) and the elegant Brunelleschian ORATORIO DELLA MADONNA DI PIÈ DI PIAZZA.

**COLLODI.** Perched on a hill ridge is Collodi, preserved almost intact. Carlo Lorenzini, the author of *The Adventures of Pinocchio*, spent his childhood here and took the name of the town as his pseudonym. The PARCO DI PINOCCHIO ● *75* takes you on a voyage of discovery through a fantastic world where you will see the monument *Pinocchio with the Fairy* (1956) by Emilio Greco and the PAESE DEI BALOCCHI, with figures by the sculptor Pietro Consagra. You can take a welcome break at the OSTERIA DEL GAMBERO ROSSO, designed in 1963 by Giovanni Michelucci, and finish with a visit to the LABORATORIO DELLE PAROLE E DELLE FIGURE, with its collection of illustrations of the famous puppet from the past hundred years. Another popular tourist attraction is the VILLA GARZONI (1633–62) ● *74*, its lovely central *salone* decorated with stuccos, frescos and paintings by the Carracci school. The splendid garden (17th–18th century), one of the finest in Italy, has an abundance of statues, fountains and water features.

**THE PAPER MILL IN PIETRABUONA**
The oldest paper mill in Italy in Pietrabuona, in the environs of Pescia, is well worth a visit. Dating back to 1224, this is still a working mill that produces the watermarked paper used for the present 5000 lire banknote.

**THE PARCO DI PINOCCHIO**
Eighty-four artists took part in the competition to design the monument to Pinocchio in 1953. The joint winners were Venturino Venturini with his *Piazzetta dei Mosaici*, a lively retelling of the main episodes from the adventures of Pinocchio, and Emilio Greco with his *Pinocchio con la fata*, a 16-foot-tall bronze symbolizing Pinocchio's real journey, the transition from a naughty *puppetto* a well-behaved boy.
Above, right: *I Conigli e la Bara (The Rabbit and the Casket)*.

The exterior of the Terme Tettuccio and the interior of the Terme Excelsior (*above, left and center*).

## From Pistoia to Abetone ◆ B E3-4-D3 C A1-2

A number of lovely towns, which are popular vacation resorts as a result of the lush countryside and healthy climate, lie along the S66 highway that, heading north, cuts through the state forest of Abetone to reach the border crossing.

**MARESCA.** Just after the Oppia Pass, you can take a detour to Maresca (2625 feet), a welcoming village on the edge of the state forest of Teso. Described neatly as 'Maresca, donne belle e acqua fresca' ('Maresca, beautiful women and fresh water'), the village is a place of natural unspoiled beauty, with an old hydraulic ironworks, perhaps of Renaissance origins, that is still in working order and well worth a visit.

**GAVINANA.** The main piazza is the site of the equestrian monument (1912) to Francesco Ferrucci, the commander killed in 1530 by Maramaldo, captain of the imperial army. Visitors can see where the bloody deed took place, and visit a small museum to find out about the battle of 1530 between the troops of the Florentine Republic ● 36 and the imperial forces of the Prince of Orange. The PARROCCHIALE has some low-reliefs by Luca della Robbia.

**SAN MARCELLO PISTOIESE.** This typical vacation resort lies below Gavinana. On September 8, in memory of the Montgolfier brothers who stayed here in the 19th century, the inhabitants launch a hot-air balloon, which until several years ago was entirely made of paper, to mark the festival of Saint Celestina. As the road descends through a mountain landscape virtually untouched by tourism, there will come into view the suspension bridge of MAMMIANO, connecting the two banks of the Torrente Lima. Nearby is the former Cini paper mill 1822–1971, a fine example of industrial archeology.

**CUTIGLIANO.** In the midst of dense woodland, Cutigliano overlooks the Lima valley. The PALAZZO PRETORIO (14th century) sports all the coats of arms from the mountain *comuni* in the territory of Pisa, while to one side stands a column topped by the Medici arms of the Marzocco.

**ABETONE.** Lower down still is the darkly brooding Abetone forest. At the highest point of the border crossing two pyramid-shaped milestones (*below*), bearing the respective coats of arms of the Duchies of Modena and Lorraine, mark the exact location of the old border. Abetone is the most famous ski resort in the Apennines. It boasts some well-developed slopes used by champions in training.

One of the coats of arms on the façade of the Palazzo Pretorio in Cutigliano; several, made of glazed terracotta, are from the della Robbia workshop (early 16th century).

**A STREET FOR ABETONE**
The resort is named after an enormous fir tree (*abete*) cut down in the 19th century to build the road between Tuscany and Emilia, a project commissioned by Francesco III Duke of Modena and Leopold I of Lorraine. The area around Abetone is ideal for hiking. Visitors can meet up at Medici fountains, intended for use by wayfarers who are addressed as follows: 'O traveler, weary of the road, stop, drink your fill, then quicken your pace.'

**THE GHOST VILLAGE OF FABBRICA**
Abandoned villages were common in the Middle Ages. In Fabbrica, in the Torbecchia valley, a ruined church emerges from a tangle of dense vegetation along with the vestiges of houses, creating the overwhelming impression that this place was full of life not so long ago. There are plans to use this atmospheric place as a possible exhibition area.

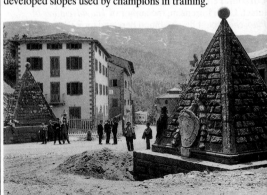

# Arezzo
# and its surroundings

**THE JOUST OF THE SARACEN**
Twice a year, in June and September, the Joust of the Saracen ● 53 takes place in the Piazza Grande. This ancient tournament, documented since the Renaissance, has been held yearly since its revival in 1931.

**FAMOUS PEOPLE FROM AREZZO**
The many artists who have secured Arezzo's fame include Guittone d'Arezzo (c. 1230–94), Pietro Aretino (1492–1556), Francesco Petrarch (1304–74) and Giorgio Vasari (1511–74) (*below*, *Vasari's bust in Corso Italia in Arezzo*). Vasari was a dominant figure: architect and historiographer, he made his mark on history as did his pupil Pietro Aretino, a hard-hitting writer.

Arezzo is fascinating both as a hill town and as a rich storehouse of well-preserved works of art. Despite the fact that urban expansion has created some extensive commercial zones, visitors to the city can still catch a tantalizing whiff of the countryside. The bastions continue to be surrounded by vineyards and besieged by olive trees, while the city's glorious works of art radiate such a glow that they seem to light the visitor's way. It is hardly surprising that Piero della Francesca became the idol of many 20th-century painters. The territory of Arezzo boasts many unique architectural gems including great Franciscan and Camaldolese sanctuaries, Etruscan strongholds such as Cortona and ideal Renaissance cities such as dazzling Sansepolcro. Arezzo is unique among the hill towns in central Italy: the city was built on the south-facing slope of a modest hill, which means that every part of the city receives an equal dappling of light and shadow. Situated at the convergence of four valleys steeped in history – the upper Arno valley, the Casentino, the Valdichiana and the Valtiberina – Arezzo has always been a meeting point and a trade forum. This strategic position meant that anyone wanting to control the region had to control this city, which is why Florence has exerted its dominion over Arezzo since 1384.

# AREZZO ▲

## AREZZO: THREE PHASES OF HISTORY ◆ C D4

The history of the city can be divided into three periods: the Etruscan period, when *Aretium* sprang up on the hill delimited by what are today the church, the fortress and the Duomo; the Roman period, when the hill town became an important military center on the Via Cassia; and its time as a *comune*, which began in 1008 with the first consuls and ended in 1384 when Arezzo was finally conquered by Florence.

## THE ARTISTIC HEART OF THE CITY

**SAN FRANCESCO.** Visitors to Arezzo generally start their tour of the city in the Piazza San Francesco, which is at the center of the oldest part of the city. Here stands the church of San Francesco, which is the custodian, among other things, of the masterpiece by Piero della Francesca, the *Legend of the True Cross* (*detail, below*), magnificently restored after fifteen years of work. This church is a 13th-century Gothic structure rebuilt between 1318 and 1377 and restored in the early 20th century. Its 15th-century campanile towers over a stone and brick façade that was never completed (parts of the facing designed in the 14th century are kept in the basement). In the

185

choir of the church of San Francesco visitors can admire the frescos by Piero della Francesca, whose works have long acted as a magnet for enthusiastic tourists. It is only natural, therefore, that visitors keen to discover Arezzo's cultural heritage should begin with these frescos, started by Piero around 1452. In his narration of the *Legend of the True Cross*, regarded as the most important icon of Christianity in the world, the artist chose to depict an extraordinary résumé of the history of mankind. Piero's narrative cycle spreads the message of the Cross down the ages, glorifying its presence in a style characterized by an air of serene detachment and a tireless quest for divine order. The frescos, taken from the *Golden Legend* by Jacopo da Varagine, can be read in a precise chronological order: 1. *The Death of Adam*, out of whose skull grew the tree from which the Cross was made; 2. *The Queen of Sheba Predicts the End of Solomon's Reign with the Cross (detail, left)*; 3. *The Sacred Wood is Moved*; 4. *The Angel Announces to Saint Helena that the Cross will be Found*; 5. *The Dream of Constantine*; 6. *The Victory of Constantine*; 7. *The Agony of Judas*; 8. *The Discovery of the Cross*; 9. *Battle of Heraclius*; 10. *Heraclius Restores the Cross to Jerusalem*. A cycle of such expressive power can be interpreted in many different ways. Looking at what D'Annunzio called 'Piero's garden', visitors will be able to find correspondences between the scenes, moving from the bottom to the top of the side walls, from one battle to another (Constantine against Maxentius, on the right, Heraclius against Chosroes, on the left), from one bipartite ceremonial scene to another (the Queen of Sheba's meeting with Solomon on the right, the recovery of the Cross on the left), from one open-air episode to another with a similar setting, as in the two opposite lunettes.

**PIAZZA GRANDE** ✪
This attractive piazza is set on a steep incline, which contributes greatly to its charm. The five roads that lead onto the square have marked differences in height, affording many different vistas and creating a variety of dramatic effects. In addition, the piazza has a delightful trapezoidal form bordered with fascinating buildings.

## AROUND THE PIAZZA GRANDE

**THE CHURCH OF SANTA MARIA.** Leading from the Piazza San Francesco, Corso Italia provides a fine view of the bell tower of the church of Santa Maria. The 'tower of a hundred holes' has always been a point of reference for the entire valley and a landmark for the city. Built between the 12th and 13th centuries, the church's façade has three tiers of loggias. The sculptures on the portals, particularly those around the central arch molding, draw their inspiration from the art of Benedetto Antelami. Inside, the mighty columns, spacious apse and high presbytery create a compelling sense of theater. Above the central altar is the glittering polyptych (*Madonna with Child and Four Saints, Annunciation, Assumption* and *Twelve Saints*) painted by Pietro Lorenzetti in 1320.

**PIAZZA GRANDE ● 65.** Behind the church lies the Piazza Grande, one of the most original squares in Italy, bordered, apart from the apse of the church, by the PALAZZO DEL TRIBUNALE (17th–18th century), approached by a flight of stairs, and by the PALAZZO DELLA FRATENITA DEI LAICI, whose original Gothic façade (1377) boasts some harmonious Renaissance additions (15th–16th centuries). On the corner is the PALAZZO DELLE LOGGE (1573–4) or LOGGE VASARIANE designed as a wing of the upper side of the piazza.

**THE PRATO.** Climbing toward the highest point of the city will bring you to the 14th-century PALAZZO PRETORIO, whose façade is covered with coats of arms, and then the CASA DEL PETRARCA (the poet Petrarch was born here in 1304) that was rebuilt in 1948. At the top there is a vast park known as the PRATO, which lies between the two massive structures of the Duomo and the Medici Fortress. This crucial vantage point affords an excellent view of the city's two-headed layout as it slopes down toward the valley with its main thoroughfares splayed like the fingers of a hand.

**THE DUOMO.** The entrance to the Prato provides a wonderful view of the polygonal 13th-century tribune of the Duomo, its eccentric early-20th-century campanile and long south-facing side. The irregular stonework of the Duomo's side wall bears witness to the three centuries it took to finish the building, begun in 1278. The Duomo contains a rich collection of Tuscan art ranging from the 13th to the 19th centuries. Anyone entering the gloomy aisle and two naves will be striped by what Dickens described as paths of emerald light. This is in fact the effect of the large brightly colored stained-glass windows created by Guillaume de Marcillat between 1518 and 1529.

**FRANCESCO PETRARCH AND HIS TIME**
In Via dell'Orto, at the top of the steep Via dei Pileati stands what is believed to be the house in which Francesco Petrarch (1304–74) ● *44* was born. This palace, rebuilt after damage caused in World War Two, marked the starting-point for the great poet's eventful life. In 1311, Petrarch moved with his family to Avignon where, in 1327, he met Laura, the woman who was to be the muse for his poetry. His collection of poems, the *Canzoniere*, started in 1335, is regarded as a true masterpiece of the Italian language. His idea of love as a force ordering all aspects of life became a characteristic part of European culture at that time.

**THE MEDICI FORTRESS**
Overlooking the Prato park, the Medici Fortress was commissioned by Cosimo I and built by the Da Sangollos in the 16th century. The construction of the fortress, designed to withstand firearms, necessitated the wholesale demolition of the medieval districts below, which, with their public and private palaces, sloped down to the level of the present Piazza Grande. The ruins were hidden by the Logge Vasariane, whose construction began in 1570.

A detail of the decoration (*left*) of the apse in the church of Santa Maria.

**THE TOMB OF SAN DONATO**
The tomb of San Donato is one of the most outstanding works of art in the Duomo. This 14th-century sculptural group, at the center of the presbytery, comprises the altar with the tomb of the city's patron saint behind it. The tomb displays different registers ranging from the mellow sculptural quality of the central relief panels to the anecdotal liveliness of the scenes from the life of the saint and the lavish decoration of molten glass and silver leaf.

**THE MUSEO DIOCESANO ✪**
Situated behind the apse of the Duomo, the museum contains works from churches and monasteries. It gives an overview of Arezzo's artistic tradition with works by Andrea de Nerio, Spinello and Parri di Spinello, Bartolomeo della Gatta, the follower of Piero della Francesca, and Vasari. It also has an outstanding collection of reliquaries, crosses and censers that charts the history of the goldsmiths' art. Works include a remarkable *S. Girolamo* by Bartolomeo della Gatta, the *Annunciation* (14th century) by Andrea di Nerio and three 13th-century crucifixes.

Regarded from both an artistic and a technical standpoint as one of the finest examples of the art of painting glass, the windows relate themes taken from the Gospel and embody Durando di Mende's definition of stained-glass windows in the late 13th century when he observed that 'stained-glass windows are the Holy Scriptures holding the brilliance of the true sun within'. Across the presbytery stands the tomb of Bishop Guido Tarlati, which dates back to 1330. The sculptors of this memorial combined the monumentality of the whole – the arcades, for example, and the curtains draped above the effigy of the bishop – with sixteen scenes illustrating Tarlati's achievements, including the warlike prelate's conquest of walled cities in the territory of Arezzo. Near the tomb is a beautiful Renaissance work, Piero della Francesca's small fresco of the *Magdalene*, an elegant solitary figure glowing as if bathed in a pool of light. This fresco, a mature work realized by Piero when he was at the height of his powers, skillfully exploits the laws of perspective: the Magdalene is set against a blue sky and framed by a decorated arch of classical Greek design.

## THE NORTHERN DISTRICTS

**SAN DOMENICO.** The church of San Domenico, begun in 1275 and completed in the early 14th century, has a single nave flooded with light that boasts a wealth of interesting pictorial decoration dating from the 14th and 15th centuries. In the choir, above the high altar, is one of the finest artistic works on earth, the huge *Crucifix* ● *78* (c. 1265) by the young Cimabue who imbued it with all the force of his innovative genius and the pathos of a deeply felt profession of faith.

**THE MUSEO D'ARTE MEDIEVALE E MODERNA.** At the end of Via XX Settembre, the stately Palazzo Bruni-Ciocchi (15th century) houses this museum of medieval and modern art, one of the leading museums in Tuscany for the variety and quality of its works and collections. The paintings exhibited here represent an excellent overview of the Renaissance artistic tradition and the form it took in and around Arezzo. There are some particularly interesting works by several 'primitive' artists including Margarito d'Arezzo, a painter who in the 13th century informed sacred representation with an unusual degree of expressive immediacy. The museum also has two admirable works by Bartolomeo della Gatta, *San Rocco che Intercede per la Città di Arezzo* (1478) and *San Rocco Davanti al Palazzo della Fraternita dei Laici* (1479).

**THE SANTISSIMA ANNUNZIATA.** A fine example of late Tuscan Renaissance architecture, the church of the Santissima Annunziata stands at the start of Via Garibaldi. The church has a rugged façade embellished by a Serlian window and an shrine with an Annunciation by Spinello Aretino. Inside, visitors will be struck first by the sense of proportion generated by da Sangallo's vestibule, then by the stately structure of the church, with its spacious nave and two aisles, that boasts some exceptionally elegant ornamentation.

**LA BADIA.** A short distance from Via Garibaldi stands the church of La Badia, dedicated to Saints Flora and Lucilla, in a small square of the same name. This building once belonged to a large conventual complex. The interior of the Gothic building has been remodeled to a design by Vasari.

## OUTSIDE THE MEDIEVAL CITY

**THE MUSEO ARCHEOLOGICO.** A stretch of Via Crispi leads to the remains of the ROMAN AMPHITHEATER, a magnificent classical monument that rises from the ground like the skeleton of a dinosaur. The Convento degli Olivetani di San Benedetto was built on an elliptical curve over the amphitheater in the late Middle Ages and given a double portico in the 17th century. The monastery now houses the Museo Archeologico dedicated to Mecenate, one of the city's illustrious citizens. This important museum contains some prestigious finds, including the red-figure Attic vase attributed to the Greek painter Euphronius and a monumental bowl that is one of the most important works of Attic pottery decoration. The museum also boasts the largest collection in existence of the famous *corallino* vases, produced exclusively in Roman Arezzo.

**SANTA MARIA DELLE GRAZIE.** From any point in the southern part of the city it is easy to reach Viale Mecenate that leads to the monumental church of Santa Maria delle Grazie with its elegant porch. The extensive lawn and wide podium provide a foil for the most elegant part of the building, the graceful porch (*below*) added by Benedetto da Maiano to the front of the church in 1478–82. Anyone arriving at the four-sided portico surrounding the church will be struck by the harmonious sight of this spacious porch that affords a spectacular view over the upper part of the city.

**THE HOME OF GIORGIO VASARI**
Near the church of San Domenico stands the house that Giorgio Vasari, the painter, architect and first art historian, personally designed and decorated, living there between working on the commissions he carried out all over Italy. The decoration of the rooms (such as the Sala del Camino, also known as the *Triumph of Virtue*, painted by the artist himself in 1548, *above*) provides a valuable insight into Vasari's development and his private life as it offers a remarkable portrait of his cultural identity.

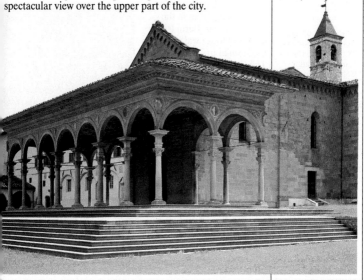

189

## TOWARD SANSEPOLCRO

Arezzo provides an ideal base for visiting Sansepolcro, the native city of Piero della Francesca, the region's most famous son. The artist painted many of the vistas you will see before you and, as Guttuso has remarked, the surrounding countryside could be a continuation of the landscapes painted on the walls of San Francesco in Arezzo.

**MONTERCHI.** Following the Cerfone valley, you will come to a short turn-off for Monterchi. The exhibition center (a former primary school) houses the *Madonna del Parto*, one of Piero della Francesca's most enigmatic works. The Madonna is seen standing at the center of a tent with her hand on her swollen belly. Once back on the road to Sansepolcro, the itinerary takes a detour to Anghiari at the top of a gentle rust-colored ridge of hills.

**ANGHIARI.** This is a perfectly preserved medieval town with its houses clustered along narrow streets that open out around the Palazzo Comunale at the top of the hill. The MUSEO STATALE in PALAZZO TAGLIESCHI is particularly interesting with its fine examples of wood carvings and a true masterpiece by Jacopo della Quercia, the *Virgin*. The museum also has a rare, fine collection of everyday objects and of items of popular devotion.

## SANSEPOLCRO ◆ C E3

Piero's city overlooks the steep Tiber valley as it opens into a vast amphitheater as varied as it is picturesque, imposing within the curve of the Apennines and more gradual as it spreads out over the hill slopes. The two major landmarks that characterize the cityscape are the pointed campaniles of the cathedral and San Francesco. Piero della Francesca established the emblematic nature of both these towers in his various paintings. The city is laid out on a symmetrical grid plan, derived from the original city center that was formed by the intersection of two thoroughfares in the Piazza Torre di Berta (the medieval tower was blown up by German troops in 1944). The city is enclosed within the MEDICI WALLS that form a quadrilateral with gates, bastions and a mighty FORTRESS designed by Giuliano da Sangallo (*right*). Visitors' first impression of this city is one of elegance and poise: a city with a long-established tradition of craftsmanship and commerce (Piero's family traded in fabrics and hides) where even the houses of the lower classes boast a certain dignified restraint and an elegant sense of proportion.

**MONTERCHI, THE ANCIENT 'MONS HERCULIS'** ★
H. V. Morton, the last of the old-style travelers, described Monterchi in 1957: 'In a labyrinth of white streets winding in various directions, to the south of the young Tiber, a hill covered with the white houses and red roofs of a town stands in the plain. Its name is Monterchi, a corruption of *Mons Herculis*, and it is the birthplace of Piero's mother. The view from its ancient bastions is magnificent. To the north it looks toward the Alpe della Luna, to the south toward Umbria.'

**IN MEMORY OF THE BATTLE OF ANGHIARI**
Not far along the main road leading from Anghiari to Sansepolcro, you will come to a small chapel on the left-hand side erected in memory of the Battle of Anghiari, fought in 1440 between Piccinino's Milanese army and that of Florence. Anghiari was defeated by Florence in this battle. This was the subject of the famous fresco painted by Leonardo da Vinci in the Palazzo Vecchio, then subsequently lost.

**DUOMO.** The structure of the cathedral is Romanesque even though it later acquired some Gothic elements. It contains a variety of works, including the beautiful *Polyptych of the Resurrection* (14th century) by Niccolò di Segna (*above*), whose risen Christ holding the standard in one hand and grasping the pink shroud in the other must have been of interest to Piero della Francesca. On the left-hand side of the presbytery is the VOLTO SANTO chapel, an impressive wooden crucifix dating from the 8th to 9th centuries. Along the left-hand aisle is an atmospheric *Ascension of Christ* based on a cartoon by Perugino, with a ring of remarkable portraits as well as a *Resurrection* (1524), the first piece of work by Raffaellino del Colle in typical Mannerist style.

**AROUND THE DUOMO.** To the left of the cathedral stands the PALAZZO DELLE LAUDI, now the town hall, remodeled in Mannerist style between 1595 and the early 17th century. The 14th-century Palazzo della Residenza, which houses the Museo Civico, is virtually opposite.

**THE MUSEO CIVICO.** The museum occupies the former town hall. The main attraction of the museum and the reason for its foundation is the fresco of the *Resurrection* (c. 1460) by Piero della Francesca which, painted in the Sala dei Conservatori del Popolo, is now regarded as a tutelary deity.

**THE CITY OF PIERO DELLA FRANCESCA ✪** Funded by a well-established mercantile bourgeoisie, Sansepolcro was an important center of artistic development in the 15th and 16th centuries. The 'quarters' of its historical center, formed by the intersection of two main axes, comprise an elegant Renaissance city filled with the works of its most illustrious son, Piero della Francesca. The Museo Civico boasts various paintings by this artist (*San Giuliano*, a fragmentary fresco from the church of Santa Chiara, *below*).

# ▲ PIERO DELLA FRANCESCA:
## IN PURSUIT OF DIVINE PROPORTION

One of the guards of Santo Sepolcro,
detail of the *Resurrection of Christ*.

Piero della Francesca was unique among Renaissance artists in that he spent most of his life in his home town of Sansepolcro and, as a result, all his works can still be found within a relatively small radius. Those who want to explore the great painter's work must follow in his footsteps, placing his views and vistas in context, identifying the hills and valleys in his paintings, discovering the reality behind his landscapes. It is also important to explore the different stages in his development, the use of geometric forms and clear, radiant colors to create and hone works completely devoid of oratory. The lasting quality of Piero's art is based on his application of the principle of divine proportion and his air of total serenity.

***The Dream of Constantine (Legend of the True Cross, AREZZO, SAN FRANCESCO ▲ 185)***
The atmospheric quality of this famous nocturnal scene is achieved by the strong artificial lighting whose fine golden rays are used effectively to emphasize the outlines of the figures. The light that fills the tent in which Constantine is sleeping alludes to the illuminating message of the angel. The use of light is offset by a liking for abstract geometric forms that can be seen in the cone of the tent, the formal repetition of this shape and the symmetrical lines formed by the curtains raised by the soldiers.

***The Victory of Constantine (Legend of the True Cross, AREZZO, SAN FRANCESCO)***
Painting the scene in which Constantine defeats Maxentius, Piero set the action in his native Valtiberina, at the first bend of the Tiber, almost as if to emphasize the new course taken by history after the event. The valley becomes an ideal microcosm mirroring the events taking place in the larger world, proving divine intervention in the history of mankind.

**POLYPTYCH OF THE MADONNA OF MERCY (SANSEPOLCRO, MUSEO CIVICO ▲ 194)**
This youthful work which took a number of years (1445–62) to complete illustrates various periods and styles in Piero's art. In contrast to the pure geometric forms that subtend the impassive figure of the Madonna, the features of the believers gathered under her cloak are portrayed with convincing realism. The iconography of the Madonna gathering believers under her cloak is widespread in the painting of central Italy, particularly in the region of Arezzo.

*Madonna del Parto* (MONTERCHI ▲ 190)
This is one of the most unusual paintings in the tradition of western figurative art: there are ceratinly few examples of pregnant Madonnas. Both noblewoman and country woman, Piero's Madonna is the protagonist in this drama, becoming a theater of flesh and blood as she parts her gown, seeming almost to lift a curtain to reveal the historic event of the Incarnation. She is in fact the tabernacle of the living God and mankind's means of salvation.

*Resurrection of Christ*
(SANSEPOLCRO, MUSEO CIVICO)
The resurrected Christ is traditionally regarded as a tutelary deity in Sansepolcro because of the emblematic way in which the painting is linked to the name of the town.
The ritual and totemic function of this painting, coupled with the geometric structure used to convey Christ's divine charisma, may explain the admiration for this painting over the centuries, from Vasari's fulsome praise to Huxley's description of it as 'the greatest painting in the world.'

The Sasso Spicco at
La Verna is a massive
fissure in the rock
where Saint Francis
used to pray.
Near the miraculously
suspended
'extraordinary
boulder', an angel
revealed to the
saint that the rocky
outcrop of La Verna
had been blasted
at the moment of
Christ's death.
Visitors should
time their visit to
enjoy the beauty of
the beech groves in
the fall.

Besides the extremely famous *Madonna of Mercy* (1445–62)
▲ *193*, the Museo Civico possesses two other works by Piero:
the detached frescos of *San Ludovico da Tolosa* and *San
Giuliano*, the latter discovered by chance in 1954. The various
rooms of the museum contain a series of works that provide an
overview of the flourishing local pictorial tradition with fine
artists like Matteo di Giovanni (*Saints Peter and Paul*),
Raffaellino del Colle (*Assumption and Coronation of the Virgin*,
1527) and the distinctive style of Giovanni de' Vecchi (*Birth of
the Virgin*, 1575–6). The extent of this region's artistic tradition
is impressive, but only a fraction of the paintings have actually
remained in Sansepolcro, with many of its more exceptional
pieces having been sold abroad. Examples include the
*Battesimo and Natività* (by Piero, now in the National Gallery in
London) and others ranging from Spinello Aretino to Sassetta.
**SAN LORENZO.** It would be a crime to leave Sansepolcro
without seeing one other major work, the *Deposition*
(1528–30) by Rosso Fiorentino in the church of San Lorenzo.
A cosmic gloom, the 'darkness that certainly occurred at the
death of Christ', in Vasari's words, envelops Mary as she
weeps over Christ's body. Flying in the face of tradition,
Rosso painted the completely naked figure of Christ, clearly
portraying his agony and death throes.

## LA VERNA, THE CASENTINO AND
### THE HERMITAGES ◆ **C** CD3

Until the age of the Grand Tour, the mountain route linking
La Verna to Camaldoli and Vallombrosa was simply famous
for being built through the heart of the most beautiful forest
in central Italy.

**THE SANCTUARY OF
LA VERNA.** The E45
highway leads to
Pieve Santo Stefano
where it starts to
climb gently toward
La Verna. Bounded
by the Arno and
Tiber valleys, La
Verna is a basalt
outcrop with a sheer
drop on three sides.
Paul Sabatier,
the historian of
Franciscanism,
described it as an
immense monolith
that had fallen from
heaven. Saint
Francis came here
for the first time in
1213 after Count
Orlando Cattani
di Chiusi gave him
this 'solitary
mountain, ideal
for contemplation'
as a gift. It was at

Typical mushrooms found in the Casentino (*below*).

La Verna, two years before his death, as Dante recorded, that he received Christ's stigmata on his limbs. The ground plan of the settlement at La Verna combined the characteristic features of the hermitage and the monastery. Peculiar to the hermitage (*left*) was an affinity with nature and forest, an affinity that can be seen in the fame of places like the Grotta di San Francesco and the Sasso Spicco, which performed a marked ritual and held a symbolic function. The layout of the communal buildings and the structure of the Chiesa Maggiore were modeled on the monastery. The latter church was consecrated in 1568 and the monastery was rebuilt in the same century after the fire of 1468. The monastery complex of La Verna boasts a remarkable collection of art that finds its highest expression in the two majolica altarpieces by Andrea della Robbia in the Chiesa Maggiore.

**THE CASENTINO.** Coming down from La Verna brings you into sight of the 'closed valley' of the Casentino, which has always been a popular destination, steeped as it is in history, haunted by the ghosts of poets, close to mountains and forests (*left, below*) and dotted with walled towns, churches and castles.

**BIBBIENA.** Lower down still you will come to Bibbiena spread out in an arc over the hill. This elegant town slopes down the hillside amid dark groves of cypress trees and is bathed at its base by the confluence of various streams with the Arno and the Archiano. Standing in solitary vigil at the valley mouth, the town's name is widely known because of Cardinal Bernardo Dovici, alias Bibbiena, a 16th-century humanist and witty playwright. He gave his name to the fine PALAZZO in Tuscan rustic style that, with the church of Santi Ippolito e Cassiano, are the main buildings of interest.

**CAMALDOLI.** From Bibbiena head in the direction of Camaldoli, a beacon of faith in the heart of the Casentino forests ● *16*. The hermitage was built by San Romualdo in 1012 just below the Apennine ridge. The monastery, also used as guest quarters, was built several years later. A large library grew up around the monastery, giving rise to a great cultural tradition that reached its apex with the presence of the court of Lorenzo de' Medici. The hermitage ● *77* has twenty monastic cells separated by paved paths that resemble small cottages in a village. At the entrance stands the church of San Salvatore, with some fine paintings by Vasari.

**THE CHURCHES OF LA VERNA**
At the entrance to the Sanctuary stands the Chiesa Maggiore (1348–1509), richly decorated with della Robbia terracottas. The oldest church is Santa Maria degli Angeli, built (1216–18) by Saint Francis. Finally, the Stimmate chapel was erected in 1263 on the spot where Francis received the stigmata.

**TRAVELERS TO THE CASENTINO**
Edward Hutton advised people to visit the Casentino (*Hermitage at Camaldoli*, Jakob-Philipp Hackert, *below*) on foot with Dante in their pocket and a sturdy cane in their hand.
D'Annunzio wrote: 'I am at the Castello di Romena, near the dried up Fontebranda of Master Adam. Tomorrow morning I will be at La Verna. I leave tonight on horseback by the light of the moon'.

The courtyard of the Castello dei Conti Guidi in Poppi. The walls are decorated with the coats of arms of Florentine commanders and vicars.

**VALLOMBROSA'S SUCCESS**
John Milton was not the only one to stay near the monastery at Vallombrosa. Mary Shelley, Vernon Lee and the American writer Edith Wharton also visited this area. Louis Gauffier and Philipp Hackert set up their easels in its glades, making it one of the most popular settings in neoclassical landscape painting. Vallombrosa continued to thrive as a renowned health resort until the early years of the 20th century.

H. Hugford, *Landscape with the Monastery of Vallombrosa and Saint John Gualberto Worshipping the Cross*.

**POPPI AND ITS CASTLE.** Once through the dense Casentino forests, Ponte a Poppi appears like a vision of historical beauty. Visitors are welcomed by a porticoed piazza on this side of the Arno which is crossed by a medieval bridge (a ritual gateway of sorts). Poppi stands opposite on the nearby hill. The entire town resembles a fortress, an impression created by the massive bulk of the CASTELLO DEI CONTI GUIDI (*left*), on which Arnolfo di Cambio collaborated in the late 13th century. The castle is Poppi's main attraction. With its postern gate, tower, picturesque courtyard and large library, it seems to exist in a time warp. The beautiful valley landscapes are equaled by the painted scenes on the 15th-century altarpieces. The whole town which, shaped like an elbow, straddles the crest of the hill, displays a compact uniformity evident in the porticoed main road and the small church of the Madonna del Morbo. At the far end of the town, on the edge of a ravine, stands the 13th-century church of San Fidele, that seems to block the traveler's path.

**AT THE FOOT OF MOUNT FALTERONA.** This itinerary continues to PRATOVECCHIO, an ancient river port on the Arno, overlooked by a conical hill, the site of the Castello di Romena and the nearby church of the same name (*below*), a favorite haunt of writers and poets and the place where D'Annunzio wrote part of *Alcyone* (1904). Heading back up the Arno you will come to STIA at the foot of Mount Falterona. This lush town, the home of the famous woolen mills, is centered about the picturesque Piazza Tanucci. This porticoed piazza narrows to a funnel shape as it slopes up the top of the town. In the dark shadows of the beautiful Romanesque church of Santa Maria Assunta you can catch the glitter of paintings with gold backgrounds by Bicci di Lorenzo and other painters from the early 15th century.

**VALLOMBROSA.** Founded by Saint John Gualberto and recognized by the Pope in 1055, the Vallombrosan order was based on two different ideals, Benedictine communes and its founder's hermitic aspirations. Dominated by a beautiful campanile and a tower that gives it the appearance of a castle, the abbey dates back to the 15th century. The main building affords views of woods and mountains, hermitages and attractive resorts, spread out in a landscape that is featured in the work of various painting schools from the 17th and the 19th centuries.

## TOWARD THE 'NEW TOWNS' ◆ C C3-4

**BETWEEN CHURCHES AND HILLS.** The towns, from Reggello to Castelfranco di Sopra, cannot compete with the beauty of the Romanesque churches on the route from Vallombrosa to the 'new towns' that include SAN PIETRO in Cascia, SAN GIOVENALE with a polyptych by Masaccio, SAN SALVATORE A SOFFENA with its fine collection of frescos, and the 11th-century SAN PIETRO A GROPINA, whose decorated capitals, along with the pulpit, furnish one of the most detailed and whimsical illustrations of the Middle Ages. An interesting port of call is LORO CIUFFENNA. The medieval bridges that cross the moat seem to mirror the arches and airy walkways of the swaying tenements in this elegant town.

**SAN GIOVANNI VALDARNO.** After Loro you leave the lowest slopes of Mount Pratomagno to reach the 'new towns' on the valley floor. Founded in the 13th century by the Florentines to check Arezzo's power, SAN GIOVANNI VALDARNO is the first on this route. The surviving monuments bear witness to the city's origins, particularly the Palazzo Pretorio, decorated with ancient majolica coats of arms that gleam in the shadowy recesses of its elegant portico. This is Masaccio's native town and visitors should make a point of going into the museum, which has an extraordinary *Annunciation* by Fra Angelico.

**MONTEVARCHI.** The disparate origins of this town can be seen in the herringbone pattern traced by the older streets as they lead off from the main road, the present Via Roma. Over the ages, Montevarchi has been a place of pilgrimage for travelers wanting to see the Sacro Latte della Vergine, a reliquary kept at the cathedral of San Lorenzo. The Museo Paleontologico with the remains of the *elephas meridionalis* is also worth a visit.

**THE INN AT LEVANELLA**
Near Montevarchi lies the village of Levanella whose inn received Montaigne's enthusiastic approval: 'You make merry here to your heart's content and they say that the noblemen of the area often meet here, as at the Moro in Paris or the Guillot in Amiens. They serve food on tin plates, which is extremely unusual. It is a house in its own right in a perfect position on the plain with its own handy spring.'

Geometric and zoomorphic decorations on the pluteus (8th century) from the church of Sant'Agata in Arfoli, near Reggello.

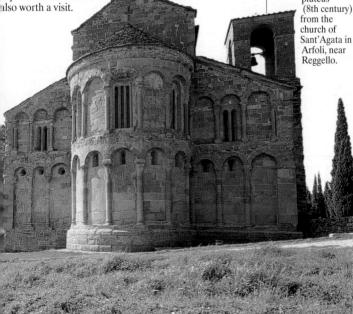

197

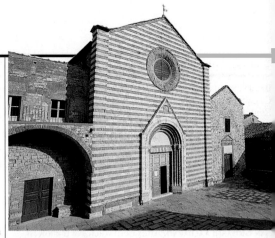

**ON THE HILLS OF THE VALDICHIANA**
The hill towns in the Valdichiana were built to keep the inhabitants safe from fever and enable them to defend themselves against raids by neighboring villages. Fortified villages such as Civitella, Monte San Savino, Marciano, Foiano and Lucignano form a picturesque sight with their old towers and ancient walls. Each one has its own little piece of history.

**WALKING TO FOIANO**
'All I can say about the road to Foiano is that it is so beautiful that it must be traveled on foot', said Edward Hutton in 1910. 'First walk down the winding road through the olive groves to the village of San Pietro, next to the station, then, on the other side of the railroad, take the road heading east across the valley and climb the hill. At Castellina descend once more into the Val d'Esse, a long estuary of the Valdichiana, and at the end climb once more toward Foiano which towers above the principal plain of the Valdichiana with Cortona opposite.'

## THE VALDICHIANA

Elegance and proportion characterize the towns, which blend perfectly with the surrounding countryside. Albert Camus was enchanted, writing at the end of his life that he would have liked to walk once more along 'the road that led from Monte San Savino to Siena, to walk by the side of that landscape of grapes and olives, crossing those hills of bluish tufa that stretch out toward the horizon'. At Levane, you can take a detour through the Valdambra, then over the wooded brow of a hill you come to GARGONZA, the epitome of the Tuscan medieval hamlet. You are now in the Valdichiana, rediscovered after a drainage program between the 18th and 19th centuries had reclaimed the pestilential swamps (one reason why medieval hamlets were built on the hills, as was the case with Monte San Savino).

**MONTE SAN SAVINO.** This town has two lovely gates in its ring of walls, one at each end of the main street that is lined with fascinating monuments. These include the Palazzo di Monte, which has a beautiful hanging garden, the LOGGIA DEI MERCANTI (1517–20), by Sansovino, who was born here, and the church of Sant'Agostino.

**LUCIGNANO.** This is a pretty town laid out on an elliptical plan, its concentric streets running around the collegiate church and its sandstone walls prettified with vegetable gardens. This peaceful hill town has some unusual works of art symbolizing ancestral hopes and fears: the fine MUSEO COMUNALE has works of the highest quality, including the outstanding *Albero di Lucignano*, an important late Gothic reliquary, symbol both of the tree of life and of the Cross; the church of San Francesco opposite (*above*) contains the fresco by the Sienese school featuring a dramatic *Triumph of Death*.

**FOIANO.** This town was once surrounded by two city walls, the older one encircling the castle and the other the hamlet. Foiano was predominantly built of brick, but the taste for ornamentation reached new heights in the colored majolica ornamentation of the octagonal dome of the church of the Santissima Trinità. The cathedral of San Martino contains the *Coronation of the Virgin*, surrounded by angels, saints and the donor (1523), believed to be Signorelli's last work.

**FARNETA.** This 11th-century abbey, with its two high thrusting apses, faces the rolling, fruitful Chiana valley, crowned on the opposite hillside by stony Cortona and Castiglion Fiorentino, with the solitary Castello di Montecchio in between.

## CORTONA ◆ C D4

To reach Cortona, you must abandon the gentler hill roads for one of those precipitous roads that cut across the valley. Although frequently besieged by tourists, Cortona still preserves a modicum of the peace and quiet that has long ensured its reputation as a lovely, historical relic left clinging to the hillside. Visitors are fascinated by the city's layout with its asymmetrical piazzas, steep streets ending in a maze of staircases and the doors of its houses overlooking the roofs of the houses below.

**THE HISTORICAL CENTER.** The upper part of the city allows you to appreciate Cortona's true nature, with its silent radiance and grassy thoroughfares – over the centuries the city has spread as if it were a natural part of the hill itself. Porta Montanina affords a dizzying view of the city and the valley. One above another, the church of Santa Margherita and the Fortezza del Girifalco seem to hold the visitor suspended in space, drinking in the entire Valdichiana from Mount Amiata to Lake Trasimeno and the Sienese hills.

**THE WALLS.** Henry James said that the Etruscan walls of Cortona are best admired through sunglasses, as the glare of history is so strong. Cortona's Etruscan origins are betrayed by its picturesque tombs, the TANELLA DI PITAGORA halfway down the slope and the MELONE DEL SODO at the foot of the hill. But this is not to mention the votive statuettes and ornaments, including the famous chandelier in the MUSEO DELL'ACCADEMIA ETRUSCA in the Palazzo Casali. This extremely rich and eclectic museum, founded in the 18th century, contains not only a large collection of Egyptian finds (funerary bark from the Middle Kingdom, c. 2055–1650 BC) and works by Etruscan goldsmiths, but also works by Tuscan painters ranging from the 12th to the 20th centuries, including Bicci di Lorenzo (*Madonna in Trono e Santi*, c. 1425–30), Pietro da Cortona (*Madonna col Bambino in Trono e Quattro*

**CORTONA'S CHANDELIER**
The most famous piece in the Museo dell'Accademia Etrusca in Cortona is a magnificent bronze chandelier dating back to the 5th–4th century BC. At its center is a gorgon's head surrounded by sixteen oil lamps in the form of satyrs and sirens (*above*). The chandelier is 24 inches in diameter and weighs 128 pounds.

**A CITY BUILT FROM ONE TYPE OF STONE**
Cortona leaves an overall impression of unity. This is due to the widespread use of *pietra serena* (soft blue-gray stone) which means that, although the city has medieval, Renaissance and baroque monuments, it seems to have been built all of a piece.

Piazza della Repubblica in Cortona.

**THE CHURCH OF SANTA MARIA AL CALCINAIO** ✪
This church was built (1485–1513) by Francesco di Giorgio Martini and commissioned by a guild of merchants. In a suburb called Il Calcinaio, an image of the Virgin had started to perform such miracles that the tanners' guild decided to erect a church to her. The interior, whose spatial unity makes it one of the finest examples of Tuscan Renaissance architecture, shows a pervasive Brunelleschian influence. A fine stained-glass window (*Madonna della Misericordia*, 1516) by Guillaume de Marcillat adds the finishing touch to the rose window on the side.

*Santi*, 1626–8) and Gino Severini, who was born here (*Maternità*, 1916).

**THE MUSEO DIOCESANO.** This museum, opposite the cathedral, possesses some first-class works, including the dazzling *Annunciation* by Fra Angelico (*detail, above*), as well as works by Pietro Lorenzetti (*Cross*, 1315–20), Bartolomeo della Gatta (*Assunta*, c. 1475) and Signorelli (*Compianto sul Cristo Morto*, 1502).

**CHURCHES AND CONVENTS.** The town has some fascinating churches: the Gothic churches of SAN FRANCESCO and SAN DOMENICO and the churches outside the city walls including SANTA MARIA AL CALCINAIO (*below*), by Francesco di Giorgio, which sparkles like a diamond against the hillside. Meanwhile, Cortona's gorgeous palaces made of *pietra serena* and sandstone are a reminder that this was the home of Berrettini, renowned as Pietro da Cortona. It was also the home of Saint Elias, a Franciscan monk and the spiritual heir of Saint Francis, so it is impossible not to visit the CONENTO DELLE CELLE (*top, left*), founded by Saint Francis in 1211 on the precipitous slopes of Mount Sant'Egidio by the banks of a fast-flowing stream.

## CASTIGLION FIORENTINO ◆ **C** D4

Having left Cortona with its head in the clouds, to quote the words of an English traveler, the road to Arezzo passes through Castiglion Fiorentino. This is a typical Tuscan walled town made of sun-kissed sandstone and overlooked by the tall tower of the CASSERO. Anyone wanting to stop here will find a fine municipal PICTURE GALLERY, with works such as *Le Stimmate di San Francesco* (1486) by Bartolomeo della Gatta, which provide a fitting end to this long itinerary.

# Chianti

# ▲ CHIANTI

1. Florentine Chianti ▲ 202
2. Sienese Chianti ▲ 205

**CHIANTISHIRE ✪**
Throughout the world, the Chianti region has become synonymous with one of the best Italian wines. However, for visitors to the rolling landscape that stretches from Florence toward Siena, this is perhaps the least of its many attractions. There are woods and fields as far as the eye can see, interrupted by rows of vines, but also, and most important, villas, churches and monasteries that stand monument to the profoundly civilized nature of this region that is as rich in culture as it is in fruit. However, Chianti has only recently become a tourist destination. The crisis in the sharecropping system caused a rural exodus which, in the 1960s, reached dangerous levels. At the same time, many foreign visitors were discovering the magic of Chianti, including artists and celebrities trying to find peace and quiet and fresh inspiration. Over the years this phenomenon has grown and in some bars English is now more common than Italian. Chianti has become so fashionable with English-speaking tourists that it is popularly described as Chiantishire.

Of all the regions in Tuscany, Chianti is probably the most famous and best loved. This hilly region extends between Florence and Siena, brushing up against the walls of the two cities that have been rivals for centuries. Chianti is traversed by steep stony roads cutting through dense woods and overlooked by smooth hills scored by lines of vineyards, dotted with silver olive groves and the occasional field of crops. Present-day Chianti has been three thousand years in the making. The families of sharecroppers and small landowners who have lived on the same small plots of land for centuries have very slowly modified this territory, a large part of which is still untamed. It is only in the last few decades that this region has seen an increase in the number of large and medium-sized businesses specializing in the production of olive oil and wine. Large families, mainly from Florence, have left their stamp on the countryside with buildings that still stand today: castles and fortified hamlets, villa-farmhouses and farms made of gray limestone or local brown marl that are so beautiful and functional they could be mistaken for noblemen's residences. There are also churches and abbeys, well kept and embellished with delightful works of art.

## FLORENTINE CHIANTI ◆ **B** F5-**C** B3 **D** E1

A strong yet vulnerable region, Chianti is characterized by buildings whose variety of styles are a product of the conflict between Florence and Siena.
**VILLAS-FARMHOUSES.** The so-called *torri appalagiate* were miniature castles, equipped not only for the purposes of subsistence, but also to ensure defense. They had a huge tower that stood at one end of the long main building used to house the residents and store the machinery. The

**VILLA L'UGOLINO**
Situated along the
Via Chiantigiana,
4 miles south of
Florence is a 17th-
century building with
an 18th-century
porch, attributed to
Gherardo Silvani.
It is now the home
of the golf course of
the same name, one
of the leading clubs
in Italy, founded
around 1930 by the
English community.

consolidation of Florence's supremacy led to the appearance
of some spacious quadrangular houses with beautiful porches
on the front, and two rows of windows. These villas,
particularly in the region of Florence (VIGNAMAGGIO, whose
VILLA has a magnificent Italian garden, VICCHIOMAGGIO,
LE CORTINE, UZZANO), drew their inspiration from Bernardo
Buontalenti's Renaissance style, and were made of lightly
whitewashed local stone. In the Sienese region of the
Berardenga, however, the farmhouses were modeled on the
work of Baldassarre Peruzzi and favored the use of brick since
there was an abundance of clay in the vicinity of Le Crete.
These villas all had barns, cellars, oil presses and mills, just
like the mightier castles and the older abbeys.

**CHIANTI PRODUCE**
Chianti is one of the
most renowned
agricultural regions in
the world: this was
where the many
consortiums were
formed to protect
typical products, such
as wine and olive oil.
One of the most
famous of these labels
is the Gallo Nero.

**BADIA DI PASSIGNANO.** Situated about 30 miles south of
Florence, is the religious complex (*below*) that boasts the
highest number of art works in the whole of Chianti.
It was first documented as early as AD 884 and shortly
after AD 1000 it was occupied by the Vallombrosan Order.
Surrounded by a strong fortification, it has accumulated
a rich and varied art collection, with works by Domenico
Cresti (1559–1638), later named Passignano because of
his long association with the monastery, and by Ghirlandaio
and Allori.

siete nel mondo
del
**gallo nero**

CONSORZIO VINO CHIANTI CLASSICO

**CHIANTI**CLASSICO

Steep narrow cobblestone streets characterize the town of Montefioralle (*top*).

A room used for the production of Vin Santo ● 29 in Greve in Chianti (*above*).

**RECOVERED TREASURES ★**
The church of San Leolino, just over half a mile from Panzano, has a Romanesque façade with a porch on Tuscan-style columns (16th century). Its interior contains fine works that were once stolen then thankfully recovered. The most important of these is without a doubt the painting of the *Madonna in Trono, i Santi Pietro e Paolo e Storie dei due Santi*, attributed to Meliore (documented c. 1260–80), one of the leading figures in Florentine art in the second half of the 13th century.

**MONTEFIORALLE.** To the east of Passignano, Montefioralle was once a thriving town because of its high, well-defended position. However, it was abandoned for the more convenient Greve after the fall of the Sienese Republic ● 37 which brought an end to centuries of border conflicts. The church of Santo Stefano possesses a rare *Madonna and Child* by a Florentine artist, a colorful work from the 13th century, while over the high altar is a 15th-century painting, *Trinità e Santi*, attributed to the Maestro dell'Epifania di Fiesole. The nearby CHURCH OF SAN CRESCI has a porch with two-light windows preceding the façade, setting it apart from all the other Romanesque architecture in Chianti.

**GREVE IN CHIANTI.** Just over a mile to the east, along the S222 highway, lies Greve in Chianti. This ancient market town is arranged around a spacious piazza, dedicated to the navigator Giovanni da Verrazzano, who was born here. The piazza is surrounded by deep arcades still used for trading, and was once a marketplace for the various surrounding regions of Chianti, the Valdarno and the Val di Pesa. Overlooking the square is the PARISH CHURCH OF SANTA CROCE, restored in the 19th century in neo-Renaissance style to a design by Luigi de Cambray-Digny. It has an interesting painting by Bicci di Lorenzo, the *Madonna and Saints* and an *Annunciation* by an unknown 14th-century Florentine artist.

**PANZANO.** Continuing along the Via Chiantigiana will bring you to this ancient town which has preserved its old walls, gate and the keep of the medieval castle. The most striking building is the CHURCH OF SANTA MARIA, situated right at the center of the town. This 13th-century structure was remodeled in the 19th century and contains some wonderful paintings, including the *Annunciation* attributed to Michele di Ridolfo del Ghirlandaio and a *Matrimonio Mistico di Santa Maria Maddalena de' Pazzi* by Pier Dandini (latter half of the 17th century).

Situated inside the
Castello di Volpaia,
the Commenda, or
Oratory, is regarded
as the sanctuary of
Chianti and has
always been a
place of pilgrimage
dedicated to the
saint most venerated
by the locals, Sant'
Eufrosino, who lived,
worked and died in
this area. It still
contains the mortal
remains of Eufrosino,
who is celebrated on
September 1; the day
when a little boy was
miraculously
resurrected.

## SIENESE CHIANTI ◆ B F6 C BC4 D E1-F2

Sienese Chianti, which is less rugged than the Florentine
region, starts after Panzano. The woods gradually thin out
toward the south until they peter out altogether in the area
of Le Crete ▲ *228*.

**CASTELLINA IN CHIANTI.** This town is situated on a hill
between the Arbia, Elsa and Pesa valleys. Etruscan in origin,
it still preserves the medieval layout of a Florentine fortified
hamlet. The quadrangular circuit of walls encloses a
cluster of sturdy buildings that converge on the ROCCA, the
present town hall, a 15th-century building topped by an
impressive tower.

**RADDA IN CHIANTI.** For a long time the chief town in the Lega
del Chianti, Radda was fortified by Florence later in the 14th
century and the Palazzo del Podestà was enlarged and rebuilt
in the following century. The Franciscan monastery of SANTA
MARIA AL PRATO, founded in ancient times then remodeled
in the 17th century, is now in the process of being converted
into a museum to house Sienese Chianti's principal works
of art. The façade of the PREPOSITURA DI SAN NICCOLÒ,
Romanesque in origin and structure, was not built until the
1930s by Carlo Coppedè, a key initiative in the historical
rehabilitation of many religious buildings in this area.

**CASTELLO DI VOLPAIA.** From the CHURCH OF SANTA MARIA
NOVELLA, which has various glazed terracottas by Santi
Buglioni, you can climb up to the nearby Castello di Volpaia
that houses the Commenda di Sant'Eufrosino. The tiny
picturesque town (*top*), situated on the most renowned slopes
in Chianti, has long been the home of some important
collections of modern art.

**BADIA A COLTIBUONO.** Founded in 1049, this abbey has
always been occupied by the Vallombrosan Benedictines.
It is situated at an altitude of 2060 feet, near the pass
linking the Valle dell'Arbia with the Valdarno. The
interior of the CHURCH OF SAN LORENZO was partly
modified and decorated in the 18th century, while the
beautiful crenelated bell tower dates back to the late
12th century.

To remedy the
scarcity of water in
the late Middle Ages,
the Sienese
constructed an
extensive network of
*bottini* (subterranean
aqueducts) that are
still in working order.
The most prolific
spring was located
in the hill of
Fonterutoli, behind
the city. During the
late 15th century, the
hill was under the
control of Florence,
being the property
of the Florentine
Mazzei family.
However, the
Sienese succeeded in
'stealing' back from
the hill the water
they needed.

**GAIOLE IN CHIANTI.** Because of its strategic position Gaiole started life as an ancient market town and has continued in that role to the present day; the piazza created as a widening of the main street was actually used as a marketplace. In the immediate vicinity stands the Romanesque CHURCH OF SANTA MARIA A SPALTENNA (12th century), whose monastery has recently been converted into a hotel, as well as some large, attractive fortified towns such as Vertine, with its stocky quadrangular embattled tower, and Barbischio.

**CASTELLI DEL CHIANTIGIANO.** Heading toward Siena through the typical Chianti landscape, where wooded areas alternate with farmsteads, you will come across the CASTELLO DI MELETO (*below, right*), an extremely old castle restored by the Ricasoli family in the 18th century. Lavishly decorated and furnished, it boasts an 18th-century toy theater and an ancient, extremely well-stocked cellar. After SAN SANO, an ancient hamlet whose small houses seem to have sprung from the stony ground, there will come into view the CASTELLO DI BROLIO (*below, left*) the largest fortified residence in the whole of Chianti. Attributed to Giuliano da Sangallo, it was restored in 1860 by the architect Giuseppe Partini. This is the headquarters of one of the leading wine-producing companies in the world. The road from Brolio leads to SAN GUSMÈ (a vulgarization of San Cosma) to whom, together with San Damiano, the local church was dedicated. This ancient town was once a stronghold of the Sienese Republic ● *37*.

**CASTELNUOVO BERARDENGA.** The chief town in the Berardenga, Castelnuovo was reinforced by the Sienese government in 1366 to exert greater control over the region's leaders. The PREPOSITURA in the main square, with its fine neoclassical façade, possesses an important painting by Giovanni di Paolo featuring the *Madonna and Child* (1426).

In the town center stands the beautiful VILLA CHIGI, set within a spacious park. Nearby is the illustrious town of PACINA, which boasts the 7th-century church of Santa Maria which has a fine cylindrical campanile. Also in Pacina is the ARCENO (now a hotel) set in beautiful romantic grounds designed by Agostino Fantastici and SANT'ANSANO A DOFANA, the church where the patron saint of Siena was martyred, with a fine hexagonal chapel.

**THE BOOZY FROG**
The emblem of San Sano is a frog drinking from a flask of wine. It is said that the wine in this area is so delicious that the frogs prefer wine from the cask to ditch water. A monument in the center of the town has even been dedicated to the boozy frog while, in the fall, various festivities are organized in its honor with plays performed by the town's inhabitants and a large art exhibition.

Giovanni di Paolo, *Madonna col Bambino* (1426), the church of Castelnuovo Berardenga.

# Siena

1. Siena ▲ 208
2. North of Siena
   ▲ 222
3. South of Siena
   ▲ 222

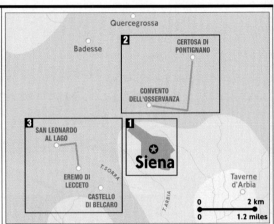

**THE SIENESE WOLF**
Siena is said to have
been founded by the
twin sons of Remus,
Senius and Ascius,
who fled to the
Tuscan hills to escape
the murderous
intentions of their
uncle Romulus. The
she-wolf suckling
the twins became the
symbol of Siena,
being featured on
the most prestigious
civic buildings. The
oldest was placed at
the entrance to the
Palazzo Pubblico.
This beautifully made
piece dates back to
the mid-15th century.

**THE COUNCIL
OF NINE**
In the latter half of
the 13th century,
Siena was suffering,
due to water
shortages and its
support of the
struggling Ghibelline
faction. This tough
period was resolved
in 1287 by the
manufacturing
classes who set up
the Council of Nine
(1287–1355). This
government oversaw
the city's building and
artistic programs: the
Campo, the Palazzo
Pubblico, the
completion of the
Duomo and the
circuit of walls.

In the streets of Siena ◆ **B** F6 **C** B4 **D** E2 time seems to have
stood still. It is easy to chart the different stages in the
history of this unique city, which appears frozen in a Gothic
reverie. Its picturesque urban plan was imposed by the
Council of Nine in the 14th century and, in subsequent
periods, new buildings were gracefully introduced into the
Gothic layout without undermining the overriding sense of
harmony that has always characterized this city. Since its
foundation, Siena has been divided into three districts called
the *Terzi*: the Terzo di Città, the oldest district packed with
works of art; the Terzo di Camollia, more vulnerable to
enemies in the north and therefore fortified; and the Terzo
di San Martino, which lies either side of the Via Francigena.
Organizing your visit to take in these three itineraries is by far
the best way to enjoy your stay in Siena.

## THE CITY'S MEDIEVAL PAST

Although at the center of a dense cluster of fairly large
Etruscan settlements, excavations in Siena have not
uncovered any written records to
document its foundation in
ancient times, even though the
city appears to have been named
after an Etruscan family. In the
Roman era, it merited various
mentions by historians such as
Tacitus, who was more interested
in stressing the ironic and
somewhat madcap nature of its
inhabitants than in listing
important territorial and
demographic characteristics.
Siena's importance grew under
the Lombard rulers who extended
the area administered by the city's
chamberlain and, in the process,
sparked off a centuries-old
dispute with the diocese of
Arezzo. In the oldest part of
Siena, so-called *Sena vetus*,

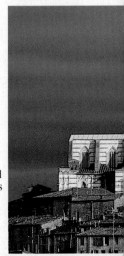

situated on the highest hill in the city, groups of residences, mainly powerful keeps, cluster around the Via Francigena. These were built by the leading feudal families who were moving to the city and wanted their new residences to be as self-sufficient as their castles. The city's increasing importance gave rise to bitter rivalry with Florence that was to last for centuries. This antagonism found expression in many bloody conflicts such as the famous battle of Montaperti in 1260 ● *33, 35* which saw 'the agony and the dreadful massacre/that made the waters of the Arba run red', as Dante recorded in his *Divine Comedy*, and the complete destruction of the Florentine army by the Sienese. The plague of 1348 created havoc, decimating the population and interrupting large-scale building projects. This marked the start of a long period of instability and savage infighting. Throughout these troubled times, a stubborn reluctance to leave the city in the hands of a single family or ruler and a dogged preference for democracy resulted, after a long siege by the Spanish and a heroic attempt to reestablish a new Sienese Republic at Montalcino, in the final clash in the mid 16th century, when Siena surrendered and was annexed to the Medici State ● *37*. The ensuing crisis left the city in a kind of time warp, a lull verging on desolation, although this was also a time when theatrical diversions such as the Palio ▲ *214* were invented: this festival assumed its present form between the 16th and 18th centuries. It was not until Italian unification that Siena regained the vigor and spirit of enterprise that had been lost for centuries. The city once again began to acquire international recognition with the 'purist school' led by Luigi Mussini and a prestigious crafts industry. Because of historical circumstances and the resilience of its inhabitants, Siena has been able to preserve the medieval urban layout and deep-rooted traditions that continue to make it a mandatory port of call for travelers.

**SIENA, 'MEDIEVAL POMPEII'** ✪
It was the exceptional integrity of Siena's urban layout and artistic heritage that caused Hippolyte Taine to come up with this description. But Siena has also created a civilization of its own, a seamless combination of art, culture and lifestyle, and, luckily, none of its achievements are buried under ash.

Sano di Pietro, *Predicazione di San Bernardo in Piazza del Campo* (1430), Museo dell'Opera Metropolitana.

## THE TERZO DI CITTÀ

**THE CAMPO** ● *64*. The main square in Siena (*above*) is one of the most emblematic and complex urban areas in the world and has served as a model for architects and city planners. The sloping piazza follows the original incline of the valley, just as its original shell shape was dictated by the garland of palaces that once stood on the old Via Francigena. The piazza therefore represents a perfect compromise between function and location. The Campo is the true heart of the city, the arena for key events over the centuries and the age-old venue for the thrilling races of the Palio. It is bordered by beautiful palaces, some of which (PALAZZO D'ELCI) still preserve their medieval aspect. Others have been remodeled in subsequent periods, either in baroque style (CASINO DEI NOBILI, PALAZZO CHIGI ZONDADARI) or early neo-Gothic (PALAZZO SANSEDONI). At the northern end of the paved brick piazza, divided into nine segments in honor of the Council of Nine, stands the FONTE GAIA.

Ambrogio Lorenzetti, *Good Government* (1337–9), Sala del Mappamondo.

**THE 'CONTRADE'**
The legally chartered neighborhoods, or *contrade*, embody the spirit of mutual aid: they exist to look after their own territory and its residents, they take a hand in matters of religion and worship and organize festivals. The names of the *contrade* are taken from the medieval bestiary and certainly predate the earliest documents that make mention of them (15th century).

This is a 19th-century copy by Tito Sarrocchi: the original, sculpted by Jacopo della Quercia in the first half of the 15th century, has been moved to the Spedale di Santa Maria della Scala ▲ *216*.

**PALAZZO PUBBLICO.** In the late 13th century, the Council of Nine decided to construct a new building to house the various state offices and departments and give themselves more space. This enabled them to cast off the yoke of the nobility and clergy, since until that time all state activities had been carried out in private palaces and churches. Between 1297 and 1308, the Palazzo Pubblico assumed what was more or less its definitive shape, although it took another forty years to complete the wing of the Podestà and the Torre del Mangia. The front of the building has a high limestone fascia with doors and windows ending in the typically Sienese pointed arch. There are two rows of three-light brick windows (the top floor of the wings was added in the late 17th century) on the upper part of the façade whose original splendor has recently been restored. The vast rooms inside, which have been converted into the MUSEO CIVICO, boast a huge collection of relics, paintings and detached frescos as well as some decorative cycles that are of paramount importance in the history of western art. The SALA DEL MAPPAMONDO, formerly used for General Council meetings and named after a large circular map of the universe created by Ambrogio Lorenzetti around 1340 and now lost, sports two famous frescos by Simone Martini. The *Maestà*, painted between 1312 and 1315 and then much altered by the painter himself, was the first large-scale painting project undertaken in the palace and Simone's earliest known work. On the opposite wall is the other famous fresco, *Guidoriccio da Fogliano all'Assedio di Montemassi* (1328, *below*), traditionally attributed to Simone Martini, although this supposition has recently been thrown into doubt. This extraordinary work, however, is completely in keeping with Simone's technique and style and is most innovative in its accurate, realistic depiction of the Maremma landscape. In the adjacent SALA DEI NOVE, or SALA DELLA PACE (Room of the Nine or Peace Room), Ambrogio Lorenzetti was commissioned by the Council of Nine to paint his masterpiece between 1337 and 1339: *Allegories of Good and Bad Government* ● *87*. This fresco, in the room used for passing decrees, clearly advocates wise government in favor of the common good.

**THE ORGAN OF THE SIGNORI CHAPEL**
The organ was placed in the Signori chapel in the early 16th century. Built by Giovanni d'Antonio Piffaro, this rare instrument is still in working order and is visited by performers and musicologists from all over the world.

**THE CAMPO ✪**
This is the loveliest Campo in Tuscany and the only large open space in the center of Siena. It was made into a fan shape in the Middle Ages and paved in bricks in 1340. The nine sections of the fan are in honor of the Council of Nine. It was built as a marketplace and serves as a link between the city's three *Terzi* (districts). According to tradition, it does not belong to any of the *contrade*.

**ACCADEMIA DEGLI INTRONATI (ACADEMY OF THE DEFEANED)** Founded in 1526 by six Sienese noblemen who wanted to withdraw into their studies because they were 'deafened' by the world, this academy is the oldest Italian institution of its kind. Its emblem is a gourd with two crossed pestles to symbolize the intelligence of its members and its motto is *meliora latent* (the best things are hidden).

**FROM THE TOWER ★** The panoramic view from the top of the Torre del Mangia extends over the city and the surrounding countryside. If you climb the 300 steps to the belfry you will be able to see the landscape featured in the *Good and Bad Government* ▲ *211* from the Palazzo Pubblico.

Other rooms of interest are the SALA DEL CONCISTORO, with its ceiling fresco by Domenico Beccafumi; the SALA DI BALIA fresco by Spinello Aretino (1407) with the *Storie di Papa Alessandro III*, and the SALA DEL RISORGIMENTO, with monumental murals by Pietro Aldi, Amos Cassioli and Cesare Maccari, dedicated to Vittorio Emanuele II. The LOGGIA DEI NOVE upstairs gives a panoramic view of the Val d'Arbia, the Val d'Orcia and Mount Amiata. The SIGNORI chapel, with a fresco by Taddeo di Bartolo (1407) of *Storie di Maria e Angeli Musicanti*, is lined along two walls with a wooden choir composed of twenty-two carved stalls decorated with intarsia work (1525–36) by Domenico di Niccolò. The ANTICAPPELLA also has frescos by Taddeo di Bartolo, *Virtù* and the *Uomini Illustri* cycle, as well as valuable objects in gold including the Golden Rose (1462) by Simone da Firenze, a gift to the city from Pope Pius II.

**TORRE DEL MANGIA.** This bell tower (1325–48) stands on the end of the left wing of the Palazzo Pubblico. It is crowned by a travertine belfry designed by Lippo Memmi to hold the *Campanone* (great bell), hung there in 1666. The bell is still used to celebrate special events and to mark key moments in the Palio.

**CAPPELLA DI PIAZZA.** Adjoining the Palazzo Pubblico, this chapel was built as an *ex voto* offering at the end of the plague in 1348 to a design by Domenico d'Agostino. Constructed in several stages, it was completed in 1468 by Antonio Federighi, who was responsible for the Renaissance crown.

**LOGGIA DELLA MERCANZIA.** This three-arched loggia supported by pilasters runs between the Campo and the Croce del Travaglio. Built between 1417 and 1428, it is one of the most elegant examples of the transition from Gothic to Renaissance style.

**VIA DI CITTÀ.** This still connects the Via Francigena ▲ *164* to the oldest part of Siena. It is lined with many fine buildings, such as the 14th-century PALAZZO PICCOLOMINI PATRIZI, seat of the Accademia degli Intronati and the PALAZZO CHIGI SARACINI, remodeled in the 18th century in early neo-Gothic style. This palace houses the ACCADEMIA MUSICALE

CHIGIANA, and has an important collection of paintings, sculptures, objects and furniture. Across the road stands the PALAZZO DELLE PAPESSE, designed by Rossellino for the sister of Pius II Piccolomini and completed in 1495, one of the few Sienese buildings in 'Florentine' style, with its broad rusticated façade. It now houses a Center of Contemporary Art. A little further on is the Gothic PALAZZO MARSILI, a typical example of a 15th-century nobleman's palace.

**DUOMO ● 78.** The cathedral of Santa Maria Assunta is one of the most outstanding monuments in Italy, even if its checkered past has in some ways undermined its stylistic unity. Many architects collaborated on this cathedral, including Andrea Pisano who created the wonderful lower section of the façade between 1285 and 1296. In the early 14th century the Sienese ambitiously decided to enlarge the already colossal structure on the side facing Via di Città, which would have made it the largest church in Christendom. However, the project had to be abandoned due to lack of space and the economic crisis caused by the plague of 1348. The gigantic skeleton of the so-called DUOMO NUOVO, its colonnade open to the sky, was left standing: an unfinished monument to an extraordinary idea. The interior of the Duomo is a glorious treasure-trove of art. Visitors will immediately be struck by the luminous striped columns that enhance the vast space. The PAVEMENT, illustrated with 56 scenes (1369–1547), boasts graffito and marble mosaic work by gifted artists such as Giovanni di Stefano, Antonio Federighi, Beccafumi and Francesco di Giorgio. The HIGH ALTAR (1532), designed by Baldassarre Peruzzi, is topped by a large CIBORIUM (1472) by Vecchietta and embellished with bronze angels by Francesco di Giorgio and Beccafumi. On the left-hand side is the famous octagonal PULPIT carved by Nicola Pisano, with his son Giovanni and Arnolfo di Cambio, between 1266 and 1268. The seven relief panels on the balustrade featuring the *Storie di Cristo* show remarkable craftsmanship and were to remain unrivaled until the masterpieces of the Renaissance. Off the left aisle is the entrance to the CHAPEL OF SAN GIOVANNI BATTISTA with the bronze statue of St John the Baptist (1457), a masterpiece by Donatello. Nearby is the entrance to the LIBRERIA PICCOLOMINI (detail of the marble group in the *Three Graces,* 3rd century, *right*), commissioned by Pope Pius III to celebrate the achievements of his uncle Enea Silvio Piccolomini, Pope Pius II. The great fresco cycle, in ten scenes, was commissioned from Pinturicchio, then at the height of his career, and completed between 1505 and 1507. The library houses some priceless illuminated codices.

**TWO WORLDS IN THE DUOMO ★**
Two elegant arches (1497) in the left-hand aisle of the Duomo serve as a doorway leading from the public Duomo into the Piccolomini Library, a private and totally secular space lavishly decorated with scenes celebrating the life of the Renaissance ruler.

# ▲ THE PALIO

**THE 'CONTRADE'**
The coats of arms of the *contrade* of
Tartuca, Istrice and Bruco.

which is extremely dangerous for both the horses and the jockeys who ride bareback, consists of three laps of the huge Piazza del Campo. This takes little more than a minute, but the celebrations can last for several days. The Palio is held on July 2 and August 16.

The Palio magically recreates the atmosphere of the medieval city, not only with the colors of the traditional costumes worn by the jockeys but by rekindling the partisan spirit and bitter rivalries between the old quarters or *contrade*. Only ten of the seventeen *contrade* can take part, each entering a horse and rider. The contest,

**THE 'CARROCCIO'**
The *carroccio* (chariot), drawn by oxen and escorted by the seven riders from the *contrade* who are not lucky enough to take part in the race, follows the parade into the Piazza del Campo. The *carroccio* bears the standard and 'palio', the so-called *cencio* (rag), that will be awarded to the winning *contrada*.

**'VA'E TORNA VINCITORE' (GO FORTH AN**
Before the race, in the local church of *contrada*, a priest blesses the horse, wh has been chosen by drawing lots, and jockey with holy water.

214

## A FRANTIC RACE

The three laps of the Piazza are completed at an incredible speed in little more than a minute. Particularly dangerous are the right angles at the downhill San Martino bend and the uphill Casato bend.

## RIDERLESS HORSES

Occasionally the jockey falls off or is unhorsed. The riderless horse continues to race and can win the Palio.

## GUEST OF HONOR

The victory celebrations are concluded with a great banquet: tables are set in the main street of the each *contrada* and thousands of people sit down to eat. At the place of honor is the horse, which is given its favorite fodder.

The squat building of the Spedale di Santa Maria della Scala (*above*). Pietro Lorenzetti, *Pala del Carmine* (1328–9), detail of the enthroned *Madonna*, Pinacoteca Nazionale (*above, right*).

**FRESCOS IN THE SALA DEL PELLEGRINAIO** ✪
The Sala del Pellegrinaio in Santa Maria della Scala, built in the second half of the 14th century and regarded as one of the most significant works of European hospital architecture, was embellished in the mid 15th century by a unique fresco cycle illustrating the hospital's activities and its treatment of the sick, the poor, pilgrims and orphans (the so-called *gettatelli* or 'little cast-offs'). Most of the frescos were executed (1440–3) by Domenico di Bartolo; the others are the work of Giovanni di Raffaele Navesi, Pietro d'Achille Crogi, Lorenzo Vecchietta and Priamo della Quercia.

**SPEDALE DI SANTA MARIA DELLA SCALA.** This hospital was originally built for travelers and pilgrims, and continued to provide some medical treatment until a few years ago. It is currently being restored to house a new museum, some of whose sections can already be visited, such as the MANTO CHAPEL, with frescos by Beccafumi, and the SACRESTIA VECCHIA, entirely painted by Vecchietta. The CHURCH OF THE SANTISSIMA ANNUNZIATA, with a magnificent fresco of the *Piscina Probatica* by Sebastiano Conca, and the MUSEO ARCHEOLOGICO are annexed to the hospital.

**PALAZZO REALE.** The right-hand side of the Piazza de Duomo is occupied by the massive palace built in the 16th century by the Medici to house the new governor just after the conquest of Siena: they did not think it expedient to use the existing Palazzo Pubblico, the symbol of Sienese liberty.

**MUSEO DELL'OPERA METROPOLITANA.** This is housed in one of the aisles of the Duomo Nuovo and has a rich collection of art works, most of them from the cathedral. The museum's true gem is the *Maestà* by Duccio di Buoninsegna, created for the Duomo's high altar between 1308 and 1311. The 'most beautiful work ever seen or created', according to a comment of the time, displays a typical formal composition featuring the enthroned *Madonna and Child* surrounded by a celestial band of angels and saints. On the reverse, Duccio depicted stories from the *Life and Passion of Christ*. The museum has many examples of Sienese painting and sculpture ranging from the 13th to the 18th century, including some wonderful statues from the façade of the cathedral and, in the Sala del Tesoro, a collection of gold objects and church ornaments.

**BAPTISTERY.** This is in the main body of the cathedral and, in addition to the fresco cycles that are thought to rank among the greatest achievements of 15th-century Siena (by Vecchietta), it contains a spectacular baptismal font. All the major Italian Renaissance sculptors contributed to this work, begun in 1416. The base is decorated with six bronze relief panels depicting the *Storie di San Giovanni Battista* by Jacopo della Quercia, Giovanni di Turino, Lorenzo Ghiberti and Donatello and six statues, also in gilt bronze, representing *Le Virtù*, by Donatello, Giovanni di Turino and Goro di Neroccio.

**PALAZZO DEL MAGNIFICO.** Commissioned by Pandolfo Petrucci, *signore* of Siena from 1487 to 1512, this palace, recently restored, had all the sophisticated trappings of an important ruler. Artists such as Pinturicchio, Luca Signorelli, Girolamo Genga and Beccafumi decorated the palace while Cozzarelli was commissioned to make the extraordinary ornamental rings and torch-holders on the façade. Unfortunately, the palace has been stripped of its treasures and its frescos are now in museums all over the world.

**PANDOLFO PETRUCCI**
According to Niccolò Machiavelli, Pandolfo was the epitome of the tyrannical Renaissance *signore*, who skillfully combined cruelty with political and diplomatic acumen. He was a 'fox and a lion' rolled into one. He succeeded in bringing Siena under his dominion and did not hesitate to murder his father-in-law who wanted him to put a stop to his dark machinations. However, his son did not possess the same talents or good luck: just after his father's death, he was exiled from Siena and the democratic form of government was reinstated.

**PINACOTECA NAZIONALE.** This gallery is housed in the 15th-century Palazzo Buonsignori which was converted to Gothic style in the 19th century. It is a must for anyone interested in Sienese painting from the late 12th century to the 17th century and contains the largest collection of gold-background paintings in the world. The collection includes works by Guido da Siena, Duccio himself (*Madonna dei Francescani*), Simone Martini (*Il Beato Agostino Novello e Quattro Suoi Miracoli*, 1330 ▲ *219*), Pietro Lorenzetti (*Pala del Carmine*, 1329) and the exponents of the Sienese Renaissance, such as Sassetta (six panels from the lost *Pala dell'Arte della Lana*) and Giovanni di Paolo (*Madonna dell'Umiltà*). Subsequent periods are also well represented with works by Francesco di Giorgio, Matteo di Giovanni, Sano di Pietro, Sodoma, Beccafumi, the baroque painters Vanni and Salimbeni and the eclectic Rutilio Manetti. In all, the collection presents a comprehensive overview of the development of Sienese art.

**CHURCH OF SANT'AGOSTINO.** The interior of this church, which is Gothic in origin, was rebuilt by Vanvitelli after a fire in the mid 18th century. A neoclassical portal was added in the early 19th century by the architect Agostino Fantastici. It contains important paintings by Francesco di Giorgio, Luca Signorelli, Francesco Vanni, Carlo Maratta and a *Crucifixion* by Pietro Perugino. The adjacent PICCOLOMINI CHAPEL contains a *Maestà* fresco by Ambrogio Lorenzetti and a lovely *Epiphany* (1535), a masterpiece by Sodoma.

**ACCADEMIA DEI FISIOCRITICI.** This academy, situated in nearby Via Mattioli, houses the Museo Naturalistico, which boasts a rich collection of paleontological, geological and zoological finds, and the Orto Botanico (Botanical Garden).

**SAN NICCOLÒ AL CARMINE.** This church stands opposite the Piano de' Mantellini. Its important works include the altarpiece by Domenico Beccafumi featuring *San Michele Che Scaccia gli Angeli Ribelli*, the second version of a work regarded by the Carmelites as improper.

Donatello, *Faith*, a bronze for the baptismal font in the baptistery.

217

Three saints in adoration of the Virgin,
detail of the *Maestà* by Duccio.

Florence was the capital of figurative art
during the Middle Ages, with artists such
as the sublime, innovative Giotto. But
Siena in the same period could pride itself
on at least four major artists, all of whom
were able to help consolidate the
supremacy of Tuscan art and boost its reputation in years to
come. Artists such as Duccio di Buoninsegna, Simone Martini
and the brothers Ambrogio and Pietro Lorenzetti developed
a new visual language that was to leave its stamp on the entire
14th century: one outcome of the harmonious understanding
that existed between skilled artists and their clients,
who were well aware of the historical role they were
playing. It is not surprising that this style of painting
was not transcended but copied, remaining unrivaled
until the discovery of the laws of perspective and
Masaccio's revolutionary work.

**MEMMO DI FILIPPUCCIO AND LIPPO MEMMI,** *Maestà*
Son of Memmo di Filippuccio, whose *Maestà* (1317) he
finished for the Palazzo Pubblico in San Gimignano
(*above*), Lippo Memmi was the brother-in-law of Simone
Martini. Memmo di Filippuccio copied young Simone's
painting in the Palazzo Pubblico in Siena (*below*), when
painting his *Maestà* in San Gimignano.

**TWO CONTRASTING
'MAESTÀS'**
Although
stylistically
very different,
the two virtually
contemporary
*Maestà*s by Duccio
(*right*) and Martini
(*below left*),
painted between
1308 and 1315,
confirmed the importance of
Siena painting. In fact, from his
first work Martini had introduced
new stylistic elements with a view
to transcending the problems
posed by the still prevalent
Byzantine style and emulating the
new Gothic vocabulary used in
the cathedrals and courts of
Northern Europe.

**SIMONE MARTINI,** *Beato Agostino Novello and Four of His Miracles*
The formal elegance of this painting subsequently led to the international Gothic style as a result of the influence exerted by Simone Martini, who was active at the Papal court in Avignon in the 1430s. Another interesting feature of this painting, now in the Museo dell'Opera Metropolitana, is the painter's choice of realistic subjects: he shows scenes of everyday life taking place in well-known and easily recognizable places in Siena.

**PIETRO LORENZETTI,** *Deposition from the Cross*
The Lorenzetti brothers were close in style to Giotto, whose language they assimilated, producing some individual works. Pietro, who was summoned to Assisi, painted this *Deposition from the Cross* (c. 1325) in the Basilica Inferiore. His dramatic portrayal of the anguish suffered by the mourners clustered around Christ's body amounts to an in-depth psychological analysis of the characters.

**AMBROGIO LORENZETTI,** *Annunciation*
His works transmit a tangible, calm view of life. In the *Annunciation* in Siena's Pinacoteca Nazionale, the Madonna, far from being surprised by the divine annunciation, seems quite aware of the task that awaits her.

**ST CATHERINE
OF SIENA**
Caterina Benincasa,
daughter of Jacopo
the wool-dyer, was
born in 1347. At the
age of sixteen she
took the veil and
entered the
Dominican order.
She was renowned
for her determined
approach to solving
the church's pressing
problems. She
succeeded in
convincing Pope
Gregory XI to move
the seat of the papacy
from Avignon back
to Rome. She died
at the age of thirty-
three, having received
the stigmata. She is
the patron saint of
Italy and Europe.

Andrea Vanni,
*St Catherine of Siena*,
church of
San Domenico.

**FONTE BRANDA**
This is the oldest
monumental fountain
in Siena. Dating from
the end of 1081, it
was remodeled in
1246 with three large
pointed arches
topped by
crenelations. Nearby
is Via della Galluzza,
one of the most
picturesque medieval
streets in Siena with
its distinctive
suspended arches.

# THE TERZO DI CAMOLLIA

This area covers the north of the city, where architectural
changes were made in the 19th and 20th centuries. It contains
various monuments to saints Catherine and Bernardino.

**ACCADEMIA DEI ROZZI.** Founded in 1531 by educated members
of the artisan classes, this academy has a fine theater,
designed by Alessandro Doveri in the early 19th century and
later enlarged by Augusto Corbi.

**COMPLESSO DI SANTA CATERINA.** Soon after her canonization
(1461) a sanctuary to Catherine was built in Fontebranda, in
the house where she was born. The oratory, built by Antonio
Federighi and Urbano da Cortona, among others, contains a
16th-century fresco cycle illustrating the saint's life (with work
by Sodoma) and a polychromatic wooden statue carved by
Neroccio di Bartolomeo in 1474.

**BASILICA OF SAN DOMENICO.** This church is perched on
the precipitous escarpment that plunges down into the
Fontebranda valley. Pure Gothic in style, despite the
remodeling of the bell tower, its CHAPEL OF SANTA CATERINA
contains a reliquary of the saint's head and some wonderful
paintings by Sodoma (*Svenimento ed Estasi di Santa Caterina*,
1526) and Francesco di Giorgio (*Adorazione dei Pastori*, 1480).

**VIA BANCHI DI SOPRA.** Siena's main street is lined with palaces
built by important families, such as the ancient PALAZZO
TOLOMEI ● *66*, which has lovely, intricate windows on the
front. This was the home of the Pia immortalized by Dante in
the *Purgatorio*. The palazzos SALIMBENI, SPANNOCCHI and
TANTUCCI are now the headquarters of the MONTE DEI PASCHI,
the oldest bank in Italy, founded in 1472 by the Sienese
government to oppose the practice of usury.

**MEDICI FORTRESS OR FORTEZZA DI SANTA BARBARA.** This
quadrangular fortress with four enormous bastions, an
impressive symbol of Florentine domination, was
commissioned by Cosimo I from Baldassarre Lanci, an
architect from Urbino, in 1560. It houses the ENOTECA
ITALIANA, founded to promote the best wines in Italy.

**VIA DI CAMOLLIA.** The heart of the *contrada* of Istrice, this
road follows the route of the Via Francigena; it is lined with
old churches such as that of SAN PIETRO ALLA MAGIONE, as
well as SANTA MARIA IN FONTEGIUSTA, built between 1482 and

1484 as an *ex voto* offering
after the battle of Poggio
Imperiale. The road ends
at the magnificent PORTA
CAMOLLIA, which is famous
for its inscription: *Cor magis
tibi Sena pandit* (Wider than
her gates Siena will open her
heart to you), a true symbol
of Sienese hospitality.

**CHURCH OF SAN FRANCESCO.**
This Gothic basilica has often
been remodeled, but it still
has some frescos by
Ambrogio Lorenzetti of
the *Storie Francescane*
and a *Crucifixion* by his
brother Pietro.

**CHURCH OF SANTA MARIA DI PROVENZANO.** In the late 16th century the new church was built to house a miraculous Madonna, a symbol of Sienese opposition to the Spanish domination. Designed by Damiano Schifardini, it shows the influence of Roman contemporary architecture and possesses some interesting works of art. The annual Palio on July 2 is raced in honor of the Madonna di Provenzano.

## THE TERZO DI SAN MARTINO

The Terzo di San Martino extends eastward from the Campo to the Porta Romana.

**PALAZZO PICCOLOMINI.** Designed by Rossellino in Renaissance style for Pope Pius II, faced with gigantic blocks of ashlar, it is now the home of city offices, including the State Archive, which exhibits the unique RACCOLTA DELLE TAVOLETTE DI BICCHERNA and various documents concerning people and events recorded in Dante's *Divine Comedy*.

**VIA DI PANTANETO.** The road is lined with impressive palaces and the baroque CHURCH OF SAN GIORGIO. Over the so-called Roman Bridge, you will come to the 19th-century PALAZZO BIANCHI, which contains some neoclassical frescos. This is also the site of the 15th-century PALAZZO DI SAN GALGANO and the CHURCH OF SAN RAIMONDO AL REFUGIO, commissioned by Pope Alexander VII and reminiscent of Bernini's style.

**PORTA ROMANA.** This is the largest gate in Siena's city walls. In the piazza in front of it stands the MUSEO DELLA SOCIETÀ DI ESECUTORI DI PIE DISPOSIZIONI which possesses a remarkable collection of art works by Sienese artists from various periods.

**CHURCH OF SANTA MARIA DEI SERVI.** This is one of the city's most important churches. The façade has never been completed, but it is the interior that is significant, supported by two rows of columns and embellished by various works of art. These include the ancient *Madonna del Bordone* by Coppo di Marcovaldo and works by Matteo di Giovanni, Giovanni di Paolo and Ambrogio and Pietro Lorenzetti.

**CHURCH OF SAN MARTINO.** Rebuilt in 1537, this has a beautiful façade dating from 1613, the work of Giovanni Fontana. The interior contains works by Guido Reni (*Circoncisione*, 1636), Guercino and Domenico Beccafumi (*Natività*).

**ORATORIO DI SAN BERNARDINO**
Erected in the 15th century on the site where the saint used to preach, this oratory houses the new Museo Diocesano. Its upper chapel contains frescos by the most renowned 16th-century Sienese painters: Domenico Beccafumi, Sodoma and Girolamo del Pacchia.

**RACCOLTA DELLE TAVOLETTE DI BICCHERNA ✪**
This is a collection of *tavolette* elegantly painted by the best Sienese painters. They were used, from 1258 to 1682, as the covers of the account books of the *Biccherna* (revenue office) and the *Gabella* (tax office). Each *tavoletta* depicts a sacred scene or a key event of the period.

221

The cloister and church of the Certosa di Pontignano (*top*). The hermitage of Lecceto (*above*).

**THE MUSEO AURELIO CASTELLI**
The musuem, housed in the Convento dell'Osservanza, has a collection from the church and monastery: paintings, sculptures, seals, choir books and incunabula. There is a fine reliquary of San Bernardino by Francesco d'Antonio (15th century).

**CASTELLO DI BELCARO**
The road through the rolling hills of the Montagnola Sienese brings you to this medieval castle standing in the midst of a splendid park. It was remodeled in the 16th century by Baldassarre Peruzzi, then 'restored' in 1868 by Giuseppe Partini.

## NORTH OF SIENA

The three ancient suburbs of Masse di Siena that used to form a natural extension of the city's *Terzi* lie within a fascinating landscape. Although heavily urbanized, their layout has remained virtually unchanged for centuries, with clusters of houses gathered around religious buildings and manor houses. You can enjoy a view of Siena's unmistakable cityscape from anywhere in the surrounding hills and there are many architectural monuments in the immediate vicinity.
**CONVENTO DELL'OSSERVANZA.** This monastery was founded by Bernardino da Siena on the Capriola hillside, the site of an ancient hermitage. Rebuilt after World War Two using surviving material, the church (1474–90) contains some important works of art, including terracottas by Andrea della Robbia and the *Madonna e i Santi Ambrogio e Girolamo*, a triptych by the Maestro dell'Osservanza.
**CERTOSA DI PONTIGNANO.** This Carthusian monastery, a 16th-century structure with three cloisters, stands on a hillside in Chianti. The church is rich in frescos by Bernardino Poccetti and Orazio Porta. The wooden choir by Atticciati (late 16th century) is particularly fine. The complex now houses various activity centers and halls of residence belonging to the University of Siena.

## SOUTH OF SIENA

**THE HERMITAGE OF LECCETO.** The dense surrounding woodland barely allows a glimpse of this extremely old hermitage with the turreted profile of a fortified monastery. Possibly founded in the 4th century and dissolved in 1810, it flourished again as an Augustinian monastery and is still dedicated to that order. Its CHURCH contains an extensive series of frescos by Sienese painters from the 14th and 15th centuries, such as Ambrogio Lorenzetti, Pietro di Giovanni d'Ambrogio. There are two cloisters in the complex, one dating from the 13th century and the other from the 15th century, with fragments of frescos painted in terre-verte on the walls.
**SAN LEONARDO AL LAGO.** San Leonardo al Lago is also found on the wooded slopes of the Montagnola Sienese. This Romanesque-Gothic CHURCH with its simple yet stately façade contains frescos of the *Storie della Vergine* (1360–70), a masterpiece by Lippo Vanni, Pietro Lorenzetti's star pupil and, in the adjoining refectory, extensive fragments of a monumental *Crucifixion* by Giovanni di Paolo.

# Around Siena

**THE COLORFUL PROVINCE OF SIENA** ✪

Siena is clothed in colors that span the centuries. Traveling through its towns and countryside you can tell which season it is just by looking at the colors. Endless green sweeps over the fields, surrounded by the sandy hills whose ocher color is now known as 'raw sienna'. The gold of arid summer follows the emerald green of spring, forming a backdrop for the red bricks of the city where the Palio is held.

Telemaco Signorini (1835–1901), *Autunno nella campagna di Siena*.

Siena epitomizes the diversity of landscape that characterizes Tuscany. The rolling countryside through which the province extends has many different faces, ranging from the lush hills of Chianti to the cultivated plains of the Val d'Arbia and the reclaimed Valdichiana, from the barren hillocks of Le Crete that gradually slope down toward the wooded Maremma to the cultivated heights of the Montagnola Sienese and Mount Amiata. A visit to the province is a constant delight, filled with surprises at every turn. And when, in the evening, you are marveling at how much you have seen in a single day, a church in isolated countryside or the rose window of a Gothic façade will suddenly appear, arousing new interest and excitement before you go on to savor the pleasures of simple, traditional fare.

## FROM SIENA TO SAN GALGANO ◆ **D** D1-E2 **C** A4-B4

Like Siena, the territory of the Val d'Elsa owed its growth to the Via Francigena, the road to Rome whose route varied depending on the historical period, deciding the shifting fortunes of the various towns.

**MONTERIGGIONI** ● *68* (*above*). Built by the Sienese in 1203 as the principal military stronghold guarding the border against Florence, it is defended by a circle of walls with fourteen embattled towers, likened by Dante Alighieri to giants in his *Inferno*. The massive hilltop fortification protects the perfectly preserved hamlet with its Romanesque-Gothic CHURCH OF SANTA MARIA. On the hillside, built on a patch of land among the marshes, stands the thousand-year-old ABBADIA ISOLA with the Romanesque church of San Salvatore.

**POGGIBONSI.** Some 19 miles north of Siena, Poggibonsi is the largest industrial town in the entire Val d'Elsa. It is fairly modern due to extensive rebuilding after taking heavy damage during World War Two, with few significant monuments except for the COLLEGIATA and the PALAZZO PRETORIO. However, the abundance of interesting sites in the surrounding countryside more than makes up for this. On the hill of Poggio Imperiale, with the remains of the Rocca (1488), commissioned by Lorenzo the Magnificent from Giuliano da Sangallo but never completed, stands the CONVENTO DI SAN LUCCHESE, apparently built after a visit by St Francis (1213). Its importance can be seen by the quality of the works inside the church: these include an outstanding painting by Memmo di Filipuccio (late 13th century) and a della Robbia altarpiece from 1514. There are some important frescos featuring the *Storie di Santo Stefano* (1388) by the Florentine Cennino Cennini, whose 14th-century *Craftsmen's Handbook* on painting techniques is more famous than his few known works. The nearby 15th-century SANTUARIO DEL ROMITUZZO contains an incredible number of *ex voto* offerings.

**SAN GIMIGNANO** ● *63*. This is one of the most famous cities in the world both for its medieval appearance – fifteen of its original seventy-two towers remain – and for the vast number of art works contained in its churches, palaces and museums. Entirely enclosed within its walls, its main monuments are found along the straight road of the Via Francigena and around the Piazza del Duomo, which is at the highest point in the city.

**THE MUSEO DI STAGGIA**
Head along the present Via Cassia after Castiglionalto, the vantage point from where, as Dante recorded, the Sienese Sapia Salvani watched complacently as his fellow citizens were routed after the battle of Colle (1269). You will come to Staggia, with its mighty ruined castle. The church of Santa Maria Assunta now houses an important small museum with works by Pollaiolo (*Assunzione di Santa Maria Egiziaca, above*) and some remarkable works by Sienese goldsmiths.

**THE MEDIEVAL CITY AND ITS TOWERS**
In the medieval city, every family wanted to flaunt its social status, setting itself above the rest. Strict laws generally prohibited or limited the wearing of costly garments or jewels, just as early city planning regulations imposed boundaries within which buildings had to be constructed. Families therefore vied with each other to build the highest tower, although they were not permitted to equal the height of civic towers. This competition resulted in the creation of cities dotted with vertical structures that were the outward signs of affluence.

**SAN GIMIGNANO AND ITS PIAZZAS** ✪
Linked by a passageway to the Piazza del Duomo, with which it forms a harmonious whole, the triangular Piazza della Cisterna is paved with brick in a herringbone pattern. At the center of this piazza bordered by medieval tower houses stands the well from which it derives its name.

**THE TREASURES OF THE COLLEGIATA**
The collegiata, which has a nave and two aisles, houses some remarkable fresco cycles from the 14th and 15th centuries by Taddeo di Bartolo (*Giudizio Universale, Paradiso* and *Inferno*), Benozzo Gozzoli (*Martirio di San Sebastiano*), Bartolo di Fredi (*Vecchio Testamento*) and scenes from the *New Testament*, for a long time attributed to Barna da Siena, then ascribed to Simone Martini's workshop, perhaps his brother-in-law Federico Memmi, assisted by his brother Lippo.

The COLLEGIATA (cathedral) has a simple original Romanesque façade although it was enlarged in 1460 by Giuliano da Maiano. Inside, the magnificent CHAPEL OF SANTA FINA, a masterpiece of Tuscan Renaissance architecture by Benedetto and Giuliano da Maiano, is decorated with important frescos by Ghirlandaio (*above, right*) illustrating stories from the life of St Fina who died in 1523 at the age of fifteen and is now patron saint of San Gimignano. The Piazza del Duomo is also bordered by the PALAZZO DEL POPOLO, built in the late 13th century together with the Torre Grossa. This building is still used for the city offices and since 1852 has also housed the MUSEO CIVICO in its upper rooms, reached through a spacious courtyard. In the Sala di Dante, so-named because the illustrious poet gave a speech here in 1300 in defense of the Guelph cause, there is a famous fresco by Lippo Memmi depicting the *Maestà* (1317) ▲ *218*, which is very similar to the one painted by Simone Martini in Siena's Palazzo Pubblico. The only difference is the addition of the donor, Nello di Mino de' Tolomei, depicted kneeling before the Virgin. The adjacent picture gallery has a rich collection of paintings by various artists, both Sienese (Memmo di Filippuccio, Niccolò di Ser Sozzo, Taddeo di Bartolo) and Florentine (Benozzo Gozzoli, Domenico di Michelino, Filippino Lippi).

In the adjoining Camera del Podestà, you can admire a unique secular fresco cycle illustrating the ups and downs of a young man's initiation into the mysteries of love by Memmo di Filippuccio (early 14th century). The CHURCH OF SANT'AGOSTINO stands on the piazza of the same name. It has a simple exterior with a single portal and Gothic windows along the sides. On the high altar is an altarpiece depicting the *Coronation of the Virgin with Saints and Musician Angels*, a masterpiece by Piero Pollaiolo (1483), although the most striking work is the fresco cycle illustrating the *Life of St Augustine*, painted by Benozzo Gozzoli and his assistants between 1464 and 1465. Particularly noteworthy in the environs of San Gimignano is the CHURCH OF SANTA MARIA A CELLOLE, in a glorious setting and decorated with some beautiful sculptures.

**COLLE DI VAL D'ELSA.** This ancient town, about 6 miles south of Poggibonsi, has managed to carve out a reputation for itself in a number of fields throughout the ages. Although in past centuries it played a leading role in the production of quality paper, exported throughout Europe, it is now a flourishing center for the production of fine glass and crystal. The lower part of the town, which has expanded over recent years because of the high level of industrialization, lies below the historical part of the town (Colle Alta). Situated outside the ancient ring of walls, the CHURCH OF SANT'AGOSTINO (13th century) contains 16th-century works by Ridolfo Ghirlandaio, Cigoli and Giovanni Battista Paggi. The old part of the town is reached by taking the steep road through the Porta Guelfa. This will bring you to the Borgo del Castello, the site of the Palazzo Pretorio with the MUSEO ARCHEOLOGICO RANUCCIO

**MUSEO CIVICO AND MUSEO D'ARTE SACRA IN COLLE DI VAL D'ELSA**
These museums house works of key importance such as the *Maestà* by the 13th-century Maestro di Badia a Isola, and the extremely rare *Tesoro di Galognano*, eucharistic vessels from the 6th century. The polychromatic wooden crucifix by Marco Romano is particularly fine.

BIANCHI BANDINELLI, and the DUOMO, which has a neoclassical façade by Agostino Fantastaci. The ancient Palazzo dei Priori has recently been converted to house the MUSEO CIVICO and the MUSEO D'ARTE SACRA. The 16th-century PALAZZO CAMPANA, separated from the rest of the city by a narrow bridge, leads into the district of the Borgo, with the CHURCH OF SANTA CATERINA and the CONVENTO DI SAN FRANCESCO. There are some interesting churches between Colle and Casole d'Elsa including the BADIA A CONEO, a fine example of Sienese Romanesque architecture.
**CASOLE D'ELSA.** This small yet picturesque hamlet is famous for the Palio delle Contrade, the most popular event in the province after the one held in Siena. In the piazza stands the CATHEDRAL which acquired its present appearance in the 15th century. It houses two extremely important funerary monuments: that of Beltramo Aringhieri del Porrina, a masterpiece by Marco Romano (early 14th century) and that of Bishop Tommaso Andrei by Gano da Siena, as well as a glazed terracotta altarpiece by Andrea della Robbia. Adjacent buildings house the MUSEO ARCHEOLOGICO E DELLA COLLEGIATA (part of the network of provincial museums) with works by Sienese and Florentine artists as well as elegant silverware and archeological finds from all over the province.

**TOMB OF THE CALISNA SEPU**
This is one of the largest Etruscan funerary complexes dating from the Hellenistic period. Some of the finds are on display at the Museo Archeologico.

**THE TOWER HOUSE OF ARNOLFO DI CAMBIO**
In Colle Alta, which still retains its medieval appearance, there are many minor residences and stately houses. Be sure to see the beautiful tower fortress of Arnolfo di Cambio, the architect and sculptor born in Colle c. 1245.

The sword that according to legend was plunged
into the rock by St Galgano (*below*).

**A STONE SKELETON**
The Abbey of San
Galgano is an
enjoyable place to
visit in the environs of
Siena. This roofless
structure is the
skeleton of a building
that is still very
beautiful (*right*). The
isolated ruins afford
the opportunity to
explore one of the
most beautiful and
unspoiled areas of
countryside in Italy.

At the end of the main street stands the Sienese FORTRESS
(14th century). The original structure is more or less intact
and is now used as the town hall. Leaving Casole, the road
winds its way through a picturesque valley and large towns
like MENSANO, RADICONDOLI and BELFORTE toward the
Metal Hills that stand before the Maremma.

**ABBEY OF SAN GALGANO ● 79.** Heading south along the
Roccastrada highway, about 12 miles below Siena you will
come to this early 12th-century abbey, a rare example of
Cistercian architecture in Italy and the only one in Tuscany.
Even older is the CHAPEL OF SAN GALGANO, on nearby
Mount Siepi. It was built by the nobleman Galgano Guidotti,
who withdrew to this region in 1180 to lead a life of penitence
(he was canonized in 1185).
The small Romanesque chapel
has an unusual cylindrical shape
with a semicircular apse.
As well as a famous sword
imprisoned in its rock, the chapel
contains frescos by Ambrogio
Lorenzetti (*Madonna and
Child, Stories from the Life of Saint
Galgano*) which, although not
perfectly preserved, are still visible.

**LE CRETE ★**
The landscape of the
Sienese Crete is

extremely unusual,
characterized by
dramatic bare hillocks
alternating with chalk
cliffs covered by
sparse vegetation.
The best time to visit
this area is in the
spring when the
flowers are in bloom
or in the summer
when it becomes a
real desert. The area
of Le Crete near
San Giovanni d'Asso
is also famous as the
home of the truffle.
In the fall, after the
harvest, a massive
market and fair is
held here.

## FROM SIENA TO CHIUSI ◆ C B4-C5-D6

To the south of Siena lies the territory of the ancient Republic
of Siena. Although, as a result of the centuries-old rivalry
between Florence and Siena, the towns between the two cities
were always bitterly disputed and subject to frequent changes
of leadership, the absence of any powerful rivals to the south
of the city allowed the Sienese state to spread as far as the
borders of Umbria and Lazio.

**ASCIANO.** About 25 miles southeast of Siena, Asciano is
regarded as the chief town in the region of Le Crete: it was an
important town in the Etruscan and Roman periods and in the
Middle Ages. As well as the TORRE CIVICA, the
Romanesque BASILICA OF SANT'AGATA and the CHURCH OF
SAN FRANCESCO, there is the interesting CASA CORBOLI that
contains a secular fresco cycle, reminiscent of the style of
Ambrogio Lorenzetti. These works include a particularly
outstanding painting of *La Natività di Maria*, attributed to the

Maestro dell'Osservanza, which is a masterpiece of 15th-century Sienese painting. In the town center, the MUSEO CASSIOLI shows works by Amos Cassioli (1832–91).

**ABBEY OF MONTE OLIVETO MAGGIORE.** This important abbey, 12 miles from Asciano, was founded in 1313 by the nobleman Bernardo Tolomei di Siena who withdrew to this secluded spot to lead a life of prayer. The main attraction of the abbey is its gorgeous setting in the lee of an enormous sandy hill, sheltered by centuries-old cypress trees, that cluster around the massive complex, virtually hiding it from sight. The abbey is a single building constructed around three cloisters. The CHIOSTRO GRANDE houses frescos ▲ 230 by Sodoma and Signorelli, depicting scenes from the life of St Benedict. In the main building is the CHURCH which, as well as some noteworthy paintings by Sodoma, boasts a carved wooden intarsia choir by Giovanni da Verona. On the upper floors there is a well-stocked LIBRARY and the PHARMACY, that now houses a rich collection of antique ceramic vases.

**BUONCONVENTO.** This town is situated on the old Via Francigena, enclosed by high walls. The PORTA SENESE leads into the main street with the PALAZZO RICCI, decorated with Art Nouveau ornaments, unusual in Siena. The palace houses the MUSEO D'ARTE SACRA DELLA VAL D'ARBIA, worth visiting for the collection of gold objects from churches in the area.

**MONTALCINO.** Overlooking the Via Cassia stands the hill town of Montalcino, the arena of many clashes due to its strategic position on the Via Francigena. It is now famous for the production of its Brunello wine. The center of this walled town is the Piazza del Popolo, the site of the PALAZZO DEI PRIORI with its fine loggia. It is dominated by the impressive tall tower of the 14th-century ROCCA, whose pioneering design heralded the new style of Renaissance military architecture. The complex of Sant'Agostino houses the new MUSEO CIVICO E DIOCESANO D'ARTE SACRA (*Vergine Annunciata*, 1369, *right*) with works mainly by Sienese painters. The DUOMO, with its neoclassical façade (1818–32), has some fine paintings by Francesco Vanni (late 16th century).

**ABBEY OF SANT'ANTIMO ● 77.** Founded, according to legend, by Charlemagne, this abbey was so wealthy and important in the Middle Ages that it entered into dispute with Siena over the control of its extensive lands. The church was built in the 12th century in Romanesque style prefiguring several themes in Cistercian architecture; the onyx and alabaster ornamentation imbues the church with a golden aura that, together with the unusual, somewhat disturbing decorative panels on the façade, is extremely atmospheric. The interior is divided into a nave and two aisles by tall columns. Those in the side aisles are surmounted by women's galleries with two-light windows. Note the beautiful capitals, many of which are made of onyx.

When Giovanni Antonio Bazzi (1477–1549), who was known as Sodoma (the Sodomite) because of his eccentric behavior, was asked to paint Beato Bernardo Tolomei, one of the famous Sienese saints featured in the Sala del Mappamondo in the Palazzo Pubblico ▲ 211, it is likely that he performed his task with particular care and gratitude because he owed his success to the monks. They had taken him in as a young man, fresh from his apprenticeship in Vercelli and Milan, and commissioned him to carry out the decoration of the chapel at Sant'Anna in Camprena ▲ 233 near Pienza. From then on, except for a Roman interlude brought to an end by the arrival of Raphael, Sodoma worked entirely in Siena, where he decorated some of the most prestigious buildings in the city. In 1506, Sodoma was summoned to enhance the glory of Monte Oliveto Maggiore ▲ 229, founded by the nobleman Tolomei. The artist was given the task of completing the work left unfinished by Signorelli in the Great Cloister of the monastery. The result is one of the finest achievements in the history of 16th-century Tuscan painting and, by extension, in the history of Western art.

### THE GREAT CLOISTER
This rectangular cloister was built between 1426 and 1433. The portico, protected by panes of glass, is decorated with frescos of scenes from the *Life of St Benedict*, as told by Saint Gregory. The Great Cloister is the most impressive space in the entire abbey complex, built on the estate of the Sienese nobleman, Bernardo Tolomei.

### LUCA SIGNORELLI, *Benedict Recognizes and Welcomes Totila*
The magnificent cycle of the stories from the life of Saint Benedict was begun by Luca Signorelli in 1497. It is not known why the master from Cortona did not start with scenes from the saint's early life, as St Gregory did in his narrative, unless one accepts the theory that the early scenes were done by a mediocre painter then painted over by Sodoma. Another mystery is why Signorelli, who began work with great enthusiasm, resigned and gave up the job, although this may have been under pressure from the monks, who had commissioned him to paint frescos in their magnificent Duomo. Nevertheless, in the scenes he painted he displays a lively narrative flair, particularly in this one where Totila is recognized.

**SODOMA,** *How the Devil Breaks the Bell*
The demon uses a rock to break the little bell
that signals the arrival of Benedict's food.

**SODOMA,** *Florenzo Sends a Group of Loose
Women to the Monastery*
Two distinct groups are seen against the
backdrop of a building.

**SODOMA,** *How Benedict Builds
Twelve Monasteries*
A scene of great industry in which the natural
landscape forms a harmonious counterpoint
to the architectural
landscape.

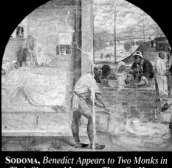

**SODOMA,** *Benedict Appears to Two Monks in
Their Sleep and Instructs Them On How to
Build a Monastery*
This scene depicts two different time frames:
on the left, the saint appears
in a dream; on the right,
the work is being
carried out.

**The prophet of Mount Amiata**
Born in Arcidosso to a humble family, Davide Lazzaretti (1834–78) worked as a carter before undergoing a spiritual crisis. He founded the Chiesa dei Giurisdavidici, a community that had a large following on Mount Amiata in the 19th century and even today boasts a certain number of supporters. The basic socialist and communitarian principles of the Giurisdavidici inevitably aroused the mistrust and suspicion of the established authorities who strongly opposed the movement. As a result, Lazzaretti was murdered with some of his companions on a march to the gates of Arcidosso.

**Abbadia San Salvatore.** The historical capital of Mount Amiata, this town sprang up around the early medieval abbey which was very powerful and owned large tracts of territory in southern Tuscany and northern Lazio. The abbey, in the town center, is Romanesque in style, although of Lombard origin. It contains a wooden crucifix reputedly presented to the Lombard king Rachis, but which dates from the 12th century. The central crypt, surrounded by beautiful columns, belongs to the original nucleus of the church. A small museum has a collection of ancient sacred objects and vestments.

**Piancastagnaio.** In a commanding position overlooking the Paglia valley, this town has two distinctive buildings: the mighty 13th–14th century Rocca degli Aldobrandeschi and the Mannerist Palazzo Bourbon Del Monte.

**Arcidosso.** To the west of Piancastagnaio, Arcidosso is an ancient hamlet that still has some narrow medieval streets and an impressive Rocca Aldobrandesca. The church of San Leonardo houses an interesting *Decollazione* (1589) by Francesco Vanni. In the immediate vicinity are the Pieve ad Lamulas, founded before AD 1000, and Monte Labbro, the site of the remains of the Chiesa Giurisdavidica built by the prophet Davide Lazzaretti.

**Castel del Piano.** This nearby town has the beautiful church of Santi Niccolò e Lucia, with paintings by Giuseppe Nicola and Francesco Nasini, who were born here, but worked in many churches in Amiata and Siena in the 17th century.

**San Quirico d'Orcia.** Heading back toward Siena, you will come to this ancient town on the Via Francigena, fortified by the Sienese in the 12th century. At the entrance to the town stands the Cathedral, rebuilt in Romanesque style at the end of the 12th century. The magnificent portal (1080) is decorated with columns and zoomorphic motifs. The side portal is supported by large caryatids standing on lions, attributed to the school of Giovanni Pisano. The interior contains a fine wooden choir by Antonio Barili (late 15th century). Behind the cathedral lies the splendid PALAZZO CHIGI, built for Cardinal Flavio Chigi by Carlo Fontana in the late 17th century. On the main street you can visit the HORTI LEONINI, a magnificent garden designed by Diomede Leoni in the mid 16th century.

**PIENZA** ● *69.* Still on the hills bordering the old Via Francigena lies Pienza (*top left*), named after Pope Pius II Piccolomini, who was born in the small town of Corsignano and was responsible for its transformation. The great architect Bernardo Rossellino accomplished one of the finest examples of 15th-century city planning here, redeveloping the city center without destroying the original medieval layout. The CATHEDRAL's façade is divided into three sections by sturdy pilasters and shows the influence of Alberti (Leon Battista Alberti was the originator of this model). It contains some important works including the altarpiece by Matteo di Giovanni and the *Assunzione*, a masterpiece by Vecchietta. The PALAZZO VESCOVILE houses the new MUSEO DIOCESANO, packed with noteworthy works including a *Madonna and Child* by Pietro Lorenzetti, the altarpiece by Vecchietta from the Spedaletto and the cope of Pius II, given to the pope by Tommaso Paleologo. There are also some important sculptures (Francesco di Giorgio) and some elegant works in gold. Along one side of the Piazza Pio II stands the massive PALAZZO PICCOLOMINI, entirely faced with ashlar.

**MONTEPULCIANO.** Continuing eastward will bring you to Montepulciano, extensively redesigned by the Florentine architect Michelozzo in the Renaissance. Some outstanding buildings were also contributed by Antonio da Sangallo and Vignola in the 16th century. Sangallo built the FORTEZZA DA BASSO, near the 14th-century CHURCH OF SANT'AGNESE that possesses, among other things, a *Madonna* by the school of Simone Martini. The Piazza Grande (*right*) is the site of the DUOMO, whose current structure was designed in the early 17th century by Ippolito Scalza; it boasts a fine *Triptych* (1401) by Taddeo di Bartolo. On the right is the PALAZZO COMUNALE modeled on the Florentine Palazzo della Signoria by Michelozzo. The PALAZZO DEL MONTE CONTUCCI and the PALAZZO NOBILI TARUGI, both by Sangallo, also border the piazza. The nearby PALAZZO NERI ORSELLI houses the Museo Civico with works by Sienese and Florentine painters ranging from the 14th to the 17th centuries and della Robbia terracottas. Just outside the city stands the CHURCH OF SAN BIAGIO ● *81,* one of the finest buildings constructed in the 16th century and a masterpiece by Antonio da Sangallo the Elder, with its Greek-cross plan, central dome and two campaniles. The interior houses a magnificent marble altar by Giannozzo and Lisandro Albertini.

**PIENZA, THE DREAM OF POPE PIUS II** It was in 1459 that Enea Silvio Piccolomini, Pope Pius II, on a visit to his native Corsignano, devised the plan of transforming the small town into a papal residence. He gave the commission to Bernardo Rossellino who produced one of the most successful examples of city planning in the 15th century, the birth of the city of Pienza.

**THE MONASTERY OF SANT'ANNA AT CAMPRENA** This monastery is 4 miles north of Pienza and was founded by the Olivetans in 1324. The refectory is famous for the decorative frescos by Sodoma.

**MONTEPULCIANO'S 'CORSO'** Via di Gracciano and Via di Voltaia, the two stretches of the 'Corso', are lined with stately palaces, including the Palazzo degli Avignonesi, attributed to Vignola, and the 16th-century Palazzo Cervini, the property of Pope Marcellus II, attributed to Sangallo. The church of Sant'Agostino designed by Michelozzo and the baroque Gesù church are also worthy of note.

The Paolozzi cinerary urn, from the 7th century BC, at the Museo Archeologico Nazionale in Chiusi.

**THE MUSEO ARCHEOLOGICO NAZIONALE IN CHIUSI**
This recently converted museum possesses some of the most important finds from the Etruscan period, unearthed in excavations of large necropolises in the territory which can still be visited (Tomba della Pellegrina and Tomba del Leone), clear proof of Chiusi's importance in ancient times.

Capital letter from Codice 'B'. Chiusi, Museo della Cattedrale.

**CHIANCIANO TERME.** Climbing the picturesque coast between the Val d'Orcia and Le Crete, you will come to this ancient health resort, famous for its therapeutic waters. The old town, surrounded by still recognizable walls, looks much as it would have done originally. The Villa Simoneschi contains the recently founded MUSEO CIVICO ARCHEOLOGICO DELLE ACQUE.

**SARTEANO.** On the road to Chiusi, Sarteano is clustered around the CASTELLO DEI MANENTI, protected by broad fortifications erected by the Sienese to designs by Vecchietta in the 15th century and Peruzzi in the 16th century. The resort has some fine palaces, such as the Palazzo dei Piccolomini, and the CHURCH OF SAN MARTINO, now neoclassical in style, with an *Annunciation* (c. 1540) by Domenico Beccafumi. The new MUSEO CIVICO ARCHEOLOGICO, belonging to the Sistema Museale Provinciale (the provincial network of museums), is housed in the Palazzo Gabrielli Galgani. It has a collection of extremely rare objects such as vases and canopic jars.

**CHIUSI.** One of the most powerful Etruscan cities, Chiusi retained its civic privileges under Rome and the Lombards and played a key role in trade negotiations between nearby Perugia and Cortona. It entered a period of irreversible decline in the 11th century, caused by encroaching marshland in the Valdichiana (*Lago di Chiusi, remains of the swamp, top*). The city is centered around the Piazza del Duomo, the site of the DUOMO dedicated to the city's patron saint, San Secondiano. Restructured in the 19th century, it contains a series of frescos painted to look like mosaics by the Sienese artist Arturo Viligiardi (1887–94). It also houses the small cathedral museum with its archeological finds and a large collection of illuminated choir books from the 15th century. An atmospheric underground passage leads from the Duomo to the CATACOMBE DI SANTA MUSTIOLA and the so-called LABIRINTO DI PORSENNA.

**CETONA.** Situated on the borders of Tuscany with Lazio and Umbria, Cetona and its nearby mountain have been inhabited since Paleolithic times, as can be seen by a visit to the GROTTE DI BELVERDE formed of long underground tunnels and recently made a Parco Archeologico e Naturalistico. The city, a select tourist resort for centuries, is centered around the rectangular Piazza Garibaldi, built in the mid 16th century.

# From Volterra to Livorno

**ARRIVING IN VOLTERRA**
At daybreak, the Val di Cecina looks unreal, suspended in the morning clouds and overlooked by the impressive shape of Volterra, a stone ship riding the waves of time. Volterra has its roots in the Etruscan civilization. It was this noble, warlike and mysterious people who discovered alabaster, the white stone that has virtually become a symbol of the city.

**THE BALZE ★**
The prevailing color, the one that stays in the memory, is the yellow ocher of the sheer cliff face. From above, you can see the stone 'park bench', the platform on which the city was first built; layers of sand and limestone are interleaved with a gray clay base. Erosion, in progress for centuries, has claimed the oldest necropolises, two early medieval churches, a monastery, several houses and has almost devoured the Camaldolese abbey. Nature has consolidated its supremacy with the *balze*.

This itinerary explores the more intimate, untouristed side of Tuscany, taking the road that winds its way from Volterra toward the Metal Hills in the direction of the 'Etruscan Riviera'. This route will please anyone who likes to take life at a leisurely pace, savoring the excitement of new discoveries like navigators of old, traveling across land and sea. The wind is muffled by the bristly Mediterranean maquis clinging stubbornly to the farthest reaches of the Maremma, while stone hamlets reach out like birds of prey toward the hilly inland region and the blue silhouettes of the Tuscan Archipelago. This itinerary is ideal for discovering the 'alternative' Tuscany: brusque and introverted like mysterious Volterra; open and sunny like the Golfo di Baratti, dynamic and impulsive like the people of Livorno. History, art and nature in this region are well-deserving of their international reputation. You will travel over wooded hills, along a stretch of coast as yet undefiled by cement and through a land as discreet and authentic as its people, as noble as its wine, as pure as its virgin olive oil.

## VOLTERRA ◆ B D6 C A4 D D2

This city, although small, is important, and proud of its history. Highly independent, it has always watched events unfolding with sublime indifference, rebelling on many occasions when imperialist Rome or Medici Florence attempted to subdue it. The stones and narrow lanes in this 'city of wind and rock' as D'Annunzio described it, betray the traces of a culture now displayed in the Museo Guarnacci, a vital port of call for anyone visiting this corner of Tuscany.

**HISTORICAL BACKGROUND.** In the 5th–4th century BC, *Velathri* was one of the twelve cities belonging to the Etruscan nation, each governed by a *lucumon*, the Etruscan ruler. At the time, it numbered around 25,000 inhabitants and was enclosed by four miles of walls. With the decline of the coastal cities, Volterra became a flourishing trading center that steadily expanded by stepping up its mining activities; iron was exported to the Mediterranean through the port of Vada. A Roman town from 90 BC, it assumed its present appearance in the Middle Ages: it became a free town in 1193 and most of its civic buildings were built in the 13th century. Volterra came under the control of Florence in 1472, when it was captured by Lorenzo the Magnificent's army. The city then

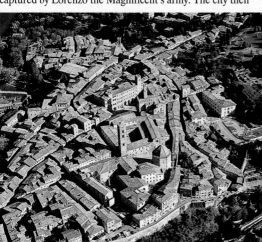

**MAGICAL ALABASTER**
The first people to work this white stone from Volterra were the Etruscans, who used it to make urns and tombs. Alabaster then disappeared from the scene until the 16th century. In the late 18th century Marcello Inghirami Fei made craftsmen more aware of its qualities by founding a school-workshop. It was still too soon to relaunch the product industrially, but this marked the start of a process still in use today.

expanded in the 19th century and some major city planning and conservation programs were implemented.

**THE BALZE.** The city is spread over the crest of a hill and built on treacherous land composed of crumbly clay that has already swallowed up buildings, churches and the mysteries of an Etruscan necropolis destroyed by landslides and erosion. The *balze*, deep clay-walled chasms, form the disturbing, mysterious and precarious face of the ancient Etruscan capital and chart the city's geological history. The massive clay wall of one cliff is dominated by the unmistakable outline of the CHURCH OF SANTI GIUSTO E CLEMENTE built between the 17th and 18th centuries, and there seems to be some truth in the theory that the ornamental columns silhouetted against its impressive façade are all that remain of a previous church that disappeared in a landslip.

**THE MEDIEVAL WALLS**
The present urban layout largely traces the outline of the medieval city, bounded by a smaller ring of walls than the boundary established by the Etruscans. There are four gates into the city which is built on an east-west axis. The Porta San Francesco in the west, the Porta a Selci in the east, the Porta Fiorentina facing north and the Porta dell'Arco facing south.

**PIAZZA DEI PRIORI.** The piazza is dominated by the façade of the PALAZZO DEI PRIORI, the oldest municipal palace in Tuscany: the first stone was laid in 1208 and work finished forty-six years later. The glazed terracottas and coats of arms (*above, left*) on the façade are highly ornamental and bear witness to the time when the city was governed by priors. The palace is topped by a tower that was partially rebuilt in 1846 after an earthquake. The marble clock (1856) is the work of Angiolo Bianchi; before that, Volterra's time had been kept by one of the oldest documented clocks: the works were probably designed and made in 1433. Another curious feature on the façade is the '*canna Volterrana*', the *comune*'s medieval gauge. On the opposite side of the piazza stands the PALAZZO PRETORIO (*above*) and the Torre del Podestà known as the TORRE DEL PORCELLINO because of the small wild boar carved on the façade. On the left-hand side of the piazza facing the Palazzo dei Priori stands the PALAZZO DEL DEMANIO whose medieval-style façade was built in the 19th century.

**DUOMO AND BAPTISTERY.** The Duomo, consecrated in 1120, was enlarged in the 13th century, possibly to a design by Nicola Pisano, while the interior was subdivided into a nave and two aisles in the 16th century. The decoration of the Duomo was modified in 1842–3. The interior contains some noteworthy pieces, including the group of the *Deposition* made of carved poplar wood, the 16th-century coffered ceiling and various decorative elements of the presbytery: the ciborium (1471) by Mino da Fiesole, who also made the angels holding candlesticks on the sides of the altar and the choir (1404). Opposite the Duomo stands the octagonal BAPTISTERY (13th century) which possesses a baptismal font created in 1502 by Andrea da Sansovino.

**D'ANNUNZIO AND ROSSO FIORENTINO**
★
In the romance *Forse che si forse che no* (*Maybe, Maybe Not*), D'Annunzio describes the emotions aroused by Rosso Fiorentino's *Deposition* and the *Madonna dal collo lungo*, a 15th-century work: 'The red garments of the woman at the Holy Mother's knees was like a cry of passion still swollen with dark blood. The uneven bars of light on the yellowish Disciple were like the sobs of the battered soul'.

**MUSEO DIOCESANO D'ARTE SACRA.** Founded to display works from the Duomo and other churches in the diocese, this museum boasts a fine sculpture section, although its two most famous works are a *Cross* painted on wood (13th century) and the *Enthroned Madonna with Sts John the Baptist and John the Evangelist* (1521) by Rosso Fiorentino.

**THE BUONPARENTI INTERSECTION.** This was the central junction in medieval Volterra. It is characterized by tower houses including those belonging to the Buonparenti (13th century) linked by a slender walkway.

**SAN FRANCESCO.** This beautiful Franciscan single-nave church was founded in the 13th century. Its stone façade has a portal and a rose window.

**PINACOTECA AND MUSEO CIVICO.** Housed in the Renaissance Palazzo Minucci-Solaini, this museum and gallery has a wonderful collection of paintings from churches, monasteries and societies in the region. Outstanding works include those by Taddeo di Bartolo (*Enthroned Madonna and Child with Saints*, 1411) and Luca Signorelli (*Annunciation*, 1491). The gem of the collection is Rosso Fiorentino's *Deposition* (1521).

**PALAZZO INCONTRI-VITI.** The palace was bought in 1850 by Benedetto Giuseppe Viti, one of the traveling alabaster salesmen. Now converted into a museum, the house has a rich collection of souvenirs collected by Benedetto Giuseppe on his travels, ranging from 13-foot tall candlesticks made for Emperor Maximilian of Habsburg to a collection of teacups.

**ROMAN THEATER.** This dates back to the 1st century AD and has a spacious *cavea* (semicircular seating area) spread out over the hilltop; nineteen rows of seats face the orchestra pit. Ionic and Corinthian columns support a large arcade behind the proscenium. Also in the monumental complex, a mosaic pavement, a *calidarium* and a *frigidarium* are all that remain of the baths dating back to the 4th century.

**MUSEO ETRUSCO GUARNACCI ▲ 240.** Since 1877, the Palazzo Desideri-Tangassi has been the home of the Etruscan Museum, which grew from the urn collection of Abbot Pietro Franceschini.

**FORTEZZA.** The upper part of Volterra is dominated by the unmistakable shape of the Renaissance fortress that stretches from east to west, with two long walls uniting the two main buildings: the trapezoidal Rocca Vecchia (1342) to the east and the Rocca Nuova (1472–5), built by Lorenzo the Magnificent, with four embattled corner towers and an impressive central keep.

**THE ACROPOLIS OF PIANO DI CASTELLO.** Be sure to visit the Parco Archeologico on the site of the Etruscan-Roman acropolis, a verdant park dedicated to Enrico Fiumi who was, until 1976, director of the Museo Etrusco Guarnacci. A system of cisterns and an Etruscan temple precinct from the Hellenistic period have been unearthed in the area that has been excavated.

La Rocca Nuova (*top left*) and the remains of the Roman Theater (*above*).

**THE LEGEND OF THE HOLY CROSS ★**
The Chapel of the Croce di Giorno, behind San Francesco, is completely covered in frescos of the *Legend of the Holy Cross*, by Cenni di Francesco Cenni, in 1410. This is the third most important fresco cycle dedicated to the legend of the Cross in Tuscany, after the one by Piero della Francesca in Arezzo ▲ 185 and the one by Agnolo Gaddi in Florence, from which Cenni drew his inspiration.

**PALAZZO INCONTRI-VITI AND THE MOVIES OF LUCHINO VISCONTI**
The city was the setting for Luchino Visconti's *Vaghe stelle dell'Orsa*, with Jean Sorel and Claudia Cardinale. The passionate emotions of the protagonists were played out against a somber, mysterious Volterra shot in black and white. Many of the scenes were filmed in the fascinating rooms of the Palazzo Incontri-Viti.

# ▲ THE MUSEO ETRUSCO 'MARIO GUARNACCI'

This museum provides an introduction to the mysteries of
the Etruscan civilization. Housed in the Palazzo
Desideri-Tangassi, it is a must for anyone
wanting to turn the clock back twenty-six
centuries: the magnificent collections owned by this
museum present visitors with a cross-section of
Etruscan life. Exhibits include funerary
equipment from the Villanovan period and from
the first ('oriental') phase of the development of the Etruscan
civilization, funerary sculpture made of stone, alabaster and
terracotta, Etruscan-Corinthian ceramics, objects in bronze and
gold, epigraphs and coins used by the Etruscan people. It was in
1761 that Monsignor Mario Guarnacci gave to the city his
remarkable collection of archeological finds, along with his
private library. These were added to the collection amassed by
the canon Franceschini, also an enthusiast. These rooms hold
the heart of the ancient, illustrious city of the *Velathri* and their
exhibits have helped to highlight some of the many enigmas
that still surround this mysterious and fascinating
nation.

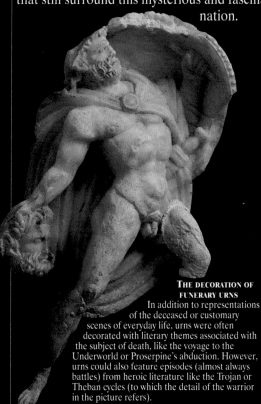

**STELE OF AVILE TIT**
Dated around c. 560
this is a funerary ste
depicting the figure c
warrior armed with
lance. The treatment
the face, headgear a
posture is typical of t
archaic period.

**THE DECORATION OF
FUNERARY URNS**
In addition to representations
of the deceased or customary
scenes of everyday life, urns were often
decorated with literary themes associated with
the subject of death, like the voyage to the
Underworld or Proserpine's abduction. However,
urns could also feature episodes (almost always
battles) from heroic literature like the Trojan or
Theban cycles (to which the detail of the warrior
in the picture refers).

## The Urna degli Sposi

This interesting item dates back to the 1st century BC and is exhibited in Room 20. Visitors will be struck by the remarkable realism of the husband and wife. The rare technical mastery of the carving is aided by the choice of terracotta, which is particularly suited to portraying fine details.

## Funerary urns

There are around 600 (*above*, the so-called Atteone urn) exhibited in the museum and they are the section that best characterizes Etruscan Volterra. The lid portrays the deceased, now immortal, reclining during a banquet in company with the gods of the Underworld.

## 'L'Ombra della Sera'

There is an air of mystical elegance about this statuette that has become the symbol (together with the *Urna degli Sposi*) of the Museo Guarnacci. The sculptural quality of this small elongated bronze is typical of *ex voto* offerings representing patrons, donors or deities found in central Italy. This statuette, discovered in early 1737, is characterized by its lack of attributes: it displays no clothes or typical poses that might indicate its social or religious status.

## MASSA MARITTIMA ◆ **C** A6 **D** D3

*Massa metallorum* was an extremely affluent city in the Middle Ages, but this golden age ended in 1335 when it was conquered by Siena. In 1555 it came under Florentine control and began a slow decline, aggravated by malaria. It experienced a recovery in the 18th century with the growth of the mining industry. Massa Marittima is a fine example of medieval city planning and an inviting place to stop before tackling the hills bordering the coastal plain.

**THE OLD CITY.** This exquisite masterpiece juggles with space and time, while light and shadow play tag among the jutting angles of the delightful medieval nucleus clustered around the remarkable PIAZZA GARIBALDI. Although the cathedral is the main focus, it seems to hold itself aloof from the piazza, engaging in a duet with the PALAZZO PRETORIO. This palace is the home of an interesting archeological museum that boasts an important collection of Etruscan funerary equipment and a *Maestà* by Ambrogio Lorenzetti. Across the square is the crenelated PALAZZO COMUNALE (13th–14th century). Stark and spare in style, the BASILICA CATHEDRAL OF SAN CERBONE was initially built in Romanesque style and later (1287) enlarged and embellished in the Gothic manner, probably by Giovanni Pisano. The magnificent decoration of the façade is equaled by the interior, which is crammed with works of interest including the travertine baptismal font (1267) carved by Giroldo da Como, the Ark of San Cerbone, a wonderful sculpture carved by Goro di Gregorio in 1324, and a *Crucifixion* (1300) by Segna di Bonaventura. In the chapel to the left of the choir is a *Madonna delle Grazie* attributed to a pupil of Duccio di Buoninsegna.

**THE NEW CITY.** A street from Piazza Garibaldi leads up to the upper part of the city, which dates back to 1228. Be sure to climb the TORRE DEL CANDELIERE (1228) for a breathtaking panoramic view from the top. If you continue walking, you will come to the Lombard portico of the PALAZZO DELLE ARMI (1443), and the church and monastery of Sant'Agostino built respectively in 1229 and 1273.

**AN IMPORTANT MINING CENTER**
After traveling through the most typical Tuscan landscapes, visitors arriving in Massa Marittima are bound to be surprised, if not flabbergasted, by the city's appearance. It looks almost like something out of a classic science-fiction movie. The first thing you see are the white fumes and enormous steel pipes that carry the steam towards the ENEL (National Electrical Company) power station (*above*), creating an outlandish landscape.

The cathedral in Massa Marittima (*top*), with the campanile, partially rebuilt in the 20th century.

## PIOMBINO AND POPULONIA ◆ **D** C3

Heading along the Tyrrhenian coast you will come to Piombino, a town that epitomizes the profound contrasts generated by the expansion of the steel industry and its impact on the gorgeous countryside in this part of Tuscany. The Piombino promontory remains, however, an area of breathtaking Mediterranean beauty.

**PIOMBINO.** A visit to one of the most beautiful historical centers in Tuscany begins at the Piazza Verdi. The 15th-century ravelin was the main gate, connected to an embattled tower (1212), another important part of the defensive system. The most outstanding monuments include the 13th-century PALAZZO COMUNALE, rebuilt in 1933–7, the Sienese Gothic CHURCH OF SANT'ANTIMO (1377), containing the tombs of the Appiani, rulers of Piombino for many years, and a fine Renaissance cloister. From PIAZZA BOVIO, which serves as a panoramic terrace, you descend toward the small harbor of Marina until you reach the marble FONTI DEI CANALI (1248), decorated with animal heads and attributed to Nicola Pisano. Above stands the CITADEL (1465–70) with a marble reservoir just in front of the Appiani Chapel.

**POPULONIA.** About 6 miles north of Piombino stands the port used by the Etruscans, who made use of the sheltered Golfo di Baratti to work Elban iron in their blast furnaces. Populonia had its heyday around the 4th century BC: its decline began in the 1st century BC when it was besieged by Sulla. On the promontory, the ROCCA (fortress) and the small town built in 1399 by Gherardo Appiani have lost none of the charm they owe to their enviable position, Here, visitors can enjoy one of the most beautiful views of BARATTI (underground tombs known as the *buche delle fate, below*) and the coastline in the area, making this place an essential port of call.

**THE PARCO ARCHEOLOGICO DI BARATTI E POPULONIA** ★
An archeological zone, part of the *Parco Archeologico di Baratti e Populonia*, lines the harbor area in the spectacular Golfo di Baratti. This is an exceptional site where you can admire buildings from various successive periods. It resembles an enormous time machine, capable of traveling from the Iron Age (9th–8th century BC) to the Roman period.

The Rocca in Populonia, with corner watchtowers and a semicircular embattled tower.

## THE TUSCAN ARCHIPELAGO ◆ D AD 3-6

The word 'archipelago' usually brings to mind a cluster of islands that to some extent form a group, coexisting in similar environmental conditions. However, the defining characteristic of the Tuscan Archipelago is its individuality: it mirrors the underlying spirit of independence and liberty that has always been the hallmark of the small towns, *comuni* and different territories that comprise the region. As a result, all the islands silhouetted against the blue sea pride themselves on their uniqueness, heightened by a sense of isolation that is not purely physical.

**THE ISLAND OF ELBA.** This is the closest island to the mainland and, as well as being the largest in the archipelago, it is also the most popular. Its varied coastal landscape affords some unforgettable sights: 90 miles of bays, beaches, rocks and crystal-clear waters. Out of season, the island is a paradise for those in search of peace and quiet while, in the summer, tourists and holidaymakers liven up the mood. In the early 20th century, the island's economy, until then based only on ancient rural and maritime traditions, developed a metallurgical industry, but after World War Two the economic recovery of the 1960s placed the focus squarely on tourism.

**ISLAND TOUR.** This tour is the best way to take in Elba's principal attractions. As this meandering itinerary covers 60 miles, you are advised to spread it over at least two days: eastern Elba and western Elba. You will leave from and return to PORTOFERRAIO (*left*). The 'eastern' itinerary follows

**FORTS AND BASTIONS**
In 1548, when the Appiani family sold Portoferraio to Cosimo I de' Medici, he built a fortified city against Barbarian invasions and renamed it Cosmopoli. The city was laid out around the natural harbor and enclosed by walls that descended to the sea from the promontory that was the site of the Forte della Stella and the Forte del Falcone. The third fort, the Linguella, stood at the sea's edge.

the coast to Magazzini, where it climbs toward Volterraio, one of the most fascinating places on the island, then descends to Cavo passing through the town of Rio nell'Elba. Heading along the coast, you come to Rio Marina then continue inland to Porto Azzurro (*below, left*) and Capoliveri, a magnificent viewpoint for the best sunsets. The 'western' itinerary (43 miles) begins by climbing the crest of the island to reach Lacona, then continues clockwise in the direction of MARINA DI CAMPO and the gorgeous inlets of Cavoli, Seccheto and Fetovaia (*opposite page, top*). Explore Elba's western 'elbow' as you climb toward the town of MARCIANA in the shadow of Mount Capanne

(3343 feet), the highest point on the island, then head back toward the sea at Marciana Marina. The road continues through Procchio and your round trip comes to an end with a final detour to Capo Enfola, a fascinating town not far from Portoferraio.

**CAPRAIA.** This distant, untamed island is a paradise for hikers. Besides the little town of Capraia, its port and just over half a mile of road, there is nothing but little paths traversing peaceful Mediterranean countryside. Until 1986, the island was the site of a penal colony and a large part of its territory is unspoiled, boasting some fascinating flora and fauna. Be sure to visit the little lake in the crater of an extinct volcano and take a boat trip around the island.

## From Campiglia Marittima to Livorno ◆ D A1-C2-3

Head for Rosignano along the 'Etruscan Riviera' taking the Strada del Vino (wine road), which could just as easily be named the oil road or any other of this region's products, from honey and cheese to bread baked in a wood oven.

**CAMPIGLIA MARITTIMA.** This town overlooks the Val di Cornia, facing the Costa di Baratti and San Vincenzo. It was first mentioned in the chronicles in 1004, when it was a castle belonging to the Counts of Gherardesca. It was then a Pisan *capitania* until 1406, when it was conquered by the Florentines. The medieval hamlet sprang up around the ROCCA (12th–13th century) and is dominated by the PALAZZO PRETORIO studded with the coats of arms of the Pisan captains. There is a panoramic view from the PORTA FIORENTINA, a wide gate in the city walls adorned with the coats of arms of Pisa, Florence, Campiglia and the counts of Gherardesca. Outside the walls stands the Romanesque CHURCH OF SAN GIOVANNI, its façade decorated with marble. There is a bas-relief on the side portal featuring *Meleager Hunting the Calydonian Boar* (12th century).

**SUVERETO.** The road through the broad Val di Cornia will bring you to Suvereto, a timeless stone gem. The ancient walls of the high Rocca guard the town. The buildings include the lovely arcaded PALAZZO COMUNALE (13th century) with its bell tower and the CLOISTER OF SAN FRANCESCO, which is all that survives of a 13th-century monastery.

**TOWARD CASTAGNETO CARDUCCI.** From Suvereto, the road of the four *comuni* resembles an asphalt ribbon winding its way through an unspoiled hilly landscape where buildings blend in perfectly with the surrounding countryside.

**THE TUSCAN ARCHIPELAGO ✪**
Seven islands and a series of tiny islets cover a combined area of about 120 square miles. These islands are almost all mountainous, with high, rocky coastlines: a national park now protects the entire area of the Tuscan Archipelago.

**THE PARCO ARCHEOLOGICO-MINERARIO DI SAN SILVESTRO**
On the hills to the north of Campiglia Marittima, this park stands monument to the tradition of mining activities in this region. You can choose between four routes (Via del Temperino, Via delle Ferruzze, Via dei Lanzi and Rocca di San Silvestro or Via dei Manienti) and an underground passage to the Temperino mine.

**THE RIFUGIO FAUNISTICO PADULE DI BOLGHERI**
Near Bolgheri, this wildlife sanctuary has been declared a wetland of international importance; it is administered by the WWF.

**THE MAQUIS OF MAGONA ★**
This magnificent woodland stretches for 4000 acres behind Bibbona; the charcoal burners used to work here producing fuel for the ironworks of Ferriere della Real Magona in Cecina. The Maquis of Magona has been classified a 'biotope' by the CNR (Italian National Research Council) because of the uniformity of its flora and fauna. It is an ideal destination for tourists interested in the environment.

The road climbs gently through the red trunks of the towering cork oaks to SASSETA, a stone town facing the Metal Hills and the distant plumes of steam from the Valle del Diavolo.

**CASTAGNETO CARDUCCI.** This is the diminutive capital of a land as rich as its oil and as noble as its wine, as wild as the Maremma and as amoral, genuine and sublime as its poet. It was a fiefdom of the Counts of Gherardesca until 1749 when it achieved autonomy. Giosue Carducci, who won the Nobel Prize for literature in 1906, spent his childhood here and at Bolgheri, but he also used to come back to this corner of Tuscany when he lived in Bologna. The Museo Archivio and the Centro Carducciano are both dedicated to this poet. The ruins of the TORRE DI DONORATICO are atmospheric and a little unsettling. The tower is associated with the life of Count Ugolino della Gherardesca, who took refuge here after the defeat at Meloria. In Canto XXXIII of the *Inferno*, Dante records how the count was starved to death in Pisa after being blamed for the defeat.

**ALONG THE STRADA DEL VINO.** The loveliest part of the Strada del Vino continues along Via Bolgherese through the monumental avenue of cypress trees (celebrated by Carducci in the ode *Davanti San Guido*) that climbs to BOLGHERI (*below*), a tiny hamlet nestling in the shadow of the 16th-century castle. This is the land of Sassicaia and Ornellaia, two universally acclaimed vines. The road winds its way between vineyards and olive groves toward BIBBONA then proceeds along the panoramic ridges that are home to the medieval hamlets of CASALE MARITTIMO (in a superb position and perfectly preserved), GUARDISTALLO and MONTESCUDAIO.

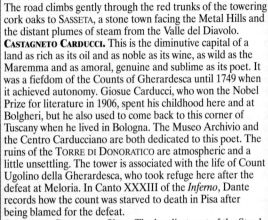

The Strada del Vino then descends toward CECINA, a modern tourist resort and commercial center, where it peters out. The 18th-century villa-farmhouse in San Pietro Palazzi La Cinquantina houses the Museo Etrusco-Romana, which exhibits archeological finds from the territory. In the adjacent farmhouse, you can pay a visit to the Museo della Vita e del Lavora della Maremma Settentrionale. Not far from the mouth of the Cecina river, in San Vincenzino, lie the remains of the Roman villa of Aulo Albino Caecina. with a magnificent underground cistern.

**THE LIVORNESI HILLS.** From Rosignano Marittimo, the road follows Livorno's coast past the towns of CASTIGLIONCELLO and QUERCIANELLA where it turns inland toward the hills that spread out behind Livorno. This has long been a forgotten land, the haunt of hermits and shepherds. It is only in the past few years that the enormous eco-tourist value of the Livornesi hills has been realized. Several years back, at a convention organized by Livorno province, this area was described as the 'island that is not an island', referring to its origins. The area was, in fact, a fossilized island, in other words a real island that was only joined to the mainland in relatively recent geological time. There is much to explore around the SANTUARIO DI MONTENERO, an impressive architectural complex with baroque decoration designed in 1712 by Giovanni del Fantasia, who built it on top of a small oratory. The church, dedicated to the Madonna delle Grazie, has been venerated since 1345, when a sick shepherd carried a picture of the Madonna here, finding peace of mind and a cure. Situated at an altitude of about 650 feet, the site affords a magnificent view over the entire city of Livorno, the sea and the islands of the Tuscan Archipelago.

## LIVORNO ◆ B C5-D B1

It was at 'XVI ⅔ hours and 8 minutes' on March 28, 1577 that the first stone of the new town around the Pisan village-castle by the sea was laid at the behest of Francesco I de' Medici. The origins of Livorno ● 69 date back to Roman times, as can be seen by various remains in the area of the Fortezza Vecchia, but the present urban layout, closely linked to the port (below), is based on the still visible octagonal plan of the Medici city. Another significant date in the history of this unique city is 1593: this was when Ferdinando I dé' Medici promulgated the 'Livornina' laws that allowed anyone, even foreigners, to leave their town or country of origin to take refuge from religious, political or racial persecution in this 'free' city. Livorno soon became a cosmopolitan town full of Jewish, Armenian, English, Dutch and Greek inhabitants. Other decrees guaranteed tax exemptions, freedom of residence and religious immunity. By the 16th century, port activities formed the mainstay of the city's economy, and it received a boost after 1625 when the Medici city was declared a free port. The number of inhabitants soared from 5000 in the 18th century to 80,000 by the end of the 18th century. In the 19th century, under the House of Lorraine, the city began to spill over beyond the city walls and, after Italian unification, its industrial sector went from strength to strength while the cosmopolitan profile of this small metropolis became less pronounced.

**LIVORNO ON THE VIA AURELIA ★**
The ancient Via Aurelia, which corresponds to the consular road laid by Claudius Aurelius Cotta in 241 BC, has recovered much of its charm now that the bulk of the traffic takes the E80 freeway. The best way to get to know the Pisan Maremma is to explore the ancient road that sometimes runs sheer above the sea and sometimes inland where farmhouses stand monument to major reclamation programs.

**THE BIRTH OF THE ITALIAN COMMUNIST PARTY**
In the Venezia Nuova district, a slab records the foundation of the party. On January 21, 1921, during the Italian Socialist Party Congress, certain delegates (including Bordiga, Gramsci and Tasca), placed in a minority, formed the Italian Communist Party, the Italian division of the Third International.

Livorno suffered greatly during World War Two: over eighty percent of the old city was destroyed by bombing.

**FROM THE PIAZZA GRANDE TO THE FORTEZZA NUOVA.** The PIAZZA GRANDE, the former 'Piazza d'Arme', formed the pivot of the Renaissance plans drawn up by Bernardo Buontalenti who, in 1576, placed this square at the intersection of the two main thoroughfares of his ideal city. Buontalenti's plan was supplemented in 1587 by the porticoed piazza (flattened in the air raids of 1943) and the church, designed by Cogorani. The Duomo, designed by Alessandro Pieroni between 1594 and 1606, was destroyed during World War Two, then rebuilt exactly as it had been, retaining the portico that precedes the façade. Crossing Piazza Cavour, one of the points of the 16th-century pentagon that traced the outline of the Fosse Reale, the ancient moat protecting the bastions, and Via Buontalenti, you will come to the CENTRAL MARKET, a spacious structure with an iron and glass roof, designed in the late 19th century by Angiolo Badaloni. Just before Piazza della Repubblica, you can take Via De Larderel to the CISTERNONE, a massive neoclassical building by Pasquale Poccianti that completed Livorno's complex water supply system. Across from the Piazza della Repubblica, you will see the mighty fortifications of the FORTEZZA NUOVA, built in 1590–4 on the marshy land of the Pisan port. The upper part of the fortress has been converted into a park area: an ideal spot to take a rest and enjoy a panoramic view over the city. Originally, this structure was linked by a long fortified wall to the Fortezza Vecchia, near the Medici port.

**THE VENEZIA NUOVA DISTRICT.** This is one of the most fascinating faces of Livorno. The area between the old and new fortresses is closely modeled on the plan of the Venetian city with its network of canals. The original design dates back to 1627 and was the work of G.B. Santi, who named this part

of the city 'Isola Ferdinanda'. Its similarity to Venice has meant that its original 'Christian name' is often abandoned in favor of the more natural 'Venezia Nuova'. As in Venice, this district is laid out in a quaint maze of canals, narrow streets and bridges that once performed the important role of connecting the warehouses with the quays in the port. Loading and unloading was made much easier by the existence of two communication routes providing access by land and water and the merchants had their living quarters on the upper floors of the warehouses. Characteristic gangways or sloping walkways connected the waterways to dry land. The thriving commercial activity of this part of the city is represented by the enormous BOTTINI DELL'OLIO, spacious buildings constructed in 1705 by Cosimo III to store the precious oil. The roof of these two structures is supported by 32 columns. You can still see the remains of some of the 304 watertight brick tanks used for storing 24,000 barrels of oil. This storage space is now given over to staging exhibitions and events. The best way to discover Venezia Nuova is to wander idly, allowing yourself to be guided by your curiosity and your taste for discovery. In this way, you are bound to find yourself admiring the CHURCH OF LUOGO PIO (churches of the Assunzione and Maria) and the CHURCH OF SAN FERDINANDO (1707) with marble statues, stucco work and sculptures by Giovanni Baratta. Among the palaces worthy of note are the PALAZZO DEL MONTE DI PIETÀ, the PALAZZO DELLE COLONNE, the PALAZZO ROSCIANO and the PALAZZO HUIGENS

**TOWARD THE DARSENA VECCHIA.** Once back on 'dry land', take Via San Giovanni from the Largo del Municipio in the direction of the FORTEZZA VECCHIA (*below*), a history book of the city hewn out of stone. Three bastions stand at the base of this fortified structure constructed by Antonio da Sangallo the Elder from 1518 onward; the Canaviglia, the Capitania and

**MODIGLIANI'S HOUSE**
A plaque at Via Roma 38 recalls the city's illustrious rebel of a son: 'Here the painter Amedeo Modigliani was given life, wit and virtue'. The artist died in Paris in 1920.

**LIVORNESE HUMOR**
'Its inhabitants are dreadfully amusing. I say dreadfully because they mock wise men and saints, friends, enemies and even their nearest and dearest; they swear on the tomb of their parents and sometimes absent-mindedly on that of their children… who are still alive.' This is how the people of Livorno are described by the Livornese humorist Davide Melodia in his guide to the city.

**THE NEW SYNAGOGUE**
Among the nationalities that arrived in Livorno after 1593 were many Jews, particularly from Spain. The synagogue they built in 1603 was destroyed in the bombings of 1943. An ultra modern synagogue was built after the war on the same site, not far from the Duomo.

**IN HONOR OF GIOVANNI FATTORI**
The 19th-century Villa Mimbelli houses the Museo Civico 'Giovanni Fattori'. This covers Livornese painting in the 19th and 20th centuries. The works by Fattori include three outstanding battle scenes: *La Signora Martelli a Castiglioncello*, *Mandrie Maremmane* and *Ritratto della Moglie*. There are also paintings by Boldini, Signorini, Lega, Corcos, Cecconi and Gordignani.

**MUSEUMS IN LIVORNO**
The neoclassical Villa Maria houses the 'Centro di documentazione e Ricerca Visiva' dedicated to the history of the city. Adjacent is the Museo Mascagnino, on the life and works of Pietro Mascagni (*a caricature, below*). The Biblioteca Labronica, in the Villa Fabbricotti, holds 360,000 volumes, making it the second largest library in Tuscany.

the Ampolletta. Towering above the fortress is the MASTIO DI MATILDE, which dates back to the late 11th century. This cylindrical tower was built by the counts of Tuscany on the remains of a Roman fortification, the *castrum Liburni*, probably dating back to the period under the rule of Pompey, Consul of the Sea (c. 67 BC). In 1377, the Pisans incorporated the *mastio* in the structure of another fortification known as the QUADRATURA DEI PISANI, attributed to Puccio di Landuccio and Francesco di Giovanni; it was partly restored after the bombings of World War Two and can be visited during the summer. At this point, having entered the port area proper, continue walking through the area around the Darsena, venturing between the fortifications of the PORTO MEDICEO, the site of the beacon attributed to Giovanni Pisano, and the TORRE DEL MARZOCCO, Livorno's outermost bulwark.

**THE LUNGOMARE.** The smell of iodine and the sound of the surf form a backdrop to the magnificent seafront promenade, Viale Italia, that leads all the way from the industrial port to the cliffs at Antignano, passing by the elegant façades of 19th-century Livorno. The promenade soon reaches the sunny Terrazza Mascagni, a spacious square facing the sea built between 1927 and 1951, and the interesting ACQUARIO COMUNALE DIACINTO CESTONI (1937) which, since 1966, has housed the Centro Interuniversitario di Biologia Marina. The 19th-century Pancaldi-Acquaviva baths can be glimpsed together with Piazza Modigliani. Once across the Canale dei Lazzaretti, the promenade runs alongside the San Jacopo neighborhood. This part of the city was built in the second half of the 16th century. It includes the BORGO DEI GRECI, as the Greeks were invited to Livorno to build the fleet for the Knights of Santo Stefano. Facing the sea stands the CHURCH OF SAN JACOPO ACQUAVIVA (18th century) and the prestigious NAVAL ACADEMY, a residential complex on the southern borders of the city. The academy, built in 1878, was commissioned by General Benedetto Brin who combined the existing naval academies of Genoa and Naples. Art Nouveau-style buildings, gardens, pavilions and bathing establishments line the front to Ardenza, a residential neighborhood built around the CASINI (1844), a group of neoclassical houses arranged in the shape of an exedra (a continuous curved shape).

# Grosseto and the Maremma

**MAREMMA'S SPANISH ORIGINS**
The name of this region, where the Etruscan civilization reached the height of its glory, is of fairly recent origin. For a long period lasting until the 15th century, this territory came under the political and military influence of Spain, and it was at this time that the term 'Maremma' was used, from the Spanish word for swamp, *marismas*.

Herd grazing in the region of Marina di Albarese (*below*).

The vast stretch of land known as the Maremma extends throughout Grosseto province to the northern borders of Lazio and boasts a remarkable natural habitat preserved in its original state. The Maremma is a wild region, alternating sea and pine forests, sunny plains and hills covered by every shade of green imaginable in a diverse landscape with an exceptional climate. This fascinating region, rich in history and time-honored traditions, is definitely worth exploring: visitors can go horse-riding through the woods or along the coast, walk through unspoiled countryside, visit health spas or savor the delights of simple, authentic food. The itinerary winds its way slowly from Grosseto toward the towns in the northeast through a land where the vestiges of different civilizations alternate with natural landscapes, untouched by man, that are almost unsettling in their rugged isolation.

## GROSSETO ◆ D D4

The major town at the heart of the entire Maremma region, Grosseto ● 70 had its heyday under the Aldobrandeschi, when the Medici were at the

height of their power, and then with the arrival of Leopold II
of Lorraine. The main monuments are clustered around the
ancient part of the city, which is enclosed by mighty walls.
**CIRCUIT OF WALLS.** The mighty buttressed walls are entirely
built of brick. They form a nearly perfect hexagonal, whose
points are shaped like pentagonal arrows. One of the points is
occupied by the MEDICI FORTRESS. There are also some
fortified buildings with roads, piazzas and brick staircases.
**DUOMO.** One of the most important monuments is the
Duomo (*above*), begun by Sozzo di Rustichino in 1294, with
its distinctive white and pink striped façade. Its interior
contains some outstanding works, including the baptismal
font and the dossal (ornamental hanging) (1470) by the
architect Antonio Ghini, as well as a painting of the *Assunta*
by Matteo di Giovanni.
**CHURCH AND MONASTERY OF SAN FRANCESCO.** These buildings
were constructed in Franciscan Gothic style using the finest
brick and wood. The interior has important frescos by the
Sienese school and a *Cross* on wood (c. 1289) attributed to
Duccio di Buonsegna. In the adjacent cloister is a travertine
well, commissioned by Ferdinando de' Medici in 1590.
**MUSEO ARCHEOLOGICO E D'ARTE DELLA MAREMMA.** This
museum has a collection of Etruscan archeological finds,
particularly from Roselle, and some important sacred works
of art, including an outstanding *Giudizio Universale* attributed
to Guido da Siena and the *Madonna delle Ciliegie* by Sassetta.

Etruscan mask from
the 5th century BC in
at the Museo
Archeologico in
Grosseto (*above*).

## FROM ROSELLE TO PUNTA ALA ◆ **D** CD4

In this area just north of Grosseto, nature and art coexist in
perfect harmony, from Etruscan archeological sites to the
Tyrrhenian coastline.
**ROSELLE.** Founded in the 7th century BC, this town expanded
in the following century in open conflict with Vetulonia. The
circuit of walls and an ancient oval house survive from the
Etruscan period. The remains of the forum and a small
amphitheater on the northern hill, a short distance from the
ruins of the thermal baths are vestiges from the Roman era.
**BURIANO.** This town, dominated by a castle, is of ancient
origin, probably Roman or Lombard. It reached the height
of its splendor between the 11th and 14th centuries. The
Romanesque church has a relic of San Guglielmo, who took
refuge in the ROMITORIO (hermitage), just outside the town.

**BUTTERI, TUSCAN COWBOYS**
The Maremma is the home of the *butteri*, the cowboys who tend the herds in the meadows near the sea. The *butteri* are renowned for winning a famous challenge issued to American cowboys in the early 20th century.

**CASTEL DI PIETRA, A BLEND OF FACT AND LEGEND**
In Canto V of the *Purgatorio*, Dante mentions Pia de' Tolomei who was murdered within the walls of Castel di Pietra ('Siena made me, Maremma unmade me…'). This building near Gavorrano, on the road to Follonica, was described in a document as early as 1067 as the property of the abbey of Sestinga. Its location was so favorable that it formed the subject, in 1203, of a treaty between Ildebrando degli Aldobrandeschi and Siena concerning the salt trade with Grosseto.

**VETULONIA.** Ruler of the territory between the 7th and 6th centuries BC, Vetulonia, about 12 miles west of Roselle, fell into oblivion until 1181, when the castle of Colonna was built. Various parts of the mighty ring of walls and the necropolis have survived from the Etruscan period. Be sure to see the TOMB OF THE DIAVOLINO II (the tomb known as Diavolino I is on display in the Museo Archeologico in Florence ▲ *132*), the TOMB OF THE PIETRERA, along the road to Buriano, and the archeological museum, which has some important finds.

**FOLLONICA.** The coastal town of Follonica does not seem to have much to offer. However, people come here for its 4 miles of fine sandy beaches, one of the most popular stretches along the entire Tyrrhenian coast. There are many bathing establishments and uncrowded beaches, all gently sloping with shallow waters and no dangerous currents.

**PUNTA ALA.** This strip of land on the southernmost tip of the Golfo di Follonica has been transformed into a peaceful, elegant resort with a picturesque marina, sheltered by a magnificent pine forest. Numerous paths lead from the town into the surrounding hills and up to the ancient castle that gives some breathtaking views. Immediately below is a line of rocks known as the Porcellini, and an islet called Troia Vecchia, with the remains of a 16th-century watchtower.

## FROM CASTIGLIONE DELLA PESCAIA TO ORBETELLO ◆ **D** D4-5 E5-6

This fascinating tourist itinerary heads south along the Maremma coast to Orbetello's lagoons, passing some magnificent viewpoints and picturesque sites on the way.

**CASTIGLIONE DELLA PESCAIA.** Of ancient Etruscan origin, this famous vacation resort has a small port and an extremely long beach bordered by a dense pine forest. In the heart of the town is the medieval hamlet, surrounded by turreted walls dating back to the period of Pisan domination (10th–13th century) and overlooked by the 15th-century Castello Aragonese.

**PARCO NATURALE DELLA MAREMMA ● 20.** Founded in 1975, the Maremma Nature Park stretches along the southern part of the coast from Pincipina a Mare to Talamone. The Trappola Marshes can be reached from the rural town of ALBERESE. The slopes of the Uccellina mountains extend along the coast for 9 miles to Talamone, where there is another entrance to the park. Here, the luxuriant Mediterranean maquis lays siege to the ancient watchtowers and ivy shrouds the picturesque ruins of the ABBEY OF SAN RABANO, founded by the Benedictines in the 11th century. There are also some ruins of the Romanesque church (11th–12th century) with its beautifully decorated exterior.

**TALAMONE.** This small town extends along a promontory overlooking the sea, hemmed in by the Uccellina mountains. The old town is enclosed by a ring of walls and overlooked by the ROCCA, situated at the highest point of the town. It was built in the 15th century by the Sienese Republic to a design by the architect Lorenzo di Pietro. The breathtaking view from the belvedere near the lighthouse takes in the whole coast from the Argentario promontory to Punta Ala and as far as Castiglione della Pescaia.

**ORBETELLO.** This town stands on a small peninsula surrounded by the Levante and Ponente lagoons, separated by an artificial dike that joins the town to the Argentario promontory. The lagoons are bordered by two tongues of sand known as the Tombolo della Feniglia and the Tombolo della Giannella, with miles of delightful beaches. The numerous historical monuments include the POLVERIERA GUZMAN, where Garibaldi stocked up on arms and ammunition, and the FORTRESS (known as *I Bastioni*) on top of which stands the keep. In the piazza, the small CHURCH OF SANTA MARIA AD PORTAM contains a delightful fresco by the Sienese school featuring the *Virgin and Child*. Nearby, the PORTA NOVA or the Porta di Medinaceli, named in honor of the Duke of Medinaceli, Spanish governor in the 16th century, is topped by the statue of San Biagio, patron saint of Orbetello. The historical center is surrounded by Etruscan

---

**TIRLI, THE CARPENTERS' TOWN**
The Maremma was also the home of carpenters, who founded attractive little towns like Tirli, nestling deep in the oaks and chestnut trees. This picturesque town with its little lanes is dominated by a fortified monastery, built around 1500, which was where the inhabitants took refuge from raids by Saracen pirates.

**THE CASALE DELLA GIANNELLA ★**
In the calm waters along the sandbar of the Tombolo della Giannella, pink flamingos are a common sight. At the center of the tombolo, in a 17th-century Spanish farmhouse (*below*), there is an environmental information center run by the WWF. On the seaward side, the tombolo stretches for miles of fine sandy beach to the mouth of the Albegna river, separated from the road that runs straight along it by dense swathes of Mediterranean maquis.

# STONE FROM THE MAREMMA

Metal and stone were two materials of vital importance to the rulers of both Etruscan and Roman civilizations. Metal was the linchpin of military power, the variable that made it possible to prevail even when armies were equally matched. Stone, however, was used as a subtle political tool, its durability making it a powerful sign of strength, of complete mastery over cities and territories. For this reason, therefore, new conquerors initially surrounded themselves with skilled stonemasons to build roads, walls, doors and towers; then with architects and artists to build amphitheaters, palaces and awe-inspiring temples whose beautiful decoration symbolized the ruler's dominion over the physical and spiritual worlds. The archeological finds discovered throughout the Maremma region chart the way in which successive civilizations have carved the emblems of their supremacy in stone.

**MASTERFUL CRAFTSMANSHIP**
Both this terracotta fragment featuring a warrior (*right*) and the marble bust (*left*), in the Antiquarium in Cosa, illustrate how late Etruscan and Roman sculptors, influenced by Hellenistic techniques, were able to shape materials to create pieces of immense expressive force.

**THE PEDIMENT OF TALAMONE**
The pediment from the *Tempio di Talamone* (a detail with Fury and demons steering Amphiaraus' horses at the bottom of the sea, *left*), that dates back to 150–130 BC, is one of the most outstanding works of Etruscan art from the Hellenistic period. The subject depicted is that of the *Seven against Thebes*.

## ROSELLE

An *opus reticulatum* from excavations at Roselle, an Etruscan city subjugated by the Romans in 294 BC. These walls faced with reticulated work still entirely encircle the city. They date back to the 6th century BC and replaced an even older fortification made of unbaked bricks.

## VETULONIA

The remains of the Roman road (3rd–1st century BC) coexist with broad stretches of the Etruscan city walls that were too strong to be demolished by the new conquerors.

## ANSEDONIA

The 'Tagliata Etrusca' is a magnificent canal carved through the rock by the Romans to allow the ebb and flow of sea water from the ancient port.

## COSA

Walls and towers from the Roman colony founded in 273 BC. The mighty ring of walls with three city gates was constructed with enormous polygonal blocks of limestone and had seventeen square towers, situated along the seaward walls.

## THE CIBORIUM FROM SOVANA

A fine example of pre-Romanesque (8th–9th century) architecture, this ciborium housed in the Romanesque church of Santa Maria embodies the lengthy struggle to gain mastery over the physical world that typified medieval culture.

walls that stretch for just over a mile. The important monuments include the ancient CATHEDRAL OF SANTA MARIA ASSUNTA, with its Tuscan Gothic façade, the former convent of the Poor Clares that contains the valuable *Frontone del Tempio di Talamone*, the PALAZZO DI SPAGNA, surmounted by a clock tower, and the PALAZZO DEL MUNICIPIO, built in the early 16th century. Walking along the sea wall you will come into sight of the spectacular MULINO SPAGNOLO, the last in a line of nine mills built by the Sienese but named after the Spanish who subsequently carried out modifications.

## FROM MOUNT ARGENTARIO TO MANCIANO ◆ **D** E5-6 F5

The Argentario promontory dominates the landscape while, in the distance, the island of Giglio floats in the crystal clear water. Further inland, the landscape becomes a succession of pastures and cultivated fields, dotted with picturesque medieval towns.

View of Porto Santo Stefano.

**THE OASIS OF BURANO**
Along the coast to the south of Ansedonia lies the oasis of Lago di Burano, another WWF project: 1000 acres incorporating a lagoon and various pools less than three feet deep are devoted to the preservation of an ecosystem that includes numerous waterbirds (teals, herons, shovelers, black-winged stilts), a rich fish fauna (eels, gray mullet, bass), as well as foxes, badgers, porcupines and other mammals.

**GIANNUTRI ISLAND**
This is the southernmost island in the Tuscan Archipelago. Particularly popular with deep-sea divers, this small island is best visited in spring when the flowers are in bloom. The ruins of the Roman Domizi Enobarbi Villa from the 1st century BC are very interesting with remains of mosaics, paved paths and columns.

**MOUNT ARGENTARIO.** Despite property speculation and some recent devastating fires, the Argentario promontory (*above*) is a fascinating place, its rugged coastline alternating cliffs with coves and little beaches affording gorgeous sea views. This landscape, occasionally wild and inhospitable, is dotted at strategic points with walls, forts and towers that formed part of the extensive defense system erected by the Spanish between the 16th and 17th centuries.

**PORTO SANTO STEFANO.** Extending between two picturesque coves along the northern shore of the Argentario, Porto Santo Stefano is a delightful seaside resort, with a commercial port which has run a ferry service to the island of Giglio since Roman times. Palaces and villas climb the slopes from the sea toward the panoramic drive that loops its way along the entire promontory. In the upper part of the port, the old houses are dominated by the RIONE FORTEZZA, which derives its name from the ancient medieval keep, first occupied by the Sienese then the Spanish.

**PORTO ERCOLE** ● *51, 70*. Probably founded by the Phoenicians, the town is dominated by the complex of the ROCCA (fortress) and encircles the natural harbor, which is now a lively tourist center. The ancient town center with its narrow alleys grew up around the fortress and the CHURCH OF SANT'ERASMO, patron saint of sailors. At the end of the main road lies the Piazza Santa Barbara, a fascinating terrace

**GIGLIO ISLAND ✪**
About 9 miles from the Argentario, this is the second largest island in the Tuscan Archipelago. Its rocky coastline interspersed with bays, little coves and sandy beaches is endlessly fascinating. In 1241 off the coast of Gigoli, Frederick II destroyed the Genoese fleet which was carrying the prelates to Rome for the ecumenical council convoked by Pope Gregory IX against the emperor.

The coastline of Giglio Island near Cala delle Cannelle (*above*).

overlooking the port dominated by the PALAZZO CONSANI, once the official residence of the Spanish governor.

**ISOLA DEL GIGLIO.** Ninety percent of this island is uninhabited and there are only three large towns. GIGLIO PORTO lies in a cove on the eastern coast bordered by houses in pastel colors and surrounded by an amphitheater of hills covered in vineyards. Further up, on the summit of a steep hill overlooking the sea, stands the fortified hamlet of GIGLIO CASTELLO, with its high medieval walls and towers that enclose narrow lanes and steep flights of steps between the stone houses to the Rocca. On the opposite slope lies the large beach of GIGLIO CAMPESE, overlooked by a squat cylindrical Medici tower.

**ANSEDONIA.** This wooded promontory extends from the sandy shores and dark green Mediterranean maquis to the end of the Tombolo della Feniglia. On its flat top stand the ruins of COSA, an ancient Roman city. Below, on the sheltered seaward slopes, villas dotted amongst the greenery form a sprawling residential area. A cliff links the beach of La Feniglia with the area known as the TAGLIATA ETRUSCA ▲ 257, a magnificent canal carved into the rock by the Romans to allow the flow of sea water from the old port.

**CAPALBIO.** Perched on the summit of a wooded hill, Capalbio is the first castled town in Tuscan Maremma, almost on the Lazio border. It is surrounded by walls with two city gates known as the Senese and the Porticina. The important buildings include the Romanesque CHURCH OF SAN NICOLA, with its bell tower at its side. The interior contains excellent frescos by the Umbrian and Sienese schools of the 15th and 16th centuries. In the northern part of the town stands the PALAZZO COLLACCHIONI, built on the remains of the ancient Rocca Aldobrandesca with its mighty 12th-century defensive tower. Outside the walls, the ORATORIO DELLA PROVVIDENZA possesses a 15th-century chapel by the Umbrian-Latian school.

**MANCIANO.** This medieval hilltop hamlet overlooks a verdant cultivated landscape with vineyards and olive groves. Be sure to see the 17th-century ORATORIO DELLA SANTISSIMA ANNUNZIATA as well as the FORTRESS (15th century) that affords a breathtaking view from Mount Amiata to the Tyrrhenian Sea. The MUSEÓ DI PREISTORIA E PROTOSTORIA is also worth a visit with its rich collection of valuable finds.

**GIARDINO DEI TAROCCHI**
Not far from Capalbio, Garavicchio is the site of the remarkable Giardino dei Tarocchi, comprising twenty-two of the principal divisions in the Tarot deck of cards. These fantastic sculptures, made from reinforced concrete and polyester and covered with locally produced ceramic mosaics, glass and mirrors, are the work of the French-American artist Niki de Saint-Phalle.

## FROM PITIGLIANO TO MONTEMERANO ◆ D EF5

There are some pretty towns bordering the road to Montemerano.

**PITIGLIANO.** This medieval hamlet (*below*, *right*, the fountain) is dominated by the 16th-century PALAZZO ORSINI, founded in the 14th century and equipped with an aqueduct in the 16th century. It now houses the Museo della Diocesi, crammed with valuable Etruscan finds. Other remarkable buildings are the CHURCH OF SANTA MARIA, near Porta di Capisotto, and the CATHEDRAL with its lovely baroque façade. A Jewish community settled in the ancient ghetto in the 15th century and you can visit the synagogue (1589), which has been restored and reopened for worship.

**SORANO.** This town, of Etruscan origin (*top*), was built of dark tufa on a sheer rock-cut terrace shaped by the Torrente Lente. It has a remarkable parish church and what remains of the Palazzo Comitale. The FORTRESS, designed by Anton Maria Lari in 1552, was linked to a defensive system whose impressive remains can be seen in Montorio, Castell'Ottieri and Vitozza.

**SOVANA.** Time seems to have stood still in this town. Each building is a monument, steeped in history and containing remarkable works, clear evidence of the town's importance in the Middle Ages. On the central piazza stands the PALAZZO PRETORIO (12th–13th century), the LOGGETTA DEL CAPITANO, the Renaissance PALAZZO BOURBON DEL MONTE and the Romanesque church of SANTA MARIA MAGGIORE, with frescos by the Sienese school and a pre-Romanesque ciborium (8th–9th century) ▲ 257. At the end of town lies the Romanesque Duomo, dedicated to saints Peter and Paul. In the immediate vicinity are several ETRUSCAN NECROPOLISES, the oldest being that of Sopraripa (7th–6th century BC).

**SATURNIA.** The thermal baths of this spa attract visitors from all over the world. Its hot springs are recommended for rheumatism, metabolic diseases, gastric and respiratory problems and stress. Historical monuments include the city walls, built by the Sienese in the 15th century on top of the remains of Etruscan and Roman walls, the ruins of the keep and, further on, those of the Porta Romana.

**MONTEMERANO.** Inside its 15th-century walls, this ancient farming town on a hilltop preserves an old medieval castle. Flanked by a 14th-century leaning tower, the CHURCH OF SAN GIORGIO is full of 15th-century works, including the polyptych of the *Madonna col Bambino in Trono e i Santi Pietro, Giorgio, Lorenzo e Francesco* (1458) by Sano di Pietro.

The Tomba Ildebranda (*above*), from the 3rd century BC, near the necropolis of Poggio Felceto, in Sovana.

**THE BATHS AT SATURNIA ★**
With its steaming springs, Saturnia has been wreathed in an atmosphere of mystery and legend for centuries: the exceptional therapeutic properties of its waters were already appreciated by the Romans. Restored around the mid 19th century, these baths are renowned for the beneficial effect of their waters.

# ◆ GETTING THERE

## USEFUL ADDRESSES

### → IN LONDON

■ **Italian Embassy**
14 Three Kings' Yard
London
W1Y 2EH
Tel. 020 7312 2200
Fax 020 7499 2283
e-mail: emblondon@
embitaly.org.uk

■ **Italian
Cultural Institute**
39 Belgrave Square
London SW1X 8HX
Tel. 020 7235 1461
Fax 020 7235 4618
ici@italcultur.org.uk

### → IN NEW YORK

■ **Italian Consulate**
690 Park Ave.
NY 10021-5044
Tel. 212 737 9100
(or 439 8600)
Fax 212 249 4945
www.italconsulnyc.org

■ **Italian
Cultural Institute**
686 Park Avenue
New York
10021-5009
Tel. 212 879 4242
Fax 212 861 4018
www.italcultny.org

## ACCOMMODATION

Tuscany boasts a
wide range of
accommodation
to satisfy all tastes
and pockets. Visitors
can choose between
luxury hotels
(including hotels in
historic buildings),
all grades of hotels,
pensions,
farmhouses
(agriturismo),
boarding houses
and hostels.
Camping is also a
popular option. In
the peak tourist
season, it is
advisable to book in
advance, particularly
in the more popular
resorts.

## BY AIR

For Florence and
other places in
Tuscany, travel to
Pisa's Galileo Galilei's
international airport
(1hr by train) and
Florence's Peretola
airport (in the
center of Florence),

also known as
Amerigo Vespucci.

### → FLORENCE – 'AMERIGO VESPUCCI' AIRPORT
Domestic flights
Tel. 055 306 1700
International flights
Tel. 055 306 1702
www.safnet.it

### → PISA – 'GALILEO GALILEI' AIRPORT
Tel. 050 20062
Flight information
Tel. 050 500 707
www.pisa-airport.com

### → FROM THE UK
There are daily
direct flights from
London and other
UK cities to Florence
and Pisa.
■ **Fares**
Fares start from
about £120 or even
less to around £600
(business). Check
with each airline
and on the internet.
■ **Travel time**
About 2hrs from
London to Florence
or Pisa.
■ **British Airways**
Tel. 0345 222 111
www.britishairways.
co.uk
■ **Meridiana**
Tel. 020 7839 2222
www.meridiana.it
■ **Alitalia**
Tel. 08705 448 259
www.alitalia.co.uk
■ **Internet**
www.cheapflights.com
www.expedia.co.uk

### → FROM THE US
There are no direct
flights from the US,
but you can fly to
Florence or Pisa via
Rome, Milan or
Venice or one of
the other main
European cities.
■ **Fares**
Fares start from
$800 (economy) to
$5,400 (business).
Check with each
airline.
■ **Travel time**
About 8–9hrs from
New York; 12–13hrs
from Los Angeles.
■ **British Airways**
Tel. 1 800 247 9297

■ **Alitalia**
Tel. 1 800 223 5730
www.alitaliausa.com
■ **American Airlines**
Tel. 1 800 433 7300
www.aa.com
■ **Continental**
Tel. 1 800 231 0856
www.continental.com
■ **Delta**
Tel. 1 800 241 4141
www.delta.com
■ **Northwest**
Tel. 1 800 225 2525
www.nwa.com
■ **TWA**
Tel. 1 800 829 4141
www.twa.com
■ **United Airlines**
Tel. 1 800 538 2929
www.unitedairlines.
com

## BY CAR

### → DOCUMENTS
Valid driving license,
car registration
papers and proof
of insurance. An
International
Driver's Permit is
recommended.
■ **American AA (US)**
Tel. 1 800 564 6222
■ **AA (UK)**
Tel. 0870 550 0600

## BY COACH FROM THE UK

### → EUROLINES
■ **Information**
Tel. 01582 40 45 11
www.eurolines.co.uk
■ **Departures**
From Victoria Coach
Terminal (London)
every day at 9am.
■ **Fares**
Return fares range
from £69–£79
(summer specials)
to £129–£139.

## BY TRAIN

Eurostar from
London Waterloo to
Paris Gare du Nord
(from £69), then the
overnight train to
Florence Santa
Maria Novella from
Gare de Lyon.
■ **Information**
RAIL EUROPE
(London):
Tel. 0990 848 848
EUROSTAR (London):
Tel. 0990 186 186
www.eurostar.com
■ **Departure point**
From Paris Gare

de Lyon: direct train
daily at 7.37pm.
■ **Fares from Paris**
Return (with sleeper)
from £160.

## CAR RENTAL

The major car hire
companies (Hertz,
Avia, Maggiore,
Europcar) all have
outlets in Florence
and Pisa airports as
well numerous
offices across the
region. You will
need a credit card
and must be over 21
years of age in order
to rent a car. Your
driving license
(preferably an
international one),
must be valid for at
least one year.

## CLIMATE

The climate can
vary considerably
between coastal
areas and
mountainous inland
regions, although
Tuscany usually
enjoys hot, dry
summers and
mostly mild winters.
The average
temperature in
Florence ranges
from 36°F (2°C) in
the winter to 86°F
(30°C) in the
summer. The best
time to visit Tuscany
is between May and
June, before the
oppressive heat of
summer (extremely
severe in inland
cities like Florence,
Arezzo and Siena),
and between
September and
October.

## ELECTRIC CURRENT

The electric current
is 220 volts. Plugs
have two or three
pins in a row.

## FORMALITIES

Valid ID cards or
passports for
European Union
members.
US visitors need a
valid passport to
enter Italy for 90
days. By law foreign

visitors should register with the police within 8 days of arriving in Italy, although this may be done for you when you check into your first hotel. Carry photo ID at all times.

## FROM FLORENCE TO...

Amsterdam: 797 miles
Berlin: 738 miles
London: 895 miles
Madrid: 955 miles
Milan: 186 miles
Paris: 676 miles
Rome: 173 miles
Vienna: 489 miles

## HEALTH

### → MEMBERS OF THE EUROPEAN UNION
Form E111, issued by Health Authorities of EU countries, entitles members to emergency medical treatment.

### → OTHER COUNTRIES
Non-EU members must take out personal medical insurance.

### → VACCINATIONS
None required, but take adequate prescription medication.

## INTERNET
■ Italian National Tourist Office (ENIT)
www.enit.it
www.piuitalia.2000.it
■ Italian Tourist Web Guide
www.itwg.com
■ Tuscany
www.turismo.toscana.it
www.giubileo.toscana.it

## MONEY
Until the official introduction of the Euro in January 2002, Italy's currency remains the lira. However prices are already given in lira and euros.
£1 = 3,000 lire
$1 = 2,100 lire
1 euro = 1,900 lire

### → CHANGING MONEY
Bureau-de-change outlets can usually be found near the major banks, in the larger railroad stations, in airports and the busiest tourist resorts.

### → CURRENCY
Bank notes come in denominations of 1000, 2000, 5000, 10,000, 50,000, 100,000 and 500,000 lire and coins are in

ROOM IN A FARM VACATION CENTER

CHIANTI

denominations of 50, 100, 200, 500, 1000 lire.

### → CREDIT CARDS
The major credit cards are now accepted almost everywhere in hotels and shops in big cities. It is advisable to check first before using your credit card in small shops and villages.

## PACKING
The clothes you pack will vary considerably depending on the season in which you are traveling and the region you are visiting. You should take short sleeves and light clothing in summer (but remember that knees and shoulders should be covered when visiting churches), a sweater, warmer clothes and perhaps a raincoat in the fall, and heavier clothes in the winter.

## STUDENT INFORMATION
The CTS (Centro Turistico Studentesco e Giovanile) gives reductions and discounts on travel, museums, hotels, restaurants, shops, etc.
■ ISIC card
An International Student Identity Card (which may be purchased from your country of residence) allows foreign students to take advantage of CTS benefits.

■ CTS, Florence office
Via dei Ginori, 25/r
Tel. 055 289721

## TELEPHONE
### → TO CALL FROM THE UK
Dial 00 + 39 + the number you wish to call (including the initial zero).

### → TO CALL FROM THE US
Dial 011 + 39 + the number you wish to call (including the initial zero).

### → MOBILE PHONES
The GSM network allows virtually all mobile phones to be used in Italy.

### → INTERNET
www.paginegialle.it
Italian Yellow Pages on the web

## TIME
Italy is on Central European Time, 1hr ahead of Greenwich Mean Time and 6hrs ahead of Eastern Standard Time. Daylight saving time (1hr ahead of CET) is in effect from end Mar. to end Sep.

## TOURIST OFFICES
■ Italian Government Tourist Office (NY)
Tel. 212 245 4822 or 212 245 5618
■ Italian State Tourist Office (San Francisco)
Tel. 415 392 6206
■ Italian State Tourist Office (Chicago)
Tel. 312 644 0990
■ Italian Tourist Office (London)
Tel. 0990 160 0280

## USEFUL NUMBERS
■ ENIT
Ente Nazionale Italiano per il Turismo, Rome
Tel. 06 49711
■ Assessorato Regionale del Turismo di Florence
Tel. 055 438 3640

# ◆ GETTING AROUND

## BY AIR

**→ 'AMERIGO VESPUCCI' AIRPORT, FLORENCE**
Via del Termine, 11 (2½ miles from Florence)
www.safnet.it
■ **Information**
(7.30am–11.30pm)
Tel. 055 373 498
■ **Airport shuttle bus service**
ATAF (No. 62)
Every 20 min between the airport and the city center, 6am–10.35pm; journey time: 20 min. Information: Tel. 055 565 0222
SITA
Hourly bus service between the airport and Via S. Caterina da Siena (alongside S. Maria Novella). Departures at 45 min past the hour (8.15am–8.05pm); journey time: 20 min. Information: Tel. 800 373 760
■ **Links with Pisa**
Train link (about 1 hour) or by SITA bus (about 3 hours).
■ **Check-in for Pisa airport, from Florence**
You can check-in for the 'Galileo Galilei' airport at the Air Terminal Firenze, inside S. Maria Novella railroad station, platform 5 (daily 6am–4.30pm)
Tel. 055 216073
■ **Car hire**
AVIS
Tel. 055 315588
EUROPCAR
Tel. 055 318609
HERTZ
Tel. 055 307370

**→ 'GALILEO GALILEI' AIRPORT, PISA**
Via dell'Aeroporto, at San Giusto
Tel. 050 500707
www.pisa-airport.com
■ **Links with the city center**
The airport is about a mile from the station piazza.
BY COACH
Coach 3 FS (every 15 min); journey time: 10 min

Information:
Tel. 050 505 511
BY CAR
Direct access to the A12 (Pisa-Genoa), A11 (Pisa-Florence) highways and the Florence-Pisa-Livorno freeway.
■ **Links with Florence**
Train link with S. Maria Novella in Florence or SITA coach service.
Stazione di S. Maria Novella FS Information:
Tel. 1478 88088 (7am–9pm)
■ **Car hire**
AVIS
Tel. 050 42028
EUROPCAR
Tel. 050 41017
HERTZ
Tel. 050 43220

## BY BICYCLE
From recommended hire outlets.
■ **CAI**
Florence division
Tel. 055 239 8580

## BY BUS
The cities are served by bus and minibus networks run by the various local authorities. Tickets, which are validated on board, can be bought at bus terminals or from newsstands, tobacconists and some bars. For special travel requirements such as day tickets or weekly passes, etc. contact the local tourist office or the bus company ticket office.

## BY CAR AND MOTORBIKE
Most Italian highways are toll roads. Seat belts are compulsory for the driver and front passenger. Motorcyclists must wear helmets. Speed limits are 50 km/h (30 mph) in town centers, 90 km/h (55 mph) on ordinary roads, 110 km/h (70 mph) on national roads and 130 km/h (80 mph) on highways. Driving and parking in the major cities can be difficult at peak hours.

## BY COACH
There are a number of different coach companies operating throughout the Tuscany region.
■ **CAP**
Routes between Prato, Pistoia, the Pistoiesi Mountains and the upper Mugello.
Tel. 055 214637
■ **Lazzi**
Links between Florence and La Spezia, Pontedera and Arezzo.
Via Mercadante 2
Tel. 055 363041
www.lazzi.it
■ **Rama**
Connects Grosseto with many provincial towns, Piombino, Siena and Florence.
Via Topazio 12
Tel. 0564 475111
■ **Sena**
Routes between Livorno, Pisa, Lucca, Florence, Siena.
Tel. 0577 283203

■ **Sita**
Local public transport, interregional lines.
Tuscany Office
Viale Cadorna, 105
Florence
Tel. 055 478 2237

## BY FERRY
There is a regular ferry service between the Tuscan Archipelago and the ports of Piombino, Livorno and Porto Santo Stefano.
Piombino-Portoferraio (1hr); Livorno-Capraia (2hr 30min); Porto Santo Stefano-Giglio Island (1hr) and Giannutri (1hr 30min)
MOBY LINES
Tel. 0565 918101
www.mobylines.it
■ **Toremar**
Tel. 0586 224511
www.toremar.it
■ **Maregiglio**
Tel. 0564 809309

## BY RAIL
The state railroad, Ferrovie dello Stato (FS), serves most of the region. Tickets can be purchased at railroad stations or travel agencies and are valid for two months. They must be validated before boarding. On some trains it may be necessary to reserve a seat in advance.

## BY TAXI
There are taxi stands outside airports, in front of railroad stations, in front of large hotels and in the city's main squares.

## FROM FLORENCE TO...
Arezzo: 48 miles
Grosseto: 89 miles
Livorno: 71 miles
Lucca: 45 miles
Massa, Carrara: 73 miles
Pisa: 56 miles
Pistoia: 22 miles
Prato: 11 miles
Siena: 42 miles

# TUSCANY FROM A TO Z ◆

Antique markets – amusement parks – banks – booking offices – food – golf courses – horse-riding
– hot-air balloons – internet – mail – motor racing – museums – period trains – pharmacies – press –
public telephones – railroad stations – scuba diving and sailing – service stations – shops – skiing
– souvenirs – taxis – theaters – thermal baths and health spas – tipping – tourist information offices
(APT) – trekking – useful numbers – wildlife parks and nature reserves – wine roads

## ANTIQUE MARKETS

There are numerous monthly markets for devotees of bric-a-brac and antiques:

■ **Arezzo**
First Sun. of the month and the Sat. before, Piazza Grande

■ **Dicomano**
Mercato del Mugello e della Val di Sieve, third Sun. of the month

■ **Florence**
– Second Sun. of the month, Piazza Santo Spirito
– Last Sun. of the month, Piazza dei Ciompi

■ **Lucca**
Third Sun. of the month and the Sat. before, Piazza Antelminelli

■ **Pisa**
Second Sun. of the month and the Sat. before, Via XX Settembre

■ **Pistoia**
Second Sun. of the month and the Sat. before, Piazza della Repubblica (except July and Aug.)

■ **Quarrata (Pistoia)**
Third Sun. of the month, Piazza Risorgimento

■ **Siena**
Third Sun. of the month, Loggiati di San Domenico

■ **Viareggio (Lucca)**
Fourth Sun. of the month, Piazza Manzoni

## AMUSEMENT PARKS

■ **Acqua**
Via Tevere 25, Cecina Mare, Livorno
Water park open until mid Sep. 10am–6pm (July, Aug. 10am–6.30pm)
For information Tel. 0586 622539

■ **Ciclilandia**
Piazza dei Fiori (north side), Tirrenia, Pisa
Tel. 050 335 73
Open Mon.–Sat. 2.30–7.30pm; Sun.

HORSE RIDING AT A FARM VACATION CENTER

TYPICAL PRODUCE

9.30am–12.30pm and 2.30–7.30pm
Everything you need to know about road safety and bicycle touring.

■ **'Città di Pistoia' zoological garden**
Open daily 9am–7pm
Tel. 0573 911219

■ **Le Cavallino Matto**
Donoratico-Castagneto Carducci, Livorno
Tel. 0565 745720

■ **Parco di Pinocchio**
Collodi – Pescia, Pistoia
Open daily 8.30am–sunset
Tel. 0572 429342

## BANKS

Open 8.30am–1pm (or 1.30pm) and 2.45–3.45pm (or 4.30pm).

## BOOKING OFFICES

■ **Box office**
– Via Alamanni, 39 Florence
Tel. 055 210804
– Chiasso dei Soldanieri, 8/r, Florence
Tel. 055 219402

■ **Easytickets**
www.tkts.it
Tel. 166 122166 (2540 lire a minute)

■ **www.ticketone.it**
Online sales

## FOOD

The choice is irresistible: typical products include wine, oil, cheese, salami and cured pork products, foodstuffs, truffles, saffron, honey and spelt.

## GOLF COURSES

■ **Castelfalfi Golf & Country Club**
Tenuta di Castelfalfi, Montaione, Florence
Tel. 0571 698093
18 holes

■ **Cosmopolitan Golf Club & Country Club**
Viale Pisorno 60, Tirrenia, Pisa
Tel. 050 33633
18 holes

■ **Esse Golf Club**
At Esse, Piazza Garibaldi 18 Bettolle, Siena
Tel. 0577 624466
18 holes

■ **Golf Club Acqua Bianca**
S146 highway, at Acqua Bianca, Chianciano Terme, Siena
Tel. 0578 31073
18 holes

■ **Golf Club Acquabona**
Island of Elba, Portoferraio, Livorno
Tel. 0565 940066
9 holes

■ **Golf Club Casentino**
at Pallazzo, Poppi, Arezzo
Tel. 0575 520167
9 holes

■ **Golf Club dell'Ugolino**
Florence
Strada Chiantigiana 3 Grassina, Florence
Tel. 055 230 1009
18 holes

■ **Golf Club Garfagnana**
at Braccicorti, Pieve Fosciana, Lucca
Tel. and fax 0583 644242

■ **Golf Club Hermitage**
Baia della Biodola, Island of Elba, Portoferraio, Livorno
Tel. 0565 969932
6 holes

■ **Golf Club Montecatini**
At Pievaccia, Via Dei Brogi, Monsummano Terme, Pistoia
Tel. 0572 62218
18 holes

■ **Golf Club Punta Ala**
Via Del Golfo 1 Punta Ala, Grosseto
Tel. 0564 922121
18 holes

■ **Golf Club Tirrenia**
Via San Guido, Tirrenia, Pisa
Tel. 050 37518
9 holes

■ **Golf Club Vicopelago**
Via del Cimitero, Vicopelago, Lucca
Tel. 0583 954014

■ **Poggio dei Medici Golf & Country Club**
Via S. Gavino 27 Scarperia, Florence
Tel. 055 843 0436
18 holes

■ **Siena Golf Club le Segalaie**
Via Grossetana 176 San Rocco a Pilli, Siena
Tel. and fax 0577 348192

■ **Versilia Golf Club**
Via della Sipe 100 Pietrasanta, Lucca)
Tel. 0584 881574
18 holes

# ◆ TUSCANY FROM A TO Z

Antique markets – amusement parks – banks – booking offices – food – golf courses – horse-riding – hot-air balloons – internet – mail – motor racing – museums – period trains – pharmacies – press – public telephones – railroad stations – scuba diving and sailing – service stations – shops – skiing – souvenirs – taxis – theaters – thermal baths and health spas – tipping – tourist information offices (APT) – trekking – useful numbers – wildlife parks and nature reserves – wine roads

ANTIQUE MARKET IN PISA

### HORSE-RIDING
Horse-riding enthusiasts will be delighted by the wide variety of options and excursions available. An increasing number of towns and farm vacation centers are providing this service in a region that cries out to be discovered on horseback.

### HOT-AIR BALLOONS
Chianti Balloon Club runs balloon flights over the region of Chianti. Departures in the morning from May to Sep. Reservations: Tel. 0577 36323

### INTERNET
To find out more about Tuscany:
– www.acpb.com/moveaboutitaly.it
– www.wonderful-italy.it
– www.itwg.com
– www.toscanainfo.it
– www.emmmeti.it/Welcome/Tuscany

### MAIL
Italian post boxes are painted red or blue (for mail to Europe). Mail services in Italy are traditionally quite slow. Post offices are open 8.30am–1pm.

### MOTOR RACING
Autodromo Internazionale del Mugello Booking and information: Scarperia, Florence, Via Senni, 15 Tel. 055 849 9111

### MUSEUMS
Opening hours vary from city to city. They are usually closed on Monday.

### PERIOD TRAINS
The Ferrovie Turistiche Italiane organizes trips on period trains and diesel-powered railcars along various stretches of track through areas of great natural beauty and artistic significance
■ **Treno degli Etruschi**
Volterra and the towns in the Val di Cecina
■ **Trenonatura Asciano e Monte Antico**
Through the Val d'Orcia
For information:
Tel. 030 740 2851
www.see.it/ok/fti

### PHARMACIES
Usually open 8.30am–12.30pm and 3–7pm.
If the pharmacy is closed, the name and address of the nearest open pharmacy will be displayed.

### PRESS
*La Nazione* is the most widely read daily paper in Tuscany, publishing news from the various provinces (www.lanazione.it). On the coast, *Il Tirreno* is sold in large quantities. Other national dailies such as *Repubblica*, *Il Giornale* and *Il Manifesto* devote pages to reporting daily news in Florence. *Tascabile TV Toscana* (weekly) and *Firenze spettacolo* (monthly) print listings of exhibitions, concerts and cultural events in Florence and Tuscany.

### PUBLIC TELEPHONES
→ **TELECOM**
Tel. 800 293 822
■ **Coins**
Some public telephones accept coins of 100, 200 or 500 lire.
■ **Telephone card**
5000, 10,000 and 15,000 lire cards sold in tobacconists, newspaper kiosks, post offices or automatic dispensers.
■ **International telephone card**
12,500, 25,000, 50,000 and 100,000 lire cards can be used for international calls. Dial 1740 in Italy to access this service.
■ **Credit cards**
Certain phones accept debit and credit cards.

| Telephone codes | |
|---|---|
| Arezzo | 0575 |
| Florence | 055 |
| Grosseto | 0564 |
| Livorno | 0586 |
| Lucca | 0583 |
| Pienza | 0578 |
| Pisa | 050 |
| Pistoia | 0573 |
| Portoferraio | 0565 |
| San Miniato | 050 |
| Siena | 0577 |

→ **INFOSTRADA**
Tel. 155
■ **Prepaid telephone card**
3000, 5000 and 10,000 lire cards sold in tobacconists, newspaper kiosks and shops that display the Infostrada logo.

→ **ALBACOM**
Tel. 800 902 942
■ **Coins**
Albacom public telephones accept coins of 100, 200, 500 and 1000 lire, 5 marks, 10 French francs and 1 English pound.
■ **Prepaid telephone cards**
5000 and 10,000 lire cards available from authorized sales outlets or automatic dispensers.

### RAILROAD STATIONS
■ **Arezzo**
– F.S. Station Piazza della Repubblica, 1 Tel. 147 888 088
– Stazione La Ferroviaria Italiana, Via Guido Monaco, 37 Tel. 0575 39881
■ **Florence** Tel. 1661 05050 and 1478 88088
■ **Grosseto** Piazza Marconi, 6 Tel. 0564 22331
■ **Livorno** Piazza Dante Tel. 1478 88088
■ **Lucca** Piazza Ricasoli Tel. 0583 47013
■ **Massa Carrara** Massa Centro, IV Novembre, 32 Tel. 0585 790791

ABETONE SKI PISTE

■ **Pisa**
Centrale, San
Rossore and
Aeroporto F.S.
stations
Tel. 1478 88088
■ **Pistoia**
Piazza Dante
Alighieri
Tel. 0573 31192
■ **Prato**
Tel. 1478 88088
■ **Siena**
Piazza Rosselli 7
Tel. 0577 280115

## SCUBA DIVING AND SAILING
The Tuscan coastline
and islands are a
paradise for scuba
divers and sailors
and there are many
centers, particularly
on Elba, Mount
Argentario, Capraia,
and Giglio Island.

## SERVICE STATIONS
Gas stations (selling
premium, green and
diesel gas) are
usually open
8.30am–1pm and
2.30–7pm, although
there are many
24-hour self-service
gas stations.

## SHOPS
Open weekday
mornings and
afternoons, but
closed Mon. am in
winter and Sat. pm
in summer. Food
stores are usually
closed on Wed. pm.
Department stores,
shopping malls and
some shops in large
city centers are open
every day 9am–7pm.

## SKIING
■ **Abetone**
Azienda di
Promozione Turistica
dell'Abetone
Abetone (Pt)
Piazzale Piramidi
Tel. 0573 60001
or 0573 360231
■ **Amiata**
Azienda di
Promozione Turistica
dell'Amiata
Via Mentana 98
Abbadia San
Salvatore, Siena
Tel. 0577 776455

## SOUVENIRS
You can buy a wide
variety of products,
ranging from
handmade crafts
items to luxury
goods from
internationally
renowned stores.
■ Clothing and
accessories: most
of the major
fashion designers
can be found in
Florence.
■ Alabaster from
Volterra.
■ Pottery and
terracotta from
Impruneta and
Montelupo
Fiorentino.
■ Knives and
scissors from
Scarperia.
■ Wrought iron.
■ Gold jewelry
from Arezzo
and Florence.
■ Carved wood.
■ Straw, wickerwork
and leather from
Florence.
■ Lace and
embroidery from
Florence and
Arezzo.
■ Paintings from
Pienza, clothing
from the Casentino.
■ Glass and crystal
from Colle di Val
d'Elsa.

## TAXIS
■ **Arezzo**
Radiotaxi
Tel. 0575 382626
■ **Florence**
Tel. 055 4499/4390
■ **Grosseto**
Tel. 0502 0005
(Station)
Tel. 0502 2478
(Duomo)
■ **Livorno**
Tel. 0586 401294
(Station)

■ **Lucca**
Tel. 0583 494989
(Station)
Tel. 0583 492691
(Piazza Napoleone)
■ **Massa Carrara**
Tel. 0585 790500
(Station in Massa)
Tel. 0585 572277
(Via Roma, Carrara)
■ **Pisa**
Tel. 050 41252
(Station)
Tel. 050 561878
(Duomo)
■ **Pistoia**
Tel. 0573 24291
(Station)
Tel. 0573 27763
(Piazza San
Francesco)
■ **Prato**
Radiotaxi 5656
■ **Siena**
Radiotaxi 49222

## THEATERS
■ **Arezzo**
Teatro Petrarca
Via Guido Monaco,
12
Tel. 0575 23975
■ **Empoli**
– Excelsior
Via Ridolfi, 75
Tel. 0571 72023
Booking Office
Tel. 0577 710746
– Centro Sociale
Coop
Via P. Veronese, 10
Tel. 0571 710746
■ **Florence**
– Teatro Romano,
Fiesole
Tel. 055 597265
– Puccini,
Piazza Puccini
Tel. 055 362067
– Verdi
Via Ghibellina, 99
Tel. 055 212320
– Pergola
Via della Pergola, 18
Tel. 055 247 9651/2
– Teatro di Rifredi
Via Vittorio
Emanuele, 303

Tel. 055 4220361
– Teatro della
Limonaia,
Sesto Fiorentino,
Via Gramsci, 426
Tel. 055 440852
– Teatro Studio di
Scandicci,
Via Donizetti, 58
Tel. 055 757348
– Teatro del Cestello,
Piazza di Cestello, 4
Tel. 055 294609
■ **Greve in Chianti**
Teatro A. Boito,
Via R. Libri, 2
Tel. 055 854 5219
and 055 240397
■ **Grosseto**
– Teatro Moderno
Via Tripoli
Tel. 0564 22429
– Teatro degli
Industri
Via Mazzini
Tel. 0564 21151
■ **Livorno**
– Teatro La Gran
Guardia
Via Grande, 121
Tel. 0586 885165
and 0586 883006
– Teatro delle
Commedie
Via G.M. Terreni, 3
Tel. 0586 404021
■ **Lucca**
Teatro del Giglio
Piazza del Giglio
Tel. 0583 467521
■ **Massa Carrara**
– Teatro Guglielmi,
Via Chiesa, 1,
Massa
Tel. 0585 41678
– Teatro Animosi,
Carrara, piazza
Cesare Battisti, 1
Tel. 0585 777226
■ **MonteCarlo (Lu)**
Teatro dei
Rassicurati,
Via Carmignani, 14
Tel. 0583 22517
■ **Pisa**
Teatro Verdi,
Via Palestro, 40
Tel. 050 941111
www.teatrodipisa.pi.it
■ **Pistoia**
Manzoni,
Corso Gramsci, 127
Tel. 0573 991609
■ **Prato**
– Fabbricone,
Via Targetti, 10
Tel. 0574 690962
– Metastasio,
Via Cairoli, 59
Tel. 0574 608501
www.metastasio.net

A WINE CELLAR

# ◆ TUSCANY FROM A TO Z

Antique markets – amusement parks – banks – booking offices – food – golf courses – horse-riding – hot-air balloons – internet – mail – motor racing – museums – period trains – pharmacies – press – public telephones – railroad stations – scuba diving and sailing – service stations – shops – skiing – souvenirs – taxis – theaters – thermal baths and health spas – tipping – tourist information offices (APT) – trekking – useful numbers – wildlife parks and nature reserves – wine roads

– Politeama Pratese, Via Garibaldi, 33
Tel. 0574 603758
– Anfiteatro Museo Luigi Pecci, Centro per l'Arte Contemporanea, Viale della Repubblica, 277
Tel. 0574 5317
www.comune.prato.it/pecci
■ **San Casciano, Florence**
Niccolini, Via Roma, 47
Tel. 055 8290146
■ **Siena**
– Teatro dei Rinnovati, Piazza del Campo, 1
Tel. 0577 292225 and 0577 292265
– Teatro dei Rozzi, Piazza Indipendenza, 15
Tel. 0577 46960

## THERMAL BATHS AND HEALTH SPAS
There are many spas and vacation resorts in Tuscany, including Chianciano, Saturnia, Montecatini and many other equally attractive smaller resorts.
■ **Bagni di Lucca**
Information: IAT
Tel. 0583 87946
■ **Bagni San Filippo**
Information: APT in Abbadia San Salvatore, Siena
Tel. 0577 775811
■ **Bagno Vignoni**
Information: IAT in San Quirico d'Orcia
Tel. 0577 897211
■ **Casciana Terme**
Information: IAT
Tel. 0587 646258
■ **Chianciano Terme**
Information: APT
Tel. 0577 63167 and 0577 63648
■ **Equi Terme**
Information: APT in Marina di Massa
Tel. 0585 240046
■ **Gambassi Terme**
Information: local tourist office
Tel. 0571 638141
■ **Monsummano Terme**
Information: APT in Montecatini Terme
Tel. 0572 772244

■ **Montecatini Terme**
Information: APT
Tel. 0572 772244
■ **Montepulciano**
Information: APT in Chianciano Terme
Tel. 0578 63167
■ **Portoferraio**
Information: APT
Tel. 0565 914671
■ **Radicondoli**
Information: APT in Siena,
Tel. 0577 280551
■ **Rapolano Terme**
Information: IAT
Tel. 0577 725541
■ **San Carlo Terme**
Information: APT in Massa Carrara
Tel. 0585 240046
■ **San Casciano dei Bagni**

Information: APT in Chianciano Terme
Tel. 0578 63167 and 0578 63648
■ **San Giuliano Terme**
Information: APT in Pisa
Tel. 050 560464
■ **Saturnia**
Information: APT in Grosseto
Tel. 0564 454510
■ **Terme di Petriolo**
Information: APT in Grosseto
Tel. 0564 454510
■ **Venturina**
Information: APT in Livorno
Tel. 0586 895320

## TIPPING
Service is usually included in restaurant bills, but extra tips are also appreciated. Hotel staff, hairdressers, tour guides and taxi drivers should be tipped (10–15%).

## TOURIST INFORMATION OFFICES (APT)
→ **AREZZO**
Piazza Risorgimento, 116
Tel. 0575 23952
Information Office
Piazza della Repubblica, 28
Tel. 0575 367678

→ **FLORENCE**
Via Manzoni, 16
Tel. 055 23320
■ Provincia-Comune
Via Cavour, 1/r
Tel. 055 290832
■ Municipal Information Office
Tel. 055 230 2124
■ Office at S. Maria Novella (building outside the station)
Tel. 055 212245
■ Office at the Airport
Tel. 055 315874

→ **GROSSETO**
Via Fucini, 43/c
Tel. 0564 454510

→ **LIVORNO**
Piazza Cavour, 6
Tel. 0586 898111
■ Information Office (seasonal)
– Medici Port
Tel. 0586 895320
– Calata Carrara Ocean terminal
Tel. 0586 210331

→ **LUCCA**
Piazzale Verdi, Vecchia Porta San Donato
Tel. 0583 419689

→ **MASSA CARRARA**
at Marina di Massa, Viale Vespucci, 24
Tel. 0585 243636 and 0585 240063

→ **PISA**
Viale Benedetto Croce, 24/26
Tel. 050 40096
■ Information office:
Via Cammeo, 2
Tel. 050 560464
Station piazza, Pisa Centrale
Tel. 050 42291
Airport
Tel. 050 500707

→ **PISTOIA**
Piazza Duomo, 4
Tel. 0573 21622

→ **PRATO**
Via L. Muzzi, 38
Tel. 0574 35141
■ Information office
Via Cairoli, 48
Tel. 0574 24112

→ **SIENA**
Via di Città, 43
Tel. 0577 42209
■ Information office
Piazza del Campo, 56
Tel. 0577 280551

## TREKKING
The various offices of the CAI (Club Alpino Italiano) dotted about the region offer courses in mountaineering, off-piste skiing and climbing. They also organize mountaineering or trekking trips.
■ **CAI**
Florence Office
Tel. 055 239 8580

■ **Trekkingitalia**
(Associazione Amici del Trekking e della Natura) Florence, Via dell'Oriuolo, 17
Tel. and fax
055 234 1040
■ **Legambiente Tuscana**
Florence,
Via G.P. Orsini 44
Tel. 055 681 0330
■ **Lega Montagna UISP**
Florence
Tel. 055 733 1814

## USEFUL NUMBERS
■ **Road Accidents** (ACI)
Florence office
Tel. 055 24861
■ **Carabinieri** (military police):
112
Information in English: 064477
■ **Public emergencies: 113**
■ **Forest rangers:** 1515
■ **Ambulance: 118**
■ **Fire service: 115**
■ **Breakdown assistance: 116**

## WILDLIFE PARKS AND NATURE RESERVES
To improve your knowledge of Tuscany's natural heritage:
■ **Cornate e Fosini**
Guided tours by the Comune of Montieri
Tel. 0566 997722
■ **Lago di Burano**
Burano,
WWF Oasis
Tel. 0564 898829
Lago di Montepulciano
Sezione Lipu di Montepulciano
Tel. 0577 241352
■ **Maremma, Parco dell'Uccellina**
Visitor Center
Via del Fante,
Alberese, Grosseto
Tel. 0564 407098
■ **Migliarino-San Rossore-Massaciuccoli**
Visitor center:
– Tenuta di Coltano,
Tel. 050 989084
– Tenuta di San Rossore
Tel. 050 539277

THERMAL POOL AT SATURNIA

■ **Orbetello, WWF Oasis**
c/o Casale della Giannella
Tel. 0564 820297
■ **Orrido di Botri**
Visitor center:
Tel. 0583 800083
■ **Padule di Bolgheri, WWF Oasis**
Visitor center:
c/o Vigili Urbani di Donoratico
Tel. 0565 777125
■ **Parchi della Val di Cornia**
Six protected areas along the coast and in the hills.
For information:
Tel. 0565 49430
■ **Parco delle Alpi Apuane**
Visitor centers:
– Forno (Massa)
ex Filanda
Tel. and fax
0585 315300
– Seravezza, Lucca
Via C. del Greco 11
Tel. 0584 756144
– Castelnuovo Garfagnana, Lucca
Piazza Erbe 1
Tel. and fax
0583 644242
■ **Parco Faunistico del Monte Amiata**
For information:
Tel. 0564 966867

## WINE ROADS
Wine Roads (Strade del Vino) are integrated tourist itineraries that involve wine-producing estates,
wine outlets, restaurants, hotels and museums. There are currently eleven approved Wine Roads in Tuscany:
The Movimento del Turismo del Vino organizes Cantine Aperte events on the last Sun. of May when the Tuscan wine shops open their doors to the public.
■ **Chianti Colli Fiorentini**
Consorzio Vino Chianti
Tel. 055 212333
Four itineraries in the suburbs of Florence and the southeastern part of the province.
■ **Chianti Rufina e Pomino**
Consorzio Chianti Rufina
Tel. 055 268204
Itinerary incorporating fifteen wine shops and various farm vacation centers.
■ **Colli di Maremma**
Comune di Scansano,
Piazza del Pretorio, 4
Tel. 0564 507122
In the southernmost part of Grosseto province, involving about 170 vineyards.
■ **Colline Lucchesi e Vino Monte Carlo**
The local tourist offices provide a printed guide to the
thirty-five wine-producing estates involved.
■ **Colline Pisane**
Piazza Vittorio Emanuele II, 4, Pisa
Tel. 050 929366
Itinerary in Pisa province from the Florence border to the Livorno border.
■ **Costa degli Etruschi**
Comune di Donoratico
Via della Repubblica, 15, Livorno
Tel. 0565 773025
Itinerary in the hinterland of the Maremma, including the island of Elba.
■ **Monteregio di Massa Marittima**
Comune di Massa Marittima,
Via Garibaldi 10
Tel. 0566 902756
Itinerary through the territory of the Metal Hills, involving over forty vineyards.
■ **MonteSpertoli**
Comune di Montespertoli,
Piazza del Popolo, 1
Tel. 0571 6001
Three itineraries: toward Empoli, toward Montelupo and toward Certaldo.
■ **Strada Medicea dei Vini di Carmignano**
Comune di Carmignano, Piazza Vitt. Emanuele II, 2
Tel. 055 871 2002
Twenty-two wine-producing estates and twelve restaurants along an itinerary that also comes under the aegis of the Comune of Poggio a Caiano.
■ **Vernaccia di San Gimignano**
Four wine roads around the historical center featuring 75 wine-producing estates.
■ **Vino Nobile di Montepulciano**
Three itineraries in the rolling hills at the mouth of the Chiana valley.

# ◆ FESTIVALS AND CULTURAL EVENTS

| | | |
|---|---|---|
| JAN.–FEB., JUNE–JULY | FLORENCE | Fashion parades and events |
| FEB. | SAN GIMIGNANO | Medieval carnival |
| | SIENA | National olive oil week in Fortezza |
| | VIAREGGIO | Viareggio Carnival |
| EASTER | FLORENCE (PIAZZA DUOMO) | Explosion of the cart and flight of the 'colombina' |
| APR.–MAY | FLORENCE (FORTEZZA DA BASSO) | Crafts market and fair Florence's Maggio Musicale |
| MAY 1 | GROSSETO | Spring festival and Alberese 'Merca' |
| LAST TWO SUN. IN MAY | LUCIGNANO MAGGIOLATA | Festival with floats bedecked with flowers |
| LAST SUN. IN MAY | FLORENCE | Cantine Aperte (open day in wine shops) (Movimento del Turismo del Vino) |
| JUNE | SIENA (FORTEZZA) | Wine Week at the Enoteca Italiana |
| | BAGNI DI LUCCA | Media Valle Canta, international folk song festival |
| 3RD SUN. IN JUNE AND 1ST SUN. IN SEP. | AREZZO | Joust of the Saracen |
| 17 JUNE | PISA | Lights festival of San Ranieri with regatta on the Arno River |
| LAST SUN. IN JUNE OR 1ST SUN. IN JULY | CHIUSI | Palio delle Torri for the festival of Santa Mustiola |
| JUNE 24 | FLORENCE (PIAZZA DELLA SIGNORIA) | Costumed historical soccer game and festival of San Giovanni |
| JUNE 26 | PISA | Gioco del Ponte |
| JULY | MONTEPULCIANO | International art workshop |
| | MONTERIGGIONI | Festa delle Torri |
| | MONTICCHIELLO | Teatro Povero di Monticchiello |
| | SAN GIMIGNANO | International festival |
| | SIENA | Settimana Musicale dell'Accademia Chigiana |
| | VOLTERRA | Volterra Teatro |
| JULY 2 AND AUG. 16 | SIENA | Palio |
| 1ST SUN. IN JULY | LIVORNO | Palio Marinaro |
| JULY 12 | LUCCA | Historical parade and Palio della Balestra |
| MID JULY– START AUG. | SIENA | Italian jazz show |
| PENULTIMATE SUN. IN JULY | PONTREMOLI | 'Bancarella' literary award |
| JULY 24 | PISTOIA | Joust of the Bear |
| JULY–AUG. | FIESOLE (ROMAN THEATER) | Estate Fiesolana |
| | MARINA DI PIETRASANTA | Festival della Versiliana |
| | TORRE DEL LAGO | Puccini Festival |
| JULY–SEP. | FORTE DEI MARMI | International festival of political satire |
| AUG. 7 | MASSA MARITTIMA | Balestro del Girifalco, crossbow contest |
| AUG. 13–15 | MONTEPULCIANO | Performance of the Bruscello |
| AUG. 28 | MONTEPULCIANO | Bravio delle Botti, barrel race |
| AUG.–SEP. | SAN QUIRICO D'ORCIA | Forme nel Verde, contemporary sculpture exhibition |
| END AUG. | VOLTERRA | Anno Domini 1398 |
| SEP. | AREZZO | International gold and costume jewelry show |
| | COLLE DI VAL D'ELSA | Cristallo Tra le Mura |
| | PRATO | International exhibition of comics and fantasy |
| 1ST SAT. AND SUN. IN SEP. | MONTALCINO | National honey fair |
| 1ST SUN. IN SEP. | VOLTERRA | Astiludium, flag-throwing tournament |
| SEP. 7 | FLORENCE | Festival of the Rificolona |
| SEP. 8 | PRATO | Historical parade and Exposition of the Sacred Girdle |
| | SAN MARCELLO PISTOIESE | Launch of the hot-air balloons |
| SEP. 13 | PISA | Lights festival of Santa Croce |
| SEP.–DEC. | SAN GIMIGNANO COLLE DI VAL D'ELSA POGGIBONSI, MONTALCINO CASOLE D'ELSA, VOLTERRA | Arte all'Arte (six contemporary artists exhibit in six historical centers) |
| OCT. 18 | IMPRUNETA | Fair in Impruneta or San Luca |
| LAST SUN. IN OCT. | MONTALCINO | Festival of the Thrush in Fortezza |
| OCT.–NOV. | PITIGLIANO | Pitigliano film festival |
| OCT.–APRIL | CHIANTI | Tuscia Electa (review of contemporary art) |
| DEC. 24–JAN 6 | PORTO ERCOLE | Presepe Marino Vivente |

Sites are listed alphabetically by *comune* within the eleven itineraries featured in this guide. For ease of reference, abbeys, churches and other isolated monuments appear under their respective *comunes*.

| FLORENCE | 50100 | ◆ A |
|---|---|---|
| **AZIENDA DI PROMOZIONE TURISTICA (APT) – FLORENCE** Via Manzoni, 16 Tel. 055 23320 Fax 055 234 6286 | e-mail: info@firenze.turismo.toscana.it | |
| **ALBERTO DELLA RAGIONE COLLECTION OF CONTEMPORARY ART** Piazza della Signoria, 5 Tel. 055 203078 | *Open 9am–1pm.* *Closed Tue.* | ▲ 123 ◆ A D4 |
| **BADIA FIORENTINA** Via del Proconsolo Tel. 055 59155 | *Open 7–11.30am and 5–7pm.* | ▲ 133 ◆ A D3-4 |
| **BAPTISTERY OF SAN GIOVANNI** Piazza San Giovanni Tel. 055 210 2885 | *Open noon–6.30pm; Sun. and public holidays 8.30am–1.30pm.* *Closed Easter and Christmas.* | ▲ 120 ◆ A D3 |
| **BIBLIOTECA LAURENZIANA** Piazza San Lorenzo, 9 Tel. 055 210760; 055 214443 Fax 055 230 2992 | *Open Mon.–Wed., Fri., Sat. 8am–1.45pm; Thur. 8am–5pm. Michelangelo's vestibule and reading room closed for restoration. Only scholars allowed access with special authorization.* | ▲ 121 ◆ A D3 |
| **BOBOLI GARDENS** Piazza Pitti Tel. 055 265171 | *Open summer 9am–7pm; winter 9am–5pm.* *Closed the 1st and last Mon. of the month.* | ▲ 125 ◆ A C5 |
| **CAMPANILE** Piazza Duomo | *Open 9am–6.50pm.* | ▲ 119 ◆ A D3 |
| **CAPPELLA BRANCACCI** Piazza del Carmine, 14 Tel. 055 238 2195 | *Open Mon., Wed.–Sat., 10am–5pm; Sun., 1–5pm.* *Closed Tue.* | ▲ 129 ◆ A B4 |
| **CAPPELLA PAZZI** Piazza Santa Croce Tel. 055 244619 | *Open winter 8am–12.30pm, weekdays 3–6pm; summer 8am–6.30pm, weekdays 8am–noon and 3–6.30pm.* | ▲ 136 ◆ A E4 |
| **CASA BUONARROTI** Via Ghibellina, 70 Tel. 055 241752 | *Open Wed.–Mon. 9.30am–1.30pm.* *Closed Christmas, New Year's Day, Easter, Apr. 24, May 1, Aug. 15.* | ▲ 136 ◆ A E4 |
| **DUOMO (SANTA MARIA DEL FIORE)** Piazza Duomo Tel. 055 294514 | *Open 10am–5pm; weekdays 1–5pm.* *1st Sat. of the month and Thur. 10am–3.30pm.* | ▲ 119 ◆ A D3 |
| **FORTE DI BELVEDERE** Via di San Leonardo Tel. 055 284571 (Office) | *Open summer 9am–8pm; winter 9am–4pm.* *Telephone for information.* | ▲ 128 ◆ A C-D 5-6 |
| **GALLERIA DELL'ACCADEMIA** Via Ricasoli, 60 Tel. 055 238 8612 | *Open Tue.–Sun. 8.15am–6.50pm.* *Closed Mon.* | ▲ 132 ◆ A D-E2 |
| **LOGGIA AND MUSEO DEL BIGALLO** Piazza San Giovanni, 1 Tel. 055 215440 | *Open 8.30am–2pm.* *Closed Sun.* | ▲ 118 ◆ A D3 |
| **MEDICI CHAPELS** Piazza Madonna degli Aldobrandini, 6 Tel. 055 238 8602 | *Open 8.30am–5pm; public holidays 8.15am–i.50pm.* *Closed 1st, 3rd, 5th Mon. and 2nd and 4th Sun. of the month* | ▲ 122 ◆ A D3 |
| **MUSEO ARCHEOLOGICO** Via della Colonna, 36 Tel. 055 247 8641 | *Open Mon. 2–7pm; Tue., Thur. 8.30am–7pm; Wed, Fri.–Sun. 8.30 am–2pm.* | ▲ 132 ◆ A E2-3 |
| **MUSEO DELL'OPERA DEL DUOMO** Piazza Duomo, 9 Tel. 055 264 7287 | *Open Mon.–Sat. 9.30am–6.30pm; Sun. 8.20am–2pm.* | ▲ 120 ◆ A D3 |
| **MUSEO DELL'OPERA DI SANTA CROCE** Piazza Santa Croce, 16 Tel. 055 244619 | *Open 10am–6pm.* *Closed Wed.* | ▲ 136 ◆ A E4 |
| **MUSEO DELLE PORCELLANE** Boboli Gardens Tel. 055 238 8710 | *Open 2nd, 4th (if not the last) Mon. of the month, Tue., Sat., 1st, 3rd, 5th Sun. of the month 9am–1.50pm.* | ▲ 128 ◆ A C-D6 |
| **MUSEO DI FIRENZE COM'ERA** Via dell'Oriuolo, 24 Tel. 055 261 6545 | *Open 9am–2pm.* *Closed Thur.* | ▲ 133 ◆ A E3 |
| **MUSEO DI SAN MARCO** Piazza San Marco, 1 Tel. 055 23885 | *Open Tue.–Fri. 8.15am–1.50pm; Sat. 8.15am–6.50pm; 2nd and 4th Sun. of the month 8.15am– 7pm; 1st, 3rd and 5th Mon. of the month 8.15am–1.50pm.* | ▲ 131 ◆ A D-E2 |
| **MUSEO MARINO MARINI** Piazza San Pancrazio Tel. 055 219432; fax 055 219438 | *Open Mon., Wed.–Sat. 10am–5pm; Sun. and public holidays 10am–1pm.* *Closed Tue.* | ▲ 129 ◆ A C3 |

| | | |
|---|---|---|
| **OPIFICIO DELLE PIETRE DURE**<br>Via degli Alfani, 78<br>Tel. 055 289414 | *Open Mon., Wed.–Sat. 8.15am–2pm; Tue.*<br>*8.15am–7pm.*<br>*Closed Sun. and public holidays.* | ▲ 132<br>◆ A D-E2 |
| **ORSANMICHELE**<br>Via Arte della Lana<br>Tel. 055 284944 | *Open 9am–noon and 2–4pm.*<br>*Closed 1st and last Mon. of the month.* | ▲ 122<br>◆ A D4 |
| **OSPEDALE DEGLI INNOCENTI**<br>Piazza SS. Annunziata, 12<br>Tel. 055 249 1708 | *Open 8.30am–2pm; public holidays 8am–1pm.* | ▲ 132<br>◆ A E2-3 |
| **PALAZZO DAVANZATI**<br>Via Porta Rossa, 13<br>Tel. 055 238 8610 | *Open 8am–1.50pm.* | ▲ 122<br>◆ A D4 |
| **PALAZZO E MUSEO NAZIONALE**<br>**DEL BARGELLO**<br>Via del Proconsolo, 4<br>Tel. 055 238 8606 | *Open 8.30am–1.50pm.*<br>*Closed 2nd and 4th Mon. of the month and*<br>*1st, 3rd and 5th Sun. of the month.* | ▲ 134<br>◆ A D3-4 |
| **PALAZZO MEDICI-RICCARDI**<br>Via Cavour, 1<br>Tel. 055 276 0340 | *Open 9am–12.45pm and 3–5pm; Sun. 9am–12.45pm.*<br>*Closed Wed.* | ▲ 121<br>◆ A D3 |
| **PALAZZO PITTI**<br>Piazza Pitti, 1<br>Tel. 055 238 8701 | | ▲ 128<br>◆ A C5 |
| **- GALLERIA D'ARTE MODERNA**<br>Tel. 055 238 8616 | *Open 8.30am–1.50pm. Closed 2nd, 4th Sun. of*<br>*month and 1st, 3rd, 5th Mon. of month.* | |
| **- GALLERIA PALATINA**<br>Tel. 055 238 8614 | *Open 8.30am–6.50pm; Sun. 8.30am–7pm.*<br>*Closed Mon.* | |
| **- MUSEO DELL'ARGENTERIA**<br>Tel. 055 238 8709 | *Open 8.30am–1.50pm.*<br>*Closed 2nd and 4th Sun. of the month and 1st, 3rd*<br>*and 5th Mon. of the month.* | |
| **- MUSEO DELLE CARROZZE** | *Currently closed; for information Tel. 055 238 8614.* | |
| **PALAZZO STROZZI**<br>Piazza Strozzi, 1<br>Tel. 055 239 8563 | *Open 8am–7pm.*<br>*Closed Sun.* | ▲ 129<br>◆ A C-D4 |
| **PALAZZO VECCHIO**<br>Piazza della Signoria<br>Tel. 055 276 8465 | *Open Mon.–Wed. and Fri.–Sat. 9am–7pm;*<br>*Thur. and Sun. 9am–2pm* | ▲ 123<br>◆ A D4 |
| **REFECTORY OF SANT'APOLLONIA**<br>Via XXVII Aprile, 1<br>Tel. 055 238 8607 | *Open 8.30am–1.50pm.*<br>*Closed 2nd and 4th Mon. of the month and*<br>*1st, 3rd and 5th Sun. of the month.* | ▲ 131<br>◆ A D2 |
| **SAN LORENZO**<br>Piazza San Lorenzo, 9<br>Tel. 055 216634 | *Open 8am–noon and 3.30–5.30pm;*<br>*Sun. 3.30–5.30pm.* | ▲ 121<br>◆ A D3 |
| **SAN SALVATORE AL MONTE**<br>Via San Salvatore al Monte, 9<br>Tel. 055 234 2640 | *Open 8am–noon and 1–5pm.* | ▲ 137<br>◆ A F6 |
| **SANTA CROCE**<br>Piazza Santa Croce, 16<br>Tel. 055 244618/9 | *Open 9.30am–12.15pm and 3–5.10pm;*<br>*Sun. 3–5.30pm.* | ▲ 136<br>◆ A E4 |
| **SANTA MARIA DEL CARMINE**<br>Piazza del Carmine<br>Tel. 055 212331 | *Open 10am–5pm; public holidays 1–5pm.*<br>*Closed Tue.* | ▲ 129<br>◆ A B4 |
| **SANTA MARIA NOVELLA**<br>Piazza Santa Maria Novella<br>Tel. 055 210113 | *Open 7am–noon; 3–6pm (Sat. and religious*<br>*holidays 3–5pm); Sun. 3–5pm.* | ▲ 130<br>◆ A C3 |
| **SAN MINIATO AL MONTE**<br>Via Monte alle Croci<br>Tel. 055 234 2731 | *Open summer 8am–noon and 2–7pm; winter*<br>*8am–noon and 2.30–6pm.* | ▲ 137<br>◆ A E-F6 |
| **SANTA TRINITA**<br>Piazza Santa Trinita<br>Tel. 055 293161 | *Open 8am–noon and 4–7pm.* | ▲ 129<br>◆ A C4 |
| **SANTISSIMA ANNUNZIATA**<br>Piazza SS Annunziata<br>Tel. 055 239 8034 | *Open 7am–12.30pm and 4–6.30pm; Sun. and public*<br>*holidays 7am–1.30pm and 4–7pm.* | ▲ 132<br>◆ A E2 |
| **SANTO SPIRITO**<br>Piazza Santo Spirito, 20<br>Tel. 055 210030 | *Open 8.30am–noon and 3.45–6pm; public holidays*<br>*9.30–10.30am and 2.45–5pm.* | ▲ 128<br>◆ A C4-5 |
| **UFFIZI GALLERY**<br>Piazzale degli Uffizi, 6<br>Tel. 055 238 8651;<br>055 294883 | *Open 8.30am–6.50pm. Closed Mon.*<br>*Visit by appointment only.* | ▲ 126<br>◆ A D4 |

| CAREGGI | 50100 | C B2 | |
|---|---|---|---|
| **MEDICI VILLA DI CAREGGI**<br>Viale Piraccini, 21<br>Tel. 055 427 7329 | *Open 9am–6pm.*<br>*Closed Sun.* | | ▲ 138 |

| CASTELLO | 50100 | C B2 | |
|---|---|---|---|
| **VILLA DELLA PETRAIA**<br>Via Petraia, 40<br>Tel. 055 451208 | *Open Nov.–Jan. 9am–4.30pm; Feb.–Mar.*<br>*9am–5.30pm; Apr.–May and Sep. 9am–6.30pm;*<br>*June–Aug. 9am–7.30pm. Closed 2nd and 3rd Mon.*<br>*of the month, May 1, Christmas, New Year's Day.* | | ▲ 138 |
| **MEDICI VILLA DI CASTELLO**<br>Via di Castello, 47<br>Tel. 055 454791 | *Open 9am–3pm (villa); 9am–4pm (garden).*<br>*Closed 2nd and 3rd Mon. of the month.* | | ▲ 138 |

| FIESOLE | 50014 | C B2 | |
|---|---|---|---|
| **DUOMO**<br>Piazza del Duomo<br>Tel. 055 23320 (APT Florence) | *Visit by appointment only.* | | ▲ 137 |
| **MUSEO ARCHEOLOGICO**<br>Via Portigiani, 1<br>Tel. 055 59477<br>Fax 055 59118 | *Open Mon.–Sun.: Mar 28–Sep. 28 9.30am–7pm;*<br>*Mar. 1–27, Oct. 1–23 9.30am–6pm; Oct. 24–Feb 28*<br>*9.30am–5pm. Closed 1st Tue. of the month.* | | ▲ 137 |
| **SAN MICHELE**<br>Via Giuseppe Mantellini<br>Tel. 055 23320 (APT Florence) | *Visit by appointment only.* | | ▲ 137 |
| **MEDICI VILLA**<br>Via Vecchia Fiesolana<br>Tel. 055 23320 (APT Florence) | *Visit by appointment only.* | | ▲ 137 |

| SETTIGNANO | 50014 | B F4 | ▲ 138 |
|---|---|---|---|
| **VILLA GAMBERAIA**<br>Via del Rossellino, 72<br>Tel. 055 697205 | *Open 8.30am–6pm (garden).*<br>*Visits by appointment Sat. and Sun.* | | |

## AROUND FLORENCE

| ARTIMINO | 59015 | B E4 | ▲ 143 |
|---|---|---|---|
| **MEDICI VILLA**<br>Tel. 055 879 2040 (villa);<br>055 871 8124 (museum) | *Open Tue. by appointment.* | | |

| CARMIGNANO | 59015 | B E4 | |
|---|---|---|---|
| **SAN MICHELE**<br>Piazza SS. Francesco e Michele<br>Tel. 055 871 2046 | *Open 7am–12.30pm and 3–7pm.* | | ▲ 142 |

| CASTELFIORENTINO | 50051 | C A3 | |
|---|---|---|---|
| **SANTA VERDIANA MUSEUM**<br>Piazza Santa Verdiana<br>Tel. 0571 64096 | *Open Sat. 4–7pm; Sun. 10am–noon and 4–7pm.*<br>*Can also be visited on request.* | | ▲ 144 |

| CERRETO GUIDI | 50050 | C A2 | |
|---|---|---|---|
| **MEDICI VILLA**<br>Via dei Ponti Medicei<br>Tel. 0571 55707 | *Open 9am–7pm.* | | ▲ 142 |

| CERTALDO | 50052 | C A3 | |
|---|---|---|---|
| **BIRTHPLACE OF BOCCACCIO**<br>Via Boccaccio<br>Tel. 0571 664208 | *Open winter 10am–noon and 2.30–5.30pm;*<br>*summer 10am–7pm. Open Tue. 10am–4.30pm.* | | ▲ 144 |

| CERTOSA DEL GALLUZZO | 50124 | C A2 | |
|---|---|---|---|
| **PICTURE GALLERY AND**<br>**CHIESA DEI MONACI**<br>Tel. 055 204 9226 | *Open winter 9am–noon and 3–5pm;*<br>*summer 9am–noon and 3–6pm.* | | ▲ 143 |

| EMPOLI | 50053 | C A3 | |
|---|---|---|---|
| **MUSEO DELLA COLLEGIATA**<br>**DI SANT'ANDREA**<br>Piazza della Propositura, 3<br>Tel. 0571 76284 | *Open Tue.–Sun. 9am–noon and 4–7pm.*<br>*Closed Mon.* | | ▲ 141 |

# ◆ PLACES TO VISIT

| | | |
|---|---|---|
| **SANT'ANDREA**<br>Piazza Farinata degli Uberti<br>Tel. 0571 72220 | *Open 8am–noon and 4–7pm.* | ▲ 141 |
| **SANTA MARIA A RIPA**<br>Via Livornese<br>Tel. 0571 80247 | *Open 8am–noon and 4–7pm.* | ▲ 141 |
| **SANTO STEFANO**<br>Via de' Neri<br>Tel. 0571 76284 | *Open Tue.–Fri. 9am–noon and 4–7pm.*<br>*Closed Sat. afternoon, Sun. and Mon.* | ▲ 141 |

| POGGIO A CAIANO | 59016 | C A2 |
|---|---|---|
| **MEDICI VILLA**<br>Via Pistoiese<br>Tel. 055 877012 | *Open Nov.–Feb. 8am–4.30pm; Mar. 8am–5.30pm;*<br>*Apr.–May and Sep.–Oct. 8am–6.30pm; June–Aug.*<br>*8am–7.30pm.* | ▲ 142 |
| **RACCOLTA COMUNALE D'ARTE**<br>Via Tilli, 41<br>Tel. 0571 64019 | *Open Tue., Thur., Sat. 4–7pm; Sun. and public*<br>*holidays 10am–noon and 4–7pm.*<br>*Closed Mon., Wed., Fri.* | |

| SAN CASCIANO IN VAL DI PESA | 50026 | C B3 |
|---|---|---|
| **MUSEUM OF THE SACRED HEART**<br>Via Roma, 31<br>Tel. 055 822 9444 | *Open public holidays 10am–12.30pm and 4–7pm;*<br>*Sat. 4.30–7pm.* | ▲ 143 |
| **SANT'ANDREA IN PERCUSSINA**<br>Via Scopeta, 46<br>Tel. 055 820351 | *Visit by appointment only.* | ▲ 144 |

| VINCI | 50059 | C A2 |
|---|---|---|
| **BIRTHPLACE OF LEONARDO DA VINCI**<br>Anchiano<br>Tel. 0571 56055 | *Open summer 9.30am–7pm; winter 9.30am–6pm.* | ▲ 142 |
| **MUSEO LEONARDIANO**<br>Via della Torre, 2<br>Tel. 0571 56055 | *Open summer 9.30am–7pm; winter 9.30am–6pm.* | ▲ 142 |

# PISA AND LUCCA

| BORGO A MOZZANO | 55023 | B C3-D |
|---|---|---|
| **SANT'JACOPO**<br>Tel. 0583 419689 (APT Lucca) | *Telephone for information and hours.* | ▲ 161 |

| CALCI | 56011 | B C3-D |
|---|---|---|
| **CERTOSA DI PISA**<br>Via Roma<br>Tel. and fax 050 938430 | *Open Tue.–Sat. 9am–6.30pm; Sun. and public*<br>*holidays 9am–noon.*<br>*Closed Mon., New Year's Day, May 1 and Christmas.* | ▲ 154 |
| **MUSEO DI STORIA NATURALE**<br>**E DEL TERRITORIO PISANO**<br>Via Roma, 103<br>Tel. 050 936193<br>Fax 050 937778 | *Open winter Tue.–Sat. 9am–6pm; Sun. and public*<br>*holidays 10am–7pm.* | ▲ 154 |
| **MUSEO STORICO E ARTISTICO**<br>**DELLA CERTOSA**<br>Via Roma<br>Tel. and fax  050 938430 | *Open 9am–7pm; public holidays 9am–1pm.*<br>*Closed Mon., New Year's Day, May 1 and Christmas.* | ▲ 154 |

| CAMIGLIANO | 55010 | B C4 |
|---|---|---|
| **VILLA TORRIGIANI**<br>Tel. 0583 928889 | *Open at all times.* | ▲ 160 |

| CASTELNUOVO DI GARFAGNANA | 55032 | B C3 |
|---|---|---|
| **DUOMO**<br>Tel. 0583 62170 | *Open every morning and 3–7pm.* | ▲ 162 |
| **ROCCA**<br>Tel. 0583 644801 | *Open 10am–1pm and 5.30–10pm.*<br>*Only part of the Rocca be visited.* | ▲ 162 |

| COREGLIA ANTELMINELLI | 55025 | B C3-D |
|---|---|---|
| **MUSEO DELLA FIGURINA DI GESSO**<br>Via del Mangano, 17<br>Tel. 0583 78082 | *Open June–Sep.*<br>*Closed Sun. during Oct. 1–May 31.* | ▲ 162 |
| **SAN MICHELE**<br>Tel. 0583 78023<br>(rector) | *Open 8.30am–6pm.* | ▲ 162 |

| DIECIMO | 55020 | B C4-D | |
|---|---|---|---|
| SANTA MARIA A DIECIMO<br>Tel. 0583 88881 (rector) | Open 8am–6pm. | | ▲ 161 |

| LUCCA | 55100 | B C4-D | |
|---|---|---|---|
| AZIENDA DI PROMOZIONE TURISTICA (APT) – LUCCA<br>Piazza Verdi<br>Tel. 0583 419689 | e-mail: aptlucca@lucca.turismo.toscana.it | | |
| CASA DI PUCCINI<br>Via di Poggio, 9<br>Tel. 0583 584 0287 | Open Tue.–Sun: Apr.–May. and Oct.–Dec. 10am–1pm and 3–6pm; June–Sep. 10am–6pm. Closed Mon. | | ▲ 157 |
| PALAZZO MANSI<br>Via Galli Tassi, 43<br>Tel. 0583 55570 | Open 9am–7pm; public holidays 9am–2pm. Closed Mon., Christmas, New Year's Day and May 1. | | ▲ 157 |
| SAN FREDIANO<br>Via Anguillara, 9<br>Tel. 0583 493627 | Open morning and afternoon. Hours vary. | | ▲ 156 |
| SAN MARTINO<br>Piazza del Duomo<br>Tel. 0583 957068 | Open summer Mon.–Fri.10am–6pm; Sat.–Sun. 10am–7pm; winter Tue.–Sun.10am–1pm and 3–6pm. Closed Mon. | | ▲ 158 |
| SAN MICHELE IN FORO<br>Piazza San Michele<br>Tel. 0583 48459 | Open morning and afternoon. Hours vary. | | ▲ 157 |
| TORRE DELLE ORE<br>Via Fillungo<br>Tel. 0583 419689 (APT Lucca) | Telephone for information and hours. | | ▲ 157 |
| VILLA GUINIGI (MUSEO NAZIONALE)<br>Via della Quarquonia<br>Tel. 0583 496033 | Open 9am–7pm; public holidays 9am–2pm. Closed Mon., Christmas, New Year's Day and May 1. | | ▲ 159 |

| MARLIA | 55014 | B C4-D | |
|---|---|---|---|
| VILLA REALE<br>Tel. 0583 30108; 0583 30009 | Open by appointment Mar.–Nov. 10am–noon and 5–7pm. | | ▲ 160 |

| MARINA DI PISA | 56013 | B C5 | |
|---|---|---|---|
| TENUTA DI SAN ROSSORE<br>Tel. 050 525500 | Open Apr.–Sep. Sun. and public holidays. | | ▲ 154 |

| PISA | 56100 | B C5 | |
|---|---|---|---|
| AZIENDA DI PROMOZIONE TURISTICA (APT) – PISA<br>Piazza della Stazione, 13<br>Tel. 050 42291 | e-mail: info@pisa.turismo.toscana.it | | |
| BAPTISTERY<br>Piazza del Duomo<br>Tel. 050 560547; 050 561820 | Open winter 9am–4.40pm; spring and fall 9am–5.40pm; summer 8am–7.40pm. | | ▲ 148 |
| CAMPANILE<br>Piazza del Duomo<br>Tel. 050 560547; 050 561820 | Not open to the public. | | ▲ 148 |
| CAMPOSANTO<br>Piazza del Duomo<br>Tel. 050 560547; 050 561820 | Open winter 9am–4.40pm; spring and fall 9am–5.40pm; summer 8am–7.40pm. | | ▲ 148 |
| DUOMO<br>Piazza del Duomo<br>Tel. 050 560547; 050 561820 | Open winter 10am–noon and 3–4.45pm, public holidays 3–4.45pm; spring and fall: weekdays 10am–7.40pm, public holidays 1–7.40pm; Apr.–Sep.: weekdays 10am–7.40pm, public holidays 1–7.40pm. | | ▲ 147 |
| MUSEO DELL'OPERA DEL DUOMO<br>Piazza Arcivescovado, 8<br>Tel. 050 560547; 050 561820 | Open winter 9am–4.20pm; spring and fall 9am–5.20pm; summer 8am–7.20pm. | | ▲ 149 |
| MUSEO DELLE SINOPIE<br>Piazza del Duomo<br>Tel. 050 560547; 050 561820 | Open winter 9am–4.40pm; spring and fall 9am–5.40pm; summer 8am–7.40pm. | | ▲ 149 |
| MUSEO NAZIONALE DI SAN MATTEO<br>Piazza San Matteo in Soarta, 1<br>Tel. 050 926511; 050 926539<br>Fax 050 500099 | Open Tue.–Sat. 9am–7pm, Sun. and public holidays 9am–2pm. Closed Mon. | | ▲ 152 |
| PALAZZO DEI CAVALIERI<br>Piazza dei Cavalieri<br>Tel. 050 509111 | Visit by appointment only. | | ▲ 149 |

| | | |
|---|---|---|
| **PALAZZO DELL'OROLOGIO**<br>Piazza dei Cavalieri<br>Tel. 050 42291 | *Visit by appointment only.* | ▲ 149 |
| **SAN FRANCESCO**<br>Piazza San Francesco, 4<br>Tel. 050 544091 | *Open morning and afternoon.*<br>*Hours vary.* | ▲ 152 |
| **SAN MARTINO**<br>Piazza San Martino, 1<br>Tel. 050 49568 | *Open morning and afternoon.*<br>*Hours vary.* | ▲ 153 |
| **SAN MICHELE IN BORGO**<br>Borgo Stretto<br>Tel. 050 541849 | *Open morning and afternoon.*<br>*Hours vary.* | ▲ 153 |
| **SAN PAOLO A RIPA D'ARNO**<br>Piazza San Paolo a Ripa d'Arno<br>Tel. 050 41515 | *Open morning and afternoon.*<br>*Hours vary.* | ▲ 153 |
| **SAN SEPOLCRO**<br>Lungarno Galileo Galilei,<br>Piazza Santo Sepolcro<br>Tel. 050 502728 | *Open morning and afternoon.*<br>*Hours vary.* | ▲ 153 |
| **SANTA CATERINA**<br>Piazza Santa Caterina<br>Tel. 050 552883 | *Open morning and afternoon.*<br>*Hours vary.* | ▲ 152 |
| **SANTA MARIA DELLA SPINA**<br>Lungarno Gambacorti<br>Tel. 050 910365;<br>055 321 5446 | *Open winter 9am–1pm; Mar.–May, Sep.–Oct.*<br>*11am–1pm, 2.30–6.30pm; June–Aug., Tue.– Fri.*<br>*11am–1pm, 2.30–6.30pm, Sat.–Sun. 11am–1pm, 2–*<br>*8pm. Closed Mon., May 1, Aug. 15, Dec. 24–Jan. 2.* | ▲ 153 |
| **SANTO STEFANO DEI CAVALIERI**<br>Piazza dei Cavalieri<br>Tel. 050 580814 | *Open morning and afternoon.*<br>*Hours vary.* | ▲ 152 |
| **PONTEDERA** | 56025 | B D4 |
| **SANTI JACOPO E FILIPPO**<br>Piazza Curtatone e Montanara<br>Tel. 0587 52017 | *Open morning and afternoon.*<br>*Hours vary.* | ▲ 155 |
| **SAN GIORGIO DI BIBBIANO** | 55100 | U B C4-D |
| **SAN GIORGIO**<br>at Vinchiana, Statale 12<br>Tel. 0583 965281 (rector) | *Visit by appointment only.* | ▲ 161 |
| **SAN MINIATO** | 56028 | B D4 |
| **DUOMO**<br>Piazza del Duomo<br>Tel. 0571 418 0171 | *Open morning and afternoon.*<br>*Hours vary.* | ▲ 155 |
| **MUSEO DIOCESANO D'ARTE SACRA**<br>Tel. 0571 418071 | *Open winter Sat.–Sun. 9am–noon, 2.30–5pm;*<br>*summer Tue.–Sun. 9am–noon, 3–6pm. Closed Mon.* | ▲ 155 |
| **SAN DOMENICO**<br>Loggiati di San Domenico<br>Tel. 0571 43150 | *Open morning and afternoon.*<br>*Hours vary.* | ▲ 155 |
| **SAN PANCRAZIO** | 55100 | C B3 |
| **VILLA GRABAU**<br>(FORMER VILLA CITTADELLA)<br>Via S. Pancrazio<br>Tel. 0583 406325 | *Visit by appointment only.* | ▲ 160 |
| **VILLA OLIVA (NOW BOTTINI)**<br>Tel. 0583 494066 | *Visit by appointment only.* | ▲ 160 |
| **SAN PIETRO A GRADO** | 56100 | B C5 |
| **ROMANESQUE BASILICA**<br>Tel. 050 42291 | *Open at all times, telephone*<br>*050 560464 (APT Pisa).* | |
| **SEGROMIGNO IN MONTE** | 55018 | B C4-D |
| **VILLA MANSI**<br>Via delle Selvette<br>Tel. 0583 920234/096/474 | *Open Tue.–Sun. 9.30am–noon and 2.30pm–sunset.*<br>*Closed Mon.* | ▲ 160 |
| **VICOPISANO** | 56010 | B C4-D |
| **SANTI MARIA E GIOVANNI BATTISTA**<br>Via Moricotti, 2<br>Tel. 050 799155 | *Hours vary.* | ▲ 155 |

| TORRE DELL'OROLOGIO<br>Tel. 050 551285<br>Fax 050 796511 | Open Sat. 3.30–7.30pm; Sun. 10am–12.30pm and 3–7pm. | ▲ 155 |

## MASSA, CARRARA AND THE APUAN ALPS

| AULLA | 54011 | B B2 |

| FORTEZZA DELLA BRUNELLA<br>Tel. 0187 409077<br>Fax 0187 420727 | Open June–Sep., Mon.–Sun. 9am–noon and 4–7pm;<br>Oct.–May, Mon.–Sun. 9am–noon and 3–6pm. | ▲ 167 |

| CARRARA | 54033 | B B3 |

| APT – MASSA CARRARA<br>Viale Amerigo Vespucci, 24<br>Tel. 0585 240046 | e-mail: apl@massacarrara.turismo.toscana.it | |
| ACCADEMIA DI BELLE ARTI<br>Piazza dell'Accademia<br>Tel. 0585 71658 | Visit by appointment only. | ▲ 165 |
| DUOMO<br>Piazza del Duomo<br>Tel. 0585 71942 | Open 8am–noon and 5–7pm. | ▲ 166 |

| MASSA | 54100 | B B3 |

| APT – MASSA CARRARA<br>Viale Amerigo Vespucci, 24<br>Tel. 0585 240046 | e-mail: apl@massacarrara.turismo.toscana.it | |
| ROCCA (CASTELLO MALASPINA)<br>Via della Rocca<br>Tel. 0585 45916 | Open 9am–noon and 4–7pm. | ▲ 165 |

| PONTREMOLI | 54027 | B B2 |

| MUSEO DELLE STATUE-STELE<br>DELLA LUNIGIANA<br>Castello del Piagnaro<br>Tel. 0187 831439 | Open winter 9am–noon and 2–5pm. | ▲ 168 |

## PRATO AND PISTOIA

| COLLODI | 51014 | B C4-D |

| PARCO DI PINOCCHIO<br>Via San Gennaro<br>Tel. 0572 429342 | Open daily 8.30am–sunset. | ▲ 181 |
| VILLA GARZONI<br>Tel. 0572 428400 | Closed for restoration.<br>Garden open daily.<br>Visit by appointment only. | ▲ 181 |

| CUTIGLIANO | 51024 | B D3 |

| PALAZZO PRETORIO<br>Tel. 0573 68383 | Open daily. | ▲ 182 |

| MONTECATINI TERME | 51016 | B D4 |

| PARCO DELLE TERME<br>Viale Giuseppe Verdi, 67<br>Tel. 0572 773295 | Toll–free number 8000 18962. | ▲ 181 |

| PESCIA | 51027 | B D4 |

| DUOMO<br>Piazza del Duomo<br>Tel. 0573 21622<br>(APT in Pistoia) | Open daily.<br>Telephone for information and hours. | ▲ 181 |
| SAN FRANCESCO<br>Piazza di San Francesco<br>Tel. 0573 368096 | Open 8.30am–noon and 4–5.45pm. | ▲ 181 |

| PISTOIA | 51100 | B E3 |

| APT – PISTOIA<br>Piazza del Duomo, 4<br>Tel. 0573 21622 | e-mail: aptpistoia@comune.pistoia.it | |

# ◆ PLACES TO VISIT

| | | |
|---|---|---|
| **BAPTISTERY**<br>Piazza Duomo<br>Tel. 0573 21622<br>(APT in Pistoia) | *Open 9.30am–12.30pm and 3–6pm; public holidays 9.30am–12.30pm.*<br>*Closed Mon.* | ▲ 179 |
| **MADONNA DELL'UMILTÀ**<br>Via della Madonna<br>Tel. 0573 22045 | *Open daily 8am–noon and 4–7pm.* | ▲ 180 |
| **MUSEO CAPITOLARE DI SAN ZENO**<br>Palazzo dei Vescovi,<br>Piazza del Duomo<br>Tel. 0573 369272 | *Open Tue., Thur. and Fri.*<br>*Visit by appointment only.* | ▲ 179 |
| **MUSEO CIVICO**<br>Piazza del Duomo, 1<br>Tel. 0573 371296<br>Fax 0573 371289 | *Open Tue.–Sat. 10am–7pm; Sun. and public holidays 9am–12.30pm.*<br>*Closed Mon.*<br>*Free admission Sat. afternoon.* | ▲ 179 |
| **SAN DOMENICO**<br>Piazza San Domenico, 1<br>Tel. 0573 28158 | *Open 6.30–11.50am and 4.30–6pm; Sun. 6.30–11.50am and 4.30–8pm.* | ▲ 180 |
| **SAN FRANCESCO**<br>Piazza San Francesco, 1<br>Tel. 0573 368096 | *Open 7.30am–noon and 4–7pm.* | ▲ 180 |
| **SAN GIOVANNI FORCIVITAS**<br>Via Cavour<br>Tel. 0573 24784 | *Open 8am–noon and 5–6.30pm.* | ▲ 180 |
| **SAN ZENO**<br>Piazza Duomo<br>Tel. 0573 25095 | *Open 9am–noon and 4–7pm; public holidays 11.20am–noon and 4–5.30pm.*<br>*Altar open weekdays 10am–noon and 4–5.45pm.* | ▲ 179 |
| **SANT'ANDREA**<br>Via Sant'Andrea<br>Tel. 0573 21912 | *Open 8am–1pm and 4–6.30pm.* | ▲ 180 |
| **SPEDALE DEL CEPPO**<br>Piazza Giovanni XXIII<br>Tel. 0573 352220 | *Visit by appointment only.* | ▲ 180 |

| **PRATO** | **59100** | **B E4** |
|---|---|---|
| **APT – PRATO**<br>Via Cairoli Benedetto<br>Tel. 0574 24112 | *e-mail: aptprato.turismo.toscana.it* | |
| **CASTELLO DELL'IMPERATORE**<br>Piazza delle Carceri<br>Tel. 0574 38207 | *Open Nov.–Feb. 10am–4pm; Mar.–May 10am–5pm; June–Sep. 10am–6.30pm; Oct. 10am–5pm.*<br>*Closed Tue.* | ▲ 178 |
| **DUOMO**<br>Piazza del Duomo<br>Tel. 0574 29339 | *Open 7am–noon and 3.30–6.30pm; public holidays 7am–noon and 3.30–8pm.* | ▲ 175 |
| **MUSEO CIVICO**<br>Piazza del Comune<br>Tel. 0574 616302 | *Open Mon., Wed.–Sat. 10am–1pm and 3.30–7pm; Sun. 10am–1pm.*<br>*Closed Tue.* | ▲ 175 |
| **MUSEO DEL TESSUTO**<br>Piazza del Comune<br>Tel. and fax<br>Fax 0574 611503 | *Open Mon. 2.30–6.30pm; Wed.–Sun. 10.30am–6.30pm.*<br>*Closed Tue.* | ▲ 175 |
| **MUSEO DELL'OPERA DEL DUOMO**<br>Piazza del Duomo, 49<br>Tel. 0574 29339 | *Closed for restoration.* | ▲ 178 |
| **PALAZZO DATINI**<br>Via Ser Lapo Mazzei, 33<br>Tel. 0574 21391 | *Open 9am–noon and 4.30–7pm.*<br>*Closed on public holidays.* | ▲ 178 |
| **SAN FRANCESCO**<br>Piazza San Francesco<br>Tel. 0574 31555 | *Open 8am–noon and 3.30–6.30pm.* | ▲ 178 |
| **SANTA MARIA DELLE CARCERI**<br>Piazza delle Carceri<br>Tel. 0574 27933 | *Open 6.30am–noon and 4–7.30pm.* | ▲ 178 |

## AREZZO AND ITS SURROUNDINGS

| **ANGHIARI** | **52031** | **C D3** |
|---|---|---|
| | | ▲ 190 |
| **MUSEO STATALE**<br>**(PALAZZO TAGLIESCHI)**<br>Piazza Mameli, 16<br>Tel. 0575 788001 | *Open Mon.–Fri. 3–7pm; Sat. and public holidays 9am–1pm and 3–7pm. Student visits by arrangement on Tue. and Thur. 9am–1pm.*<br>*Closed on: Christmas, New Year's Day and May 1.* | |

| AREZZO | 52100 | C D4 |
|---|---|---|
| **APT – AREZZO**<br>Tel. 0575 23952<br>Fax 0575 28042 | *e-mail: info@arezzo.turismo.toscana.it* | |
| **CASA DEL PETRARCA**<br>Via dell'Orto, 28<br>Tel. and fax 0575 24700 | *Visit by appointment only.* | ▲ 187 |
| **CASA DI VASARI**<br>Via XX Settembre<br>Tel. 0575 409040 | *Open 9am–7pm; public holidays 9am–12.30pm.* | ▲ 189 |
| **DUOMO**<br>**(CATHEDRAL OF SAN DONATO)**<br>Piazza Duomo<br>Tel. 0575 23991 | *Open 7am–noon and 3–6.30pm.* | ▲ 187 |
| **LA BADIA**<br>Piazza di Badia<br>Tel. 0575 356612 | *Open 8am–noon and 4–7pm; public holidays<br>7am–12.30pm.* | ▲ 189 |
| **MEDICI FORTRESS**<br>Tel. 0575 23952 (APT Arezzo) | *Open Mar. 28–Oct 30 7am–8pm; Oct. 31–Mar. 27<br>7.30am–6pm.* | ▲ 187 |
| **MUSEO ARCHEOLOGICO**<br>Via Margaritone, 10<br>Tel. 0575 20882 | *Open 9am–2pm; public holidays 9am–1pm.* | ▲ 189 |
| **MUSEO D'ARTE**<br>**MEDIEVALE E MODERNA**<br>Via San Lorentino, 8<br>Tel. 0575 409050 | *Open 8.30am–7.30pm; June–Sep. Sat. 8.30am–11pm.<br>Closed Mon.* | ▲ 188 |
| **MUSEO DIOCESANO**<br>Piazzetta dietro il Duomo<br>Tel. 0575 23991 | *Open Thur.–Sat. 10am–noon.* | ▲ 188 |
| **PALAZZO DELLA FRATERNITA DEI LAICI**<br>Piazza Grande<br>Tel. 0575 377678<br>(Tourist information office) | *Not open to the public.* | ▲ 187 |
| **PALAZZO PRETORIO**<br>Tel. 0575 377678<br>(Tourist information office) | *Not open to the public.* | ▲ 187 |
| **SAN DOMENICO**<br>Piazza San Domenico<br>Tel. 0575 22906 | *Open 3.30–7pm.* | ▲ 188 |
| **SAN FRANCESCO**<br>Piazza San Francesco<br>Tel. 0575 20630 | *Open 8.30am–noon and 2–7pm.* | ▲ 185 |
| **SANTA MARIA**<br>Corso Italia<br>Tel. 0575 22629 | *Open 8am–1pm and 3–6.30pm.* | ▲ 187 |
| **SANTA MARIA DELLE GRAZIE**<br>Via Santa Maria<br>Tel. 0575 323140 | *Open 8am–noon and 4–7pm.* | ▲ 189 |
| **SANTISSIMA ANNUNZIATA**<br>Via Garibaldi, 185<br>Tel. 0575 26774 | *Open 8am–12.30pm and 3.30–7pm.* | ▲ 188 |
| BIBBIENA | 52011 | C D3 |
| **INFORMATION OFFICE**<br>Via Berni, 25<br>Tel. and fax. 0575 593098 | | |
| **SANTI IPPOLITO E CASSIANO**<br>Via Rosa Scoti, 41<br>Tel. 0575 593079 | *Open 7.30–1pm and 3–7pm.* | ▲ 195 |
| CAMALDOLI | 52010 | C D2 |
| **SAN SALVATORE**<br>Tel. 0575 556013 | *Open Nov 16–Mar. 31 9am–12.30pm and 2.30–6pm;<br>Apr. 1–Nov.15 9am–12.30pm and 2.30–6pm.<br>Closed Wed.* | ▲ 195 |
| CASTELFRANCO DI SOPRA | 52020 | C C3 |
| **SAN GIOVENALE** | *Visit by appointment only.* | ▲ 197 |
| **SAN PIETRO A GROPINA** | *Visit by appointment only.* | ▲ 197 |
| **SAN SALVATORE A SOFFENA**<br>Via di Soffena<br>Tel. 055 914 8055 | *Open Mon.–Sat. 8am–2pm.* | ▲ 197 |

# ◆ PLACES TO VISIT

| CASTIGLION FIORENTINO | 52043 | C D4 |
|---|---|---|
| **PICTURE GALLERY** (CHURCH OF SAN ANGELO) Via del Cassero Tel. 0575 657466 Fax 0575 659457 | *Open Apr. 1–Sep. 30: 10am–12.30pm and 4–6.30pm; Oct. 1–Mar 31 10am–noon and 3.30–6pm.* | ▲ 200 |

| CORTONA | 52044 | C D4 |
|---|---|---|
| **APT – CORTONA** Via Nazionale, 42 Tel. 0575 630352 | *www.valdichiana.net* | |
| **CONVENTO DELLE CELLE** at Celle, 73 Tel. 0575 603362; 0575 601017 | *Open 8am–7pm.* *Church open 8am–noon and 3–7pm.* | ▲ 200 |
| **FORTEZZA DEL GIRIFALCO** Tel. 0575 603793 | *Open Apr. 1–Sep. 30 10am–6pm.* *Closed Mon.* | ▲ 199 |
| **MELONE DEL SODO** Tel. 0575 637235 | *Open May–Oct. 9.30am–5.30pm.* *The tombs can be visited by appointment.* | ▲ 199 |
| **MUSEO DELL'ACCADEMIA ETRUSCA** (PALAZZO CASALI) Piazza Signorelli, 9 Tel. 0575 630415 Fax 0575 637248 | *Open Nov.– Apr. 10am–5pm; May–Oct. 10am–7pm.* *Closed Mon.* | ▲ 199 |
| **MUSEO DIOCESANO** Piazza Duomo, 1 Tel. 0575 62830 | *Open Apr. 1–Sep. 30 9am–1pm and 3–6.30pm; Oct. 1–Mar. 31 9am–1pm and 3–5pm.* *Closed Mon.* | ▲ 200 |
| **SAN DOMENICO** Largo Beato Angelico Tel. 0575 603041 | *Open 9am–noon and 3–6pm.* | ▲ 200 |
| **SAN FRANCESCO** Via Berrettini Tel. 0575 603217 | *Open 8am–noon and 3–6.30pm.* | ▲ 200 |
| **SAN NICCOLÒ** Via San Niccolò Tel. 0575 604591 | *Open  9.30am–noon and 3.30–6.30pm.* | |
| **SANTA MARGHERITA** Piazzale Santa Margherita Tel. 0575 603116 | *Open 7.30am–noon and 3–7.30pm.* | ▲ 199 |
| **SANTA MARIA AL CALCINAIO** Tel. 0575 62537; 0575 604830 | *Open morning and afternoon.* *Hours vary.* | ▲ 200 |
| **TANELLA DI PITAGORA** at Cinque Vie Tel. 0575 603083 | *Open May–Oct. 9.30am–5.30pm. The tombs can be visited by appointment.* | ▲ 199 |

| CHIUSI DELLA VERNA | 52010 | C D3 |
|---|---|---|
| **SANCTUARY OF LA VERNA** Church of La Verna Tel. 0575 5341; 0575 553 4002; 0575 553 4004 | *Open 6.30–7.30pm.* | ▲ 194 |

| FOIANO | 52045 | C D5 |
|---|---|---|
| **SAN MARTINO** Piazza della Collegiata Tel. 0575 648888; 0575 643236 (Comune di Foiano) | *Open 8.30am–noon and 3–6.30pm.* | ▲ 198 |
| **SANTISSIMA TRINITÀ** Via SS.Trinità | *Currently closed.* | ▲ 198 |

| LUCIGNANO | 52046 | C C5 |
|---|---|---|
| **MUSEO COMUNALE** Piazza del Tribunale, 22 Tel. 0575 838001 Fax 0575 838026 | *Open Oct.–Mar. 10.30am–12.30pm and 3.30–5.30pm; Apr. 10.30am–12.30pm and 3.30–6.30pm; May–Sep. 10.30am–12.30pm and 3.30–7pm.* | ▲ 198 |
| **SAN FRANCESCO** Piazza del Tribunale Tel. 0575 583801 (Comune di Lucignano) | *Open 9am–sunset.* | ▲ 198 |

| MONTERCHI | 52035 | | C D4 |
|---|---|---|---|
| **CAPPELLA DI SANTA MARIA** in Momentana Via della Regina, 1 Tel. 0575 70713 | *Open Sep. 27–Mar. 31 9am–1pm and 2–6pm; Apr. 1–Sep. 26 9am–1pm and 2–7pm; July–Aug. 9am–1pm, 2–7pm and 9pm–midnight.* | | |
| **'MADONNA DEL PARTO' EXHIBITION CENTER** Via Reglia, 1 Tel. and fax 0575 70713 | *Open July–Aug. Tue.–Sun. 9am–1pm, 2–7pm and 9pm–midnight; June, Sep. Tue.–Sun. 9am–1pm and 2–7pm; Oct.–May Tue.–Sun. 9am–1pm and 2–6pm. Closed Mon.* | ▲ 190 | |

| MONTEVARCHI | 52025 | | C C4 |
|---|---|---|---|
| **MUSEO PALEONTOLOGICO** Via Poggio Bracciolini, 36 Tel. 055 981227 Fax 055 982670 | *Open Tue.–Sat. 9am–12.30pm and 4–6pm; Sun. 10am–noon. Closed Mon.* | ▲ 197 | |
| **SAN LORENZO** Piazza Varchi Tel. 055 980468 | *Open 8am–noon and 4–7pm.* | ▲ 197 | |

| POPPI | 52014 | | C C3 |
|---|---|---|---|
| **CASTELLO DEI CONTI GUIDI** Tel. and fax 0575 529964 | *Open winter 9.30am–12.30pm and 2.30–5.30pm; summer 9.30am–12.30pm and 3.30–6.30pm.* | ▲ 196 | |

| PRATOVECCHIO | 52015 | | C C2-D |
|---|---|---|---|
| **CASTELLO DI ROMENA** Via Romena, 12/a (at Romena) Tel. 0575 581353 | *Open 3–6pm.* | ▲ 196 | |
| **CHURCH OF ROMENA** at church of Romena 0575 583725 | *Visits only by arrangement.* | ▲ 196 | |

| SAN GIOVANNI VALDARNO | 52027 | | C C3 |
|---|---|---|---|
| **TOURIST INFORMATION** Tel. 055 912 6321 | *www.comune.san-giovanni-valdarno.ar.it* | | |
| **MUSEO DI SANTA MARIA DELLE GRAZIE** Piazza Masaccio Tel. 055 912 2445 Fax 055 941265 | *Open Tue.–Fri. 11am–1pm and 3–5pm; Sat. 11am–1pm and 3–6pm; Sun. 3–6pm. Closed Mon.* | | |
| **PALAZZO PRETORIO** Piazza Cavour, 1 Tel. 055 126300 | *Open Mon., Tue, Fri. 9am–1pm; Tue.–Thur. 2.30–6.30pm. Closed Sat. and Sun.* | ▲ 197 | |

| SANSEPOLCRO | 52037 | | C E3 |
|---|---|---|---|
| **INFORMATION OFFICE** Piazza Garibaldi, 2 Tel. and fax 0575 740536 | *www.sansepolcro.net/index.asp* | | |
| **BIRTHPLACE OF PIERO DELLA FRANCESCA** Via Niccolò Aggiunti, 71 Tel. 0575 740411 | *Visit by appointment only.* | ▲ 191 | |
| **MUSEO CIVICO** Via Niccolò Aggiunti, 65 Tel. 0575 732218 Fax 0575 740338 | *Open Jan.–May. 9.30am–1pm and 2.30–6pm; June–Sep. 9.30am–1.30pm and 2.30–7.30pm; Oct.–Dec. 9.30am–1pm and 2.30–6pm. Closed Christmas, New Year's Day and August 15.* | ▲ 191 | |
| **SAN LORENZO** Via Santa Croce Tel. 0575 740536 | *Visit by appointment only.* | ▲ 194 | |

## CHIANTI

| BROLIO | 53010 | | C C4 |
|---|---|---|---|
| **CASTELLO** Tel. 0577 747156; 0577 747104 | *Open winter 10am–noon and 2.30–4.30pm; summer 10am–noon and 3–6pm.* | ▲ 206 | |

| CASTELLINA IN CHIANTI | 53011 | | C B4 |
|---|---|---|---|
| **ROCCA (TOWN HALL)** Piazza del Comune, 1 Tel. 0577 742311 | | ▲ 205 | |

# ◆ PLACES TO VISIT

| CASTELNUOVO BERARDENGA | 53019 | | C C4 |
|---|---|---|---|
| VILLA CHIGI<br>Tel. 0577 355500 | Open winter Sun. and public holidays 10am–5pm;<br>summer Sun. and public holidays 10am–8pm. | | ▲ 206 |
| **GAIOLE IN CHIANTI** | **53013** | | **C B4-C** |
| COMUNE DI GAIOLE IN CHIANTI<br>Via Ricasoli<br>Tel. 0577 749365 | | | |
| BADIA A COLDIBUONO<br>Tel. 0577 749498<br>Fax 0577 49235 | Hours vary. | | ▲ 205 |
| SANTA MARIA A SPALTENNA<br>Via Spaltenna, 13<br>Tel. 0577 749483 | Visit by appointment only. | | ▲ 206 |
| **GREVE IN CHIANTI** | **50022** | | **C B3** |
| SANTA CROCE<br>Piazzetta Santa Croce<br>Tel. 055 853085 | Open at all times. | | ▲ 204 |
| **MELETO** | **52020** | | **C C4** |
| CASTELLO<br>Tel. 0577 749496 | Visit by appointment only. | | ▲ 206 |
| **MONTEFIORALLE** | **50022** | | **C B3-4** |
| SAN CRESCI<br>Tel. 055 853085 | Visit by appointment only. | | ▲ 204 |
| SANTO STEFANO<br>Tel. 055 853057; 055 853085 | Visit by appointment only. | | ▲ 204 |
| **PANZANO** | **50020** | | **C B3-4** |
| SANTA MARIA<br>Tel. 055 852037 | Open at all times. | | ▲ 204 |
| **PASSIGNANO** | **50020** | | **◆ C B3-4** |
| BADIA DI PASSIGNANO<br>Tel. 055 807 1622 | Open Sun. 3–7pm. | | ▲ 203 |
| **RADDA IN CHIANTI** | **53017** | | **C B4** |
| INFORMATION OFFICE<br>P. Ferrucci, 1<br>Tel. 0577 738494 | email: proradda@chiantinet.it | | |
| SANTA MARIA AL PRATO<br>Tel. 0577 738003 | Visits only by appointment. | | ▲ 205 |
| **SIENA** | **53100** | | **C B4** |
| APT – SIENA<br>Il Campo, 56<br>Tel. 0577 280551<br>Fax 0577 270676 | e-mail: aptsiena@siena.turismo.toscana.it | | |
| ACCADEMIA DEGLI INTRONATI<br>Via di Città, 75<br>Tel. 0577 284073 | | | ▲ 212 |
| ACCADEMIA DEI FISIOCRITICI<br>Prato di S.Agostino, 4<br>Tel. 0577 47002 | Open Mon.–Fri. 9am–1pm and 3–6pm.<br>Closed Thur. afternoon, Sat. and Sun. and public<br>holidays. | | ▲ 217 |
| ACCADEMIA DEI ROZZI<br>Via di Città, 36<br>Tel. 0577 280122 | Not open to the public. | | ▲ 220 |
| ACCADEMIA MUSICALE CHIGIANA<br>Via di Città, 89<br>Tel. 0577 46152 | Visits only by appointment. | | ▲ 212 |
| BAPTISTERY<br>Piazza San Giovanni<br>Tel. 0577 283048<br>Fax 0577 280626 | Open Mar. 15–Sep. 30 9am–7.30pm; Oct. 9am–<br>6pm; Nov. 1– Mar. 14 10am–1pm and 2.30–5pm. | | ▲ 216 |
| BIBLIOTECA COMUNALE<br>DEGLI INTRONATI<br>Via della Sapienza, 5<br>Tel. 0577 280704<br>Fax 0577 44293 | Open Sep.–June, Mon.–Fri. 9am–7pm; Sat.<br>9am–2pm; July–Aug. 9am–2pm.<br>Closed Sun. and public holidays. | | |

| | | |
|---|---|---|
| **CAPPELLA DI PIAZZA**<br>Piazza del Campo<br>Tel. 0577 280551 (APT Siena) | *Not open to the public.* | ▲ 212 |
| **CHURCH OF FONTEGIUSTA**<br>Via Fontegiusta<br>Tel. 0577 280551 (APT Siena) | *Open 8am–noon and 3–7pm.* | ▲ 220 |
| **DUOMO**<br>Piazza del Duomo<br>Tel. 0577 283048; 0577 280626<br>Fax 0577 226265 | *Open Nov. 1–Mar. 15 7.30am–1pm and 2.30–5pm;<br>Mar. 16–Oct. 31 9am–7.30pm.<br>Send a fax for information and to arrange a visit.* | ▲ 213 |
| **MEDICI FORTRESS**<br>**(ENOTECA ITALIANA)**<br>Viale Vittorio Veneto<br>Tel. 0577 288497<br>Fax 0577 270717 | *Open Tue.–Sat. noon–9pm; Mon. noon–8pm.<br>Closed Sun.* | ▲ 220 |
| **MONTE DEI PASCHI**<br>Piazza Salimbeni, 3<br>Tel. 0577 294758 | *Visit by appointment only.* | ▲ 220 |
| **MUSEO ARCHEOLOGICO**<br>Piazza del Duomo<br>Tel. and fax 0577 49153 | *Open Mon., Thur. 8am–5pm; Tue., Wed., Fri., Sat.<br>8am–2pm; Sun. and public holidays 8am–1pm.<br>Closed 1st and 3rd Sun. of the month* | ▲ 216 |
| **MUSEO CIVICO PALAZZO PUBBLICO**<br>Piazza del Campo, 1<br>Tel. 0577 41169 | *Open Nov. 1–Mar. 15 10am–6.30pm; Mar. 16–Oct.<br>31 10am–7pm; Easter Mon. 9.30am–7.45pm.* | ▲ 211 |
| **MUSEO DELL'OPERA**<br>**METROPOLITANA**<br>Piazza del Duomo, 8<br>Tel. 0577 42309 | *Open Mar. 15–Sep. 30 9am–7.30pm; Oct. 9am–6pm;<br>Nov. 1–Mar. 14 9am–1.30pm.* | ▲ 216 |
| **MUSEO DELLA SOCIETÀ DI ESECUTORI**<br>**DELLE PIE DISPOSIZIONI**<br>Via Roma, 71<br>Tel. 0577 284300<br>Fax 0577 284347 | *Visit by appointment only.* | ▲ 221 |
| **MUSEO NATURALISTICO**<br>Prato di S. Agostino, 4<br>Tel. 0577 47002 | *Open Mon.–Fri. 9am–1pm and 3–6pm.<br>Closed Thur. afternoon, Sat. and Sun.* | ▲ 217 |
| **ORTO BOTANICO**<br>Prato di S. Agostino, 4<br>Tel. 0577 298874 | *Open Mon.–Fri. 8am–5pm; Sat. 8am–noon.* | ▲ 217 |
| **OSPEDALE DI SANTA**<br>**MARIA DELLA SCALA**<br>Piazza del Duomo<br>Tel. 0577 41169<br>(Centro Servizi Comune<br>di Siena) | *Open Nov. 1–Dec. 24 10.30am–4.30pm; Dec.12–<br>Jan. 6 10am–6pm; Jan. 7–Mar. 15 10.30am–4.30pm;<br>Mar. 16–Oct. 31 10am–6pm.* | ▲ 216 |
| **PALAZZO CHIGI SARACINI**<br>Via di Città, 89<br>Tel. 0577 46152 | *Visit by appointment only.* | ▲ 212 |
| **PALAZZO CHIGI ZONDADARI**<br>Piazza del Campo<br>Tel. 0577 280551 (APT Siena) | *Visit by appointment only.* | ▲ 210 |
| **PALAZZO D'ELCI**<br>Via di Città, 43<br>Tel. 0577 280551 (APT Siena) | *Visit by appointment only.* | ▲ 210 |
| **PALAZZO DEL MAGNIFICO**<br>Piazza San Giovanni<br>Tel. 0577 280551 (APT Siena) | *Visit by appointment only.* | ▲ 217 |
| **PALAZZO DELL'UNIVERSITÀ**<br>Via Sallustio Bandini, 25<br>Tel. 0577 280551 (APT Siena) | *Visit by appointment only.* | |
| **PALAZZO DELLE PAPESSE**<br>Via di Città, 126<br>Tel. 0577 41169 (Centro Servizi) | *Open Mon.–Sun. noon–7pm; July 17–Sep. 15<br>noon–11pm.* | ▲ 213 |
| **PALAZZO DI SAN GALGANO**<br>Via Roma, 47 | *Not open to the public.* | ▲ 221 |
| **PALAZZO MARSILI**<br>Via di Città, 132<br>Tel. 0577 280551 (APT Siena) | *Visit by appointment only.* | ▲ 213 |
| **PALAZZO PICCOLOMINI**<br>Via Banchi di Sotto, 52<br>Tel. 0577 247145 | *The museum is closed for restoration.<br>Open Mon., Fri. 8am–1.45pm. Sala di Studio open<br>Tue., Wed. and Thur. 8am–5.30pm.* | ▲ 212 |

# ◆ PLACES TO VISIT

| | | |
|---|---|---|
| **PALAZZO PUBBLICO**<br>Piazza del Campo, 1<br>Tel. 0577 226265 | *Open Nov. 1–Mar. 15 10am–6.30pm; Oct. 31–*<br>*Mar. 16 10am–7pm; Easter Mon. 9.30am–7.45pm.* | ▲ 211 |
| **PALAZZO REALE OR PALAZZO DEL GOVERNO**<br>Piazza del Duomo | *Information from the APT.* | ▲ 216 |
| **PALAZZO SPANNOCCHI**<br>Via Banchi di Sopra<br>Tel. 0577 280551 (APT Siena) | *Visit by appointment only.* | ▲ 220 |
| **PALAZZO TOLOMEI**<br>Piazza Tolomei, 11<br>Tel. 0577 280551 (APT Siena) | *Visit by appointment only.* | ▲ 220 |
| **PINACOTECA NAZIONALE**<br>Via San Pietro, 29<br>Tel. 0577 281161 | *Open Mon. 8.30am–1.30pm; Tue.–Sat. 9am–7pm;*<br>*Sun. and public holidays 8am–1pm.* | ▲ 217 |
| **RACCOLTE DELLE TAVOLETTE DI BICCHERNA**<br>Via Banchi di Sotto, 52<br>Tel. 0577 41271 | *Closed for restoration.* | ▲ 221 |
| **SAN BERNARDINO**<br>Piazza San Francesco<br>Tel. 0577 41169 (Centro Servizi) | *Open Mar. 15–Oct. 31 10.30am–1.30pm and*<br>*3–5.30pm.* | ▲ 221 |
| **SAN DOMENICO**<br>Piazza San Domenico<br>Tel. 0577 280893 | *Open daily.*<br>*Hours vary.* | ▲ 220 |
| **SAN FRANCESCO**<br>Piazza San Francesco<br>Tel. 0577 289081 | *Open daily.*<br>*Hours vary* | ▲ 220 |
| **SAN GIORGIO**<br>Via di Pantaneto | *Information from the APT .* | ▲ 221 |
| **SAN MARTINO**<br>Via del Porrione, 47<br>Tel. 0577 289178 | *Open 8am–noon and 4.30–7.30pm.* | ▲ 221 |
| **SAN NICCOLÒ AL CARMINE**<br>Pian de' Mantellini<br>Tel. 0577 280551<br>(APT Siena) | *Open 8am–noon and 4.30–7.30pm.* | ▲ 217 |
| **SAN PIETRO ALLA MAGIONE**<br>Via Camollia, 10<br>Tel. 0577 47226 | *Open daily.*<br>*Hours vary.* | ▲ 220 |
| **SAN RAIMONDO AL REFUGIO**<br>Via Roma<br>Tel. 0577 280551 (APT Siena) | *Open 8am–noon and 4.30–7.30pm.* | ▲ 221 |
| **SANT'AGOSTINO**<br>Prato di Sant'Agostino<br>Tel. 0577 41169 (Centro Servizi)<br>Fax 0577 226265 | *Open Mar. 15–Oct. 31 10.30am–1.30pm and*<br>*3–5.30pm.* | ▲ 217 |
| **SANTA CATERINA**<br>Costa di S. Antonio, 10<br>Tel. 0577 44177 | *Open winter 9am–12.30pm and 3.30–6pm; summer*<br>*9am–12.30pm and 2.30–6pm.* | ▲ 220 |
| **SANTA MARIA DEI SERVI**<br>Piazza Manzoni, 5<br>Tel. 0577 222633 | *Open 8am–noon and 4–7pm.* | ▲ 221 |
| **SANTA MARIA DI PROVENZANO**<br>Piazza Provenzano Salvani<br>Tel. 0577 285223 | *Open 8am–noon and 4.30–7.30pm.* | ▲ 221 |
| **SANTISSIMA ANNUNZIATA**<br>Piazza del Duomo<br>Tel. 0577 280551<br>(APT Siena) | *Open 8am–noon and 4.30–7.30pm.* | ▲ 216 |
| **STATE ARCHIVES**<br>Via Banchi di Sotto, 52<br>Tel. 0577 247145 | *Open Mon.–Sat. 9am–1pm.* | ▲ 221 |
| **TORRE DEL MANGIA**<br>Piazza del Campo, 1<br>Tel. 0577 41169 (Centro Servizi) | *Open Nov. 1–Mar. 15 10am–4pm; Mar. 16–Oct. 31*<br>*10am–7pm; July–Aug. 10am–11pm.* | ▲ 211 |

| PONTIGNANO | 53010 | C B4 |
|---|---|---|
| **CERTOSA DI PONTIGNANO**<br>Tel. 0577 356851 | *Visit by appointment only.* | ▲ 222 |

## AROUND SIENA

| ABBEY OF MONTE OLIVETO MAGGIORE | 53020 | C C6 |
|---|---|---|
| At Chiusure<br>Tel. 0577 707017;<br>0577 707106; 0577 707611 | *Open 9.15am–noon and 3.15–5pm; summer 9.15am–noon and 3.15–5.45pm.* | ▲ 229 |

| ABBEY OF SAN GALGANO | 53012 | C B5 |
|---|---|---|
| At Chiusdino<br>Tel. 0577 756738 | *Open at all times.* | ▲ 228 |

| ABBADIA SAN SALVATORE | 53021 | C C6 |
|---|---|---|
| **ABBEY**<br>Via del Monastero<br>Tel. 0577 778083 | *Open 5am–7pm.* | ▲ 232 |

| ABBEY OF SANT'ANTIMO | | C C6 |
|---|---|---|
| Tel. 0577 83565 | *Open Mon.–Fri. 10.30am–12.30pm and 3–6.30pm; Sun. and public holidays 9.15–10.45am and 3–6pm.* | ▲ 229 |

| ARCIDOSSO | 38031 | C C6 |
|---|---|---|
| **SANTA MARIA AD LAMULAS**<br>At Pieve Montelaterone<br>Tel. 0564 967045 | *Visit by appointment only.* | ▲ 232 |
| **ROCCA ALDOBRANDESCA**<br>Tel. 0564 966438 | *Only open to the public for exhibitions.* | ▲ 232 |
| **SAN LEONARDO**<br>Piazza della Chiesa<br>Tel. 0564 966140 | *Open at all times except during mass (5.30pm).* | ▲ 232 |

| ASCIANO | 53041 | C C5 |
|---|---|---|
| **CASA CORBOLI**<br>Vicolo Sant'Agostino, 1<br>Tel. 0577 719510 | *Visit by appointment only.* | ▲ 228 |
| **MUSEO CASSIOLI**<br>Via Mameli<br>Tel. 0577 718745 | *Open 10am–12.30pm; summer also 4.30–6.30pm. Closed Mon.* | ▲ 229 |
| **SAN FRANCESCO**<br>Via San Francesco<br>Tel. 0577 719510; 0577 71441 | *Hours vary.* | ▲ 228 |
| **SANT'AGATA**<br>Piazza Bandiera<br>Tel. 0577 719510 | *Hours vary.* | ▲ 228 |

| BUONCONVENTO | 53022 | C C5 |
|---|---|---|
| **MUSEO D'ARTE SACRA DELLA VAL D'ARBIA**<br>Via Soccini, 17<br>Tel. and fax 0577 807181 | *Temporarily closed.* | ▲ 229 |

| CASOLE D'ELSA | 53031 | ◆ C B4 |
|---|---|---|
| **TOURIST OFFICE**<br>Via Consolani, 32<br>Tel. 0577 948705 | | |
| **CATHEDRAL**<br>Piazza della Libertà<br>Tel. 0577 948705<br>(Municipal Tourist Office) | *Visit by appointment only.* | ▲ 227 |
| **MUSEO ARCHEOLOGICO E DELLA COLLEGIATA**<br>Piazza della Libertà, 1<br>Tel. 0577 948705 | *Open winter Tue.–Sat. 3–7pm, Sun. and public holidays 10am–noon and 3–6pm; summer 10am–noon and 4–7pm.* | ▲ 227 |
| **TOWER HOUSE OF ARNOLFO DI CAMBIO**<br>Via del Castello, 63<br>Tel. 0577 948705 (Tourist Office) | *Visit by appointment only.* | ▲ 227 |

| CASTEL DEL PIANO | 58033 | C C6 |
|---|---|---|
| **SANTI NICCOLÒ E LUCIA**<br>Piazza Madonna<br>Tel. 0564 955272 | *Visit by appointment only.* | ▲ 232 |

# ◆ PLACES TO VISIT

| CETONA | 53040 | C D6 | |
|---|---|---|---|
| PARCO ARCHEOLOGICO E NATURALISTICO (BELVERDE) Tel. 0578 238004 | *Visit by appointment only.* | | ▲ 234 |

| CHIANCIANO TERME | 53042 | C D6 | |
|---|---|---|---|
| MUSEO CIVICO ARCHEOLOGICO DELLE ACQUE Viale Dante; Tel. 0578 30471 | *Open Apr.–June, Sep.–Oct. 10am–7pm; July–Aug. 10am–1.30pm, 4–7.30pm and 9–11pm; Nov.–Mar. 10am–1pm and 3–7pm.* | | ▲ 234 |

| CHIUSI | 53043 | C D6 | |
|---|---|---|---|
| CATACOMBE DI SANTA MUSTIOLA AND LABIRINTO DI PORSENNA (ETRUSCO-ROMAN UNDERGROUND TUNNELS) Piazza del Duomo Tel. 0578 226490 | *Guided tour 11am; Sun. and public holidays 11am and 4pm.* | | ▲ 234 |
| DUOMO Piazza Duomo Tel. 0578 226490 | *Open 9am–1pm and 3–7pm.* | | ▲ 234 |

| COLLE DI VAL D'ELSA | 53034 | C A4 | |
|---|---|---|---|
| TOURIST INFORMATION OFFICE Via Campana, 43 Tel. 0577 922791 | | | |
| MUSEO CIVICO AND MUSEO D'ARTE SACRA Via di Castello, 31 Tel. 0577 92388 | *Open winter Sat., Sun. and public holidays 10am–noon and 3.30–6.30pm; summer 10am–noon and 4–7pm. Closed Mon.* | | ▲ 227 |
| MUSEO ARCHEOLOGICO RANUCCIO BIANCHI BANDINELLI Piazza del Duomo Tel. 0577 922954 | *Open Tue.–Fri. winter 3.45–5.45pm, summer 10am–noon and 4.45pm–6.45pm; Sat., Sun. and public holidays 10am–noon and 4.30–7.30pm.* | | ▲ 227 |
| PALAZZO CAMPANA At the entrance to the Castello Tel. 0577 922791 (Tourist information office) | *Telephone for information.* | | ▲ 227 |
| PALAZZO PRETORIO Piazza del Duomo Tel. 0577 922791 (Tourist information office) | *Telephone for information.* | | ▲ 227 |
| SANT'AGOSTINO Via dei Fossi Tel. 0577 922791 (Tourist information office) | *Telephone for information.* | | ▲ 227 |
| SANTA CATERINA Piazza Santa Caterina Tel. 0577 922791 (Tourist information office) | *Telephone for information.* | | ▲ 227 |

| MONTALCINO | 53024 | C C5 | |
|---|---|---|---|
| MUSEO CIVICO E DIOCESANO D'ARTE SACRA Via Ricasoli, 31 Tel 0577 846014 | *Open Jan.–Mar. 10am–1pm and 2–5.30pm; Apr.–Oct. 10am–6pm. Closed Mon.* | | ▲ 229 |
| ROCCA Piazzale della Fortezza Tel. 0577 849211 | *Open winter 9am–1pm and 2–6pm; summer 9am–1pm and 2.30–8pm.* | | ▲ 229 |

| MONTEPULCIANO | 53045 | C D5 | |
|---|---|---|---|
| DUOMO Piazza Grande Tel. 0578 757556 | *Open 9am–6pm.* | | ▲ 233 |
| PALAZZO COMUNALE Piazza Grande Tel. 0578 7121 | *Open weekdays 8am–1pm. Closed Sun. and public holidays. Only the tower can be visited.* | | ▲ 233 |
| PALAZZO DEL MONTE CONTUCCI Piazza Grande Tel. 0578 757006 | *Visit by appointment only.* | | ▲ 233 |
| PALAZZO NERI ORSELLI Via Ricci, 10 Tel. 0578 716935 | *Visit by appointment only.* | | ▲ 233 |

| PALAZZO NOBILI TARUGI<br>Piazza Grande<br>Tel. 0578 758687 | Visit by appointment only. | ▲ 233 |
|---|---|---|
| SAN BIAGIO<br>Tel. 0578 757556 | Open daily.<br>Hours vary. | ▲ 233 |
| SANT'AGNESE<br>Tel. 0578 758687 | Open weekdays 9am–noon and 3–6pm;<br>Sun. 3–6pm. | |

| MONTERIGGIONI | 53035 | C B4 |
|---|---|---|
| PRO LOCO TOURIST OFFICE<br>Largo Fontebranda, 3<br>Tel. 0577 304810 | | |
| ABBADIA ISOLA | Inquire at the information office next to the<br>church or contact the custodians to arrange a visit. | ▲ 225 |
| SANTA MARIA<br>Tel. 0577 304810 | Hours vary. | ▲ 225 |

| PIANCASTAGNAIO | 53025 | C C6 |
|---|---|---|
| ROCCA AND MUSEUM<br>Rocca degli Aldobrandeschi<br>Tel. 0577 786024 | Visit by appointment only. | ▲ 232 |

| PIENZA | 53026 | C C5 |
|---|---|---|
| INFORMATION OFFICE<br>Corso Rosellino, 59<br>Tel. and fax. 0578 749071 | www.ctnet.it/pienza | |
| CATHEDRAL<br>Piazza Pio II<br>Tel. 0578 749071 | Open 7.30am–1pm and 2.30–7pm. | ▲ 233 |
| MONASTERY OF SANT'ANNA<br>IN CAMPRENA<br>Tel. 0578 74 8303 | Visit by appointment only. | ▲ 233 |
| MUSEO DIOCESANO<br>Corso Rossellino, 30<br>Tel. 0578 749905 | Open Nov. 3–Mar. 13 Sat., Sun. and public holidays<br>10am–1pm and 3–6pm; Mar. 14–Nov. 2 10am–1pm<br>and 2–6.30pm. | ▲ 233 |
| PALAZZO PICCOLOMINI<br>Piazza Pio II<br>Tel. 0578 748503 | Open Oct.–May 10am–12.30pm and 3–6pm;<br>June–Sep. 10am–12.30pm and 4–7pm. | ▲ 233 |

| POGGIBONSI | 53036 | C B4 |
|---|---|---|
| TOURIST SERVICE VALDELSA SRL<br>Via Borgaccio, 23<br>Tel. 0577 987017<br>Fax 0577 992775 | email: info@comune.poggibonsi.si.it | |
| COLLEGIATA<br>Piazza Cavour<br>Tel. 0577 987017; 0577 986203 | Visit by appointment only. | ▲ 225 |
| PALAZZO PRETORIO<br>Via Marmocchi, corner Via della<br>Repubblica<br>Tel. 0577 987017; 0577 986203 | Visit by appointment only. | ▲ 225 |
| SAN LUCCHESE<br>Near Via Cassia, at San Lucchese<br>Tel. 0577 936219 | Visit by appointment only. | ▲ 225 |

| SAN GIMIGNANO | 53037 | C B4 |
|---|---|---|
| INFORMATION OFFICE<br>Piazza Duomo, 1<br>Tel. 0577 940008 | e-mail: prolocsg@tin.it | |
| MUSEO CIVICO<br>Piazza del Duomo<br>Tel. 0577 990340 | Open Apr.–Oct. 9.30am–7.30pm; Nov.–Mar.<br>Tue.–Sun. 9.30am–5pm, closed Mon. | ▲ 226 |
| PALAZZO DEL POPOLO<br>AND TORRE GROSSA<br>Piazza del Duomo<br>Tel. 0577 940008<br>(Information office) | Nov.–Feb. open 10.30am–4.20pm, closed Fri.;<br>Mar.–Oct. open 9.30am–7.20pm. | ▲ 226 |
| SANT'AGOSTINO<br>Piazza Sant'Agostino<br>Tel. 0577 940008<br>(Information office) | Open winter 7am–noon and 3–6pm; summer<br>7am–noon and 3–7pm. | ▲ 226 |

| | | |
|---|---|---|
| **SANTA FINA**<br>Piazza del Duomo<br>Tel. 0577 940008<br>(Information office) | *Open Jan. 21–Feb. 28: Mon.–Sat. 9.45am–noon and 3.15–4.30pm, Sun. and public holidays 3.15–4.30pm; Mar.: Mon.–Sat. 9.30am–5pm, Sun. and public holidays 1–5pm; Apr.–Oct.: Mon.–Fri. 9.30am–7.30pm, Sat. 9.30am–5pm, Sun. and public holidays 1–5pm; Nov. 3–Jan. 20 Mon.–Sat. 9.30am–5pm Sun. and public holidays 1–5pm.* | ▲ 226 |
| **SAN QUIRICO D'ORCIA** | 53027 | C C5 |
| **MUNICIPAL TOURIST OFFICE**<br>Via Alighieri, 33<br>Tel. 0577 8972111 | *Open 8am–sunset.* | |
| **HORTI LEONINI**<br>Piazza della Libertà<br>Tel. 0577 898303; 0577 898247 | *Visit by appointment only.* | ▲ 233 |
| **SARTEANO** | 53047 | C D6 |
| **CASTELLO DEI MANENTI**<br>Via della Rocca<br>Tel. 0578 2691 | *Open Nov. 1–May 31 Sat. and Sun. 10am–noon and 4–7pm.* | ▲ 234 |
| **MUSEO CIVICO ARCHEOLOGICO**<br>Via Roma, 29<br>Tel. 0578 269261 | *Contact the parish priest for information.* | ▲ 234 |
| **SAN MARTINO**<br>Piazza San Martino<br>Tel. 0578 265573 | *Visit by appointment only.* | ▲ 234 |
| **STAGGIA** | 53038 | C B4 |
| **MUSEUM**<br>Piazza Grazzini<br>Tel. 0577 930901 (rector) | *Open Apr. 13–Oct.31 Sat. 3–5.30pm. For other times, visit by appointment only.* | ▲ 225 |

## FROM VOLTERRA TO LIVORNO

| | | |
|---|---|---|
| **CAMPIGLIA MARITTIMA** | 57021 | D C3 |
| **PALAZZO PRETORIO**<br>Via Cavour<br>Tel. 0565 838958<br>(Tourist information office) | *Visit by appointment only.* | ▲ 245 |
| **ROCCA**<br>Monte Calvi<br>Tel. 0565 838958<br>(Tourist Information Office) | *Visit by appointment only.* | ▲ 245 |
| **SAN GIOVANNI**<br>Via di Venturina<br>Tel. 0565 838958<br>(Tourist information office) | *Visit by appointment only.* | ▲ 245 |
| **CASTAGNETO CARDUCCI** | 57022 | D C2 |
| **MUNICIPAL TOURIST OFFICE**<br>Via Marconi<br>Tel. 0565 763624 | *email: castagneto.turismo@infol.it* | |
| **CENTRO CARDUCCIANO**<br>Via Carducci<br>Tel.0565 777868 | *Open summer 10.30am–12.30pm.*<br>*Closed Sat.–Mon.* | ◆D C2<br>▲ 246 |
| **MUSEO ARCHIVIO**<br>**DI CASTAGNETO CARDUCCI**<br>c/o Municipal Tourist Office | *Open summer 10.30am–12.30pm.*<br>*Closed Sat.–Mon.* | ◆D C2<br>▲ 246 |
| **LIVORNO** | 57100 | D B1 |
| **APT – LIVORNO**<br>Piazza Cavour, 6<br>Tel. 0586 898111 | | |
| **ACQUARIO COMUNALE**<br>Tel. 0586 820111 | *Open Nov.–Jan. 9.30am–12.30pm and 2.30–5.30pm; Feb.–Oct. 9.30am–12.30pm and 4–7pm. Closed Mon.* | ▲ 250 |
| **CISTERNONE**<br>Tel. 0586 242111 | *Visit by appointment only.* | ▲ 248 |

| DUOMO<br>Piazza Grande<br>Tel. 0586 884642 | Open 7.15am–noon and 5–7pm. | ▲ 248 |
|---|---|---|
| FORTEZZA NUOVA<br>Via Scali della Fortezza Nuova<br>Tel. 0586 802518 | Open 8am–8pm. | ▲ 248 |
| FORTEZZA VECCHIA AND<br>MASTIO DE MATILDE<br>Darsena Nuova, Medici Port | Visit by appointment only: contact Litoral Sindi<br>(tel. 058 689 7071), Toscatravel (tel. 0586 898444)<br>or Vietu (tel. 0586 897020). | ▲ 249 |
| SAN FERDINANDO<br>Piazza del Luogo Pio<br>Tel. 0586 888541 | Visit by appointment only. | ▲ 249 |
| SAN JACOPO ACQUAVIVA<br>Via San Jacopo<br>Tel. 0586 800590 | Open 8am–noon and 4–8pm. | ▲ 250 |
| SYNAGOGUE<br>Piazza Benamozegh, 1 | Visit by appointment only: contact Communita<br>Ebraica (Via del Tempio, 3, tel. 0586 896290). | ▲ 249 |
| TORRE DEL MARZOCCO<br>Via Mogadiscio<br>Tel. 0586 802454; 0586 820132<br>(Livorno Tourist Office) | Not open to the public. | ▲ 250 |

| MASSA MARITTIMA | 58024 | D D3 |
|---|---|---|
| PALAZZO COMUNALE<br>Piazza Garibaldi<br>Tel. 0566 902051 | Not open to the public. | ▲ 242 |
| PALAZZO PRETORIO<br>Piazza Garibaldi<br>Tel. 0566 902289 | Open winter Tue.–Sun. 10am–12.30pm and 3–5pm;<br>summer Tue.–Sun. 10am–12.30pm and 3.30–7pm<br>(July–Aug. daily 10am–1pm and 3.30–10.30pm). | ▲ 242 |
| SAN CERBONE<br>Piazza Garibaldi<br>Tel. 0566 902237 (rector) | Open winter 8am–noon and 3.30–6.30pm; summer<br>8am–noon and 3.30–7pm. | ▲ 242 |
| TORRE DEL CANDELIERE<br>Piazza Matteotti<br>Tel. 0566 902289 | Open 11am–12.30pm and 5–7pm. | ▲ 242 |

| PIOMBINO | 57025 | D C3 |
|---|---|---|
| PALAZZO COMUNALE<br>Piazza Bovio<br>Tel. 0565 83111 | Visit by appointment only. | ▲ 243 |
| SANT'ANTIMO<br>Piazza Curzio Desideri<br>Tel. 0565 83111 | Visit by appointment only. | ▲ 243 |

| POPULONIA | 57020 | D C3 |
|---|---|---|
| ROCCA | Open 9.30am–12.30pm and 2.30–5pm. | ▲ 243 |

| SAN PIETRO IN PALAZZI | 57010 | D C2 |
|---|---|---|
| MUSEO ETRUSCO-ROMANA<br>Via Guerrazzi<br>Tel. 0586 660411; 0586 680145 | Open Tue., Thur., Sat. 1–5.30pm; Mon., Wed., Fri.<br>and Sun. visits by appointment, telephone. | ▲ 246 |

| SUVERETO | 57028 | D C3 |
|---|---|---|
| PALAZZO COMUNALE<br>Via Piave<br>Tel. 0565 829923 | Open 10am–12.30pm.<br>Closed on public holidays. | ▲ 245 |
| SAN FRANCESCO<br>Via del Crocifisso<br>Tel. 0565 829923 | Visit by appointment only. | ▲ 245 |

| VOLTERRA | 56048 | D D1 |
|---|---|---|
| CONSORZIO TURISTICO VOLTERRA<br>VALDICECINA<br>Piazza dei Priori, 20<br>Tel. and Fax. 0588 87257 | www.volterra.it<br>email: ced@sirt.pisa.it | |
| BAPTISTERY<br>Piazza San Giovanni<br>Tel. 0588 87654 | Open 7.30am–12.30pm and 3–6pm. | ▲ 238 |
| DUOMO<br>Piazza San Giovanni<br>Tel. 0588 87654 | Open 7.30am–12.30pm and 3–6pm. | ▲ 238 |

# ◆ PLACES TO VISIT

| | | |
|---|---|---|
| **MUSEO DIOCESANO D'ARTE SACRA**<br>Via Roma, 1<br>Tel. 0588 86290 | *Open Mar. 15–Nov. 2 Mon.–Sun. 9am–1pm and 3–6pm; Nov. 3–Mar. 14 Mon.–Sun. 9am–1pm.* | ▲ 238 |
| **MUSEO ETRUSCO GUARNACCI**<br>Via don Minzoni, 15<br>Tel. 0588 86347 | *Open Nov. 3–Mar. 14 9am–2pm; Mar. 16–Nov. 2 9am–7pm.* | ▲ 239 |
| **PALAZZO DEI PRIORI**<br>Piazza dei Priori<br>Tel. 0588 86050 | *Open Tue., Thur. 10am–1pm and 3–6pm; Mon., Wed., Fri. 10am–1pm.* | ▲ 238 |
| **PALAZZO INCONTRI-VITI**<br>Via dei Sarti, 41<br>Tel. 0588 84047; 0588 87801 | *Open Mar. 16–Sep. 30 Mon., Wed.–Fri. 9am–1pm; Sat., Sun. and public holidays 9am–1pm and 3–5.30pm. Closed Tue.* | ▲ 239 |
| **PALAZZO PRETORIO**<br>Piazza dei Priori | *Closed.* | ▲ 238 |
| **PINACOTECA AND MUSEO CIVICO**<br>**(PALAZZO MINNUCCI SOLAINI)**<br>Via Sarti, 1<br>Tel. 0588 87580 | *Open Nov. 3–Mar. 15 9am–2pm; Mar. 16–Nov. 2 9am–7pm.* | ▲ 239 |
| **ROMAN THEATER**<br>Porta Fiorentina | *Open Mar. 16–Nov. 2 11am–5pm.*<br>*Closed in the event of rain.* | ▲ 239 |
| **SANTI GIUSTO E CLEMENTE**<br>Via Borgo San Giusto<br>Tel. 0588 86302 | *Visit by appointment only.* | ▲ 237 |
| **TORRE DEL PORCELLINO**<br>Piazza dei Priori | *Closed.* | ▲ 238 |

## GROSSETO AND THE MAREMMA

**ALBERESE**                      U D D5

| | | |
|---|---|---|
| **ABBEY OF SAN RABANO**<br>at Poggio Lenci<br>Parco dell'Uccellina<br>Tel. 0564 407098<br>Pro Loco: tel. 0564 860447 | *Visit by appointment only.* | ▲ 255 |

**ANSEDONIA**        58016              D E6

| | | |
|---|---|---|
| **RUINS OF THE CITY OF COSA**<br>Tel. 0564 881421 | *Open Oct.–Apr. 8am–5pm; May–Sep. 8am–8pm.* | ▲ 259 |

**CAPALBIO**        58011              D E5

| | | |
|---|---|---|
| **ORATORIO DELLA PROVVIDENZA**<br>Tel. 0564 896018<br>(Tourist office) | *Visit by appointment only.* | ▲ 259 |
| **PALAZZO COLLACCHIONI**<br>Via Collacchioni, 1<br>Tel. 0564 896611<br>(Tourist office) | *Visit by appointment only.* | ▲ 259 |
| **SAN NICOLA**<br>Centro Urbano<br>Tel. 0564 896018 | *Visit by appointment only.* | ▲ 259 |

**GIARDINO DEI TAROCCHI**        58011          D E6 F

| | | |
|---|---|---|
| At Garavicchio-Capalbio<br>Tel. 0564 895122<br>Fax 0564 895700 | *Open May–Oct., 2.30–7.30pm; Nov.–Apr., only by appointment (via fax).*<br>*Closed Sun. and public holidays.* | ▲ 259 |

**GROSSETO**        58100              D D4

| | | |
|---|---|---|
| **APT – GROSSETO**<br>Via Monte Rosa, 206<br>Tel. 0564 462611 | *e-mail: aptgrosseto@grosseto.turismo.toscana.it* | |
| **DUOMO**<br>Piazza del Duomo<br>Tel. 0564 414303<br>(Information office) | *Telephone for information and hours.* | ▲ 253 |
| **MUSEO ARCHEOLOGICO E**<br>**D'ARTE DELLA MAREMMA**<br>Piazza Baccarini, 3<br>Tel. 0564 417629 | *Open winter Tue.–Sun. 9am–1pm and 4–6pm; summer Tue.–Sun. 10am–1pm and 5–8pm.*<br>*Closed Mon.* | ▲ 253 |
| **SAN FRANCESCO**<br>Piazza Indipendenza<br>Tel. 0564 414303 | *Hours vary.* | ▲ 253 |

| MANCIANO | 58014 | D F5 | |
|---|---|---|---|
| **MUSEO DI PREISTORIA E PROTOSTORIA**<br>Via Corsini, 5; Tel. 0564 629222 | *Open winter Tue., Fri. 10.30am–1.30pm; Sat. 10.30am–1pm and 2.30–4.30pm.* | ▲ 259 | |

| ORBETELLO | 58015 | D E5 | |
|---|---|---|---|
| **TOURIST INFORMATION**<br>Via dell'Unione<br>Tel. 0564 860447 | *www.orbetellonline.it* | | |
| **PALAZZO DEL MUNICIPIO**<br>Piazza Plebiscito<br>Tel. 0564 861111 | *Closed for restoration.* | ▲ 258 | |
| **PALAZZO DI SPAGNA**<br>Piazza Garibaldi<br>Tel. 0564 861111 | *Closed.* | ▲ 258 | |
| **POLVERIERA GUZMAN**<br>Tel. 0564 861111 | *Closed.* | ▲ 255 | |
| **SANTA MARIA AD PORTAM**<br>Piazza IV Novembre<br>Tel. 0564 861111 | *Closed.* | ▲ 255 | |
| **SANTA MARIA ASSUNTA**<br>Piazza Duomo<br>Tel. 0564 867480 | *Open 7am–12.30pm and 3–8pm.* | ▲ 258 | |
| **PARCO NATURALE DELLA MAREMMA**<br>Head Office at Pianacce<br>(Alberese) Tel. 0564 407098 | *Visit by appointment only.* | ▲ 255 | |

| PITIGLIANO | 58017 | D F5 | |
|---|---|---|---|
| **CATHEDRAL**<br>Piazza San Gregorio VII<br>Tel. 0564 614433<br>(Information office) | *Open daily.* | ▲ 260 | |
| **MUSEO DELLA DIOCESI**<br>**(PALAZZO ORSINI)**<br>Piazza della Fortezza Orsini<br>Tel. 0564 615568 | *Open Apr.–Sep. 10am–1pm and 3–8pm; Oct.–Dec. 10am–1pm and 3–7pm.* | ▲ 260 | |
| **SANTA MARIA**<br>Via Orsini<br>Tel. 0564 614433<br>(Information office) | *Open daily.* | ▲ 260 | |

| ROSELLE | 58100 | D E4 | |
|---|---|---|---|
| **ARCHEOLOGICAL EXCAVATIONS**<br>Tel. 0564 402403 | *Open Nov.–Feb., 9am–5.30pm; Mar.–Apr., 9am–6.30pm; May–Aug., 9am–7.30pm.* | ▲ 253 | |

| SORANO | 58010 | D F4 | |
|---|---|---|---|
| **FORTRESS**<br>Via San Marco<br>Tel. 0564 633767 | *Open Fri., Sat., Sun. and public holidays 10am–4pm (Oct.–Mar.); Mon.–Sun. 10am–7pm (Apr.–Sep.).* | ▲ 260 | |

| SOVANA | 58010 | D F5 | |
|---|---|---|---|
| **DUOMO**<br>Piazza del Pretorio | *Open winter Sat. and Sun.; summer daily. Information from the APT in Grosseto.* | ▲ 260 | |
| **ETRUSCAN NECROPOLIS**<br>Poggio di Sopra Ripa | *Open daily. Information from the APT in Grosseto.* | ▲ 260 | |
| **ROCCA ALDOBRANDESCA**<br>Via del Pretorio | *Closed.* | | |
| **SANTA MARIA MAGGIORE**<br>Piazza del Pretorio | *Open daily. Information from the APT of Grosseto.* | ▲ 260 | |

| TALAMONE | 58010 | D D5 | |
|---|---|---|---|
| **ROCCA**<br>Tel. 0564 861111<br>(Comune di Orbetello) | *Visit by appointment only.* | ▲ 255 | |

| VETULONIA | 58040 | D D4 | |
|---|---|---|---|
| **MUSEO ARCHEOLOGICO**<br>Via Garibaldi<br>Tel. 0564 927432 | *Visit by appointment only.* | ▲ 254 | |
| **TOMB OF DIAVOLINO II AND TOMB OF PIETRERA**<br>Tel. 0564 949587 | *Visit by appointment only.* | ▲ 254 | |

The grid references (e.g. ◆ B F4)
refer to the map section.
The key for the symbols is on page 261.

**HOTELS**
- ⬚ < 100,000 lire
- ⬚ 100,000–200,000 lire
- ⬚ 200,000–300,000 lire
- ⬚ > 300,000 lire

## FLORENCE

### FIESOLE

◆ B F4
→ HOTELS

**Villa Aurora ****
Piazza Mino, 39
Tel. 055 59100
Fax 055 59587
*19th-century villa in the city center with period furnishings and modern facilities.*
⬚Ⅲ🄿🄰🍽🄾🅐

**Villa Fiesole ***
Via Frà Angelico, 35
Tel. 055 597252
Fax 055 599133
*This hotel, situated in a residential area, enjoys a breathtaking panoramic view of Fiesole and Florence.*
⬚Ⅲ🄿🄰🍽🄾🅐
⬚

**Villa San Michele ****
Via Doccia, 4
Tel. 055 59451
Fax 055 598734
*15th-century former monastery with a façade and loggia reputedly designed by Michelangelo. Now converted into a stunning hotel, set in a lovely Tuscan garden. Extremely high prices, but if money is no object, this must be one of the best choices of hotel in Tuscany.*
⬚Ⅲ🄿🄰🍽🄾🍸
⬚

### FLORENCE

◆ B F4
→ HOTELS

**Aprile ***
Via della Scala, 6
Tel. 055 216237
Fax 055 280947
*A peaceful garden in a former Medici palace. Frescoed ceilings, antique furniture and paintings; quiet rooms, individually decorated.*
⬚Ⅲ🄿🄲🄾🄰

**Bellettini ***
Via dei Conti, 7
Tel. 055 213561

VILLA SAN MICHELE, FIESOLE

Fax 055 283551
*Family-run hotel; the star attraction is the buffet breakfast with homemade biscuits and cakes.*
⬚Ⅲ🄰🄾🅐

**Botticelli ***
Via Taddea, 8
Tel. 055 290905
Fax 055 294322
*A stone's throw from San Lorenzo market and the church of the same name, this 16th-century palace has frescos in the public rooms and a covered terrace.*
⬚Ⅲ🄰🄿🄲🄾🅐🄰

**Casci ***
Via Cavour, 13
Tel. 055 211686
Fax 055 2396461
Closed for part of Jan.
*Set in a 15th-century building that was once the home of Gioacchino Rossini.*
⬚Ⅲ🄿🄾🅐

**Desirée ***
Via Fiume, 20
Tel. 055 238 2382
Fax 055 291439
Closed for part of Aug.
*The owner of this small hotel with large air-conditioned bedrooms is the soul*

*of courtesy. Excellent value for money.*
⬚Ⅲ🄰🄾🅐

**✪ Excelsior *****
Piazza Ognissanti, 3
Tel. 055 264201
Fax 055 210278
*Gracious, Renaissance-style palace in the historical center; easily the most luxurious hotel in Florence. Smart roof garden with a splendid view over the Arno river. It has a popular restaurant, 'Il Castello'.*
⬚Ⅲ🄿🄲🍽🄾🅐⬚

**Grand Hotel Baglioni ****
Piazza Unità Italiana, 6
Tel. 055 23580
Fax 055 235 8895
*A classic hotel that meets contemporary requirements yet retains an air of old-world refinement and glamour.*
⬚Ⅲ🄿🄾🅐⬚

**✪ Grand Hotel Minerva ****
Piazza Santa Maria Novella, 16
Tel. 055 284555
Fax 055 268281
*Classy hotel right in*

*the center. This haven of peace has a swimming pool on the terrace, a porch, and a garden overlooked by the restaurant.*
⬚Ⅲ🄿🄲🄰🄾🍽🅐
⬚

**✪ Grand Hotel Villa Cora *****
Viale Machiavelli, 18
Tel. 055 229 8451
Fax 055 229086
*Nobility, royalty, ambassadors and artists from all over the world have stayed in this villa, built by Baron Oppenheim in the latter half of the 19th century. Extremely comfortable rooms in plush, peaceful surroundings. The 'Taverna Machiavelli' is a must.*
⬚Ⅲ🄿🄾🅐🍽⬚

**✪ Helvetia & Bristol *****
Via de' Pescioni, 2
Tel. 055 287814
Fax 055 288353
*In the heart of Florence, opposite Palazzo Strozzi, this hotel stands in the most elegant area of the city. Built in the second half of the 19th century, it was long frequented by artists and writers. Now remodeled, it combines traditional hospitality with modern facilities.*
⬚Ⅲ🄿🄲🄾🅐⬚

**Hermitage ***
Vicolo Marzio, 1
on the corner of Piazza del Pesce
Tel. 055 287216
Fax 055 212208
*Close to the Ponte Vecchio, this hotel has the comfortable atmosphere of an old manor house. Delightful honeysuckle-covered terrace with a view over the Arno river.*
⬚Ⅲ🄿🄰🄲🍽🄾🅐

**RESTAURANTS**
- 🅴 < 50,000 lire
- 🅴 50,000–80,000 lire
- 🅴 90,000–120,000 lire
- 🅴 > 120,000 lire

**○ J and J ★★★★**
Via di Mezzo, 20
Tel. 055 234 5005
Fax 055 240282
*There is a lovely view over the roofs and courtyards of Florence from the sumptuously furnished rooms of this peaceful hotel set in a former monastery.*
🅴🅴🅴🅴🅴🅴🅴🅴

**Kraft ★★★★**
Via Solferino, 2
Tel. 055 284273
Fax 055 239 8267
*Neo-baroque hotel with a terrace and swimming pool. Superb view.*
🅴🅴🅴🅴🅴🅴🅴

**○ Rivoli ★★★★**
Via della Scala, 33
Tel. 055 282853
Fax 055 294041
*In the historical center, this former convent renovated in the 1990s combines tradition and modernity. The small swimming pool and patio are very quiet and restful.*
🅴🅴🅴🅴🅴🅴🅴🅴

**○ Loggiato dei Serviti ★★★**
Piazza Santissima Annunziata, 3
Tel. 055 289592
Fax 055 289595
*Built in 1527 by Antonio da Sangallo the Elder, this gem of a hotel has huge fresco-painted lounges and bedrooms furnished with English and Italian antiques. View of the piazza and the small inner courtyards.*
🅴🅴🅴🅴🅴🅴

**○ Regency ★★★★★**
Piazza Massimo d'Azeglio, 3
Tel. 055 245247
Fax 055 2346735
*This charming and intimate 19th-century villa is set on the edge of a plane-tree shaded park.*

*It has an elegant town garden and a superb restaurant. Classic cuisine.*
🅴🅴🅴🅴🅴🅴🅴🅴🅴

**Residenza Apostoli B&B**
Borgo Santi Apostoli, 8
Tel. 055 284837
or 055 288432
Fax 055 268790
*Each of the bedrooms in this 14th-century palazzo are individually and tastefully decorated. This is more a hotel than a bed and breakfast. The best bedroom is number 3 overlooking the loggia. Children under two stay for free.*
🅴🅴🅴🅴

ENOTECA PINCHIORRI, FLORENCE

**Residenza Hannah e Johanna B&B**
Via Bonifacio Lupi, 14
Tel. 055 481896
Fax 055 482721
*This well-kept hotel is housed in a 19th-century palazzo near the Duomo. Its light, airy rooms have been stylishly redesigned. Children under two stay for free.*
🅴🅴🅴🅴🅴🅴🅴

**Residenza Johanna B&B**
Via delle V Giornate, 12
Tel. and fax 055 473377
*Small early-19th-century villa in the city center with a delightful little garden. Warm*

*atmosphere and a well-stocked library. Each bedroom has a kettle and everything you need for a DIY breakfast.*
🅴🅴🅴

**○ Splendor ★★★**
Via San Gallo, 30
Tel. 055 483 427
Fax 055 461 276
*This tastefully restored old building is ideal for a romantic interlude. Superb terrace and inviting reading room furnished with period furniture.*
🅴🅴🅴🅴🅴🅴🅴🅴

**Villa Azalee ★★★**
Viale Fratelli Rosselli, 44
Tel. 055 214242
Fax 055 268264

*This romantic hotel with intimate floral decor will charm you with the warmth of its welcome. Bicycle hire in summer.*
🅴🅴🅴🅴🅴🅴🅴🅴

→ **RESTAURANTS**
**○ Alle Murate**
Via Ghibellina, 52/r
Tel. 055 240618
Closed Mon. lunchtime and Christmas.
*Intimate and sophisticated atmosphere, soft background music. This is an ideal place to spend a quiet evening, buoyed up by superb wines from one of the best wine cellars in the city featuring the*

*leading national labels and some of the most prestigious French vintages.*
🅴🅴🅴

**Al Lume di Candela**
Via delle Terme, 23/r
Tel. 055 294566
Fax 055 283815
Closed Sun. and Mon. lunchtime.
*Romantic restaurant in a 14th-century tower. The sensational desserts are a must.*
🅴🅴🅴🅴

**Don Chisciotte**
Via Rodolfi, 4/r
Tel. 055 475 4430
Fax 055 485305
Closed Sun., Mon. lunchtime and Aug.
*Tastefully furnished and decorated with pictures inspired by the adventures of Don Quixote, this restaurant serves dishes with the emphasis on tradition.*
🅴🅴🅴

**○ Enoteca Pinchiorri**
Via Ghibellina, 87
Tel. 055 242777
Fax 055 244983
Closed Sun., Mon. lunchtime and Wed.
*Set in a beautiful palazzo in the historical center, this elegant restaurant boasts an award-winning cuisine celebrating 25 successful years. Beautifully prepared dishes and an outstanding selection of cheeses and desserts. Extensive wine cellar with some 80,000 bottles of the best French and Italian wines.*
🅴🅴🅴🅴

**Il Cibreo**
Via dei Macci, 118/r
Tel. 055 234 1100
Fax 055 244966
Closed Sun., Mon.
*One of the best restaurants in*

# ◆ USEFUL ADDRESSES
## FLORENCE

**HOTELS**
- ⬚ < 100,000 lire
- ⬚ 100,000–200,000 lire
- ⬚ 200,000–300,000 lire
- ⬚ > 300,000 lire

Florence. Il Cibreo welcomes gormets in a refined yet relaxed atmosphere and in the best of Florentine tradition. Simple Tuscan dishes are reinvented and turned into delicacies: bean soup, dogfish, liver and bacon, tripe in vinegar. Popular with artists who jostle around the large wooden tables.
⬚ ⬚ ⬚

IL CIBREO, FLORENCE

**La Baraonda**
Via Ghibellina, 67
Tel. 055 234 1171
Closed Sun., Mon. lunchtime, first week in Jan. and Aug.
*In the historical Santa Croce district, this discreet, peaceful restaurant only has a limited number of tables; meals are served in the garden in the summer.*
⬚ ⬚ ⬚ ⬚ ⬚

**La Baruciola**
Via Maggio, 61/r
Tel. 055 218906
Closed Sun. and Aug. 15.
*A lively young eatery in an old street in the Oltrarno district, a stone's throw from the Piazza Pitti.*
⬚ ⬚ ⬚ ⬚

**Loggia**
Piazzale Michelangelo, 1
Tel. and fax 055 234 2832
Closed Mon.
*Restaurant renowned both for its location overlooking the city and for its food.*
⬚ ⬚ ⬚ ⬚ ⬚ ⬚

**Marione**
Via della Spada, 27/r
Tel. 055 214756
Closed Sun. and part of Aug.
*Simple traditional trattoria, in business since the 1960s.*
⬚ ⬚ ⬚

**Oliviero**
Via delle Terme, 51/r
Tel. 055 212421
Fax 055 230 2407
Closed Sun. and Aug.
*Tuscan cuisine by an acclaimed chef who uses fish and homemade products to create a blend of classic dishes and innovative creations.*
⬚ ⬚ ⬚

### → CAFÉS
**❂ Caffè Rivoir**
Piazza della Signoria, 5/r
Tel. 055 214412
Closed Mon.
*Attractive café selling the best hot chocolate in the city.*

**Giacosa**
Via Tornabuoni, 83/r
Tel. 055 239 6226
Closed Sun.
*Elegant tearoom, selling homemade ice-cream, cakes and biscuits.*

**Gilli**
Piazza della Repubblica 39/r
Tel. 055 213896
Closed Tue.
*Founded in 1733: a delightful atmosphere and top quality service.*

**Giubbe Rosse**
Piazza della Repubblica, 13/14/r
Tel. 055 212280
*One of Florence's early-20th-century literary cafés, it is now renowned for its Pratese cantucci and its Vin Santo.*

**Il Latini**
Via dei Palchetti, 6/r
Tel. 055 210916
Closed Mon.
*For three generations the Latini family has been serving homemade Tuscan recipes in the Palazzo Rucellai; good value for money.*
⬚

**Il Sasso di Dante**
Piazza delle Pallottole, 6/r
Tel. 055 282113
*This small, distinctive restaurant has an attractive façade bedecked with flowers. Typical Tuscan cuisine.*

**Osteria del Caffè Italiano**
Via Isola delle Stinche, 11–13/r
Tel. 055 289368
*'Tuscan wine and cooking' is the slogan of this restaurant on the first floor of the historical Palazzo Salviati which still has its period architecture and décor.*
⬚ ⬚

**Paszkowski**
Piazza della Repubblica, 6/r
Tel. 055 210236
Closed Mon.
*Piano bar all year round and orchestra on the terrace during the summer.*
⬚ ⬚ ⬚

**Sabatini**
Via de' Panzani, 9/a
Tel. 055 212559
Fax 055 210 2293
Closed Mon.
*For long one of the finest and most expensive restaurants. Traditional and delicious.*
⬚ ⬚ ⬚

### → ICE-CREAM PARLORS
**Antartide**
Via Ponte di Mezzo, 40/b
Tel. 055 366859
Closed Mon.

**Vivoli**
Via Isola delle Stinche, 7/r
Tel. 055 292334
Closed Mon.
*Regarded as the best in Florence.*

### → NIGHT LIFE
**Jazz Club**
Via Nuova de' Caccini, 3
Tel. 055 247 9700
Closed Mon.
*Warm welcome. Live music every evening.*

**Rex Caffè**
Via Fiesolana, 23/25/r
Tel. 055 248 0331
Closed Tue.
*You can get a bite to eat during the day and enjoy a beer in the evening in this café decorated with blue mosaics.*

**Tenax**
Via Pratese, 46
Tel. 055 308160
Closed Tue.

**Zoe**
Via Dei Renai, 13/r
Tel. 055 243111
*Ultra-fashionable bar that puts on shows and exhibitions.*

### → WINE SHOPS
**Enoteca Ognissanti**
Borgo Ognissanti, 133/r
Tel. 055 287505
*Truffle specialties.*

**RESTAURANTS**
◼ < 50,000 lire
◼ 50,000–80,000 lire
◼ 90,000–120,000 lire
▦ > 120,000 lire

**Il Cantinone
del Gallo Nero**
Via di Santo Spirito,
6/r
Tel. 055 218898

**La Cantinetta
Antinori**
Piazza Antinori, 3
Tel. 055 292234

**La Cantinetta
del Verrazzano**
Via di Tavolini, 18/20
Tel. 055 268590
Tastings of Tuscan
ham and salami.

**→ FOOD STORES
Cibreo**
Via Andrea del
Verrocchio, 8/r
Tel. 055 2341094
Oil, wine, aromatic
vinegar, brandy,
jams, recipe books...
This shop sells
everything! A little
pricey, but very good
quality.

**Pegna**
Via dello Studio, 8
Tel. 055 282701
Luxury delicatessen
selling salami
and cured pork
produce, dairy
produce, wine,
biscuits and various
types of preserves.

**Procacci**
Via Tornabuoni, 64/r
Tel. 055 211656
Specialty rolls filled
with truffles.

**→ OLIVE GROWERS
Marchesi Antinori**
Piazza Antinori, 3
Tel. 055 235 9848

**→ WINE OUTLETS
Casa del Vino**
Via dell'Ariento, 16/r
Tel. 055 215609

**Fuori Porta**
Via Monte alle
Croci, 10/r
Tel. 055 234 2483

**Le Volpi e l'Uva**
Piazza dei Rossi, 2/r
Tel. 055 239 8132

**Zanobini**
Via Sant'Antonino,
47/r
Tel. 055 239 6850

**→ ANTIQUE DEALERS
Bartolozzi**
Via Maggio, 18/r
Tel. 055 215602
Medieval artefacts.

**Campolmi**
Via Maggio, 5
Tel. 055 295367
16th- and 17th-
century furniture
and paintings.

**Carnevali**
Borgo San Jacopo,
64/r
Tel. 055 295064
Clothes.

**Piselli**
Via Maggio, 23/r
Tel. 055 239 8029
Pictures and antique
fabrics.

**Pratesi**
Via Maggio, 13
Tel. 055 239 6568
17th-century and
neoclassical
paintings and
sculpture.

**Romano**
Borgo Ognissanti, 36
Tel. 055 239 6006
17th- and 18th-
century objects.

**Studio Santo Spirito**
Via dello Sprone,
19/21/r
Tel. 055 214873
Restorers of
porcelain and
majolica.

◆ B F4
**→ RESTAURANT
Cave di Maiano**
Via delle Cave, 16
Tel. 055 59133
Closed Mon.
lunchtime.
This ancient
trattoria, founded
in 1897, has a
panoramic terrace
with tables made
of pietra serena.
◼ ▦ ✦

◆ B E4
**→ HOTEL
✿ Paggeria
Medicea ****
Viale Papa Giovanni
XXIII, 3

Tel. 055 871 8081
Fax 055 871 8080
This hotel, in 16th-
century converted
servants' quarters, is
surrounded by lush
olive groves and
vineyards. The
'Biagio Pignatta'
restaurant, housed
in the residence of
Ferdinando de'
Medici's first major-
domo, serves dishes
with a Renaissance
touch.
◼ ▦ ⯀ ▣ ♟ ⛖ ⯀ ✦
♿ ▦

**→ RESTAURANT
✪ Delfina**
Via della Chiesa, 1
Tel. 055 871 8074
Fax 055 871 8175
Closed Sun. eve. and
Tue., Aug., Jan. 1
and Epiphany.
A stronghold of
authentic Tuscan
cuisine specializing
in dishes such as
ribollita and spit-
roasted meat.
◼ ▣ ♟ ⯀ ✦

◆ B E4
**→ OIL PRODUCERS
Tenuta di Capezzana**
Via di Capezzana,
100
Tel. 055 8706 0065
Capezzana label.

◆ B E5
**→ HOTEL
La Speranza ***
Borgo Garibaldi,
80
Tel. 0571 668014
Comfortable,
inexpensive hotel
situated in the
lower part of
the town.
◼

**→ RESTAURANT
Osteria del Vicario**
Via Rivellino, 3
Tel. 0571 668228
Closed Wed.
This 13th-century
building in the
historical center
serves creative
Tuscan cuisine. Some
accommodation
available.
◼ ▦ ♟ ⯀ ✦

◆ B E4
**→ HOTEL
Il Sole ***
Piazza Don Minzoni,
18
Tel. 0571 73779
Small family-run
hotel located
opposite the station.
◼ ▦ ⯀ ⛃ ✦

**→ RESTAURANTS
Bianconi**
Via Tosco
Romagnola, 92
Tel. 0571 590558
Closed Wed.
Spacious restaurant
with open ovens for
barbecue specialties.
◼ ▦ ▣ ♟ ✦

**Galeone**
Via Curtatone e
Montanara, 67
Tel. 0571 72826
Closed Sun.
Classic family-run
restaurant. Fish
dishes and pizzas.
◼ ▦ ✦

◆ B D4
**→ HOTEL
La Campagnola ***
Viale Colombo, 144
Tel. 0571 260786
This family-run hotel
in the open
countryside provides
laid-back hospitality.
◼ ▦ ▣ ♟ ✦

**→ RESTAURANT
Vedute**
Via Romana
Lucchese, 121
at Le Vedute
Tel. 0571 297498
Closed Mon.
Former country
trattoria, now a cozy
restaurant serving
seasonal dishes.
◼ ▣ ✦

◆ B E4
**→ HOTEL
Baccio da
Montelupo ***
Via Don Minzoni, 3
Tel. 0571 51215
Closed Aug.
Typical Tuscan
building with
modern facilities.
◼ ▦ ▣ ⯀ ⛃ ✦

# ◆ USEFUL ADDRESSES
## PISA AND LUCCA

→ **RESTAURANT**
**Agriturismo Fattoria Petrognano**
Via Bottinaccio, 116
Tel. 0571 913795
Fax 0571 913796
*This hillside restaurant boasts a superb view and a traditional cuisine.*
□ ▣

→ **POTTERY**
**Ceramiche Artistiche Brogi**
Via della Pesa, 30
Tel. 0571 542652
Fax 0571 911811

**Ellegi Porcellane**
at Camaioni
Via Tosco Romagnola Nord, 3/b
Tel. 0571 910107
Fax 0571 910140
info@ellegi.it

**Fercolor**
Via Caverni, 87
Tel. 0571 541626
Fax 0571 1910894
info@fercolor.com

### SAN CASCIANO IN VAL DI PESA
◆ B F5
→ **RESTAURANTS**
✪ **Il Salotto dei Chianti**
Via Sonnino, 92
at Mercatale (3 miles)
Tel. 055 821 8016
Closed Wed. and weekday lunchtimes; part of Jan.
*A quiet restaurant serving Tuscan cuisine with an innovative twist. First-class cheeses, sliced ham and salami and an extensive wine list.*
□ ▥ ▤ ▣

✪ **Tenda Rossa**
Piazza del Monumento, 9
at Cerbaia (4 miles)
Tel. 055 826132
Fax 055 882 5210
Closed Sun. and Mon. lunchtime; part of Aug.
*Refined Tuscan cuisine (with particular emphasis on fish) for one of the best restaurants*

*in Italy. The warm welcome makes up for the nondescript décor.*
□ ▥ ▤

→ **OIL PRODUCERS**
**Consorzio Olio Extravergine Terre del Chianti**
Tel. 055 822 8245
Fax 055 822 8173
**Fattoria di Cigliano**
Via di Cigliano, 17
Tel. 055 824 8032

### VINCI
◆ B E4
→ **HOTELS**
**Alexandra ★★★**
Via dei Martiri, 38/40
Tel. 0571 56224
*Modern, comfortable hotel providing a haven of peace and quiet.*
□ ▥ ▤ ▣ ▤ ▣ ▤ ▣ ▣

**Gina ★★★**
Via Lamporecchiana, 27/29
Tel. 0571 56266
*Comfortable rooms in a recently built hotel.*
□ ▥ ▤ ▣ ▣

### PISA AND LUCCA
### BAGNI DI LUCCA
◆ B D3
→ **HOTELS**
**Bridge ★★★**
Piazza Ponte a Serraglio, 5/a
at Ponte a Serraglio (1 mile)
Tel. 0583 805324
*Small, comfortable hotel with simple, well-kept rooms.*
□ ▥ ▤ ▣ ▤ ▣ ▤ ▣

**Corona ★★★**
Via Serraglia, 78
at Ponte a Serraglio (1 mile)
Tel. 0583 805151
Fax 0583 805134
*An early 19th-century palace on*

the banks of the Torrente Lima.
□ ▣ ▤ ▣ ▣

### CASTELNUOVO DI GARFAGNANA
◆ B C3
→ **HOTEL**
**Hambros Parco Hotel ★★★**
at Lunata
Tel. and fax 0583 935355
*Late-18th-century villa with a sophisticated ambiance.*
□ ▣ ▤ ▣ ▣

→ **RESTAURANT**
**Da Carlino**
Via Garibaldi, 15
Tel. 0583 644270
Closed Mon.
*Restaurant with terrace and garden serving kid, spelt and homemade pasta; wine from various Italian regions.*
□ ▣ ▣

### LUCCA
◆ B C4
→ **HOTELS**
**Grand Hotel Guinigi ★★★★**
Via Romana, 1247
Tel. 0583 4991
Fax 0583 499800
*Efficient, functional hotel complex, bedrooms and suites equipped with modern conveniences and excellent facilities. Rooms for special occasions and restaurant serving Tuscan and international cuisine.*
□ ▥ ▤ ▣ ▤ ▣ ▣

✪ **La Luna ★★★**
Via Fillungo corner Corte Compagni, 12
Tel. 0583 493634
*Situated in the historical center of*

the city, this family-run hotel with experienced and attentive staff guarantees a comfortable, welcoming stay.*
□ ▥ ▤ ▣ ▤ ▣ ▤ ▣ ▣

✪ **Locanda l'Elisa ★★★★★**
Via Nuova per Pisa 1952
at Massa Pisana (2½ miles)
Tel. 0583 379737
Fax 0583 379019
*A Napoleonic villa converted into an ultra-luxurious hotel. Careful attention to detail and opulent surroundings. The 'Gazebo' restaurant is very good.*
▤ ▥ ▤ ▣ ▤ ▣ ▣

**Piccolo Hotel Puccini ★★★**
Via di Poggio, 9
Tel. 0583 55421
*Modern, functional rooms in a Renaissance palace in the heart of the city.*
□ ▣ ▤ ▣ ▣

**Stipino ★★**
Via Romana, 95
Tel. 0583 495077
Fax 0583 490309
*Simple but comfortable family-run hotel. Each room is individually furnished.*
□ ▥ ▤ ▣ ▤ ▣ ▤ ▣ ▣

✪ **Villa San Michele ★★★★**
Via della Chiesa, 462
at San Michele in Escheto (2½ miles)
Tel. 0583 370276
Fax 0583 370277
Closed mid Nov.–Feb.
*A beautiful 14th-century villa in the woods and olive groves. The annex is divided into mini-apartments.*
□ ▥ ▤ ▣ ▤ ▣ ▥ ▤ ▣ ▣
▤ ▣

→ **RESTAURANTS**
**Antico Caffè delle Mura**
Piazza Vittorio

AGRITURISMO FATT. PETROGNANO, MONTELUPO

**RESTAURANTS**
- 🔲 < 50,000 lire
- 🔲 50,000–80,000 lire
- 🔲 90,000–120,000 lire
- 🔲 > 120,000 lire

Emanuele, 2
Tel. 0583 467962
Closed Tue.;
part of Jan.
*Old-world eatery
that provides a
period setting for a
traditional style of
cuisine. Meals are
also served beneath
the trees in the
garden.*
🔲 🔲 🔲 🔲

**✪ Buca di
Sant'Antonio**
Via della Cervia, 3
Tel. 0583 55881
Closed Sun. eve.
and Mon.; part
of July.
*Good wholesome
food plus a friendly
welcome from the
owner and a highly
respected wine
cellar.*
🔲 🔲

**✪ La Mora**
Via Sesto
di Moriano, 1748
at Ponte a Moriano
(6 miles)
Tel. 0583 406402
Closed Wed.;
part of Jan.
*Regarded as the
best restaurant
for traditional
Lucchese cuisine,
La Mora serves an
exciting selection
of perfectly-
presented classic
dishes with a
modern touch.
Excellent choice of
oils and interesting
wine list.*
🔲 🔲 🔲

**Puccini**
Corte San Lorenzo,
1/3
Tel. 0583 316116
Fax 0583 316031
Closed Nov.–Feb.,
Tue. and Wed.
lunchtime.
*Comfortable,
modern restaurant
housed in a 15th-
century palazzo;
fresh seafood is
delivered daily from
the market in
Viareggio. Meals
are served outside in
the summer.*
🔲 🔲 🔲 🔲

ANTICO CAFFÈ DI SIMO, LUCCA

BUCA DI SANT'ANTONIO, LUCCA

**→ CAFÈS**
**✪ Antico Caffè
di Simo**
Via Fillungo, 58
Tel. 0583 467148
*Art Nouveau décor
that harks back to
a time when
animated literary
gatherings were
held here. Highly
recommended.*

**Taddeucci**
Piazza
San Michele, 34
Tel. 0583 494933
*Typical pastry shop
famous for its
Buccellato (wreath-
shaped cake).*

**→ WINE SHOPS**
**Enoteca Lucca
in Tavola**
Via San Paolino, 130
Tel. 0583 581022
*Prestigious
traditional wines
from Tuscany.*

**→ DELICATESSENS**
**La Cacioteca**
Via Fillungo
*A mecca of cheese,
from mild young
cheeses to the ripest,
most pungent
pecorino (ewe's
milk cheese).*

**La Grotta**
Piazza Anfiteatro, 2
*Store housed in an
old salt warehouse;*

as well as peppered
prosciutto, it sells
biroldo, a local
salami made from
pork blood and
sultanas.*

**PISA**

**◆ B** C4-5
**→ HOTELS**
**D'Azeglio ****
Piazza Vittorio
Emanuele II, 18
Tel. 050 500310
Fax 050 28017
*A centrally-located,
modern but
comfortable bed and
breakfast hotel.*
🔲 🔲 🔲 🔲 🔲 🔲 🔲

**Roma ****
Via Bonanno
Pisano, 111
Tel. 050 554488
Fax 050 550164
*Hotel with good,
functional facilities
guaranteeing an
adequate standard
of comfort.*
🔲 🔲 🔲 🔲 🔲 🔲

**Verdi ****
Piazza Repubblica, 5
Tel. 050 598947
Fax 050 598944
*A bed and breakfast
hotel equipped with
all mod cons, housed
in a completely
renovated period
palazzo in the
historical center.*
🔲 🔲 🔲 🔲 🔲 🔲 🔲

**→ RESTAURANTS**
**✪ Artilafo**
Via Volturno, 38
Closed Sun.
lunchtime,
and Aug.
*In a secluded narrow
street, this
restaurant is
renowned for its
authentic and
creative cuisine, as
well as its good
selection of cheeses
from Italy and
abroad.*
🔲 🔲 🔲 🔲

**Ristoro dei Vecchi
Macelli**
Via Volturno, 49
Tel. 050 20424
Fax 050 506008
Closed Wed. and
Sun. lunchtime;
part of Aug.
*Traditional cuisine
and authentic
service in a
typical setting,
accompanied
by fine bottles from
the wine cellar.*
🔲 🔲 🔲

**Osteria dei Cavalieri**
Via San Frediano,
16
Tel. 050 580858
Closed Sat. lunchtime
and Sun., first week
in Jan. and part of
July–Aug.
*Welcoming
restaurant housed
in a period palazzo.
It offers seafood,
vegetarian and
meat set menus,
as well as an à la
carte option.*
🔲 🔲 🔲

**→ CAFÈS**
**Caffè Dell'Ussero
Palazzo Agostini**
Lungarno Pacinotti,
27
Tel. 050 581100

**Pasticceria Salza**
Borgo stretto, 44
Tel. 050 580144

**→ WINE SHOP**
**Marcellino...
Pane e Vino**
Piazza Bartolo
da Sasso Ferrato,
16
Tel. 050 544559

▫ *< 100,000 lire*
▪ *100,000–200,000 lire*
✦ *200,000–300,000 lire*
▦ *> 300,000 lire*

→ **DELICATESSEN**
**La Bottega della Pasta Fresca**
Piazza delle Vettovaglie, 28
*The products sold by this store are in great demand abroad. Its specialties include filled ravioli.*

→ **OIL PRODUCERS**
**Olio delle Colline Lucchesi**
c/o Camera di Commercio
at Corte Campana
Tel. 0583 9765
Fax 0583 9765529

### PONTEDERA
◆ B D5
→ **HOTELS**
✿ **Armonia** ★★★★
Piazza Caduti di Cefalonia e Corfù, 11
Tel. 0587 278511
Fax 0587 278540
*In the heart of the historical center, this ancient hotel has been remodeled in early 20th-century lavish and gilded style.*
▫ ▥ ▣ ▢ ▤ ▨ ▦

**La Rotonda** ★★★
Via Dante, 52
Tel. 0587 52287
Fax 0587 55580
*A bed and breakfast hotel in an excellent location for business tourism.*
▫ ▥ ▢ ▫

→ **RESTAURANTS**
**Aeroscalo**
Via Roma, 8
Tel. 0587 52024
Closed Mon. and Aug.
*A welcoming restaurant which has been run by the same family for almost one hundred years.*
▫ ▥ ▣ ▫

**La Polveriera**
Via Fratelli Marconcini, 54
Tel. 0587 54765
Closed Mon.
*Friendly restaurant, with tastefully furnished rooms, serving excellent seafood dishes with an artistic flourish.*
▫ ▣ ▫

### SAN MINIATO
◆ B D5
→ **HOTEL**
**Miravalle** ★★★
Piazza del Castello, 3
Tel. 0571 418075
Fax 0571 419681
*Atmospheric hotel with good facilities housed within an old castle.*
▫ ▥ ▢ ▤ ▫

### MASSA, CARRARA AND THE APUAN ALPS
### CAMAIORE
◆ B C4
→ **HOTEL**
✿ **Locanda le Monache** ★★★
Piazza XXIX Maggio, 36
Tel. 0584 989258
Fax 0584 984011
*Sensitively restored residence in the historical center. The restaurant serves mainly mushroom dishes and game.*
▫ ▣ ▢ ▤ ▫

→ **RESTAURANT**
✿ **Emilio e Bona**
at Lombrici (2 miles)
Tel. 0584 989289
Closed Mon. and for a time Jan.–Feb.
*Housed in an old oil mill. Serves typically Tuscan cuisine with the emphasis on mushrooms and truffles.*
▫ ▥ ▣ ▫

### CARRARA
◆ B B3
→ **HOTEL**
**Michelangelo** ★★★
Corso Fratelli Rosselli, 3
Tel. 0585 777161
Fax 0585 74545
Closed mid Dec.– mid Jan.
*Each room is furnished with period furniture in different styles.*
▫ ▣ ▢ ▫

→ **RESTAURANT**
**Enoteca Ninan**
Via Bartolini, 3
Tel. 0585 74741
Closed Sun.
*This restaurant only has limited seating so it is advisable to book in advance. Regional cuisine and a wine cellar with a good selection of wines.*
▫ ▥ ▣ ▫

### COLONNATA
◆ B-C3
→ **RESTAURANT**
**Venanzio**
Piazza Palestro, 3
Tel. 0585 758062
Closed Sun. eve. and Thur.
*A delightful restaurant situated among the quarries. As well as lardo, it also serves simple, tasty local dishes.*
▫ ▫

### FORTE DEI MARMI
◆ B B3
→ **HOTELS**
✿ **Byron** ★★★★★
Viale Morin, 46
Tel. 0584 78052
Fax 0584 787152
*Two 19th-century villas overlooking the sea: old-world hospitality plus the outstanding 'La Magnolia' restaurant (a must).*
▫ ▥ ▣ ▢ ▤ ▨ ▦

**Franceschi** ★★★
Via XX Settembre, 19
Tel. 0584 787114
Fax 0584 787471
Closed Nov.–mid Mar.
*Sophisticated hotel in a stately villa furnished with period furniture. It also boasts a private beach.*
▫ ▥ ▣ ▢ ▤ ▦

✿ **Il Negresco** ★★★★
Lungomare Italico, 82
Tel. 0584 787133
Fax 0584 787535
*Elegant, welcoming hotel with a lovely panoramic view.*
▫ ▥ ▣ ▢ ▨ ▤ ▦

✿ **Ritz Forte dei Marmi** ★★★★
Via Gioia, 2
Tel. 0584 787531
Fax 0584 787522
*Handsome, recently renovated Art Nouveau building, a stone's throw from the sea.*
▫ ▥ ▣ ▢ ▨ ▤ ▦

→ **RESTAURANTS**
**Alberto**
Via Alpi Apuane, 33
at Querceto (2 miles)
Tel. 0584 742300
Closed Tue. and for part Oct.–Nov.
*Restaurant decorated in an elegant-rustic style, serving good food.*
▫ ▣ ▤ ▫

✿ **La Magnolia**
Viale Morin, 46
Tel. 0584 787052
Closed Nov.
*Sophisticated restaurant, decorated in Art Nouveau style; excellent Tuscan cuisine, particularly fish dishes.*
▫ ▥ ▣ ▫

✿ **Lorenzo**
Tel. 0584 66961
Fax 0584 84030
Closed Mon., lunchtime in July and Aug., mid Dec.–Jan.
*Simple, unfussy recipes using regional produce; excellent fish, cooked while you wait.*
▫ ▥ ▫

### LIDO DI CAMAIORE
◆ B B-C4
→ **HOTEL**
✿ **Villa Ariston** ★★★★
Viale Colombo, 355
Tel. 0584 610633
Fax 0584 610631
Closed Nov.–Feb.
*Art Nouveau-style residence set in a park sandwiched between the sea and a pine forest. 'D'Annunzio' restaurant.*
▫ ▥ ▲ ▣ ▢ ▨ ▤ ▦

### MASSA
◆ B B3
→ **RESTAURANT**
**Ruota**
Via Bergiola Nuova, 2

**RESTAURANTS**
▪ < 50,000 lire
▪ 50,000–80,000 lire
▪ 90,000–120,000 lire
▪ > 120,000 lire

at Bergiola Maggiore
Tel. 0585 42030
Closed Mon. off
season.
*Well-established
family-run
restaurant, rustic
in style.*
▪ P ▪ ▪

### PIETRASANTA
◆ B C3
→ **HOTELS**
**Palagi ***
Piazza Carducci, 23
Tel. 0584 70249
Fax 0584 71198
*In a central location,
this efficient,
functional hotel is
air-conditioned and
soundproofed.*
▪ ▪ P ▪ C ▪ ▪

✪ **Pietrasanta ****
Via Garibaldi, 35
Tel. 0584 793726
Fax 0584 793728
*Convenient, modern
hotel situated in the
town center. Housed
in a 16th-century
palazzo, it has
frescoed rooms
furnished in
different styles. The
hotel also boasts a
winter garden.*
▪ ▪ P ▪ C ▪ ▪ ▪

→ **RESTAURANTS**
✪ **Enoteca Marcucci**
Via Garibaldi, 40
Tel. 0584 791962
Closed Mon.
lunchtime, (except
July and Aug.)
and Nov.
*Prestigious wines,
cheeses, sliced ham
and salami; excellent
lardo.*
▪ ▪ ▪

**Martinatica**
Via Martinatica, 20
Tel. 0584 792534
Closed Tue.
*Delightful restaurant
serving elaborate
Tuscan cuisine.*
▪ ▪ ▪ ▪

**Rocchetta**
Via Montiscendi, 172
at Strettoia
Tel. 0584 799728
Fax 0584 4799840
Closed Tue.
*This characterful
restaurant, built on*

the remains of an
old fortress, serves
local cuisine.
▪ ▪ ▪

### PONTREMOLI
◆ B B2
→ **HOTEL**
**Golf Hotel ***
at La Pineta
Tel. 0187 831573
*Comfortable,
spacious rooms;
meals are also served
on the porch.*
▪ ▪ P ▪ ▪ ▪

→ **RESTAURANTS**
**Ca' del Moro**
Via Casa Corvi
Tel. 0187 830588

ENOTECA MARCUCCI, PIETRASANTA

Closed Sun. eve.
and Mon.; part
Jan.–Feb.; July
*Housed in the
barn of a former
farmhouse under
the shade of the
chestnut trees,
this restaurant
serves traditional
cuisine from the
Lunigiana in the
peaceful intimacy of
its dining rooms.*
▪ P ▪ ▪

**Da Bussè**
Piazza Duomo, 31
Tel. 0187 831371
Closed eves
and Fri.
*The classic,
traditional kitchen
serves regional
dishes. Try their
sensational herb
tarts.*
▪ ▪

→ **BOOKS**
**Città del Libro**
at Santissima

Annunziata, 21
Tel. 0187 830676

**Libreria del
Campanone**
Piazza Repubblica, 5
Tel. 0187 830092

→ **TYPICAL PRODUCE**
**Il Fungo**
Via 1° Maggio, 8
*As well as selling the
more obvious
regional specialties,
this shop also stocks
chestnut flour,
preserves and
testaroli (regional
type of pasta) from
the Lunigiana
region.*

### TORRE DEL LAGO PUCCINI
◆ B C4
→ **RESTAURANTS**
**Butterfly**
Belvedere
Puccini, 24/26
at Lake Massaciuccoli
Tel. 0584 341024
Closed Thur.,
part of Oct.–Nov.
*Hotel-restaurant
with light, airy
rooms and a
spacious garden.
Not far from the
Casa di Puccini.*
▪ P ▪ ▪

**Da Cecco**
Belvedere
Puccini 10/12
at Lake Massaciuccoli
Tel. 0584 34022
Closed Sun. eve. and
Mon.; part of July
and in Nov.
*Rustic, simple
surroundings;
traditional fish and
meat recipes.*
▪ ▪ ▪

**Lombardi**
Via Aurelia, 127
Tel. 0584 341044
Closed Tue.
*This spacious
restaurant has
traditional décor
and cuisine.*
▪ ▪ P C ▪

### VIAREGGIO
◆ B B-C4
→ **HOTELS**
**Grand Hotel
& Royal ***
Viale Carducci, 44
Tel. 0584 45151
Fax 0584 31438
Closed Nov.–Mar.
*Situated between
the sea and a pine
forest, this hotel
has a delightful
'turreted' structure
dating from the turn
of the 20th century.*
▪ P ▪ ▪ ▪ ▪ ▪ ▪

**Palace Hotel ****
Via Gioia, 2
Tel. 0584 46134
Fax 0584 47351
*Art Nouveau
building built in the
early 20th century
and equipped with
modern facilities.*
▪ ▪ ▪ P ▪ ▪

**Plaza e de Russie
****
Piazza D'Azeglio, 1
Tel. 0584 44449
Fax 0584 44031
*This recently
renovated hotel,
built in 1871, was
the first in Viareggio.
Well-kept bedrooms
and public rooms
furnished with
period furniture.*
▪ ▪ C ▪ ▪ ▪

→ **RESTAURANTS**
✪ **Oca Bianca**
Via Coppino, 409
Tel. 0584 388477
Closed lunchtime in
July and in Aug.;
Tue. and Wed.
lunchtime during the
rest of the year.
*Very attractive,
elegant restaurant
with a superb view
over the port. A
selection of unusual
fish dishes. Good
value for money.*
▪ ▪ P ▪ ▪

# ◆ USEFUL ADDRESSES
## PRATO AND PISTORIA

HOTELS
- ▪ < 100,000 lire
- ▪▪ 100,000–200,000 lire
- ▪▪▪ 200,000–300,000 lire
- ▪▪▪▪ > 300,000 lire

GRAND HOTEL & LA PACE, MONTECATINI TERME

**✪ Romano**
Via Mazzini, 122
Closed Mon.,
part of Jan.
*An extremely
friendly restaurant
that offers a warm
welcome, good
service and wide
choice of desserts.
Excellent wine list.*
▫ ▥ ▨

**→ WINE OUTLETS**
**Magazzino
del Vino-Novi**
Via Zanardelli, 116
Tel. 0584 45581

**Taverna
dell'Assassino**
Viale Manin, 1
Tel. 0584 45011

### PRATO AND PISTOIA
#### ABETONE

◆ B D3
**→ HOTELS**
**Bellavista ★★★★**
Via Brennero, 383
Tel. 0573 60028
Fax 0573 60245
Closed mid Sep.–
Nov. and May–June
*This welcoming
hotel has well-
equipped rooms
and a view of the
mountains.*
▫ ▥ ▣ ▤ ▨ ▧ ▫

**Primula ★★**
Via Brennero, 195
Tel. 0573 60108
Fax 0573 60254
Closed mid Sep.–Nov.
*Very comfortable
rooms and informal
atmosphere; close to
all the main tourist
attractions.*
▫ ▣ ▤ ▨ ▫ ▫

**Regina ★★★**
Via Uccelliera, 9
Tel. 0573 60007
Fax 0573 60257
Closed mid
Apr.–June and mid
Sep.–Christmas.
*Welcoming, informal
hotel housed in a
late 19th-century
villa.*
▫ ▣ ▤ ▫ ▫

**→ RESTAURANTS**
**Capannina**
Via Brennero, 520
Tel. 0573 60562
Closed Mon.; part of
May and in Oct.
*Traditional,
unpretentious
cuisine in informal
surroundings.*
▫ ▨

**Pierone**
Via Brennero, 556
Tel. 0573 60068
Closed Thur.;
part of June
and in Oct.
*Simple, authentic
restaurant
specializing in the
preparation of
mushrooms and
truffles. Advance
booking is advisable.*
▫ ▨ ▨

#### COLLODI

◆ B D4
**→ RESTAURANT**
**Osteria del Gambero
Rosso**
Via San Gennaro, 1
Tel. 0572 429364
Closed Mon. eve.
and Tue.; part of
Nov. and in Jan.
*Spacious restaurant
within the Parco di
Pinocchio with
rooms suitable
for banquets and
special occasions.*
▫ ▥ ▣ ▨

#### MONTECATINI TERME

◆ B D4
**→ HOTELS**
**✪ Adua ★★★**
Viale Manzoni, 46
Tel. 0572 78134
Fax 0572 78138
Closed mid Nov.–mid
Mar. (open Jan. 1)
*Near the thermal
baths, this recently
renovated, family-
run hotel has a*
classical décor.
▫ ▥ ▣ ▤ ▫ ▨ ▧ ▫

**✪ Grand Hotel
& La Pace ★★★★★**
Via della Torretta,
1/a
Tel. 0572 9240
Fax 0572 78451
Closed Nov.–Mar.
*Comfortable Art
Nouveau hotel with
a wide range of
amenities and
facilities.*
▫ ▥ ▣ ▤ ▫ ▨ ▧ ▨ ▨

**Parma e Oriente ★★★**
Via Cavallotti, 135
Tel. 0572 78313
Closed Nov.–Mar.
*Art Nouveau hotel
with good facilities,
run by the same
family since the
1920s.*
▫ ▥ ▣ ▤ ▫ ▨ ▧ ▨ ▨

**Palo Alto ★★**
Via Bruceto, 10
Tel. 0572 78978
Closed Nov.–Mar.
*Small, friendly
hotel, run by the
owners. Recently
renovated.*
▫ ▥ ▫ ▫

**Tettuccio ★★★★**
Viale Verdi, 74
Tel. 0572 78051
Fax 0572 75711
*Refined, luxurious
hotel in an early-
20th-century
palazzo. Close to the
thermal baths.*
▫ ▥ ▣ ▤ ▧ ▨

**→ RESTAURANTS**
**Gourmet**
Via Amendola, 6
Tel. 0572 771012
Closed Tue.; part of
Aug. and in Jan.
*This restaurant
boasts Art Nouveau
décor, a central
location and
reasonably priced
menus.*
▫ ▥ ▨

**Il Cucco**
Via del Salsero, 3
Closed Tue.
*Clean, modern
restaurant,
open kitchen and
simple regional
dishes.*
▫ ▥ ▣ ▨

**→ WINE SHOP**
**Enoteca Giovanni**
Via Garibaldi, 25
Tel. 0572 71695
*Rustic wine shop
that also serves
traditional Tuscan
dishes.*

#### PESCIA

◆ B D4
**→ HOTELS**
**Dei Fiori ★★★**
Via VIII Settembre,
10
Tel. 0572 477871
Fax 0572 490021
*Simple building
providing a
good standard
of comfort.*
▫ ▥ ▫ ▫

**San Lorenzo ★★★**
At San Lorenzo
Tel. 0572 408340
Fax 0572 408333
*Renovated 19th-
century palazzo;
some residential
apartments
available.*
▫ ▣ ▤ ▫ ▫

**RESTAURANTS**
- ▪ < 50,000 lire
- ▪▪ 50,000–80,000 lire
- ▪▪▪ 90,000–120,000 lire
- ⊞ > 120,000 lire

## → RESTAURANTS

**Cecco**
Via Forti, 96/98
Tel. 0572 477955
Closed Mon.; part
of Jan. and in July
*This restaurant has
been in business for
100 years and the
excellent cuisine
reflects its illustrious
past.*
▪ ▥ ▪

**Fortuna – Da Piero
e Franca**
Via Colli per
Uzzano, 32/34
Closed Mon., Aug.
*This restaurant
serves fish dishes
in informal
surroundings under
the shade of the
olive trees.*
▪ ▥ P ▨ ▪

### PISTOIA

◆ B E3-4
## → HOTELS

**Leon Bianco ***
Via Panciatichi, 2
Tel. 0573 26676
Fax 0573 26704
*A traditional bed
and breakfast hotel
in the pedestrian
precinct of the
historical center.*
▪ ▣ ▤ ▪

**Patria ***
Via Crispi, 6/8
Tel. 0573 25187
Fax 0573 368168
*An authentic
family-run hotel
housed in a
refurbished 17th-
century palazzo in
the historical center.*
▪ ▣ ▤ ▪

## → RESTAURANTS

✪ **Castagno di Pier
Angelo**
Via del Castagno, 46
at Castagno di
Piteccio (7 miles)
Tel. 0573 42214
Closed Mon., part of
Jan. and Oct.–Nov.
*Restaurant on the
wooded slopes of
the Apennines
serving regional
cuisine, particularly
fish, and innovative
dishes. Sensational
desserts.*
▪ ⊞ ▣ ▪

**Manzoni**
Corso Gramsci, 112
Closed Sat.
lunchtime, Sun.
and in Aug.
*Right in the center,
opposite the theater
of the same name,
offering excellent
fish dishes in an
elegant setting.*
▪ ▥ ▣ ▪

**San Jacopo**
Via Crispi, 25
Closed Mon. and
Tue. lunchtime;
part of Aug.
*Informal restaurant
in a refurbished
period house serving
traditional Tuscan
cuisine. You can
order à la carte or
choose one of the
set menus.*
▪ ▥ ▪

## → CAFÉ

**Caffè Pasticceria
Valiani**
Via Cavour, 55
Tel. 0573 23034
*Torte della Bisnonna,
Cassata Valiani.*

### PRATO

◆ B E4
## → HOTELS

**Flora ***
Via Cairoli, 31
Tel. 0574 33521
Fax 0574 40289
*An elegant hotel
that offers good*

*facilities and a
pleasantly informal
atmosphere; the
'Salomè' restaurant
serves a vegetarian
menu at the bar or
on the terrace.*
▪ ▥ P ▣ ▪

**Giardino ***
Via Magnolfi, 4
Tel. 0574 606588
*In a 14th-century
palazzo overlooking
the Piazza del
Duomo, this air-
conditioned, sound-
proofed hotel
guarantees a
restful stay.*
▪ ▥ P ▣ ▣ ▣ ▪

## → RESTAURANTS

**Baghino**
Via Accademia, 9
Tel. 0574 427920
Closed Sun. and
Mon. lunchtime;
part of Aug.
*Period rooms
attractively
decorated in rustic
style. Meals are
served in the garden
in summer.*
▪ ▣ ▪

**Osvaldo Baroncelli**
Via Fra Bartolomeo,
13
Tel. 0574 23810
Closed Sat.
lunchtime and Sun.;
part of Aug.
*Quiet, modern,*

*elegant setting; the
kitchen serves
traditional dishes.*
▪ ▥ ▪

**Piraña**
Via Valentini, 110
Tel. 0547 425746
Closed Sat.
lunchtime, Sun.
and Aug.
*Near the Firenze-
Mare highway: two
elegant, comfortable
dining rooms.
Wonderful for fish
and seafood.*
▪ ▥ ▣ ▪

## → CAFÉS

**Pasticceria Caffè
Nuovo Mondo**
Via Garibaldi, 23
Tel. 0574 27765
*Raspberry pastries,
pasticceria mignon,
warm cremini.*

**Pasticceria Luca
Mannoni**
Via Lazzerini, 2
Tel. 0574 216228
*Torte Sette Veli,
Abbraccio di Venere,
Orient Express.*

## → TYPICAL PRODUCE

**Biscottificio Antonio
Mattei**
Via Ricasoli, 20/22
Tel. 0574 25756
*Since 1858, typical
Pratese biscotti: a
variation on cantucci
made with bread
and aniseed.*

## → FABRICS

**Profilo**
Via Marradi, 43
Tel. and fax
0574 692297

**Remo Ferrario&Figli**
Via Galcianese,
39/a
Tel. 0574 27312
Fax 0574 27298

**Startex**
Via Fonda di
Mezzana, 21
Tel. 0574 505796
Fax 0574 582254
startexl@lanificio
startex.it

**Tegitex**
Via Matteo degli
Organi, 40
Tel. 0574 663473

CAFFÉ PASTICCERIA VALIANI, PISTOIA

BAGHINO, PRATO

# ◆ USEFUL ADDRESSES
## AREZZO AND ITS SURROUNDINGS

HOTELS
- < 100,000 lire
- 100,000–200,000 lire
- 200,000–300,000 lire
- > 300,000 lire

### AREZZO AND ITS SURROUNDINGS
#### AREZZO

◆ C D4
→ HOTELS
**Continentale ***
Piazza Guido Monaco, 7
Tel. 0575 20251
Fax 0575 350485
*Comfortable, modern hotel in the heart of Arezzo. Small and medium-sized conference facilities.*

**Etrusco Palace Hotel ****
Via Fleming, 39
Tel. 0575 984067
Fax 0575 382131
*Six-story parallelepiped, with comfortable, well-equipped rooms.*

**Europa ***
Via Spinello, 43
Tel. 0575 357701
Fax 0575 357703
*Traditional bed and breakfast hotel offering a good standard of comfort in a central location.*

→ RESTAURANTS
**Antica Trattoria al Principe**
Piazza Giovi, 25
at Giovi (5 miles)
Closed Mon.; Aug. and part of Jan.
*Traditional Casentino dishes in typical Aretine surroundings with coffered ceilings and period furniture.*

**Buca di San Francesco**
Via San Francesco, 1
Tel. 0575 23271
Closed Mon. eve. and Tue.; part of July
*Wood paneled, frescoed walls and floors paved with Etrusco-Roman slabs. Authentic, simple and tasty fare.*

**Le Tastevin**
Via de' Cenci, 9
Tel. 0575 28304
Closed Sun.; part of Aug.
*Three dining rooms with a piano bar in the center. Wide selection of wines.*

→ TYPICAL PRODUCE
**Bottega dell'Alveare**
Via N. Aretino, 19
Tel. 0575 20769
*All types of honey, bee-glue, royal jelly.*

**La Macelleria Gastronomia Aligi Barelli**
Via della Chimera, 22
Tel. 0575 357754
*Chianina beef, salami and cured pork products from the Casentino and Chianti, lardo and cheeses.*

→ OIL PRODUCERS
**Fattoria San Fabiano**
Via San Fabiano
Tel. 0575 370368
*Laudemio label.*

#### BIBBIENA
◆ C D3
→ HOTEL
**Borgo Antico ***
Via Dovizi, 18
Tel. 0575 536445
Fax 0575 536447
Closed part of Nov.
*A small hotel in the historical center with a restaurant offering authentic homemade food.*

#### CAMALDOLI
◆ C D2
→ HOTEL
**Il Rustichello ***
Via Corniolo, 14
Tel. 0575 556020
Fax 0575 556046
*This peaceful hotel is situated deep in the Camaldolese forest; high standard of comfort.*

→ RESTAURANT
**Cedro**
Via di Camaldoli, 20
at Moggiona (3 miles)
Tel. 0575 556080
Closed Mon. except in summer.
*Situated in a beautiful hamlet, specializing in game dishes.*

#### CASTELFRANCO DI SOPRA
◆ C C3
→ RESTAURANTS
**Vicolo del Contento**
at Mandri (½ mile)
Tel. 055 914 9277
Fax 055 914 9906
Closed lunchtime (except Sun.), Mon., Tue. and in Aug.
*Innovative dishes firmly rooted in traditional regional cuisine. Exciting wine cellar.*

#### CASTIGLION FIORENTINO
◆ C D4
→ HOTELS
**Park ***
Via Umbro-Casentinese, 88
Tel. 0575 680288
Fax 0575 680008
*Welcoming family-run hotel that has been recently refurbished.*

**Relais San Pietro in Polvano ***
at Polvano
Tel. 0575 650100
Fax 0575 650255
Closed mid Nov.–mid Feb.
*Housed in an ancient country house in the woods, this hotel is renowned for its peaceful atmosphere and warm hospitality.*

→ RESTAURANT
**Da Muzzicone**
Piazza San Francesco, 8
Tel. 0575 680346
Closed Tue.
*Strictly local cuisine; this restaurant also caters for banquets and special occasions.*

#### CORTONA
◆ C D4-5
→ HOTELS
**Oasi Neumann ***
Via Contesse, 1
Tel. 0575 630354
Fax 0575 630354
Closed Nov.–Mar.
*A peaceful old house in extensive grounds with panoramic views. Ideal for banquets.*

**Portole ***
Via Umbro Cortonese, 39
at Portole
Tel. 0575 691008
Fax 0575 691035
Closed mid Nov.–Mar.
*Typical Tuscan villa in lush countryside, with a large restaurant serving traditional dishes.*

**San Michele ****
Via Guelfa, 15
Tel. 0575 604348
Fax 0575 630147
Closed mid Jan.–Feb.
*Welcoming, characterful hotel housed in a Renaissance palazzo.*

→ RESTAURANTS
**Il Cacciatore**
Via Roma, 11/13
Tel. 0575 63 0552
Closed Wed., Epiphany–mid Feb.
*Two dining rooms in*

RELAIS SAN PIETRO IN POLVANO, CASTIGLION F.

302

**RESTAURANTS**
- 🔲 < 50,000 lire
- 🔲 50,000–80,000 lire
- 🔲 90,000–120,000 lire
- 🔲 > 120,000 lire

18th-century surroundings: serves regional cuisine.
🔲 🔲 🔲

FIORENTINO, SANSEPOLCRO

**☼ Il Falconiere**
at San Martino a Bocena (2 miles)
Tel. 0575 612679
Fax 0575 612927
Closed Mon.
Seafood and meat dishes, with a sizable wine list, set in a lemon-house.
🔲 P 🔲 🔲 🔲

**Osteria del Teatro**
Via Maffei, 5
Tel. 0575 630556
Closed Wed. in winter.
Efficient family-run restaurant serving traditional cuisine in rustic surroundings.
🔲 🔲 🔲

---

**LORO CIUFFENNA**
◆ C C3
→ **OIL PRODUCERS**
**Azienda Agricola Rossi Bandino**
at Levane
Via Sette Ponti
Tel. 055 977635
Fax 055 977538

---

**POPPI**
◆ C C3
→ **HOTEL**
**☼ Campaldino ★★**
Via Roma, 93
at Ponte a Poppi (½ mile)
Tel. 0575 529008
Fax 0575 529032
Limited number of well-kept, excellently furnished rooms. Warm, welcoming surroundings, lavishly decorated.
🔲 🔲 🔲 🔲

**Parc Hotel ★★★**
Via Roma, 214
at Ponte a Poppi (½ mile)
Tel. 0575 529994
Fax 0575 529984
Family-run hotel with functional, welcoming rooms.
🔲 🔲 P 🔲 🔲 🔲 🔲 🔲

→ **RESTAURANT**
**La Loggia**
at Lierna (3 miles)
Tel. 0575 520365

---

Closed Mon. and Tue. in winter; part of Jan.
Rustic-style restaurant serving a wide variety of seasonal products.
🔲 🔲 P 🔲 🔲 🔲

---

**REGGELLO**
◆ C C3
→ **HOTEL**
**☼ Villa Rigacci ★★★★**
Via Manzoni, 76
at Vaggio (3 miles)
Tel. 055 865 6718
Fax 055 865 6537
This hotel, in an old country house, has rooms furnished with Provençal and Tuscan period furniture. 'Le Vieux Pressoir' restaurant.
🔲 🔲 🔲 P 🔲 🔲 🔲 🔲
🔲

---

**SANSEPOLCRO**
◆ C E3
→ **HOTELS**
**Borgo Palace ★★★★**
Via Senese Aretina, 80
Tel. 0575 736050
Fax 0575 740341
Business hotel on the outskirts of town; good amenities.
🔲 🔲 🔲 🔲 🔲 🔲 🔲

**Fiorentino ★★★**
Via Pacioli, 60
Tel. 0575 740350

---

Fax 0575 740370
This welcoming hotel in the historical center radiates a delightful old-world atmosphere.
🔲 P 🔲 🔲 🔲

→ **RESTAURANTS**
**☼ Oroscopo di Paola e Marco**
Via Togliatti, 66/68
at Pieve Vecchia (½ mile)
Tel. 0575 734875
Closed lunchtime, Sun., Jan. 1– Epiphany, mid June–mid July
This hotel, in a refurbished 19th-century manor house, is furnished in 'English style' and offers an innovative style of cuisine by gourmet chefs.
🔲 🔲

**Ventura**
Via Aggiunti, 30
Tel. 0575 742560
Closed Sat.; part of Jan. and in Aug.
Three rustic-style dining rooms with exposed beams in the historical center. Experienced management.
🔲 🔲

---

**CHIANTI**
**BADIA A COLTIBUONO**
◆ C B-C4
→ **RESTAURANT**
**Badia a Coltibuono**
Tel. 0577 749424
Closed Mon. (except May–Oct.), Feb.–Mar.
Spacious rooms for receptions and banquets; garden in the summer.
🔲 🔲 🔲 P 🔲 🔲 🔲

→ **WINE OUTLET**
**Tenuta di Coltibuono**
Tel. 0577 74 9498

---

**CASTELLINA IN CHIANTI**
◆ C B4
→ **OIL PRODUCERS**
**Rocca delle Macie**
at Rocca delle Macie
Tel. 0577 743220
Fax 0577 743150
Rocca delle Macie label.

---

**CASTELNUOVO BERARDENGA**
◆ C C4
→ **HOTELS**
**Posta del Chianti ★★★**
at Colonna del Grillo (3 miles)
Tel. 0577 353000
Fax 0577 353050
A family-run hotel set in an old mill in the midst of the Sienese countryside.
🔲 🔲 P 🔲 🔲 🔲 🔲 🔲

**☼ Relais Borgo San Felice ★★★★**
at San Felice (6 miles)
Tel. 0577 359260
Fax 0577 359089
Closed Nov.–Mar.
A superb hotel (with the equally excellent 'Poggio Rosso' restaurant) situated in a restored medieval hamlet. It also has twelve suites.
🔲 🔲 🔲 P 🔲 🔲 🔲
🔲 🔲

**☼ Villa Arceno ★★★★**
in San Gusmè (3 miles), at Arceno
Tel. 0577 359292
Fax 0577 359276
Closed Dec.–mid Mar.
Amidst the Chianti hills, a 16th-century villa that is now an

# ◆ USEFUL ADDRESSES
## SIENA

**HOTELS**
- ▪ < 100,000 lire
- ▪ 100,000–200,000 lire
- ▪ 200,000–300,000 lire
- ▪ > 300,000 lire

*elegant, refined hotel.*

▪▥▦▪▣▪▪▪▩
▪▦

→ **RESTAURANT**
**Da Antonio**
Via Fiorita, 38
Tel. 0577 355321
Closed Mon.
*Extremely fresh fish dishes. Excellent wine list.*
▪▪

→ **WINE SHOPS**
**Dievole**
at Dievole
Tel. 0577 322613
*17th-century villa surrounded by an estate of about 1000 acres. For fans of the great Chianti Classico reserves.*

**Enoteca Bengodi**
Via Società Operaia, 11
Tel. 0577 355116

**Fattoria dell'Aiola**
at Vagliagli
Tel. 0577 322615

### GAIOLE IN CHIANTI
◆ C B-C4
→ **HOTELS**
**Castello di Spaltenna ★★★★**
at Pieve di Spaltenna
Tel. 0577 749483
Fax 0577 749269
Closed mid Nov.–mid Mar.
*An ancient fortified monastery, now a simple, elegant hotel.*
▪▥▦▪▣▪▪▪▩
▪▦▦

**L'Ultimo Mulino ★★★★**
at La Ripresa dei Vistarenni
Tel. 0577 738520
Fax 0577 738659
Closed Epiphany–Feb.
*This hotel is housed in a completely refurbished mill in a country setting.*
▪▥▦▪▣▪▪▪▩
▪▦

→ **WINE OUTLETS**
**Barone Ricasoli**
at Brolio
Tel. 0577 7301

**Capannelle**
at Capannelle
Tel. 0577 749691

### GREVE IN CHIANTI
◆ C B3
→ **HOTEL**
✿ **Villa le Barone ★★★**
Via San Leolino, 19
at Panzano (3 miles)
Tel. 055 852621
Fax 055 852277
Closed Nov.–Mar.
*This former patrician villa with all the mod cons is a haven of peace among the olive groves. Comfortable rooms.*
▪▪▩▪▣▪▪▩▪
▪▪

### RADDA IN CHIANTI
◆ C B4
→ **HOTELS**
✿ **Relais Fattoria Vignale ★★★★**
Via Pianigiani, 8

PODERE CAPACCIA, RADDA IN CHIANTI

Tel. 0577 738300
Fax 0577 738592
Closed Epiphany–mid Mar.
*Lavishly frescoed, welcoming rooms with 19th-century fireplaces and furnishings.*
▪▥▦▪▣▪▪▩▪
▦

**Vescine ★★★**
at Vescine (4 miles)
Tel. 0577 741144
Fax 0577 740263
Closed mid Nov.–mid Mar.
*This renovated medieval hamlet exudes an air of refinement.*
▪▪▩▪▣▪▩▪▪

→ **RESTAURANTS**
**Vignale**
Via XX Settembre, 23
Tel. 0577 738094
Closed Thur.,

Epiphany–mid Mar.
*Ancient renovated oil mill. Regional cuisine with a modern twist.*
▪▥▦▪

→ **WINE SHOP**
**Enoteca Dante Alighieri**
Piazza Dante Alighieri, 1
Tel. 0577 738059
Fax 0577 738732
*In the city center, with a spacious terrace overlooking the piazza.*
▪▪

→ **WINE OUTLETS**
**Castello d'Albola**
Via Pian d'Albola, 31
Tel. 0577 738019

**Colle Bereto**
at Collebereto
Tel. 0577 738083

**Fattoria Castello di Volpaia**
at Volpaia
Tel. 0577 738066
*Farm vacation center; sells Chianti Classico as well as locally produced oil and vinegar.*

**Le Bonatte**
at Le Bonatte
Tel. 0575 738783

**Piccolo Museo del Chianti**
Fattoria di Montevertine
Tel. 0577 738009
*Offers authentic red table wines.*

**Podere Capaccia**
at Capaccia
Tel. 0577 738385
capaccia@chiantinet.it

**Podere Terreno**
Via della Volpaia, 21

Tel. 0577 738312
podereterreno@chiantinet.it

**Poggerino**
at Poggerino
Tel. 0577 738232

### SIENA
◆ C B4
→ **HOTELS**
✿ **Antica Torre ★★★**
Via Fieravecchia, 7
Tel. and fax
0577 222255
*Eight comfortable, picturesque rooms housed in a 16th-century restored tower.*
▪▪▣▪▪▩▪

✿ **Certosa di Maggiano ★★★★**
Via Certosa, 82
Tel. 0577 288180
Fax 0577 288189
*One of the most remarkable establishments in Italy. Housed in one of the oldest Carthusian monasteries (14th century) in Tuscany, this hotel combines beauty and elegance with modern facilities.*
▪▥▦▪▣▪▣▪▩▪▪
▪▦

**Piccolo Hotel il Palio ★★**
Piazza del Sale, 19
Tel. 0577 281131
Fax 0577 281142
*The brick vaults betray the 15th-century origins of this comfortable hotel. A little way from the center but easily accessible by car.*
▪▥▦▪▣▪▪▪▩▪

**Piccolo Hotel Oliveta ★★★**
Via Enea Silvio Piccolomini, 35
Tel. 0577 283930
Fax 0577 270009
Closed Epiphany–Feb.
*Just outside the Porta Romana, this 19th-century stone cottage has been renovated preserving its*

**RESTAURANTS**
🔲 < 50,000 lire
🔲 50,000–80,000 lire
🔲 90,000–120,000 lire
🔳 > 120,000 lire

*original architecture and atmosphere. The hotel has two separate buildings: attractively furnished public rooms in one and well-kept bedrooms in the other. Breakfast is served in the large garden.*
🔲🔲🔲🔲🔲🔲🔲

**Santa Caterina ★★★**
Via Enea Silvio Piccolomini, 7
Tel. 0577 221105
Fax 0577 271087
*Renovated building from the second half of the 18th century. Breakfast is served on the porch.*
🔲🔲🔲🔲🔲

✪ **Villa Scacciapensieri ★★★★**
Via di Scacciapensieri, 10
Tel. 0577 41441
Fax 0577 270854
Closed Epiphany–mid Mar.
*Elegant country hotel in a 19th-century palazzo with a lovely view, especially at sunset. Spacious rooms and excellent facilities. It also has several suites.*
🔲🔲🔲🔲🔲🔲🔲🔲
🔲

→ **RESTAURANTS**
**Antica Trattoria Botteganova**
Via Chiantigiana, 29
Tel. 0577 284230
Closed Monday; part of Jan. and in Aug.
*Traditional dishes in modern guise. Reasonably priced lunch menus.*
🔲🔲🔲🔲

**Antica Osteria da Divo**
Via Franciosa, 25
Tel. 0577 286054
*Unusual picturesque restaurant; Etruscan surroundings with an ancient well.*
🔲🔲🔲

**Enzo**
Via Camollia, 49
Tel. 0577 281277

Closed Mon.; part of July
*Traditional family-run restaurant in a period palazzo; meat and fish menus with a good selection of wines.*
🔲🔲

**Olivo**
Via di Marciano, 18
Tel. 0577 44803
Fax 0577 49020
*Elegant decor with an old-world feel; regional cuisine with Mediterranean influences.*
🔲🔲🔲🔲🔲🔲
🔲🔲

→ **TYPICAL PRODUCE**
**Enoteca Italiana**
Fortezza Medicea
Tel. 0577 288497
Fax 0577 270717
www.enotecaitaliana.it
*Leading national organization for the promotion of quality wines. This wine shop represents 400 wine-producing estates as well as various varieties of extra virgin olive oil.*

**Il Magnifico**
Via dei Pellegrini
*Long-established food store with ancient adjoining bakery*

**Palazzo della Chigiana**
Via di Città
*Renowned showcase of salami, cured pork products and cheese.*

**AROUND SIENA**
**CASOLE D'ELSA**
◆ **C** A4
→ **HOTEL**
✪ **Relais la Suvera ★★★★**

Via della Suvera at Pievescola (8 miles)
Closed Nov.–Mar.
*This elegant hotel is opulently decorated: it is housed in the villa of Pope Julius II, one of the protagonists of the Italian Renaissance.*
🔲🔲🔲🔲🔲🔲🔲🔲
🔲🔲

**CHIANCIANO TERME**
◆ **C** D5-6
→ **HOTELS**
**Ambasciatori ★★★★**
Viale della Libertà, 512
Tel. 0578 64371
Fax 0578 64371
*This renovated hotel near the thermal baths is comfortable and offers good amenities.*
🔲🔲🔲🔲🔲🔲🔲
🔲

**Chianciano ★★★**
Via Buozzi, 51
Tel. 0578 63649
Fax 0578 64121
Closed Nov.–Mar.
*Functional and comfortable family-run establishment right in the center.*
🔲🔲🔲🔲🔲🔲

✪ **Grand Hotel Terme ★★★★**
Piazza Italia, 8
Tel. 0578 63254
Fax 0578 62014
Closed part of Jan.
*Hotel in the city center. It has several suites and various health and fitness facilities. 'Bellevue' restaurant.*
🔲🔲🔲🔲🔲🔲🔲🔲
🔲

**Sole ★★★**
Via delle Rose, 40
Tel. 0578 60194
Fax 0578 60196
Closed Nov.–Mar.
*Peaceful, sunny modern complex that has been recently refurbished.*
🔲🔲🔲🔲🔲🔲🔲

→ **RESTAURANT**
**Lory**
Tel. 0578 63704
Fax 0578 61100
*Popular and reliable family-run restaurant; Tuscan cuisine.*
🔲🔲

**CHIUSI**
◆ **C** D6
→ **HOTELS**
✪ **Il Patriarca ★★★**
at Querce al Pino (2½ miles)
Tel. 0578 274407
Fax 0578 274594
*Housed in an old villa set in superb grounds, this hotel offers good hospitality.*
🔲🔲🔲🔲🔲🔲🔲

**La Sfinge ★★**
Via Marconi, 2
Tel. 0578 20157
Fax 0578 222153
Closed mid Jan.–Feb.
*Simple, pleasant hotel located in the historical center.*
🔲🔲🔲🔲🔲

→ **RESTAURANTS**
**Osteria La Solita Zuppa**
Via Porsenna, 21
Tel. 0578 821006
Closed Tue., mid Jan.–Feb.
*Intimate, welcoming restaurant with brick vaults; traditional and seasonal cuisine.*
🔲🔲

**Zaira**
Via Arunte, 12
Tel. 0578 20260
Closed Mon.; part of Nov.
*In a medieval palazzo, this restaurant serves regional cuisine and boasts a very well-stocked wine cellar.*
🔲🔲

VILLA SCACCIAPENSIERI, SIENA

# ◆ USEFUL ADDRESSES
## SIENA

HOTELS

- ⊡ < 100,000 lire
- ⊡ 100,000–200,000 lire
- ⊞ 200,000–300,000 lire
- ⊞ > 300,000 lire

---

**COLLE DI VAL D'ELSA**

◆ C A-B4

→ **HOTEL**

**La Vecchia Cartiera ★★★**
Via Oberdan, 5/9
Tel. 0577 921107
Fax 0577 923688
*Efficient, modern hotel-restaurant housed in a 13th-century structure.*
⊡ �III P ⊡ ⊡ ⊡ ⊡

→ **RESTAURANTS**

✪ **Arnolfo**
Via XX Settembre, 50/52a
Tel. 0577 920549
Closed Tue.;
part of Jan.–Feb.
*Cozy restaurant serving elegant and rarefied cuisine. Superb wine cellar, excellent desserts.*
⊡ III ⊡ ⊡ ⊡

**L'Antica Trattoria**
Piazza Arnolfo, 23
Tel. 0577 923747
Closed Tue. and Christmas–Epiphany.
*Family-run restaurant offering first-class menus.*
⊡ ⊡ ⊡

---

**MONTALCINO**

◆ C B-C5

→ **HOTELS**

**Al Brunello di Montalcino ★★★**
at Bellaria
Tel. 0577 849304
Fax 0577 849430
*This recently built hotel is comfortable and has good facilities.*
⊡ III P ⊡ ⊡ ⊡ ⊡ ⊡

**Bellaria ★★★**
Via Osticcio, 19
Tel. 0577 848668
Fax 0577 849326
*New building designed to resemble a Tuscan cottage: Arte Povera décor and welcoming atmosphere.*
⊡ III P ⊡ ⊡ ⊡ ⊡ ⊡

**Dei Capitani ★★★**
Via Lapini, 6
Tel. 0577 847227
Fax 0577 847239
Closed mid Jan.–Feb.
*Simple, peaceful*

*hotel right in the historical center.*
⊡ III P ⊡ ⊡ ⊡ ⊡
⊡ ⊡

→ **RESTAURANTS**

**Pieve di San Gismondo**
at Poggio alle Mura (11 miles)
Podere La Pieve, 19
Tel. 0577 816026
Closed Tue.; part of Jan.–Feb.
*This recently*

AZIENDA AGRICOLA BARBI E CASATO, MONTALCINO

LA VECCHIA CARTIERA, COLLE DI VAL D'ELSA

*refurbished restaurant serves mouthwatering Tuscan specialties in a rural setting.*
⊡ III P ⊡ ⊡

✪ **Poggio Antico**
in Poggio Antico (2½ miles)
Tel. 0577 849200
Closed Sun. eve. and Mon.
*Elegant restaurant in the lush countryside, serving sophisticated, ambitious and imaginative cuisine.*
⊡ P ⊡ ⊡ ⊡

→ **FARM VACATION CENTER**

**Azienda Agricola Barbi e Casato**
at Pordenovi
Tel. 0577 841111
Fax 0577 849356

*A farm vacation center offering tastings of local products; craft courses.*

→ **WINE SHOPS**

**Bacchus**
Via Matteotti, 15
Tel. 0577 847054

**Dalmazio**
Via Traversa dei Monti, 214
Tel. 0577 849019

**Franci**
Piazzale Fortezza, 6
Tel. 0577 848191

**La Casa del Vino**
Piazza del Popolo, 16
Tel. 0577 849113

**La Fortezza**
Piazzale Fortezza
Tel. 0577 849211

→ **OIL PRODUCERS**

**Tenuta Col d'Orcia**
at Sant'Angelo in Colle
Tel. 0577 814232
Fax 0577 864018
*Col d'Orcia label.*

→ **WINE OUTLETS**

**Castello Poggio alle Mura Banfi**
at Casenove, 222
in Sant'Angelo in Colle
Tel. 0577 840111
*This outlet has a fine*

*wine cellar and a small museum of glass and bottles, but its main attraction remains its Brunello label.*

---

**MONTEPULCIANO**

◆ C D5

→ **HOTELS**

**Gran Ducato ★★★**
Via delle Lettere, 62
Tel. 0578 758610
Fax 0578 758597
*Next to the historical center, furnished in modern style and run by the owners.*
⊡ ⊡ ⊡ C ⊡ ⊡ ⊡

✪ **Il Marzocco ★★★**
Piazza Savonarola, 18
Tel. 0578 757262
Fax 0578 757530
Closed part of Nov.–Dec.
*A 16th-century palazzo in the city center. Understated décor, beautiful terraces with panoramic views.*
⊡ P ⊡ C ⊡

→ **RESTAURANTS**

**La Grotta**
at San Biagio
Tel. 0578 757607
Closed Wed. and Epiphany–end Feb.
*This restaurant is located in the home of the famous architect Antonio da Sangallo; good wine list.*
⊡ ⊡ ⊡

→ **WINE SHOPS**

**Enoteca Piccoli Produttori Vino Nobile**
Piazza Pasquino da Montepulciano
Tel. 0578 788444

**Fattoria della Talosa**
Via Talosa, 8
Tel. 0578 758277

**Fattoria di Palazzo Vecchio**
Via Terrarossa
Tel. 0578 724170

**Oinochoe Enoteca Antichità**
Via Voltaia nel Corso, 82
Tel. 0578 757524

**RESTAURANTS**
◾ < 50,000 lire
◾ 50,000–80,000 lire
◾ 90,000–120,000 lire
▦ > 120,000 lire

**Redi**
Via di Collazzi, 5
Tel. 0578 757166
*In a Renaissance palazzo: sells Nobile, Rosso di Montepulciano, Valdichiana, Vin Santo.*
◾ ▥ P ⌂ ⚏ ▣ ⚌ ⚒ &
🖥 ▦

**Tenuta Sant'Agnese**
Viale Calamandrei, 27
Tel. 0578 757266

◆ C B-C5
→ OIL PRODUCER
**Agricola Campriano**
at Campriano
Tel. 0577 814232
Fax 0577 281937
*Campriano label.*

PIENZA
◆ C C5
→ HOTEL
**Relais Il Chiostro di Pienza ***
Corso Rosellino, 26
Tel. 0578 748400
Fax 0578 748440
Closed Jan.–mid Mar.
*Comfortable, functional rooms in a former 15th-century cloister that has now been refurbished.*
◾ P ⌂ ⚏ ▣ ⚌ ⚒ &
▦

→ RESTAURANT
**Buca delle Fate**
Corso Rosellino, 38/A
Tel. 0578 748272
Closed Mon.; part of Jan. and in June
*This restaurant, housed in the Palazzo dei Gonzaga, serves authentic traditional cuisine with a good selection of wines.*
◾ ◾

POGGIBONSI
◆ C B4
→ HOTEL
**Villa San Lucchese ****
at San Lucchese (½ mile)
Tel. 0577 934231
Fax 0577 934729
Closed mid Jan.–mid Feb.
*Residence set in a panoramic location with modern*

*facilities and good standard of comfort.*
◾ ▥ P ⌂ ⚏ ▣ ⚌ ⚒ &
🖥 ▦

→ RESTAURANTS
**Galleria**
Galleria Vittorio Veneto, 20
Tel. 0577 982356
Closed Sun.
*Authentic traditional cuisine, with the emphasis on fish dishes, in modern, comfortable*

*Castello Poggio alle Mura Banfi, Montalcino*

*Poggio Antico, Montalcino*

*surroundings. Meals served outside in summer.*
◾ ▥ ⚒

**Sole**
Via Trento, 5
Tel. 0577 936283
Closed Mon.; part of Aug.
*Perhaps the oldest restaurant in the city, serving traditional Tuscan cuisine with a certain amount of creative innovation.*
◾ ◾

SAN GIMIGNANO
◆ C A4
→ HOTELS
**Bel Soggiorno ***
Via San Giovanni, 91
Tel. 0577 940375
Fax 0577 943149
Closed mid Jan.–mid Feb.
*14th-century house*

*with mod cons and reproduction furnishings.*
◾ ▥ P ⚌ ▣ ⚒ ⚏

**Da Graziano ***
Via Matteotti, 39/a
Tel. 0577 940101
Fax 0577 940655
Closed Epiphany–Feb.
*Simple, basic hotel; evening meals are served on the terrace by candlelight.*
◾ ⬆ 🖥 ▣

**La Cisterna ***
Piazza della Cisterna, 24
Tel. 0577 940328
Fax 0577 942080
Closed Epiphany–mid Mar.
*Former 14th-century palazzo furnished in Florentine style; period atmosphere and modern facilities.*
◾ ▥ P ⌂ ⚏ ⚌ ▣ & 🖥
▣

◙ **La Collegiata ****
on Strada 27
Tel. 0577 943201
Fax 0577 940566
Closed Jan.–beg. Feb.
*16th-century villa with views over the superb surrounding countryside. Excellent restaurant.*
◾ ▥ ⌂ P ⚏ ⚌ ▣ ⚒
▦

◙ **Villa San Paolo ****
Strada per Certaldo (2½ miles)
Tel. 0577 955100
Fax 0577 955113
Closed Epiphany–mid Feb.
*19th-century villa standing in a centuries-old park, just north of the city.*
◾ ▥ ⌂ P ⚏ ⚌ ⚒ &
🖥 ▣

→ RESTAURANTS
**Dorandò**
Vicolo dell'Oro, 2
Tel. 0577 941862
Closed Mon. (off season) and mid Jan.–Feb.
*Intimate, welcoming restaurant, serving historical recipes.*
◾ ▥ ▣ ⚏

**La Griglia**
Via San Matteo, 34/36
Tel. 0577 940005
Closed Thur. and mid Dec.–Feb.
*This restaurant derives its name from its open grill; terrace with pergola and panoramic views.*
◾ ▥ ⚒ ▣ ⚏

→ WINE SHOPS
**Enoteca Bruni**
Via Quercecchio, 61
Tel. 0577 940442

**Enoteca Casa del Caffè**
Via San Matteo, 2
Tel. 0577 940371

**Enoteca Gustavo**
Via San Matteo, 29
Tel. 0577 940057

**Enoteca La Botte e il Frantoio**
Via San Giovanni, 56
Tel. 0577 940353

**Guicciardini Strozzi**
at Cusona
Tel. 0577 950028
*Sells the famous Vernaccia and San Gimignano Rosso.*

# ◆ USEFUL ADDRESSES FROM VOLTERRA TO LIVORNO

**HOTELS**
< 100,000 lire
100,000–200,000 lire
200,000–300,000 lire
> 300,000 lire

**SAN QUIRICO D'ORCIA**
◆ **C** C5-6
→ **HOTEL**
**Le Terme** ***
Tel. 0577 887150
Fax 0577 887497
Closed part of Nov. and Dec.
*The Pope's former summer house has been converted into a welcoming hotel. There is a large heated pool at the entrance.*

**FROM VOLTERRA TO LIVORNO**

**CAMPIGLIA MARITTIMA**
◆ **D** C3
→ **RESTAURANTS**
**Dal Cappellaio Pazzo**
Via di San Vincenzo
Tel. 0565 838358
Closed Tues (off season) and for part of Jan. and Feb.
*In a 19th-century house, this restaurant has two dining rooms, their walls attractively decorated with a profusion of hats. Meals served under a pergola in summer.*

**Enoteca Pizzica**
Via della Vittoria, 2
Tel. 0565 838383
Closed Mon.; part of Oct.
*Rustic family-run restaurant with a good selection of wines; lovely terrace with panoramic views.*

**CAPRAIA**
◆ **D** A3
→ **HOTEL**
**Il Saracino** ****
Via Cibo, 40
Tel. 0586 905018
Fax 0586 905062
*Elegant, comfortable hotel in the ancient village with a sea view.*

**CASTAGNETO CARDUCCI**
◆ **D** C2-3
→ **HOTELS**
✪ **I Ginepri** ***
Viale Italia, 13
in Marina di Castagneto (5 miles)
Tel. 0565 744027
Fax 0565 744344
Closed Nov.–Feb.
*Near the sea, with good amenities in the rooms.*

✪ **Nuovo Hotel Bambolo** ***
at Il Bambolo, 31
in Marina di Castagneto (5 miles)
Tel. 0565 775206
Fax 0565 775346
Closed part of Feb.
*Housed in a refurbished grocery store, this hotel offers excellent rooms and a swimming pool in the garden.*

PARK HOTEL NAPOLEONE, PORTOFERRAIO

→ **RESTAURANTS**
**Da Ugo**
Via Pari, 3/a
Tel. 0565 763746
Closed Monday (except July and Aug.); part of Nov.
*For almost thirty years this restaurant has been serving tasty meat and fish dishes.*

**Il Bambolo**
at Il Bambolo, 31
in Marina di Castagneto (5 miles)
Tel. 0565 775055
Closed Mon. (off season) and mid Dec.–mid Jan.
*Furnished with rustic furniture, this typical family-run Tuscan restaurant is renowned for its warm welcome. Interesting fish dishes.*

**ISOLA D'ELBA**
◆ **D** A-B4
→ **HOTELS**
✪ **Antares** ***
at Capoliveri
Tel. 0565 940131
Fax 0565 940084
Closed mid Oct.–Apr.
*Modern complex boasting excellent facilities and a beautiful panoramic view of Montecristo Island.*

✪ **Barracuda** ***
at Marina di Campo
Viale Elba, 2
Tel. 0565 976893
Fax 0565 977254
Closed mid Oct.–mid Apr.
*Hotel set in a beautiful palm grove; caters particularly for children. Spacious rooms and an elegant winter porch.*

✪ **Del Golfo** ****
at Marciana
in Procchio (9 miles)
Tel. 0565 907565
Fax 0565 907898
Closed Oct.–mid May
*A complex of villas in a lush pine forest. Privacy guaranteed.*

✪ **Hermitage** ****
at Portoferraio
in La Biodola (6 miles)
Tel. 0565 936911
Fax 0565 969984
Closed mid Oct.–Apr.
*Village-like resort with pretty little cottages clustered together in the countryside, a stone's throw from the sea.*

**Park Hotel Napoleone** ****
at Portoferraio
in San Martino (4 miles)
Tel. 0565 918502
Fax 0565 917836
*A late-19th-century villa set in extensive grounds.*

**Marinella** ***
Viale Margherita, 38
at Marciana Marina
Tel. 0565 99018
Fax 0565 996895
Closed Oct.–Mar.
*Informal hospitality.*

**Maristella** ***
Via Kennedy
at Rio Marina
in Cavo (4 miles)
Tel. 0565 931109
Fax 0565 949859
Closed mid Sep.–mid May
*Light and welcoming, directly overlooking the sea. Spacious garden.*

**Riva del Sole** ****
Via degli Eroi, 11
at Marina di Campo
Tel. 0565 976316
Fax 0565 076778
Closed mid Oct.–mid Apr.
*Rustic-style rooms and unostentatious hospitality.*

✪ **Villa Ottone** ****
at Portoferraio
in Ottone (6 miles)
Tel. 0565 933042
Fax 0565 933257
Closed Oct.–mid May
*A 19th-century villa with several bungalows, set in a beautiful park.*

→ **RESTAURANTS**
**Bologna**
Via Firenze, 27
at Marina di Campo

**RESTAURANTS**
- ⊞ < 50,000 lire
- ⊞ 50,000–80,000 lire
- ⊞ 90,000–120,000 lire
- ⊞ > 120,000 lire

Tel. 0565 976105
Closed Tue. and
Nov.–mid Mar.
*Traditional Tuscan
restaurant, built in
the late 19th
century, serving
typical island cuisine.*
⊟ Ⅲ 🅿 ✖

**Canocchia**
Via Palestro, 1
at Rio Marina
Tel. 0565 962432
Closed Mon. and
Nov.–Jan.
*Central restaurant
offering simple,
classic cuisine.*
⊟ Ⅲ ✖

**Capo Nord**
at Marciana Marina
in La Fenicia, 89
Tel. 0565 996983
Closed Mon. and
Jan.–mid Mar.
*Offers menus
based on the daily
catch; polished,
courteous service.*
⊟ Ⅲ ⛾ ✖

**Da Vittorio**
Via dell'Amore, 54
at Portoferraio
Tel. 0565 917446
Closed Wed. and
Epiphany–Feb.
*Creative fish dishes
in informal
surroundings.*
⊟ Ⅲ ✖

LIVORNO
◆ B C5
→ **HOTELS**
**Boston** ✳✳✳
Piazza Mazzini, 40
Tel. 0586 882333
Fax 0586 882044
*Modern bed and
breakfast hotel
offering a good
standard of comfort
situated near the
boarding stage for
the island ferries.*
⊟ 🅿 🔲 🔀 ✖

**Gran Duca** ✳✳✳
Piazza Micheli, 16
Tel. 0586 891024
Fax 0586 891153
*In a central location
facing the sea,
this welcoming,
comfortable
complex is housed
in a Medici fortress.
It also has five suites.*

View of the Darsena.
⊟ Ⅲ 🅿 ⛾ 🔲 🔀 ♿ ✖

→ **RESTAURANTS**
**Antico Moro**
Via E. Bartelloni, 59
Tel. 0586 884659
Closed Wed.
lunchtime, and part
of Aug. and Sep.
*Typical restaurant
serving classic
Livornese dishes; run
by the Bulletti family
who have been in
catering since 1918.*
⊟ Ⅲ ✖

✪ **Ciglieri**
Via O. Franchini, 38
Tel. 0586 508194
Fax 0586 589091
Closed Wed.;
part of Jan.
*The best restaurant
in the city. Excellent
freshly-caught fish
and top quality
ingredients; the*

CIGLIERI, LIVORNO

*acclaimed wine
cellar is full of
interesting surprises.*
⊟ Ⅲ ✖

**Gennarino**
Via Santa
Fortunata, 11
Tel. 0586 888093
Closed Wed.;
part of Oct.
*Regional cuisine
in an informal
atmosphere;
traditional Tuscan
fish and meat dishes.*
⊟ Ⅲ ✖

**La Barcaiola**
Viale Carducci, 63
Tel. 0586 402367
Closed Sun.
*Lively, informal*

*restaurant near the
railroad station;
beautifully prepared
fresh fish and local
specialties; well-
stocked wine cellar*
⊟ ✖

→ **WINE SHOPS**
**Enoteca Doc
Parole e Cibi**
Via Goldoni, 40
Tel. 0586 887583

**Enoteca Faraoni**
Via Mentana, 85
Tel. 0586 886078

**Enoteca Nardi**
Via Cambini, 6
Tel. 0586 808006

→ **TYPICAL PRODUCE**
**Azienda Bioagricola
Marcantoni Sante**
Via del Vecchio
Lazzaretto, 110
Tel. 0586 500669
*'Organic' pigeon
farming.*

**Macelleria
di Bonelli Paolo**
Via Monte
Grappa, 7/9
Tel. 0586 886344
*Chianina beef, oil,
pecorino from the
Sienese Crete,
gastronomic
products.*

**Torteria Gagarin**
Via D. Cardinale, 24
Tel. 0586 884086

MASSA MARITTIMA
◆ D D3
→ **HOTEL**
**Il Sole** ✳✳✳
Via della Libertà, 43
Tel. 0566 901971
Fax 0566 901959
*Bed and breakfast*

*hotel in a
refurbished medieval
building.*
⊟ Ⅲ ♿ ✖

→ **RESTAURANT**
✪ **Bracali**
at Ghirlanda (1 mile)
Tel. 0566 902318
Fax 0566 940302
Closed Mon. eve,.
Tue.; part of Jan. and
Feb. and in Nov.
*This old family-run
trattoria has passed
into the hands of the
new generation who
pride themselves on
creating imaginative
versions of regional
dishes. Extensive
wine list and a wide
selection of brandies
and liquors.*
⊟ Ⅲ ⬆ 🅿 ⊞

→ **OIL PRODUCER**
**Frantoio Sociale
Massa Marittima**
at Valpiana
Tel. and fax
0566 919211

VOLTERRA
◆ D1-2
→ **HOTELS**
**San Lino** ✳✳✳✳
Via San Lino, 26
Tel. 0588 85250
Fax 0588 80620
Closed Nov.
*This hotel, housed in
a former convent,
has all the mod cons.*
⊟ Ⅲ 🅿 🔲 🔀 ♿ ✖

✪ **Sole** ✳✳✳
Via dei Cappuccini,
10
Tel. 0588 84000
Fax 0588 84000
*This new family-run
hotel is on the
outskirts of town;
only ten rooms, but
guaranteed peace
and quiet.*
⊟ 🅿 🔲 🔀 ♿ 🔀 ✖

✪ **Villa Nencini** ✳✳✳
Borgo Santo
Stefano, 55
Tel. 0588 86386
Fax 0588 80601
*In a late-16th-
century villa, this
hotel has attractive,
functional rooms.*
⊟ 🅿 ⛾ ⛾ 🔲 🔀 ♿
✖

# ◆ USEFUL ADDRESSES
## GROSSETO AND THE MAREMMA

**HOTELS**
- ⚀ < 100,000 lire
- ⚁ 100,000–200,000 lire
- ⚂ 200,000–300,000 lire
- ⚃ > 300,000 lire

**→ RESTAURANTS**

**✪ Il Vecchio Mulino**
Via del Molino
at Saline (6 miles)
Tel. 0588 44060
Closed Mon. (except
July and Aug.)
*Picturesque,
atmospheric
restaurant housed in
an old mill, serving
dishes with a strong
regional bias.*
▨ ▥ ✪ ▩ ▨

**Vecchia Osteria
dei Poeti**
Via Matteotti, 55
Tel. 0588 86029
Closed Thur. and
mid Jan.–mid Feb.
*Right in the center,
this restaurant serves
strictly traditional
Tuscan recipes.*
▨ ▨

**→ ALABASTER**
Società Cooperativa
Artieri Alabastro
Via Provinciale
Pisana, 28
Tel. 0588 86135
Fax 0588 86224

### GROSSETO AND THE MAREMMA

#### ANSEDONIA
◆ D E6
**→ RESTAURANT**
**Pitorsino**
Via Aurelia, 40
Tel. 0564 862179
Closed Wed.
(in winter).
*Authentic regional
cuisine; meals are
served in the garden
in summer.*
▨ ▥ ✪ ▨

#### CAPALBIO
◆ D E-F5
**→ HOTEL**
**Valle del Buttero ***
Via Silone, 21
Tel. 0564 896097
Fax 0564 896518
Closed Christmas.
*This hotel is mainly
divided into small
apartments.*
▨ ▣ ✪ ▨ ▨ ▨ ▨

**→ RESTAURANTS**
**Da Maria**
Via Comunale, 3
Tel. 0564 896014
Closed Tue. and
Epiphany–beg. Feb.

*Rustic-style
restaurant offering
classic Tuscan cuisine.*
▨ ▥ ▨

**Porta**
Via Vittorio
Emanuele II, 1
Tel. 0564 896311
Closed Tue.;
part of Dec.
*Large restaurant
in the historical
center serving
regional specialties,
particularly
barbecued meat.*
▨ ▨

SOC. COOP. ARTIERI ALABASTRO

#### CASTIGLIONE DELLA PESCAIA
◆ D D4
**→ HOTEL**
**✪ L'Approdo ***
Via Ponte Giorgini,
29
Tel. 0564 933466
Fax 0564 933086
*In a panoramic
location on the port-
canal, this hotel has
views of the sea and
the pine forest.*
▨ ▥ ▣ ▨ ▨ ▨ ▨
▨

#### FOLLONICA
◆ D C4
**→ HOTEL**
**Parco dei Pini ***
Via delle
Collacchie, 7
Tel. and fax
0566 53280
*A stone's throw from
the sea, this hotel
has modern,
comfortable rooms.*
▨ ▥ ▣ ▨ ▨

**→ RESTAURANT**
**Leonardo Cappelli
Già Paolino**
Piazza XXV
Aprile, 33
Tel. 0566 57360
Closed Sun. eve. (off

season) and Mon.;
part of Jan. and Feb.
*Seafood in intimate
surroundings.*
▨ ▥ ▨

#### GROSSETO
◆ D D4
**→ HOTELS**
**✪ Bastiani
Grand Hotel ****
Piazza Gioberti, 64
Tel. 0564 20047
Fax 0564 29321
*Early-20th-century
palazzo with a
marble hall, a fine
staircase leading to
the second floor,
rooms with English-
style furnishings
and a roof-garden.
The hotel is close
to the historical
center.*
▨ ▥ ▣ ▨ ▨ ▨

**Maremma ***
Via F. Paolucci de
Calboli, 11
Tel. 0564 22293
Fax 0564 22051
*In a pedestrian
precinct, this bed
and breakfast hotel
has air-conditioned
rooms. The adjoining
restaurant is under
separate
management.*
▨ ▥ ▣ ▨ ▨ ▨

**→ RESTAURANTS**
**Terzo Cerchio**
Piazza del Castello, 2
at Istia d'Ombrone
(4 miles)
Tel. 0564 409235
Closed Mon. and
Nov.
*Elegant rustic-style
restaurant, housed
in the former
Palazzo Pretorio;
serves regional
cuisine.*
▨ ▨

**Canapone**
Piazza Dante, 3
Tel. 0564 24546
Closed Sunday;
part of July and Aug.
*Well-established
restaurant situated
in the city's central
piazza. Specialties:
fish and spit-roasted
meat.*
▨ ▨

**→ TYPICAL PRODUCE**
Enrico Ombronelli
Via Telamonio, 61
Tel. 0564 4943327
*Local meat, Chianina
beef and salami
from Castel del
Piano.*

#### GIGLIO ISLAND
◆ D D6
**→ HOTELS**
**✪ Il Saraceno ***
Via del Saraceno, 69
at Giglio Porto
Tel. 0564 809006
Fax 0564 809007
Closed Sep.–Apr.
*Directly on the
seashore, this hotel
offers excellent
rooms and a good
standard of comfort.*
▨ ▥ ▣ ▨ ▨ ▨ ▨

**✪ Pardini's
Hermitage ****
at Cala degli Alberi
Tel. 0564 809034
Fax 0564 809177
*This hotel can
only be reached by
sea or after an hour's
walk: privacy
guaranteed.*
▨ ▥ ▣ ▨ ▨ ▨

**→ RESTAURANT**
**Da Santi**
Via Marconi, 20
in Giglio Castello
Tel. 0564 806188
Closed Mon. and
Christmas–Jan.
*Excellent tasty and
authentic fish dishes.
In the historical
center.*
▨ ▥ ▨

#### MONTEMERANO
◆ D E-F5
**→ HOTEL**
**✪ Villa Acquaviva
****
at Acquaviva
Tel. 0564 602890
Fax 0564 602895

**RESTAURANTS**
- ▪ < 50,000 lire
- ▪ 50,000–80,000 lire
- ▪ 90,000–120,000 lire
- ⊞ > 120,000 lire

*In a panoramic location among the hills, this hotel provides attentive hospitality and an informal atmosphere.*
▪ ▥ ⌂ P ⇄ ⋇ ▣ ⤢ ▪

→ **RESTAURANT**
✪ **Caino**
Via Canonica, 3
Tel. 0564 602817
Fax 0564 602807
Closed Wed.
*Small, attractive restaurant with a limited number of elegantly laid tables. Top quality regional cuisine.*
▪ ▥ ⊞

**ORBETELLO**
◆ D E5-6
→ **HOTEL**
✪ **Vecchia Maremma ★★★**
at Quattrostrade (4 miles)
Tel. 0564 862147
Fax 0564 862347
*This hotel feels like a private villa with its high standard of comfort, excellent facilities and faultless hospitality. The restaurant of the same name in the building is under separate management.*
▪ ▥ P ⇄ ▣ ⋇ ⤢ ⤢ ▪

→ **RESTAURANT**
**Ruota**
at Orbetello Scalo (2½ miles)
Tel. 0564 862137
Closed Thur.
*Situated in a small Maremman farmhouse, a well-established restaurant serving traditional dishes at inexpensive prices. It is also a hotel.*
▪ P ⇄ ▪

**PITIGLIANO**
◆ D F5
→ **HOTEL**
**Corano ★★**
Statale 74
Maremmana Ovest
Tel. 0564 616112
Fax 0564 614191

Closed part of Jan. *Simple, peaceful surroundings in the lush Maremman countryside.*
▪ P ⇄ ⌂ ▣ ⋇ ⤢ ▪

→ **RESTAURANT**
**Il Tufo Allegro**
Vicolo della Costituzione, 2
Tel. 0564 616192
Closed Tue.; part of Jan. and Feb. and in July
*The food served at this small restaurant constructed of tufa is cooked personally by the owner. Excellent choice of wine.*
▪ ▥ ▪

**PORTO ERCOLE**
◆ D E6
→ **HOTEL**
✪ **Il Pellicano ★★★★**
at Cala dei Santi
Tel. 0564 858111
Fax 0564 833418
Closed mid Oct.–

mid Apr.
*Self-contained cottages amidst ancient olive groves; the complex feels almost like a private residence with hotel amenities and facilities of the highest standard. It also has some suites.*
▪ ▥ P ⇄ ⋇ ▣ ⋇ ⤢
⤢ ⊞

→ **RESTAURANT**
**Gambero Rosso**
Lungomare Andrea Doria, 70
Tel. 0564 832650
Closed Wed. and Feb.
*Fish cuisine served with great care and courtesy. Lovely sea view.*
▪ ⋇ ▪

**PUNTA ALA**
◆ D C4
→ **HOTELS**
✪ **Cala del Porto ★★★★**
Via del Pozzo
Tel. 0564 922455
Fax 0564 920716
Closed Sep.–May
*This modern, complex next to the tourist port, boasts a rural setting and has an elegant décor and excellent facilities.*
▪ ▥ P ⇄ ⋇ ▣ ⤢
⊞

✪ **Piccolo Hotel Alleluja ★★★★**
Via del Porto
Tel. 0564 922050
Fax 0564 920734
Closed Nov.–Mar.
*A welcoming country house with good facilities in the center of a park. Three good restaurants.*
▪ ▥ ⌂ P ⇄ ⋇ ▣ ⤢
⊞

**SATURNIA**
◆ D E-F5
→ **HOTEL**
✪ **Terme di Saturnia ★★★★**
Via della Follonata
Tel. 0564 601061
Fax 0564 601266
*This hotel stands in its own grounds and also comprises an exclusive spa institute.*
▪ ▥ P ⇄ ▣ ⤢ ⤢
⊞

→ **RESTAURANT**
**Due Cippi-Da Michele**
Piazza Vittorio Veneto, 26/a
Tel. 0564 601074
Fax 0564 601074
Closed Tue.; part of Dec.
*Former nobleman's residence with classic furnishings; the kitchen serves typical Maremman dishes.*
▪ ▪

**SOVANA**
◆ D F5
→ **RESTAURANT**
**Scilla**
Via Rodolfo Siviero, 1/3
Tel. 0564 616531
Closed Tue., Nov. or Feb.
*Spacious recently renovated restaurant, rather touristy in style. It serves traditional dishes based on mushrooms and game. It is also a hotel.*
▪ ▥ P ⇄ ▪

**TALAMONE**
◆ D D-E5
→ **HOTEL**
✪ **Corte dei Butteri ★★★★**
at Fonteblanda (2½ miles)
Via Aurelia, 97 miles
Tel. 0564 885548
Fax 0564 886282
Closed mid Oct.–Apr.
*Several yards from the sea, with a private beach, this hotel is a long horizontal building reminiscent of Maremman farmhouses.*
▪ ▥ P ⇄ ⋇ ▣ ⤢ ▪

## HISTORY

◆ BARKER, GRAEME, *The Etruscans*, Blackwell Publishers, 1998
◆ BRATCHEL, M.E., *Lucca 1430–1494*, Clarendon Press, 1995
◆ BURCKHARDT, JACOB, *The Civilization of the Renaissance in Italy*, Penguin Books, 1990
◆ BURKE, PETER, *The Italian Renaissance*, Polity Press, 1999
◆ CIPOLLA, CARLO M, *Faith, Reason and the Plague in 17th Century Tuscany*, Norton 1981
◆ GETTY TRUST PUBLICATIONS, *Etruscan Civilization: a Cultural History*, 2000
◆ GOLDTHWAITE, RICHARD, *Wealth and the Demand for Art in Italy 1300–1600*, John Hopkins University Press, 1995
◆ HALE, J.R. (ed), *Encyclopedia of the Italian Renaissance*, Thames and Hudson, 1983
◆ HIBBERT, CHRISTOPHER, *The House of Medici: its Rise and Fall*, Quill (Harper), 1980; *Florence: The Biography of a City*, Penguin Books, 1994.
◆ HOLMES, GEORGE, *Oxford History of Mediaeval Europe*, Oxford Paperbacks, 1992
◆ ROBSON, MARK, *Italy: Liberalism and Fascism 1870–1945*, Hodder and Stoughton, 2000
◆ SOUTHERN, R.W., *The Making of the Middle Ages*, Pimlico, 1993
◆ TIME LIFE EDUCATION, *Etruscans: Italy's Lovers of Life*, 1995

## ART AND ARCHITECTURE

◆ BELLOSI, LUCIANO, *Duccio: the Maesta.*, Thames and Hudson, 1999
◆ BECK, JAMES, *Michelangelo: The Medici Chapel*, Thames and Hudson, 2000
◆ BERENSON, BERNARD, *Drawings of the Florentine Painters*, Casa Editrice Leo S. Olschki, 1938; *Italian Painters of the Renaissance*, Ursus Press, 1997
◆ CANEVA, CATERINA, *Treasures of Uffizi*, Abbeville Press, 1999
◆ CHELAZZI, GIULETTA, *Sienese painting: From Duccio to the Birth of*

*the Baroque*, Harry N. Abrams Inc., 1998
◆ CHIARELLI, CATERINA, *The Pitti Palace, Museums and Galleries*, Borechi Edizioni 'il Turismo s.r.l.,1999
◆ GIBSON, KATHARINE, *Goldsmith of Florence: A Book of Great Craftsmen*, Ayer Co Publishers Inc, 1929
◆ KENT, DALE, *Cosimo de' Medici and the Florentine Renaissance*, Yale University Press, 2000
◆ KENT, DIANA, *Siena and the Virgin*, Yale University Press, 1999
◆ KING, ROSS, *Brunelleschi's Dome*, Chatto and Windus, 2000
◆ LAVIN, MARILYN ARONBERG, *Piero della Francesca: San Francesco, Arezzo*, George Braziller Publishers, 1994
◆ LIGHTBOWN, RONALD, *Piero della Francesca*, Abbeville Press Inc, 1992
◆ MARANI, PIETRO C., *Leonardo da Vinci: The Complete Paintings*, Harry N. Abrams Inc, 2000
◆ MURRAY, PETER, *Architecture of the Italian Renaissance*, Batsford, 1963
◆ PALLOTTINA, MASSIMA, *Etruscan Painting*, Skira, 1952
◆ PIO, ROSALYND C., *Masterpieces of the Bargello*, Borechi Edizioni 'il Turismo s.r.l.,1999
◆ PLUMB, J. H., *The Penguin Book of the Renaissance*, Penguin Books, 1991
◆ VASARI, G., *The Lives of the Artists*, Peter Smith Publishers, 1993

## LITERATURE

◆ BOCCACCIO, GIOVANNI, *The Decameron, trans.* G.H.McWilliam, Penguin Books, 1995
◆ BROWNING, ELIZABETH BARRETT, *Complete Poems*, Lightyear Press, 1992
◆ BROWNING, ROBERT, *Complete Works*, Ohio University Press, 1969
◆ CALVINO, ITALO, *Italian Folktales*, Penguin, 1982
◆ DANTE, *The Divine Comedy, trans.* Allen Mandelbaum, Everyman's Library, 1995
◆ DICKENS, CHARLES, *Pictures from Italy*

*(1844-45)*, Penguin Books, 1998
◆ FORSTER, E.M., *A Room with a View*, Harper Collins, 1999
◆ HESSE, HERMANN, *Dall'Italia*, Milan, 1990
◆ JAMES, HENRY, *Portrait of a Lady*, W.W. Norton, 1995
◆ JENNINGS, ELIZABETH, *Collected Poems*, Carcanet Press, 1987; *Sonnets of Michaelangelo (trans.)*, Carcanet Press, 1988
◆ LAWRENCE, D. H., *Etruscan Places*, Viking Penguin, 1999
◆ MACHIAVELLI, NICCOLO, *The Prince*, Cambridge University Press, 1988
◆ LEE, LAURIE, *I Can't Stay Long*, Andre Deutsch Ltd, 1975
◆ ORIGO, IRIS, *Merchant of Prato*, Penguin Books, 1992; *Images and Shadows*, John Murray, 1998; *Leopardi: A Study in Solitude*, Turtle Point, 2000
◆ POUND, EZRA, *The Cantos of Ezra Pound*, Faber and Faber, 1987
◆ RUSKIN, JOHN, *Selected Writings*, Penguin 1991
◆ SHELLEY, P. BYSSHE, *Complete Poems*, Modern Library, 1994
◆ STENDHAL, *Rome, Naples and Florence*, trans. R. N. Coe, John Calder Ltd, 1959
◆ WOOLF, V., *A Writer's Diary*, Harcourt, 1973

## TRAVEL AND DESCRIPTION

◆ ACTON, HAROLD, *Florence, A Traveller's Companion*, Constable, 1986
◆ CONNELL, W.J., ZORZI, ANDREA, *Florentine Tuscany*, Cambridge University Press, 2000
◆ GERVAIS, PAUL, *A Garden in Lucca: Finding Paradise in Tuscany*, Hyperion, 2000
◆ HEINE, HEINRICH, *Journey to Italy*, Marsilio Publishers, 1998
◆ LASDUN, JAMES, DAVIS, PIA, *Walking and Eating in Tuscany and Umbria*, Penguin Books, 1997
◆ LEVEY, MICHAEL, *Florence: A Portrait*, Jonathan Cape, 1997
◆ MELVILLE, HERMAN, *Journal of a Visit to Europe and the Levant 1856–57*, Greenwood Press, 1977

◆ MORTON, H.V., *A Traveller in Italy*, Methuen, 2001
◆ MATE, FERENC, *The Hills of Tuscany: A New Life in an Old Land*, Albatross Publishers, 1998
◆ MCCARTHY, MARY, *The Stones of Florence and Venice Observed*, Penguin Books, 1985
◆ PALMER, HUGH, BENTLEY, JAMES, *The Most Beautiful Villages of Tuscany*, Thames and Hudson, 1955
◆ PRICE, GILLIAN, *Walking in Tuscany*, Cicerone, 1998
◆ RAISON, LAURA, *Tuscany, An Anthology*, Ebury Press, 1983
◆ SMOLLETT, TOBIAS, *Travels Through France and Italy*, Marlboro Press, 1997
◆ TWAIN, MARK, *Innocents Abroad or The New Pilgrims Progress*, Signet Books, 1981
◆ SERPELL, CHRISTOPHER, SERPELL, JEAN, *Elba and the Tuscan Archipelago*, Salem House Publications, 1988

## FOOD AND WINE

◆ ASHLEY, MAUREEN, *Wine Touring Tuscany*, Mitchell Beazley, 2000
◆ BEARD, JAMES, *Beard on Pasta*, Papermac, 1983
◆ CERMILLI, DANIELE, SABELLICO, MARCO, *The New Italy: A Complete Guide to Contemporary Italian Wine*, Mitchell Beazley, 2000
◆ DAVID, ELIZABETH, *Italian Food*, Penguin Books, 1954
◆ GAVIN, PAOLA, *Italian Vegetarian Cookery*, Little, Brown, 1997
◆ GRAY, PATIENCE, *Honey from a Weed: Feasting and Fasting in Tuscany*, Harper Row, 1987
◆ HAZAN, MARCELLA, *Marcella's Kitchen*, Papermac, 1987
◆ JOHNSON, HUGH, *Tuscany and its Wines*, Chronicle Books, 2000
◆ REDON, OTILE, *The Mediaeval Kitchen, Recipes from France and Italy*, University of Chicago Press, 1998
◆ ROOT, WAVERLEY, *The Food of Italy*, Vintage Books, 1992
◆WRIGHT, JENI, *Tuscan Food and Folklore*, Advantage Publishers Group, 1998

# LIST OF ILLUSTRATIONS ◆

# ◆ LIST OF ILLUSTRATIONS

# LIST OF ILLUSTRATIONS ◆

# ◆ LIST OF ILLUSTRATIONS

# LIST OF ILLUSTRATIONS ◆

# ◆ LIST OF ILLUSTRATIONS

We would like to thank the following publishers and copyright holders for permission to reproduce the quotations on pages 98–108:
◆ Extract from *A Writer's Diary* by Viginia Woolf published by Hogarth Press. Used by permission of the executors of the Virginia Woolf Estate and The Random House Group Limited.
◆ Extract from *A Room With a View* by E.M. Forster. Reproduced by permission of The Scholars and Provost of King's College, Cambridge and the Society of Authors as the Literary Representatives of the Estate of E.M. Forster.
◆ Extract from *Selected Prose and Poetry* by Giacomo Leopardi, edited, translated and introduced by Iris Origio and John Heath-Stubbs. Reproduced by permission of Oxford University Press.
◆ Extract from *Images and Shadows* by Iris Origo. Reproduced by permission of John Murray (Publishers) Ltd.

We would also like to thank: the Museo Pecci in Prato; the Museo Marino Marini in Florence; Dr. F. Comanducci at the Museo Civico in Sansepolcro; Mr. A. Neri at Villa Balmain, Island of Elba; Ristorante Venanzio, Piazza Palestro 3, Colonnata Carrara; Mr. F. Anichini at the Centro Culturale e Sociale San Sano, Gaiole in Chianti (Siena), the Azienda Zootecnica F.lli Fabbrini, Vico d'Arbia (Siena); Azienda Giannetto

Cugusi, Montepulciano; Caseificio Cooperativo della Val d'Elsa, Casole d'Elsa; the Associazione 'Pro Anghiari'; Mr. E. Polverini at the Fondazione Città del Libro, Premio Bancarella; Arch. M. Ragone at IMM. Carrara spa.

We have not been able to trace the heirs or publishers of certain documents. An account is being held open for them at our offices.

# PEOPLE

## A

# ◆ INDEX

# ◆ INDEX

# ◆ INDEX

# Map section

A  Florence
B  Northern Tuscany
C  Central Tuscany
D  Southern Tuscany
   and the Tuscan Archipelago

## Key

- Freeway
- Primary road
- Secondary road
- Other roads
- Ferry link
- Railroad
- Provincial boundary
- Urban area
- Main town
- Secondary town
- Place of interest
- Cemetery
- Hospital

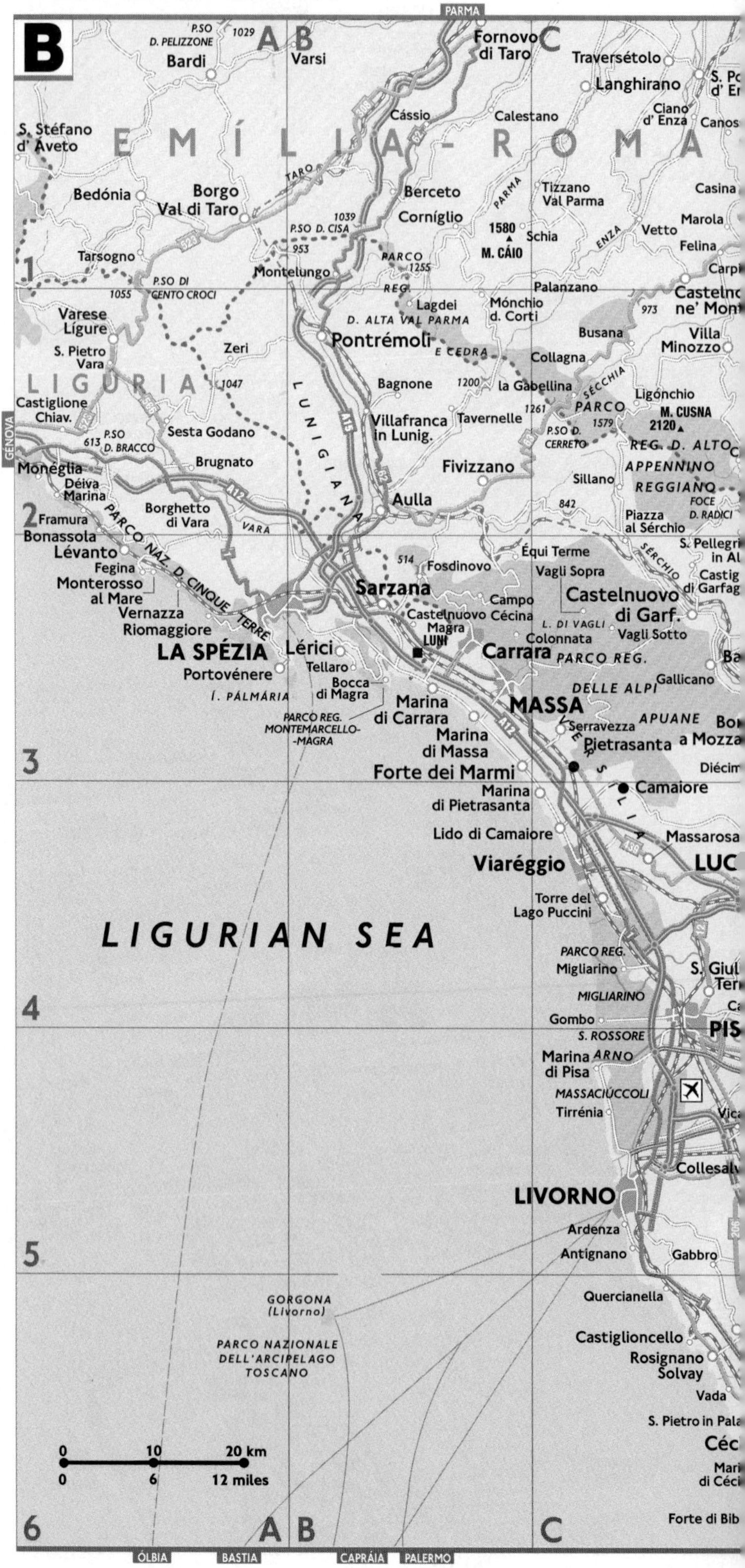

B

A B C

PARMA

**EMÍLIA-ROMA**

P.SO
D. PELIZZONE 1029
Bardi
Varsi
Fornovo
di Taro
Traversétolo
S. Po
d' Er
Cássio
Calestano
Langhirano
Ciano
d' Enza
Canos
S. Stéfano
d' Áveto
Bedónia
Borgo
Val di Taro
Berceto
Tizzano
Val Parma
Casina
TARO
Corníglio
PARMA
Marola
Vetto
Tarsogno
P.SO D. CISA 1039
953
1580
▲ M. CÁIO
Schia
Felina
Carpi
Montelungo
PARCO 1255
REG
Palanzano
Castelno
ne' Mon
973
1055
P.SO DI
GENTO CROCI
Lagdei
D. ALTA VAL PARMA
Mónchio
d. Corti
Busana
Villa
Minozzo
Varese
Lígure
Zeri
1047
Pontrémoli
E CEDRA
Collagna
la Gabellina
1200
SECCHIA
Ligónchio
PARCO
S. Pietro
Vara
Bagnone
1261
M. CUSNA
2120▲
LIGURIA
Castiglione
Chiav.
613
P.SO
D. BRACCO
Sesta Godano
LUNIGIANA
Villafranca
in Lunig.
Tavernelle
P.SO D.
CERRETO 1579
REG. D. ALTO
APPENNINO
Monéglia
Déiva
Marina
Brugnato
Fivizzano
Sillano
REGGIANO
842
FOCE
D. RADICI
2 Framura
Bonassola
Lévanto
Borghetto
di Vara
VARA
Aulla
Piazza
al Sérchio
S. Pellegri
in Al
Fegina
Monterosso
al Mare
Vernazza
Riomaggiore
PARCO NAZ. D. CINQUE TERRE
514
Fosdinovo
Équi Terme
Vagli Sopra
SÉRCHIO
Castig
di Garfag
Sarzana
Campo
Castelnuovo
Cécina
Castelnuovo
di Garf.
Vagli Sotto
LA SPÉZIA
Lérici
Tellaro
Castelnuovo
Magra
LUNI
Colonnata
Carrara
PARCO REG.
Gallicano
Ba
Portovénere
Bocca
di Magra
DELLE ALPI
MASSA
I. PÁLMÁRIA
PARCO REG.
MONTEMARCELLO-
-MAGRA
Marina
di Carrara
Serravezza
APUANE
Bon
a Mozza
3
Marina
di Massa
Pietrasanta
S
Diécim
Forte dei Marmi
Camaiore
Marina
di Pietrasanta
Massarosa
Lido di Camaiore
LUC
Viaréggio
Torre del
Lago Puccini
**LIGURIAN SEA**
PARCO REG.
Migliarino
S. Giul
Ter
MIGLIARINO
C
4
Gombo
S. ROSSORE
PIS
Marina
di Pisa
ARNO
MASSACIÚCCOLI
Tirrénia
✈
Vic
Collesalv
**LIVORNO**
5
Ardenza
Antignano
Gabbro
GORGONA
(Livorno)
Quercianella
PARCO NAZIONALE
DELL'ARCIPELAGO
TOSCANO
Castiglioncello
Rosignano
Solvay
Vada
S. Pietro in Pala
Céc
0        10        20 km
0        6        12 miles
Mari
di Céci
6
A        B        C
Forte di Bib

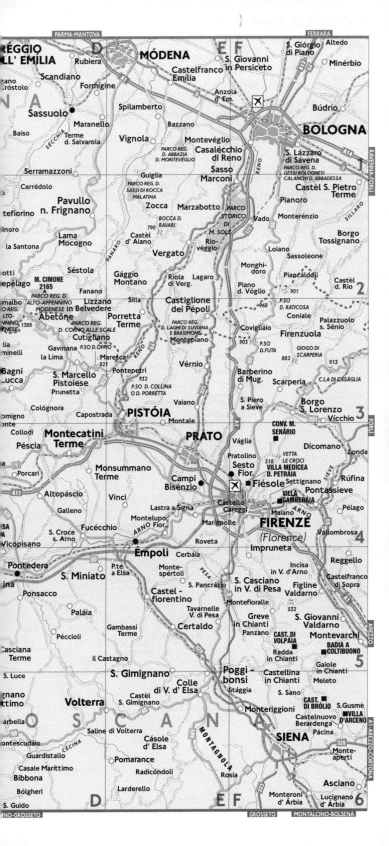

**C**

BOLOGNA — BOLOGNA

A   B   C   D

Gággio Montano
Fanano
Lizzano in Belvedere
Silla
Riola di Verg.
Lagaro
Monghidoro
Piancáldoli
Castél d. Rio
Cásola Valsenio
Brisighell
Modig

PARCO REG. D. CORNO ALLE SCALE
Porretta Terme
Castiglione dei Pépoli
Piano d. Vóglio
968
901
P.SO D. RATICOSA
Palazzuolo s. Sénio
LAMO

Cutigliano
Gavinana la Lima
P.SO D'ÓPPIO
Maresca
932
821
Montepiano
PARCO REG. D. LAGHI DI SUVIANA E BRASIMONE
Coviglláio
903
Coniale
Firenzuola
P.SO D. FUTA
GIOGO DI SCARPERIA
882
Marradi
Tre

Pontepetri
Vérnio
Barberino di Mug.
913
C.LA DI CASÁGLIA
Pórti di Romag

**1**
S. Marcello Pistoiese
Prunetta
P.SO D. COLLINA O D. PORRETTA
Vaiano
S. Piero a Sieve
Scarperia
Borgo S. Lorenzo
S. Benedetto in Alpe
907

Capostrada
**PISTÓIA**
Montale
Váglia
Vícchio
S. Godenzo
P.SO D. MURAGL
MO

**Montecatini Terme**
**PRATO**
Pratolino
CONV. M. SENÁRIO
Dicomano
Londa
**M. FALTERONA 1654**
Ca
129

Monsummano Terme
Campi Bisénzio
Sesto Fior.
VILLA MEDÍCEA D. PETRAIA
518
VETTA LE CROCI
Settignano
Rúfina
Stia

**2**
Vinci
Castello Careggi
Fiésole
VILLA GAMBERÁIA
Pontassieve
Consuma
1060
Prato- vécchio

Lastra a Signa
ARNO Fior.
Morignolle
**FIRENZE** (Florence)
Maiano
Pélago
Borgo alla Collina

S. Croce s. Arno
Fucécchio
Montelupo
Roveta
Impruneta
Vallombrosa

**Émpoli**
Cerbáia
Incisa in V. d'Arno
Reggello
Pc

S. Miniato
P.te a Elsa
Monte- spértoli
PESA
S. Casciano in V. di Pesa
Figline Valdarno
Castelfranco di Sopra
PARCO NAZ. D. FORESTE CASENTINESI -MONTE FALTERONA- -CAMPIGNA
Loro Ciuffenn

Paláia
Castel- fiorentino
S. Pancrázio
Montefioralle
532
Grópina
67

**3**
Gambassi Terme
Certaldo
Tavarnelle V. di Pesa
Greve in Chianti
Panzano
S. Giovanni Valdarno
Terranuova Bracciolini

il Castagno
CAST. DI VOLPÁIA
Radda in Chianti
Montevarchi
Lévane
BADIA A COLTIBUONO

S. Gimignano
Colle di V. d'Elsa
Castellina in Chianti
Gaiole in Chianti
Meleto
Capánnole

**Volterra**
Castèl S. Gimignano
Stággia
S. Sano
CAST. DI BRÓLIO
S. Gusmè
Pi al To

Saline di Volterra
CÉCINA
Monteriggioni
Castelnuovo Berardenga
VILLA D'ARCENO

**4**
Pomarance
Radicóndoli
Rosia
MONTAGNOLA
**SIENA**
Pácina
Monte- aperti
Gargonza
Monte S. Savino
N

Larderello
MERSE
Asciano
Rapolano Terme
Lucigna

Canneto
Castelnuovo di V. di Cécina
Monteroni d'Árbia
Lucignano d' Árbia
ABB. M. OLIVETO MAGGIORE
Sinalunga
To di

Terme d. Bagnolo
Montieri
ABBAZIA DI S. GALGANO
S. Lorenzo a Merse
Buonconvento
S. Giovanni d' Asso

Monterotondo Maríttimo
Gabellino
Monticiano
Bagni di Petriolo
Torrenieri

**5**
**Massa Maríttima**
Roccatederighi
Roccastrada
Montalcino
S. Quírico d'Órcia
Pie

Valpiana
Civitella Maríttima
S. ÁNTIMO
Castiglione d' Órcia

BRUNA
Pagánico
ÓRCIA
Abbadia S. Salvatore
**M. AMIATA 1738**

**Follónica**
Gavorrano
Monte- pescali
Cinigiano
Castèl del Piano
Arcidosso

Vetulónia
Batignano
S. Fiora
Pian- castag

**6**
Punta Ala
Buriano
Roselle
OMBRONE
Arcille
S. Fiora

A   B   C

AT-LUCCA · AT-PISA-LIVORNO · LIVORNO

RENO · SIEVE · ARNO · ARNO · PESA · CÉCINA · MERSE

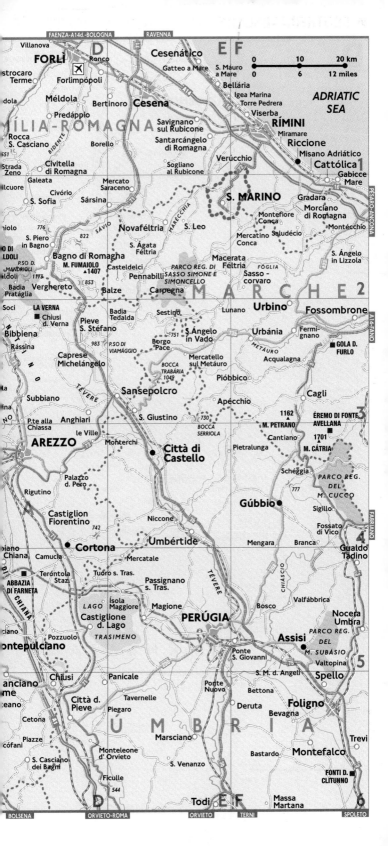

**D**

PISA-LUCCA — PISA — ÉMPOL

A   B   C

Tirrénia

Vicarello · Ponsacco · Pontedera · Pa

Collesalvetti · Péc

**LIVORNO**

Ardenza

Antignano · Gabbro

Casciana Terme

Quercianella · S. Luce

GORGONA (Livorno)

**1**

Castiglioncello

Rosignano Maríttimo

Rosignano Solvay

Vada

Riparbella

S. Pietro in Palazzi

Montescudáio

**Cécina**

Guardistallo

Marina di Cécina

Casale Maríttime

Bibbona

Forte di Bibbona

Bólgheri

S. Guido · Canne

BASTIA

**2**

Marina di Castagneto-Donorático

Donorático

Monteve Maritt.

Castagneto Carducci

312 Sassetta

S. Vincenzo · **S. SILVESTRO** ■ · Suveret

Campíglia Maritt.

P. D. TÉIA

Capráia

CAPRÁIA (Livorno)

P. D. ZENÓBITO

Venturina

Populónia

**3**

**Piombino**

Follónic

CANALE DI PIOMBINO

ELBA (Livorno)

C. D. VITA

Cavo

**Portoferráio**

Marciana Marina

Rio Marina

P. ALA

Marciana

S. Martíno

Punt

Chiessi

Prócchio

Porto Azzurro

Marina di Campo

Capolíveri

BASTIA

**4**

P. DI FETOVÁIA

P. D. RIPALTI

PARCO NAZIONALE DELL'ARCIPELAGO TOSCANO

P. D. MARCHESE

PIANOSA (Livorno)

Pianosa

P. BRIGANTINA

# T Y R R H E N I A N   S.

PORTO-VECCHIO

**5**

MONTECRISTO (Livorno)

la Villa

P. ROSSA

| 0 | 10 | 20 km |
| 0 | 6 | 12 miles |

**6**

A   B   C

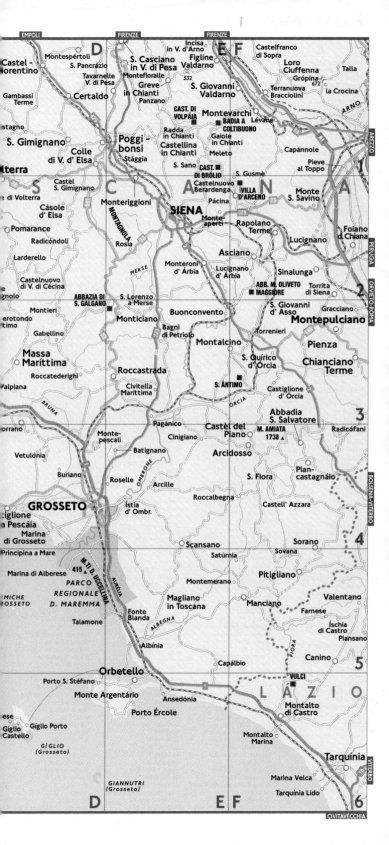

# ◆ MAP INDEX

Langhirano
Sassuolo
Maranello
Castelnovo ne'Monti
Vignola
EMÍLIA - ROMAG
Sasso Marconi
Pso. d. Cerreto 1261
Pavullo nel Frignano
ENZA
SÉCCHIA
Modena
RENO
Bolo
Pievepélago
Abetone
Porretta Terme
PARCO REG. DELLE ALPI APUANE
Castelnuovo di Garfagnana
Fi
dei Marmi
Pistóia
Prato
Lucca
Montecatini Terme
Fiés
Viaréggio
Pisa
Émpoli
Flore
Pontedera
ARNO
S. Miniato
CO REG. ARINO - ÖSSORE - CIÚCCOLI
Collesalvetti
Livorno
Casciana Terme
Poggibonsi
S. Gimignano
CH
Castiglioncello
Colle di V. d'Elsa
Volterra
Si
Cecina
Larderello
TUSCANA
Monticiano
S. Vincenzo
Massa Maríttima
223
Suvereto
Roccastrada
Populónia
Piombino
Follónica
OMBRONE
rtoferráio
Porto Azzurro
Castiglione della Pescáia
Grosseto
PARCO REG. D. MAREMMA
Porto Azzurro
TUSCAN ARCHIPELAGO
GÍGLIO
Orbetello
SEA
Porto Ércole
GIANNUTRI
sto

TUSCANY

# MAP INDEX ◆